Equipping Modern Patriots

New Beginnings

Book 3

By:

Jonathan Hollerman

EMP: Equipping Modern Patriots is a work of fiction. Names, characters, places, and incidents are the products of the author's imagination or are used fictitiously. Any resemblance to actual events, or persons, living or dead, is entirely coincidental.

Published in the United States by:

APOC PUBLISHING
PO Box 99331
Pittsburgh, PA 15233
www.apocpublishing.com

Apoc Publishing mass market 1st Edition: November 2017
1st Edition Edited by: C. M. Hollerman

Cover Photo: Contributor: Konstanttin/ BigStock

ISBN: **0-692-97862-3**
ISBN 13: **978-0-692-97862-7**

Note to Reader:

Although every precaution has been taken to verify the accuracy of the information contained herein, the author and publisher assume no responsibility for any errors or omissions. No liability or responsibility is assumed for damages, losses, or injuries that may result from the use or misuse of information or ideas contained within. This book is published for entertainment purposes only and is not a substitute for an actual survival manual or instruction with qualified professional consultants.

To contact author or for personalized consulting go to:
www.GridDownConsulting.com

Books by Jonathan Hollerman:

EMP: EQUIPPING MODERN PATRIOTS
"A STORY OF SURVIVAL"
Book 1

EMP: EQUIPPING MODERN PATRIOTS
"THE AFTERMATH"
Book 2

EMP: EQUIPPING MODERN PATRIOTS
"NEW BEGINNINGS"
Book 3

SURVIVAL THEORY
A PREPAREDNESS GUIDE:
How to Survive the End of the World on a Budget

ALONE: BETH ANN'S STORY OF SURVIVAL
Co-Authored with C.M. Hollerman

Forthcoming Works

SURVIVAL THEORY II
A follow-up to Survival Theory, A Preparedness Guide

DARK SKIES
The first novel in a new series inside the Equipping Modern Patriots world. It will follow a new character while describing life inside the Green Zones.

Dedication

This book is dedicated to the newest addition to our family,
our beautiful and uproarious daughter, Hannah.
I hope and pray you never experience the world I write about.

Psalm 91

Prologue

Nine months post EMP

The man was a shadow on a shadowless night. Deeper than black, the trees and outcroppings of the Allegheny National Forest provided the perfect backdrop for prowling in the pre-dawn hours…but only for a man who knew how to bend the darkness to his will. Each silent footstep through the damp underbrush released a new waft of pungent moss and decay. Imperceptible droplets of moisture from the late summer thunderstorm that had rolled through earlier in the evening permeated the tight weave of his cloak, seeping through onto shoulders and into his bones. He ignored the chill. His discomfort was not relevant to the task at hand.

Gently placing his right heel on the ground, he slowly rolled his foot forward. Halfway through the motion, he felt a small twig under his arch through the soft leather sole of his hand-sewn moccasins. He rolled his foot back onto the heel, shifting his weight onto his left foot. Slightly picking up his right foot, he calmly led with his toe and slid it underneath the offending twig, gradually rolling his weight back onto his right leg. It was a slow and deliberate type of movement, but even the slightest crack from the twig could alert the two men who stood watch only ten yards away.

Only a few short hours ago, the man had spotted two vehicles parked horizontally across the road, completely blocking any passage into the next town on his list. He had surveilled the men on watch through his priceless Swarovski binoculars, but that only provided him with a sliver of the information he sought. The two men were perched opposite the roadblock, concealing themselves just inside the tree line, quietly talking and occasionally using their own binoculars to peer down the roadway in his direction. He wasn't concerned. There was no way they could spot him in his concealed location. There was a third individual behind the wheel of a late sixties Chevy Impala facing away from their position. This person, asleep inside the vehicle, would likely have been missed by someone less experienced: someone who didn't possess the shadowy figure's experience navigating the dangerous open road of the new world. Under the rising moon of late twilight, it was difficult to see through the hazy rear window of the Impala, even with the sizeable binoculars possessing 56mm objective lenses. But the dark, bulbish shape sticking up above the driver's seat had been unmistakable.

Confident in his map reading and navigating skills, he knew that he was roughly a mile outside the next sleepy mountain town and he needed to determine if these men were a part of that town or just another random ambush. His first assumption, which was usually correct, was that they were advanced scouts put into place to give warning to the townspeople if a large band of raiders came barreling down the road. If these men were locals trying to set an ambush, they were clearly botching it. Two cars parked across the road in that manner was a clear sign of danger to anyone travelling these days. Any desperate brigands using a technique of such obvious nature would have been eradicated by smarter and better trained travelers long before his arrival into the area. These days, the occasional ambushes the dark figure encountered were considerably more deceptive in their attempt to catch travelers unaware and loot their food and provisions. Even with his level of training and experience, there were a few times he'd come close to getting caught in some elaborate ambush…but not yet.

After an hour of surveilling the three watchmen from a distance, a dense fog had pushed through the sharply angular valley. Its slow intrusion masked the moonlight and stars and enveloped him in its suffocating density. The fog, combined with the darkening sky, made any further use of the binoculars hopeless. He'd made some notes on the men's appearance and the weapons they carried using his Write-In-The-Rain tablet, which he studiously carried inside his pants cargo pocket. His annotations complete, the dark figure had stashed his pack and battle rifle under a nearby log, readjusted his sidearm's holster, and begun his creeping stalk forward.

He had spent over an hour in his passage through the tangled underbrush of the Allegheny National Forest. Even now, only a stone's throw from the roadblock, the men's whispered conversation was still muffled. The dense fog seemed a living thing, dampening the sound of voices to an inaudible hum. He cautiously suspended his advance, studying his path forward. His destination was a decaying hollowed-out stump protruding from the earth like a mossy tombstone, its position conveniently adjacent to where the two men sat, unaware of his presence. Their backs were to him and they lounged on red nylon folding chairs as if waiting for burgers to finish cooking at a lazy summer barbeque. Despite the foggy night, the bright colored chairs stood out like a sore thumb amongst the muted tones of the forest surrounding them. Each time one of them shifted in his seat, it produced a low scratching sound like sandpaper over plastic. The men obviously had no professional training or understanding on the basic principles of keeping watch: Don't be seen and don't be heard. It was that simple. The shadowy figure felt embarrassed for them.

How easy it would be for him to evade right up to where they sat and slit both of their throats. He was taken aback by the disturbing thought and let it dissolve from his mind. Once he'd established the path of least resistance to his final place of concealment, he slowly lifted his right foot and gently placed it on the base of the fern in front of him. Feeling no resistance, he leaned his body weight forward.

Another quarter hour passed before he covered the last few steps to reach his destination. At the base of the large moss-covered stump he eased himself into a squat, his insufferable left knee popping in protest. It was an incessant reminder that he was no longer a youthful man. He froze and listened intently, but the men continued their discussion without a pause. The shadowy figure furrowed his brow as he remained motionless, concentrating on his other senses and awaiting discovery. Perhaps the men had heard the click from his knee and continued their dialogue as a ruse while waiting for more sound emanating from his direction. He smiled at the absurd idea. He was giving these amateurs *way* too much credit.

He returned his attention to the task at hand. Using measured movements, his chill-stiffened fingers gathered every crinkly leaf and brittle twig beneath where he crouched, repositioning them away from where he intended to sit. It was a long and arduous process, but eventually he was able to silently hunker down on the damp moss with his back to the decomposing stump. Quads throbbing, his leg muscles twitched from the exertion of the hunt. The edges of his mouth turned up as he leaned his head back against the soft stump, closing his eyes and engrossing himself in the men's conversation. He interlaced his fingers over his stomach, tapping his thumbs together in timely cadence.

After close to an hour of aimless chatter, the huskier of the two men stood and tromped through the underbrush to the road, his work boots thudding on the pavement. With a rap on the Impala's window, he woke his sleeping friend. They conversed briefly while making no attempt to keep their voices low. The thud of the car door signaled the swapping of their positions. After occupying the empty red chair, this new character was chattier than the other two men had been. His partner interrupted the man's ceaseless story telling with biting quips and sharp retorts while unsuccessful in slowing the man's ramblings.

The never-ending sound of the man's nasally voice permeated the fog, washing away the otherwise peaceful sounds of nighttime forest.

The shadowed figure lounged against the mossy stump in silence until he'd obtained all the information he would need. Daybreak would soon be upon them, and if he didn't start his retreat before long, he would surely be discovered in the early morning light...even by these greenhorns. He peeled his back off the stump and sat up. Listening intently, he gently placed his hands on the damp ground and pushed himself upright, hoping his bum knee wouldn't give him away.

The dark figure carefully picked his way back to where he'd stashed his pack and rifle earlier that night. The first hints of orange hue invading the darkness were now visible on the eastern horizon. In a short time, the rising sun would burn away the morning fog, most likely leaving the humidity behind for another oppressively hot day. Quietly opening the outside pocket of his Eberlestock Little Brother pack, he pulled out a stale chocolate chip granola bar and scarfed it down in two ravenous bites. Finished with his meager breakfast, he slowly peeled the wet leather moccasins off of his aching feet and using some para cord, tied them securely to the outside of his pack so they could dry out over the course of the day. He double checked that his knots were tight to be sure he wouldn't lose them along his trek. Propping his feet up on a fallen log, he pulled the waterproof notebook from his cargo pocket once more. He scribbled numerous notations while allowing his sodden, wrinkled feet to dry. Then he donned a fresh pair of fluffy Merino wool socks and retrieved his Danner boots from inside his pack, lacing them onto his feet. Standing with a stifled groan, he stretched his aching muscles for a few moments and listened to the scuffling sounds of a gray squirrel as it emerged to greet the new day. The dark figure led a mostly nocturnal existence and would soon find a place to sleep away the daylight hours. He threw the sturdy pack over his shoulders with a purpose and set off at a forty-five-degree dogleg, silently gliding through the woods around the roadblock. He'd finally made it to his objective…the tiny town of Tionesta.

Chapter 1

Sean sat quietly in the tall grass, slowly crushing the soft petals of a Black-Eyed Susan between his index finger and thumb until his fingers were glistening with its sweet smelling moisture. August was turning out to be rather cool compared to years past and Sean closed his eyes, feeling the light breeze waft through his growing beard. "I'm not even sure where to begin…" he began. "The baby is doing really well. I can't believe how chubby he's getting," Sean chuckled introspectively. "That boy just eats and eats and eats. However, he *has* been sleeping through the entire night now for a couple weeks, which is nice. It's the only time Maria gets a break from nursing. It was funny—she's been getting a little thin lately, so at the last meeting, my mom insisted her food rations need to be increased to compensate." Sean snickered once more before continuing. "Maria was really embarrassed about my mom discussing how nursing can be taxing on a mother's body in front of everyone….

"But it's cool… the two of them have been getting along really well the last couple weeks. Not that they didn't before. It's just different now that Maria has a baby. My mom is always poking around, offering suggestions and the like. Maria has been taking it in stride, but I also wonder for how long." Sean paused for a minute. He thought about Jacob's dark brown eyes and the way they seemed to bore into his soul each time he held his son. His light copper complexion was purely from his wife's Guatemalan heritage and Sean didn't think James resembled him in the least. Most disagreed.

"I wish I would have mentioned it to you before…, but Maria wants to have another baby. In fact she's adamant about it. The idea scares me to death, especially after the attack last month. I just don't know what to do. I'm worried, Buddy…Should I be?" Sean thought back a few months, to the day Maria had given birth in the guest room of the cabin. He couldn't imagine going through that whole process again, watching his wife in so much pain. And then there was the screaming and the bleeding…. Sean didn't receive an audible answer to his question. "At some point, I'm fairly sure I'm going to have to relent. You know Maria…," he trailed off with a wry grin.

"By the way, Brody and Beth Ann's wedding was epic!" Sean changed the subject to something more cheerful. A subject that didn't stress him out. "I can't even describe to you how amazing Pastor Dan and the others in town made their wedding. The church was entirely scrubbed down, there were ribbons everywhere, and they even decorated the gazebo out at Sherman Island Park." Sean paused remembering back to the candle stands that had been placed on the podium next to him where he had stood as Brody's best man. Half of Brody's groomsmen had been killed in the attack a week before his wedding. Sean could still smell the sweet vanilla scent of the candles that were next to him as he had stood on the dais waiting for Beth Ann to walk down the aisle. He wasn't being very successful at keeping this conversation positive and cheerful like he'd promised himself.

Time to change the subject once more. "Colonel Harris attended and brought a diesel generator with him which they used to power a bunch of Christmas lights hung on the gazebo. There was even a dance with a band and everything." He ran a hand through his brittle hair. He was forgetting something. "Oh yeah, one of the town's patrols stumbled across two deer the night before the wedding, so we had smoked venison for the reception! It was crazy how it all worked out. I haven't seen a single deer in three months and their hunting team shot two on the same day… big does at that. The wedding was really, really nice. I wish you could have been there."

Sean paused, picking another Black-Eyed Susan to begin his slow, deliberate process of flower ruination once more. Several minutes ticked by. "I think the soldiers up there in Warren are starting to go hungry. Colonel Harris was at last week's board meeting in Tionesta. He didn't say as much, but he sure asked a lot of questions about the town's gardening abilities. It was unusual for him." His brows drew together as he said, more to himself than anyone, "I think those soldiers of his are starting to go hungry." He huffed and flung the crumbled flower away. "We worried about this day, remember? Working with Colonel Harris was always going to be a double-edged sword. On one hand, they helped us get rid of the prison gang but on the other, if they can't keep their soldiers fed…well, we could be in for some trouble soon."

Screams of a young child caught Sean's attention, and he immediately turned to look over his shoulder. It turned out to be one of Caleb's little ones squealing in delight, being chased through the backyard by Randy's oldest daughter, untamed hair flying as they ran. Evidently the women were giving the children a break from their morning lessons. The overgrown lawn was soon full of children of various ages. Most were playing some version of tag that Sean didn't recognize, while the oldest ones worked their way to the edge of the woods where they sat in the shade of a large willow tree to discuss…teenager things.

Sean took a deep breath, continuing his previous line of thought. "Colonel Harris is supposed to come back tomorrow night for this week's board meeting. I might try and push him a little on why he asked so many questions about the town's food last week. I told Pastor Dan after the last meeting it's vital the townspeople keep their food production private. He agreed but seems way more trusting of Colonel Harris than I am. I don't think the Colonel would do anything shady, but he is also responsible for keeping his entire Regiment fed…and that's a lot of mouths to feed." Sean received silence in response to his speculations. "Heck, I'm only trying to help organize the four dozen members of our retreat and that man has to keep a whole Regiment in line…. I wouldn't want to be in his shoes. Still, the questions he was asking last week have me concerned." Sean trailed off once more.

He wasn't being very successful in keeping this conversation positive. He gave up. It wasn't really a conversation anyways, and he wasn't getting any response or feedback from his old friend that would help him. "I should probably be getting back soon. We're still working on plans to tighten up security around here. I've got a couple new ideas I want to run by Brody." Sean stood silently, brushing off the seat of his pants before closing his eyes once more and relishing the late summer breeze. Silence. All was calm on the home front.

"I'm sorry it took so long for me to come up here and talk to you…." He felt a tear slide down his sun-ripened cheek. "I promise I'll talk to you again soon." Sean rubbed the moisture off his cheek before he lowered his fingers, sliding them across the rough wooden cross that bore Damian's name. He turned and strode back toward the East Homestead's cabin.

He walked a circuitous route around the garden area on his return. Although he wasn't an overly proud man, he'd still be uncomfortable if the children saw his red eyes or the tears he couldn't seem to prevent. Damian hadn't been Sean's closest friend before the EMP, but he had grown on him over the last year with his disarming smile, his logical view on life, and the designer clothes he'd continued to wear even after the collapse. His long auburn hair had always seemed to be combed perfectly. With all the blood, sweat, hard work, and stress, everyone looked dirty and unkempt except Damian, who always appeared as if he'd had just stepped out of an ad in GQ magazine.

Sean stood at the corner of the garden, subconsciously peeling some paint off the garden's corner post with his fingernail. He thought about Andrew and his wife, who'd also lost their lives on that fateful night. Sean wondered why wasn't he as torn up over Andrew as he was with Damian. He'd known Andrew considerably longer as he had gone to the same small high school as Sean, albeit a few years his junior. Sean felt guilty that his tears were only falling for Damian. What was wrong with him? There were five other retreat members who had lost their lives during the battle over East Homestead. Two were locals that had joined the retreat in the spring but they were still members of their tight-knit community. They were people with faces, names, personalities, and little idiosyncrasies that Sean would never forget.

A sharp banging sound came from his left and Sean quickly turned, looking across the large field toward Peter's farm house. He covered his eyes with his calloused hand to shield the mid-morning sun. From a distance, he could make out a couple men at the front door of Peter's farm house. One of them swung his arm over his head and Sean heard another loud bang from the man's hammer as the sound reverberated across the open field. They were finally getting around to replacing the front door which had been blown off its hinges as the military made entry during the horrific attack. While the same had happened to the main retreat cabin, its door had been a standard size and a replacement was easily pilfered from one of the vacant farm houses nearby. Peter's front door had probably been there for close to a hundred years and hand hewn to fit the old oak door casing. Apparently, someone had finally located another door that could be trimmed down and retrofitted into place.

The members of East Homestead were still picking up the pieces and making repairs after the battle with the men from Bradford Prison only three weeks earlier. It would be impossible to completely erase any trace of the battle as all three structures on the homestead were permanently riddled with bullet holes. Those holes would be a constant reminder of how dangerous a world they now lived in. Sean felt lucky he would be returning to his family soon at the North

Homestead. Mr. Andrews' retreat wasn't peppered with constant reminders of the terrible battle and the lives lost.

Sean had merely witnessed the scene and hadn't really taken part even though he'd been shot in the calf while opening the gate for the convoy of MRAPs and soldiers that had come to East Homestead's rescue. He flexed his calf muscle and a small twinge of discomfort worked its way up his leg. He'd been off his crutch for the last week, but the East Homestead's doctor, Darren, had insisted he still take it easy for the next few months: "No hard work for you Sean. Doctor's orders!"

It was tough for Sean to sit on the sidelines and not take part in the harder work details. Even though the other members of his extended family assured him it was fine, he still felt lousy and unproductive at not being able to do more. Initially, he'd busied himself with inspecting and re-inspecting every square inch of the North Homestead, trying to find any gaps in their security or ways they could improve on the existing infrastructure, but he hadn't found anything significant. Mr. Andrews had been very thorough in his preparations and the planning of his survival retreat. Mainly, Sean found little nit-picky tasks that usually involved someone else to accomplish.

His father had finally come to him, pleading with Sean to cease his over-analyzation of the retreat. All he was doing was making more work for everyone else. Embarrassed, Sean acquiesced and moved to helping with the cooking and laundry chores. He was swiftly kicked off those duties by his sister who was in charge of logistics at the North Homestead. Apparently, he wasn't very good at either of the tasks. After that, he'd spent two days taking as many extra shifts at watch as he was permitted but was prevented from taking as many as he would have liked. The retreat's by-laws were rigid and forbid anyone from taking more than six eight-hour watches per week. Watch duty was a tedious thing and it was vital that the person on watch stay sharp and focused on their surroundings. Too many shifts on watch was dangerous. The person would likely start day-dreaming or nodding off, putting the whole retreat at risk. After the two days of extra shifts, Sean meandered around North Homestead finding himself getting more and more agitated at the slightest things.

"Why don't you just get out of here and go bother the others at East Homestead for a few days?" Maria had "suggested" after he'd snapped at her over something trivial. He felt like a puppy being chided by its master but conceded that she was probably right, even though he was reluctant to go. He knew it meant facing Damian's and Andrew's graves. It was something he had been trying to avoid as long as he possibly could, knowing it would be tough to face those wooden crosses. He'd been correct.

Visiting trips between the two retreats had been restricted now that locating gas for the Bronco was growing more difficult. Besides, they had ham radio communication between the retreats now, even if it did mean having to relay messages through the operator in Tionesta. With standard movement agreements at both retreats insisting that no one was permitted to leave the retreat alone, Randy had volunteered to accompany Sean and visit their old friends. That led to Randy's wife Emily and their two young daughters tagging along, glad to visit the other children and old friends at the East Homestead where they had spent the winter. The ride had been an uncomfortable and noisy one as the two rival sisters argued incessantly, forcing Emily to raise her voice in warning every few minutes. It also added one more checkmark to his list of reasons for not wanting another child.

Sean waited by the garden post a few more minutes, composing himself, before continuing on. Randy's youngest, Penelope, saw Sean sauntering toward them and raced in his direction with Caleb's daughter close on her heals. Penelope wrapped her arms around Sean's thigh with a squeal of delight and tried to use his leg as a shield against the rapidly approaching threat. Sean smiled and quickly lifted his friend's daughter high up in the air above his head and placed her on his broad shoulders. She laughed hysterically as Sean fended off the other girl's efforts to tag Penelope's dangling legs.

After a minute of futile attempts to get past Sean's defenses, Caleb's daughter stomped off in the direction of one of the other children who had taken the opportunity of her distraction with Sean to flee from his hiding spot behind a tree. The young boy headed for the wood pile releasing a squeal as the girl bore down on him. Sean jogged toward the side door of the cabin as Penelope held on to his forehead and bounced along with a steady stream of giggles. When he reached the short wooden stairs, he gently lowered his passenger down to the ground, held a finger to his lips, and pointed to a good hiding place underneath the edge of the steps. She winked at him and disappeared beneath his feet as he climbed the three steps into the side entrance.

Sean entered the open living area through the kitchen with a forced smile on his face. He found Brody sitting in the reclining chair talking quietly to Randy who was splayed out on the couch relaxing. Sean strolled up to them and roughly pushed Randy's leg off the couch and sat down facing Brody.

"Excuse me." Randy said sarcastically. Sean just grinned back at his friend.

"How'd it go?" Brody asked.

"How'd what go?" Sean asked, trying to avoid his friend's concerned eyes.

Brody jerked his thumb in the direction of the graveyard they had built after the attack. "I saw you headed up there at first light." Brody and Randy exchanged a quick glance.

Sean now surmised they had been talking about him when he entered. He drew his lips to a tight line. "It is what it is."

"It is what it is," Brody agreed somberly.

The room fell silent for a moment and Sean changed the subject. "I have an idea for the watchtowers that might come in handy if the place gets overrun again." Brody tilted his head and lifted an eyebrow.

He had stepped up at the East Homestead and basically taken over Damian's leadership role after his death. Even if it had never been discussed or voted on, the retreat members always looked to Brody when it came to security measures because of his experience as an Army Ranger QRF. He was also a very calm and deliberative individual. After the wedding, Brody had planned to live at the North Homestead with his bride, Beth Ann. However, the attack on East Homestead and Damian's death had changed all that. After discussing it with Beth Ann, to Sean's disappointment, they had decided they could be of better use staying at the East Homestead.

"While I was on my walk yesterday evening," Sean began, "I swung by each of the watchtowers to see if there were any ways we could bolster their defenses and prevent those on watch from getting pinned down up there like Andrew and Vita did." He saw their faces shadow and he frowned at himself for wording it so callously. "I know we discussed this last winter when we built them and I agree that encircling the platform with sandbags would add too much weight to the existing structures. Short of completely re-engineering the platforms and a lot of bracing, I was thinking we could just add a layer of sandbags on the floor of the watchtower. It would only have to be big enough for the watchmen to huddle together on top of in case the enemy made it directly underneath the tower again. They have protection from perimeter fire but we need to give them some ballistic protection from directly below. I considered using a couple of the AR500 silhouette targets we had, but Peter told me that they were all being used in other locations. What do you say about a single layer of sandbags maybe six feet long by four feet wide, right next to the hatch?"

Brody considered it a moment before opening his mouth to speak, when suddenly a voice emanated from directly over Sean's head. Sean flinched in surprise as he hadn't heard Caleb enter the room. He looked up to hear his input. "Sean, I was the one who drew up the plans for those towers. While telephone poles and excess lumber were easy to come by last winter, large structural bolts to hold everything together weren't. That platform is only held up there by a crap load of sixteen penny nails and a handful of spikes. That being said, what you are talking about might be okay, however, if we have two separate three-foot by four-foot sections of sandbags on opposite corners of the platform to better spread out the weight."

"That makes sense," Sean agreed. He turned back to Brody. "Well, what do you think? Are there enough sandbags left in storage to get that done?"

"Yes, that is one item we have plenty of. We'll get some guys on that right away." Before being attacked, their plan had been to use the floor hatch and return gunfire to anyone below the watchtower. That strategy hadn't panned out so well. By opening the hatch, they only gave away their position on the platform.

"I can help...," Sean started to say, but was instantly cut off by Brody.

"Not on that leg you can't. You don't need to be climbing those forty-foot extension ladders anytime soon." Brody crossed his arms, not leaving any room for discussion.

Sean huffed as Randy jumped in. "Sean can help me organize it. He can fill sandbags or something. I'll keep his feet on the ground."

"I'll help too," Caleb offered.

"Don't you have next watch?" Brody asked.

"Yeah, but it's not for another two hours." Caleb stretched his arms over his head, making a show that he was ready for the hard labor of carrying sandbags up the tall ladders to the watchtower platforms.

"By the time everything is organized, you're not going to be much help. I'll do it." Brody countered.

"Are you sure you wanna do that? Friend, that little physique of yours was never meant for manual labor." Caleb grinned at Brody, who just shook his head in exasperation. "You could always trade me and take my shift on watch. Maybe take Beth Ann to keep you company…if she's not busy." Sean and Randy both chuckled at

Caleb's implication, causing Brody's cheeks to redden. "Whoop, whoop!" Caleb added.

"Keep going and I just might take you up on that offer. There are four towers to get done. Since Sean and I need to be at Tionesta's council meeting this evening, I was figuring on doing two towers today and letting you do the other two tomorrow. If you really want to carry sandbags up those ladders both days, I'm fine with that." Caleb's smile vanished as he realized the amount of hard work he was getting himself into. Brody noticed the realization on Caleb's face and continued with a smile of his own. "Maybe I will go see what Beth Ann is up to." Sean and Randy both laughed and turned to see how Caleb would respond.

"No, no, that's okay. I reckon you could probably use the exercise. I'll wait till tomorrow."

"Very well then," Brody said with a fake sigh.

Sean took the pause in the action to bring up his second point. "There was a second idea I had as well." The guys turned to him in unison. Suddenly, Sean thought back to what his father had told him a week prior about making more work for others. He clamped his mouth shut, wondering if he should continue.

The others noticed his indecision. "Just spit it out," Randy said.

"Well," Sean began, "I was also considering ways of installing an escape route off the towers if you found yourself pinned down up there. Even with the sandbags, it's just a matter of time till they get a round through the floor from a weird angle."

"Are you thinking about a rappel line?" Brody asked. "We already considered that. We don't have enough rappelling hardware for eight people. Plus, you'd just be rappelling straight down the line into incoming fire."

"No, I remember that discussion with Damian when we built the towers." Sean frowned at himself for bringing Damian's name up again. "I was thinking of a zip line."

The others fell silent for a minute, pondering the idea. It was Randy who finally spoke up. "You realize they make specific hardware for zip lines with internal braking systems and the like, don't you? I don't know where we would even find something like that short of fabricating it ourselves. Besides, the zip lines I've ridden don't go all that fast and then you'd have to unclip at the bottom. It just seems dicey to me."

"I wasn't thinking about a formal zipline. We could easily pull enough wire from the various power poles in the area. I thought you might be able to just clip a large carabiner over the line and have a small wooden seat that would dangle below it. The wire could be attached to a tree in the woods and have some slack in the line about five feet off the ground. You slide just down and jump off. It would probably be a single-use type of system. Without any braking, you'd probably fly down the line. There's a good chance you'd only get one or two uses out of each carabiner before it was trashed, but it might be worth trying out on one of the towers." There was an uncomfortable silence as everyone pondered the idea.

"Sounds like fun." Randy broke the silence with a big grin.

"Are you volunteering to take the maiden voyage?" Brody asked.

"Well no, not exactly," Randy backtracked. "But I'll definitely go second if the first guy doesn't die."

"It was my idea, I'll do it," Sean insisted, accepting the responsibility and the risk.

"No!" All three yelled in unison at Sean.

"Seriously Sean! You have to stay off that leg or it's never gonna heal," Brody demanded. "Besides, we've only got a handful of carabiners in storage with the climbing equipment."

"There's a whole box of them in storage at our place," Sean offered. "Probably three dozen of them at least—all different sizes."

Brody leaned back in his chair. "It's probably worth the extra work to try it out on one of the towers." He looked at Caleb first who nodded back and then looked to Randy.

"Yeah, let's try it," Randy said. "Just remember, I got dibs on riding it second."

Brody ignored him. "I don't want to focus on that project just yet, though. We've got enough stuff going on right now. I think the sandbags are more important in the near term, so trying out the zip line idea can wait. Besides, we don't even have the carabiners here yet and who knows when we'll see you guys again."

Caleb had been standing silently with his hand on his chin. "There may also be some issue with the horizontal stress a long section of cable like that could put on the watchtower. I imagine we'll have to run another cable down to the ground in the opposite direction and anchor it into the ground or attach it to something heavy. I get the gist of what you are implying Sean, I just need to think it through a bit. We didn't build the roof structure above the watchtowers to handle stress like that. I'm going to have to draw something up on paper." Sean nodded in understanding. Caleb had been a contractor before the collapse and anything building related was deferred to his judgement. Sean hadn't considered the horizontal stress a zip line could have as it pulled on the watchtower.

"Maybe you can think about it while you are on watch today," Brody added with a smile, returning to their earlier banter. Caleb just rolled his eyes. "Any other ideas, Sean? Randy?" Brody asked.

"Not right now," Sean answered. "That was just what I came up with on my walk earlier."

"I've got an idea how you guys might be able to water the garden more efficiently, but I want to run the concept by Sean's uncle Nathan first," Randy added.

"Alright then," Brody said as he stood and stretched his arms. "Let's get to it. Our six o'clock meeting in Tionesta is going to get here fast if we don't get a move on." The men stood and headed for the back door with Caleb walking alongside Randy, pressing him for more information about his concept for changing how they water the garden. Sean waited while the others exited and turned back to the cold hearth. It was late summer and the fireplace stood empty and free of ash. Sean closed his eyes. He could see a blazing fire and feel the heat of the flames radiating on his cheek and even smell the sweet smoke. For a brief second, he had a flashback to a meeting they'd had in early spring before the attack. Damian was leaning up against the mantle with his elbow and laughing hard at something funny Caleb had said. Sean couldn't even remember the joke.

"You comin'?" Brody asked from the kitchen entrance. Sean snapped out of his trance.

"Yeah, I'm coming," he answered with a forced smile. Sean worked his way around the couch toward Brody who'd already turned back through the door. Sean gave a final glance over his shoulder. The fireplace was a cold dark cave and Damian was gone.

Chapter 2

Lt. Col. Bruce Harris sat at his desk and rhythmically clicked his pen. He'd been admonished relentlessly by his teachers in grammar school for the distracting habit, but the reprimands clearly hadn't stuck. He thumbed through Major "Sammy" Samuelsson's report on the 31st Infantry Regiment's recent supply drop and current food inventory. Bruce reached up and rubbed his hand over his face. The gesture revealed a prickly five o'clock shadow forming on his chin. His frown deepened. He'd skipped shaving that morning as he hadn't planned on leaving his office and being seen by his men. Now that he was being forced to visit the supply room, he'd have to shave. He was completely out of shaving cream and hated scraping the dull razor across his face each morning. The clicking of his pen picked up pace.

With the overall lack of shaving equipment, he had long ago issued a Regiment Directive allowing his men to keep short trimmed beards. Even so, he felt it was important that he, as regiment commander, stick to the original Army Regulation 670-1 which governed standard hair and grooming practices. Even if it wasn't practical to enforce the standards on his men now, senior officers still needed to keep up their appearance. Reaffirming his men's belief in the bedrock of military structure was hard enough in these unusual times. Not being able to keep them fed properly could end up being the final straw that broke the camel's back.

Reports of AWOL soldiers were becoming a normal routine. Just three days past, a small group of soldiers had even stolen an MRAP and raided the mess hall before they fled. That had been a first. Bruce couldn't really blame them. Regardless, he had sent out patrols to track the men down. If he hadn't done so, his men might get the wrong impression that stealing transportation and food on your way out the back door was acceptable. The AWOL soldiers hadn't been located which had been a relief to Bruce. The thought of having to incarcerate men for being hungry wasn't a decision he wanted to make…though he would have forced himself to do it had they been captured.

With the lack of food, long-term incarceration was just a waste of resources. As it was, Col. Harris still had 8 men imprisoned. The same men who'd surrendered during the battle with the gang of looters from the Bradford Prison. It had been weeks and he still hadn't been able to bring himself to make a final decision on their fate. Bruce set the food supply report aside and grabbed the stack of manila files from the corner of his desk. They contained handwritten notes from each of the imprisoned men's interrogations. He had read through each of them dozens of times now and felt as if he knew the men personally. His executive officer, Maj. Samuelsson, had been growing ever more relentless in pressuring him to make a decision on the men's fate. Bruce continued to procrastinate the inevitable. Sammy was insistent that keeping the prisoners fed while incarcerated would soon anger the men in the Regiment who resented the perceived waste of food on criminals. But the captured men weren't all hardened criminals; at least, not in the murderers and rapist sense. Only one man had actually been incarcerated for murder. He had tried to hide that fact but enough of the other seven prisoners knew about his background to force the truth out of him. Of the other seven prisoners, their crimes had been serious but non-violent.

Colonel Harris struggled with what to do with them. Just turning them loose seemed unfair and absolved them of their previous crimes, as well as many of the terrible things they had stood by and watched the prison gang do to the locals. Even though all eight men claimed they weren't involved with the more horrific atrocities like the sexual slave girls that had been captured and kept at the prison, they had not done anything to stop it either. They claimed when the prison gates opened they had nowhere else to go and just "followed the crowd." But it was no excuse in Bruce's eyes. He simply refused to let them go free, yet executing them also seemed extreme. Lately, he was leaning toward forced labor, like digging latrines. That way his troops couldn't complain about wasting food on them. However, putting them on a work detail outside the security of their cells also increased the chance they might escape. There was also the risk they might hurt or kill one of his men in their escape attempt. Bruce kept convincing himself that he just needed more time to weigh the risks involved.

The last nine months had been an astounding education on how hunger, overall human desperation, and lack of law and order could affect the psychology of a once great nation full of mostly respectable people. The horrible things he had witnessed one human committing against another completely boggled his mind. Humanity had disappeared and survival of the fittest was now the norm. A sudden knock at his door interrupted his thoughts, and he looked up as Sammy let himself in. Bruce set the prisoners' folders aside and picked up the supply and food report…but not fast enough. Sammy raised an eyebrow and started to say something as Bruce raised his hand: "No Sammy, I haven't made a decision yet. Don't even ask me about the prisoners today…seriously." Sammy paused for a moment before nodding his head and walking across the room, unceremoniously plopping down into the chair across from Bruce.

"So what do you think?" Bruce's friend and closest advisor asked.

"I'm going to assume you are talking about the supply report you gave me this morning," Bruce stated matter-of-factly, knowing that his

XO was itching to get rid of the prisoners one way or another. "I've spent most of the afternoon going over it. I think we need to consider some drastic courses of action."

Sammy sat up in the chair and leaned forward. "Such as?"

"I'm thinking a reduction of our forces and the amount of mouths we are responsible for feeding," Bruce said blandly.

"And send them where?" Sammy asked curiously. "Per my source at HQ, we are one of the best fed Regiments in the entire country right now. Sending them to another location isn't really helping them."

"I wasn't planning on relocating them. I'm talking about releasing them from service."

Sammy let out a long slow whistle between his teeth. "Good luck getting that approved through headquarters." He ran his hand through his shaggy grey hair at the thought.

Bruce noticed that his friend needed a haircut…and a shave, but he let it go for now. "I wasn't planning on discussing it with HQ."

Sammy quickly stood up in frustration, his hands balled into fists. "My word, Bruce! You are just hell bent on getting us arrested, aren't you?" He slowly regained his composure as Bruce just sat staring back at him. Sammy slumped back down into the chair and turned his face away from Bruce. "How we've gone this far without getting caught is beside me. You realize it would only take one hungry, disgruntled soldier out there with the right information to turn us in…to make a deal for some food or something. Heck, I'd turn you in myself if I knew I could get a solid meal out of it!" Bruce gave his friend a lopsided grin. "There has to be a better way Bruce. C'mon man! You know as well as I do that releasing soldiers from duty without permission is a court martial offense. The whole military is under Stop Loss. Sure, they may look the other way about releasing a couple soldiers here or there on personal or humanitarian grounds, but a large reduction of men without approval from headquarters is crazy talk."

"You got a better idea?" Bruce asked, rubbing the back of his neck.

Sammy thought about it a moment. "No, but this one sucks." Then he chuckled. "That's why *you* get payed the big bucks, Colonel. I don't have to make these types of decisions; my job is to advise you—"

"Then advise me," Bruce stated flatly.

"…AND to keep you out of trouble," Sammy finished emphatically at his friend's interruption. He flicked a loose piece of foam on the chair's armrest with his forefinger. "What about trying to acquire some food from the local towns that are thriving?"

"It's out of the question. You've seen Kane and Tionesta. The word thriving doesn't even come close to describing them. They are barely keeping their own populace fed…."

"But they *are* staying fed," Sammy cut him off, "which is more than I can say about what we're doing here."

"It doesn't matter." Bruce crossed his arms across his chest. "We are going to need cooperation with the local towns if we want to get through the months and years ahead. Confiscating their food is going to have the opposite effect."

"Bruce, you know I wasn't talking about confiscation. We aren't looters. I was talking about buying it from them or trading for it."

"Buying it with what? Trading what? Besides, they're not going to have any food to spare, I'm almost sure of it." Bruce reached up, once more scratching at his scruffy chin. "Also, how would it look for us to come begging from them?"

"It's worth a shot."

"It *is* worth a shot…," Bruce finally relented, but reluctantly. "I want to be careful how it's phrased. We don't want to look like we are coming to them with our hat in hand or, more importantly, that we are compelling them to help feed us."

"Pastor Dan is a good leader. I don't think he would take it that way and I'm sure he'd be willing to offer their aid," Sammy said, referring to Tionesta's mayor by the name everyone else used.

"I agree, but it's not just Pastor Dan we're dealing with. Sean, Brody and the other members of those two nearby homesteads will likely be there and I know they have the ear of the mayor. They're not naïve and they won't be easily persuaded. They are a lot more reluctant and suspicious of outsiders than the town council members, but I can't really say that I blame them. Seriously, how would you react if you found out there were almost 1,000 professionally trained soldiers stationed right next to your farm and they're on the verge of starving?" Sammy bobbed his head in acknowledgement of the optics behind their request. Bruce continued, "I'm just saying we've got to be careful how we approach this. Considering the fact that we received *another* short shipment of supplies from HQ yesterday, I don't see how we can hide the fact that our men are going hungry much longer. I think being honest and up front with them is the best policy right now. We are going to need their help." Bruce sighed, having finally said out loud what he had known for weeks.

"I don't think we need to get too specific though." Sammy rubbed at his temples.

"No, of course not, but we do need to let them know it's somewhat urgent. To be honest, I think the better way to approach this would be to seek assistance in getting our gardens up and growing while—"

"That doesn't help us keep the soldiers fed in the near term," Sammy interjected.

"No, Sammy…. It doesn't." Bruce narrowed his eyes at the interruption. "That is where the reduction in forces comes in." Sammy threw up his arms in exasperation, but Bruce continued. "We'll need to keep HQ in the dark; otherwise, they may short us even further on our future shipments. I estimate we can properly feed about two-thirds of our current forces in the near term. With the large raiding force from Bradford Prison gone, I think we could easily manage security in the area with seventy percent of the men."

Sammy pursed his lips. "I seriously can't believe you are considering flat-out releasing a third of our forces to the wind." He leaned forward to grab the supply report off Bruce's desk and scanned it for a few minutes before slumping back in the chair. The amount of food sent in their most recent supply run clearly wasn't enough to feed their men for the next two weeks. "I agree with you that we could feed about two-thirds of the regiment on what they've been sending us. But if we're going that route—and let's assume for two seconds that I'm even considering going along with this hair-brained scheme of yours—why go through all the hassle of training our soldiers how to be farmers?"

"Two reasons," Bruce began. "One, I don't trust that HQ is going to continue sending us the same level of food all winter. For all we know, food shipments could stop entirely at some point. We need a fallback plan."

"Okay, I agree that a fallback plan is warranted."

"Two…." Bruce's fingers thrummed on the desk while he tried to find the best way to phrase what he was going to say next. "I don't know how long HQ is going to be able to keep things from *completely* falling apart." Sammy raised an eyebrow.

"You've seen how the civilians in the Green Zones react when they begin to *really* starve. Do you seriously think it's going to be much different when our own soldiers start to starve? You are talking about impulsive twenty-year-olds with plenty of weapons training, loads of ammunition, and a good deal of recent battle experience. I think that if we start training them how to farm, we will be teaching them a life skill that they can use in the years to come. If all they know is how to kill…well, Sammy, they are going to use whatever life skills they have to survive these hard times."

"You are painting a pretty bleak picture there, Colonel. Unless you've heard information from HQ that I haven't...?" Bruce shook his head and Sammy continued. "Then I don't have any reason to believe that the whole military structure is going to fall apart. I believe having effective leadership going forward is important. We definitely have that, especially here. Not that I think training how to grow food is a bad idea either," Sammy added as an afterthought.

"Let me ask you a simple question, Sammy. Why did our country fall apart?"

Maj. Samuelsson furrowed his brow at his boss, perplexed at the question. He made a stab at it. "Because we elected Congressmen who refused to act and harden the electric grid, and then we elected a moron as President who refused to see the threat and pissed off the North Koreans who in turn smacked us in the mouth with an EMP...."

Bruce raised his hand to stop Sammy's political rambling. "Hold on Sammy. You know I agree with all of that. But that was the catalyst, not the actual reason why things fell apart afterwards. I'll rephrase it. Why did social order in this country completely fall apart after the EMP?"

Sammy thought about it for another moment. "I'm going to go back to what I said earlier: leadership...and the lack of law and order. Plus, there was poor organization responding to the—"

"No." Bruce cut him off once more. "Food!" Bruce bellowed. "No amount of leadership, law and order, planning, or anything else under the sun could have stopped things from falling apart when the food ran out. The American people relied upon and trusted the US Government to keep them fed by making sure our country and its infrastructure was protected from a threat that most didn't even know existed. Americans have grown lazy over the last hundred years with just-in-time delivery of anything and everything they wanted, right to their front door within two days' time. They completely forgot how to live without electricity. Right now, you and I are doing the same thing. We are being every bit as naïve as the average American was before the EMP. We are willingly putting our lives into the hands of our superiors at HQ and trusting that they are going to keep this great big military machine running smoothly. We are trusting them that they are going to keep us fed. Do you not see the irony in this?" Bruce leaned forward over the desk. "We have a mission here to restore the electric grid and get that refinery up and running. I intend to complete that mission to the best of our ability. At the same time, my men look to me for leadership and to keep them fed and keep things orderly. I'm telling you right now, Sammy, if we don't turn this ship around soon, the amount of AWOL soldiers we've been seeing the last few weeks is going to double and then triple and then…well, before long we aren't going to have any soldiers left."

Sammy sneered. "C'mon Bruce. I keep a good pulse of the men. There is some grumbling and complaining going around, but if we just—"

"Food!" Bruce slammed his open palm down on the desk.

"What?" Sammy asked, eyes wide in surprise.

Bruce lowered his voice. "The answer is still food, Sammy. Don't you get it? Yes, there is only grumbling and complaining right now but that is because every one of the men ate this morning. Now it may not be as generous a portion as they're accustomed to, but it's still something. What's their alternative? They know what's out there." Bruce jerked his thumb over his shoulder toward the dirty window. "There's nothing out there for them. They know there's no food left in this country and my men have honor. They know if they head out on their own, they will likely have to do some nasty stuff to survive. Right now, their alternative here is better. We have to keep it that way. It's not perfect, but two small meals a day is a lot better than what they are going to find out there on their own." Bruce held eye contact with Sammy to stress his next point. "But if you think for one second that we are going to maintain control of this Regiment without food, then you haven't learned a single thing from watching this country destroy itself over the last nine months. The world we live in is all about survival. And if you want to survive you HAVE to have food! If those food shipments from HQ slow down any further or stop altogether, we will lose control of this Regiment. I promise you. No amount of

food. The military is hording all the food, right?" Bruce asked Sammy sarcastically, reflecting the thoughts of most people who lived in the Green Zones. They didn't understand how the food shipments from NATO were actually distributed; all they knew is that they were hungry and starving and the soldiers weren't.

"If the bases start to fall apart and the men here get word, we are likely to lose half our men wanting to get back to their families. I'm still considering how this would work, though. If they just showed up back at Aberdeen with their hats in hand asking about their family members, they'd get arrested for desertion and sooner or later our secret would be out. It's a timing issue. We would need to find out immediately after Aberdeen falls apart and release the men with families stationed on the base to retrieve their loved ones and bring them back here. That's where reviving the town of Warren, with a reliable farming and food infrastructure, would benefit us. It's a humanitarian issue and I don't think HQ would make a big stink about it, especially if we were producing our own food and taking the responsibility of feeding a bunch of civilians off their hands. If we're successful in getting the grid and the refinery up and running, that would only help our cause. Besides, if the food runs out and our military forces start falling apart to the point that bases are getting overrun, they'll have a lot more to worry about than disciplining me for taking a single matter into my own hands."

"I hope you're right about that." Sammy squinted his eyes, not entirely convinced.

"Me too," Bruce smiled dryly. "I'll just tell them I didn't want to concern them over a trivial matter like that and I knew they were busy."

Sammy sneered. "Did I ever tell you you're crazy, Bruce?"

Bruce grinned. "A time or two."

They sat in silence for a few moments before Sammy spoke up. "I know of eight mouths we could stop feeding right now…."

Bruce narrowed his eyes at Sammy and was getting ready for a sharp rebuke when a loud crackling sound came from outside, somewhere in the town. "What the hell?" Bruce said as he raced Sammy to the open window.

Chapter 3

Bruce hopped down from the Humvee, closing the heavy armor-plated door behind him. A small stream of smoke was trickling from a second-floor window of the power plant. There were two groups of men in the high weeds of the front lawn arguing emphatically. The first group was made up of uniformed soldiers while the other group was entirely civilians. Captain Barnes, who was in charge of the men from the Army Corps of Engineers, stood nose to nose with Consolidated Edison's Chief Engineer, a man Bruce only knew as "Cameron." They were screaming profanities at each other, and Bruce could clearly see the veins in Cameron's neck bulging. He could tell it was only minutes away from coming to blows. One of the electricians behind Cameron held a large pipe wrench in his hand and was slowly inching forward as the two sides faced off.

"What the hell is going on here, Captain?" Bruce bellowed as he approached. The men either ignored him or didn't hear him as they continued their argument. It was quickly escalating as Cameron gave Captain Barnes a shove.

"Get out of my face!" Cameron screeched as Bruce pushed his way into the fray.

Captain Barnes was far larger than Cameron and responded by shoving him back even harder. The civilian with the wrench made a move forward but was roughly horse-collared by Sergeant Timms who was Bruce's security escort for the day. The man spun angrily to see who'd grabbed him and then hesitated as he saw the sergeant's hand lightly resting on his side arm. "I wouldn't do that if I were you," Timms said in an icy tone. "Drop it!" The man glared back at the steely eyed soldier before slowly letting the wrench drop from his greasy fingers and turning his attention back to the argument. Col. Harris forced himself between the two men, pushing Captain Barnes back a step or two while Sgt. Timms faced off with Cameron, staring him down with a "just try me" look.

"What the hell is going on here?" Bruce demanded of them. Capt. Barnes just glared at Cameron over Bruce's shoulder. "I'm not going to ask you again, Captain!"

"That idiot just destroyed half the work we've done over the past two months!" Cameron hollered out with a clenched fist raised in Captain Barnes direction.

Bruce spun his head toward Sgt. Timms. "Shut him up, please!" Timms took another step toward Cameron who quickly reacted by taking a step back and raising his hands up submissively.

Captain Barnes gave Cameron a final icy glare before turning his hard eyes to Col. Harris. He let out a long sigh. "There was a miscommunication between our teams on which breaker we were to engage and…some stuff got damaged."

Cameron let out a loud huff behind Bruce. "Some stuff? Damaged? You fried the entire master control board and damn near killed me in the process!"

Bruce turned to see Cameron literally shaking in rage. "You done?" Bruce asked rhetorically. Cameron folded his arms across his chest, took in a deep breath, and slowly let it out before nodding. He turned his head to stare off in the direction of the river.

"How is this even possible?" Bruce asked angrily. "How could you guys blow something up without any electricity? We heard the explosion from all the way over on the other side of town!"

"We tied three of our 60-kilowatt diesel generators together and hooked them up to the main. Boy Genius over there insisted on running diagnostics before we tried to fire up the entire plant tomorrow." Captain Barnes said in a snarky tone. "I told him it was a bad idea and the loads were completely different…."

"It wasn't a bad idea and the smaller load had nothing to do with it!" Cameron suddenly jumped in to defend himself. "It was bad execution on his part. I gave his men simple instructions!"

"We followed your stupid instructions!" Capt. Barnes snapped back.

"Aren't you Army boys supposed to be good at following orders?" Cameron responded, and the two of them were once again yelling over each other.

"Shut up!" Bruce roared. "Both of you! Seriously, I'm about to lock both of you up for the next couple days…in the same cell," he added. "But that's not going to solve the problem here. I don't care what happened, how it happened, or why it happened, all I care about is fixing it and moving forward! I'm scheduled to call in and give HQ an update tomorrow on how things are going. From our meeting last week, they're expecting to hear that you guys have fired this thing up or at least tried to."

"Well that's not gonna happen now," one of the other men behind Bruce muttered under his breath.

Col. Harris spun around, looking for the man who'd spoken. "Who said that? What do you mean, 'That's not going to happen now?'" The men all looked off in other directions, none of them wanting to make eye contact with the furious commander.

Cameron unclenched his fists, some of the tension draining from his face. "What he means is it's not gonna—"

Consolidated Edison's Chief Engineer was interrupted as an MRAP suddenly appeared in the distance, barreling down the road and turning into the power plant's driveway at a high rate of speed. The heavy truck's wheels locked up as it skidded to a stop in the soft grass, only ten feet from the crowd of greasy men. QRF (Quick Response Force) soldiers poured out of the truck and rushed forward. Bruce's driver had evidently called in for back up after witnessing Bruce approach the irate mob of arguing men. Bruce raised his hand to the approaching soldiers, keeping them on the outskirts of the fray.

Bruce addressed the mob, turning in a circle and making eye contact with all the men surrounding him. "I don't want to hear it's not going to happen. We are going to get this grid up and running, and we are going to do it soon. It only took me five minutes to get here after the explosion, so I know there is no possible way either one of you could have had time to diagnose what's broken in there. I don't care whose fault it is. I care about getting the problem fixed. All of you are going to go back in there and work together to figure it out." He waited for a response, and a few of the men started bobbing their heads.

In the awkward silence, Bruce turned back to Barnes and Cameron. "I want both of you in my office in four hours to report where we are at with all of this." He used his "commander" voice, which didn't leave any room for discussion.

"I'm also sending a squad of my men in there to watch over you with specific instructions that if any more of this pushing and shoving crap takes place, they are to hogtie the men involved and deliver them to me personally. That goes for you civilians as well!" Bruce turned toward Cameron and stared him in the eye. Cameron stood defiant for a moment before breaking the Colonel's gaze and looking down at his shoes. "Forget what happened and why because that ship has sailed. Work together and figure out how to fix it!" Bruce turned to address the half-dozen QRF soldiers standing off to the side. "And I'm serious about what I just said. If any of these guys gets out of hand, I want them hogtied and brought to my office immediately! That's a direct order."

The sergeant standing out front of his men grinned. "You got it, sir."

Bruce glanced down at his watch and muttered to himself before turning his attention back to Captain Barnes and Cameron. "I'm not going to make you two shake hands like you're school kids on the playground, but I want both of your words that this arguing is over. I want you to work together to fix this mess. Understood?"

Captain Barnes responded first. "Understood, Colonel."

Bruce turned to Cameron who sighed again. "Yeah, we'll figure it out."

Bruce huffed. "Okay then, I want both of you in my office no later than 1600 hours with a report of where we are. I have somewhere else to be this evening, so don't be late! Now get on with it." Bruce didn't even wait to see how they responded. He just turned on his heel and stomped back toward his ride, Sgt. Timms at his side.

The dark figure awoke to the sound of a car door slamming. He slowly opened his eyes, letting them adjust to the late day sun while trying to figure out its position relative to the horizon. After establishing it was late afternoon, he spent a few minutes lying perfectly still, listening to his surroundings and allowing his senses to come fully awake. When he was sure no one was nearby, he slowly lifted his head and peered around. Nothing to see. After the previous night of stalking the men from the roadblock, he had made his way through the forest paralleling the road until he found what he was looking for and settled in for a few hours of shuteye. Picking up the binoculars that rested by his side, he slowly rolled over into a prone position. He focused the binoculars on the six men below him who weren't making much effort to be quiet or hide their movements. They were being reckless. He had assumed that someone from the group would have walked a small perimeter of their area, but no one had left the road to wander through the woods near him. Tionesta's main roadblock needed serious work. This was too easy.

He studied the men for a few more minutes before rolling his body back behind the cover of the fallen pine tree he was halfway burrowed under. He quietly sat up and slid his pack out from underneath the tree limbs to his left. He opened the main compartment and pulled out his uniform. It was a dark brown pair of pleated pants and a matching short-sleeve button-down shirt with a rectangular UPS patch on the chest. He'd discovered that the muted brown uniform blended in with the forest fairly well and he preferred it over the Fed Ex uniform he had originally worn. After changing his clothes, he re-packed his bag. Sitting on the stump in front of him were various implements he had removed from his other clothing and he quickly inventoried them.

The first item he picked up was a small shiny handcuff key he'd painstakingly made with a square file. It had a small clip on it, and he reached behind his back to clip onto his rear belt loop that he always intentionally skipped. This method kept the small key well hidden, even during a pat down. Next, he took the razorblade with the cardboard protector still in place and slid it inside the flap that buttoned down over his back pocket. He'd made a small incision on the inside of the pocket flap where he could hide it. If his hands were handcuffed or zip tied behind his back, he'd easily be able to free himself when the time was right. He had another, smaller handcuff key that was attached to the end of his bootlace and covered with a piece of skinny rubber tubing. At a glance, no one would notice it was any different than the typical aglet. He had also replaced his laces with 550 cord, enabling him to use them as a friction saw on zip ties if need be. He reached down to feel the hidden pocket inside the front of his belt to be sure the second razorblade was still in place. That same pocket he had sewn on the inside of his belt also held a small hook pick, a rake, and a tension wrench. They all had their small plastic handles melted off and cut down as short as practicably possible. The last detention escape item was a Master padlock bump key that he stashed inside the small coin pocket of his pants. He snatched the important letter he was carrying protectively inside a ziplock baggie and stuffed it in his front left pocket. Last, he picked up the final item off the log and clipped his Kershaw Camber pocket knife onto his front pants pocket.

He pondered whether or not he should take his notebook and finally grabbed it from his pack, sticking it in his back pants pocket. Typically, he never brought it along on an initial meeting, but for some reason he decided to bring it anyway. He stood up, inspected himself, and found he had missed one of the buttons on his shirt. First impressions were important. He took a large black contractor's garbage bag and gently placed his pack inside, being careful not to rip the plastic. Next, he unchambered his AR and Glock 17 handgun before removing the AR's upper receiver from the lower and wrapped all three items inside his cloak to protect them. Last, he carefully placed them in the garbage bag on top his pack and covered his livelihood with a few branches and leaves. He turned and quietly walked back through the trees in the opposite direction of the roadblock until he could walk down to the road unseen. He slowly edged his way out onto the road, looking in both directions to be sure no one was visible. Once on the road, he smoothed out his wrinkled shirt as best he could and ran his fingers through his hair a few times before walking forward at a casual pace.

"Halt right there!" a man yelled from behind one of the cars, pointing his battle rifle threateningly.

The dark figure quickly raised his hands over his head and turned three hundred and sixty degrees so they could see he didn't have a weapon on him. "I'm unarmed, please don't shoot me!"

A couple of the men behind the roadblock of cars were having a discussion, motioning in his direction. The dark figure stood as still as stone, not wanting to move should it be perceived as threatening.

Another man, older than the others, with gray wispy hair and bushy eyebrows stepped forward and called out, "Keep your hands above your head and walk forward to the vehicles!"

The dark figure complied, slowly walking forward with his hands raised. He noticed a couple men scrambling up the hillside through the trees and taking elevated positions to his left. He pretended not to notice and kept his eyes forward. Two of the men took positions behind some pre-set logs, while two others continued paralleling the road back in the direction he'd come from. "Okay," the dark figure thought. "Maybe they aren't as incompetent as I thought." They had set up a cross firing security team while they sent men to determine if he was actually alone. He considered his hidden pack for a moment but let the thought drift away. It was well hidden.

When the dark figure was only three paces from the car the older man, who he assumed was in charge, challenged him in a firm voice, "Okay, stop right there." He stopped compliantly and tried to look as casual as possible. He had been in this position numerous times now and it was important not to appear nervous. It was just as important though not to look too confident or arrogant. "Are you carrying any weapons on you?" the man asked.

"No, sir," he responded politely. "Just a small pocket knife in my front pocket." He made sure to keep his hands still as he spoke and not motion toward the pocket with his hand as one of the security guards might mistake the movement as reaching for it.

"Where's the rest of your supplies?" the old man inquired. "I know you aren't travelling the open roads with just a small pocket knife and a prayer. Are you local?"

"This is all I brought with me." It was always best not to tell an outright lie as they could be hard to get out of if you needed to. Speaking in half-statements and misdirection was best.

"Yeah, whatever you say." The man's eyes narrowed. "I'm going to send two men out to search you for weapons. If you make any sudden or threatening movements, you'll likely end up dead. Keep your hands up in the air and everything will be fine. Are we clear?" There was a reason the old man was in charge. He was good at giving instruction and taking control of a situation, while at the same time not escalating an already tense encounter with a stranger.

"That will be fine," the dark figure quickly responded, reassuring the man in charge with a slight smile and a nod. Two men walked around the back of the car and slowly approached him. One of the men walked in front of him and held a pistol pointed at his chest from a few feet away. "That's a little too close," the dark figure thought. If he had wanted, he could probably juke to his left and close the distance fast enough to grab the man's pistol before he could place his finger on the trigger and squeeze. It would have been safer if the man had stayed back a few more feet.

His musings were interrupted by the second man who had approached from his right and reassuringly gave his shoulder a squeeze. "Just relax, Buddy. This will only take a second," he said calmly before patting him down, being careful not to place his body in between the dark figure and his friend with the pistol. When he was done, the man pulled the pocket knife out of his front pocket and looked it over briefly before sliding it into his own pocket. "Nice knife," he commented as he stepped back a pace or two. The dark figure stared at the man's front pocket longingly, pretending to be upset at the confiscation of his beloved pocket knife.

Noticing the look on the dark figure's face, the man in charge spoke up. "Don't worry, you'll get it back when we're done here." He motioned at the two men, who quickly retreated to the protection of the vehicles while the pistol stayed trained on the dark figure's chest. The old man motioned to the others next to him to lower their weapons and waved the stranger forward. He complied and walked forward till he was on the opposite side of the car hood from the old man. He slowly lowered his hands with a questioning look, placing them on the hood of the car. The old man just nodded his assent.

"We don't see too many travelers these days. Where ya comin' from, son?"

"I've been travelling from the east," he answered.

"Where's all your stuff? You don't look like you're starving, so I assume you must have stashed your gear before you approached us." The old man must have had numerous conversations just like this with other travelers. He obviously wasn't naive.

"No, I'm not really hungry right now, thank you for asking. I am kinda thirsty though," he hedged again, not wanting to acknowledge the man's suspicions about stashing his pack up the road. The old man paused, weighing his response before gesturing to the teenager next to him. The young man removed a green plastic military-surplus canteen from the pouch on his belt and leaned over the car, placing it halfway across the faded hood. The dark figure nodded his appreciation at the lad and leaned forward to grasp the canteen. He took a long draw from its contents. The water was lukewarm but it was clean and clear. The taste of the fresh, non-iodine-flavored water made him realize how thirsty he actually was. He took another long swig before winking his thanks to the teen and placing the canteen back down on the center of the hood where it stayed.

"I've been polite so far with you mister, yet you keep dodging my questions," the old man said flatly. "So let's try again. Where are you headed?"

"The town of Tionesta."

The old man waited for more information. When it was apparent that the stranger wasn't going to offer any, he continued. "Well, you've found us. How can we help you?"

Chapter 4

The mayor of Tionesta dumped his bicycle over on its side and strolled up to the current watch leader at the East Roadblock. "What's the situation?" he asked with a frown, huffing as he spoke. His work had been interrupted by the radio call, and then he was forced to ride the rusty bicycle up to the roadblock. The mayor peered at the stranger suspiciously. At first glance, he was a middle-aged man clad in a deep brown uniform, casually leaning against the hood of one of the vehicles making up the road block.

"Well, this stranger here approached on foot about a half hour ago," Victor, the road block's captain, began. "He doesn't have any supplies on him and he won't tell us anything about himself or where he's coming from. He insisted on speaking with you directly. He said he has a message for you."

The dark figure, who had been pretending not to listen, cut the watch leader off. "I apologize to interrupt the honorable watch commander here, but for the record, I never said I had a message for the mayor. I just said 'I *have* a message' and I needed to 'speak with the mayor.' Two separate things."

The old man rolled his eyes in annoyance and ignored the interruption, continuing his report. The mayor was still listening to the watch leader, but he was also now studying the stranger with interest.

"Anyways, he won't say who the message is from or what it's about," Victor finished. He glanced at the stranger across the vehicle and made sure his next comment was clearly overheard. "He also likes to play word games, so you'll need to read between the lines of anything he says."

"Okay, Victor, thank you," the mayor said softly to the older gentleman with a light squeeze to the shoulder. He shuffled over to the figure with a reassuring smile. "What's your name, friend?"

"I'm The Postman." The uniformed man waited for some recognition from the mayor, but it never came. "You know, like the movie, *The Postman*…with Kevin Costner?" He held his arms out and spun around, showing off his uniform.

The mayor's face was blank. "I'm sorry, friend, but I'm not real sure what you're talking about."

One of the other men on watch stepped forward. "I've seen the movie a time or two...."

The mayor cocked his head in the man's direction.

"It's a post-apocalyptic movie where Kevin Costner finds a mailman's outfit and goes from town to town delivering messages between the various surviving villages in trade for room and board. He ends up getting captured by this warlord who….." He trailed off as Pastor Dan began to lose interest. "Well, it's a long movie," he added sheepishly.

The mayor turned his attention back to the wiry figure. "Okay, Mr. Mail Man, what's your real name and how can I help you?"

"It's *the Postman*," the wiry figure emphasized. He realized it was going to be much harder to explain since the mayor hadn't seen the movie.

"But you're wearing a UPS uniform?"

The uniformed man just waved the idea away. "Never mind all that. My friends just call me Willy." He offered the mayor his deepest smile. Considering the mayor's reaction, it might have been a bit too deep. His wife, Angel, had always loved his big smile, but others had told him not to smile so much as he looked silly with his big blocky teeth. He dropped the smile and tried to force his face to go back to normal, which produced another awkward look from the mayor.

"I go by Pastor Dan around here, and I'm the acting Mayor of Tionesta. How can I help you, Willy?" the mayor asked with a forced smile in return, still trying to determine if the man before him was completely sane.

"I already told you, I'm the Postman. I have a letter to deliver," Willy said matter-of-factly, pulling the ziplock bag out of his pocket, retrieving the handwritten letter and showing it to the mayor. Pastor Dan began to lean forward, but Willy pretended not to notice and quickly placed the letter back into the safety of the baggie, returning it to the relative safety of his front pocket.

The mayor turned to the men behind him with a completely bewildered look on his face before turning back to Willy. "Okay, Willy. Who is your message addressed to?"

"Well it's not exactly addressed, per se, as most people don't have any envelopes and most addresses aren't very accurate these days with people being scattered to the four winds, an' all. I also don't require stamps as that wouldn't really be fair with no post offices around to buy them from. My delivery fees are typically a bartering system depending on the distance I have to travel and how dangerous the route will be. I also—" Willy trailed off as he realized he was babbling again. He took a big breath and gave the mayor another a big smile. "Too big again," he thought to himself as he pressed his lips tightly together. The mayor just looked back at him in awe and wonder at the strangeness of the entire conversation. Willy quickly answered the mayor's original question. "The message is for a Mr. Hank Keefer."

Willy saw the instant recognition on the Mayor's face and was suddenly excited about the prospect of delivering his message. But then a deep sadness filled Pastor Dan's eyes. Willy didn't need to hear what came next as he'd seen that same look a dozen times.

"I'm sorry to tell you, Willy, but Hank passed away a month ago," the mayor said in a somber tone as he glanced down at his feet.

Willy's shoulders slumped. "I understand, Reverend."

"It's just Pastor. Pastor Dan," the mayor corrected him before continuing. "Can I ask who the letter was from?"

"Sure, you may."

The mayor stood there for an awkward moment, waiting for Willy to continue. "Okaaaay, who was the letter to Hank from?"

"Oh, I'm sorry, but I can't divulge that information. The United States Postal Service has a very strict privacy policy. I could get in a lot of trouble if…well, you understand." Willy shifted his stance onto his other foot while the mayor was trying to determine if the man was messing with him.

"But you just said I could ask who it was from." The mayor was growing annoyed.

"Sure, I was being polite and saying that *you could* ask me if you'd like. But unfortunately, because of the official USPS privacy policy, I'm unable to provide you with that information at this time."

"But you're wearing a UPS uniform," Pastor Dan pointed out. "I don't think the United States Postal Service's privacy policy applies to the UPS."

Willy looked down at his uniform, suddenly aware of the mayor's confusion and chuckled. "Oh, you mean these old things?" he asked, pulling at the collar of his dark brown button-down shirt. "I haven't been able to find an actual United States Postal Service uniform yet…or at least one that fit properly." Willy raised his hand and scratched at his chin for a moment. "I once found a female's Postal Service uniform that fit my height okay. Unfortunately, it had a bunch of extra fabric up in this region here…." Willy tugged on the chest area of his uniform. "It looked kinda silly with all that loose cotton dangling limp out in front of me." He chuckled. "I think the woman must have had—" He paused in horror, looking up at Pastor Dan's face. "I'm so very, very sorry, Reverend. I truly didn't mean to offend you." He paused uncomfortably for a moment before adding. "Please forgive me." Willy's face contorted in obvious pain at the possible offense he may have caused to the man of God.

"Sure, Willy. It's no problem. Just try and relax a bit." The mayor didn't seem offended in the least. "I'm sorry that I couldn't help you deliver that message, but if you don't have any other official United States Postal Service business with our town, I'm afraid I'll need to get back to what I was working on," he added politely.

Pastor Dan was turning to leave when Willy blurted out, "But I do have other official business in town!"

The mayor stopped and sighed deeply, shaking his head. He seemed to be in a rush to leave. "Lord, give me strength to be patient with this poor man," Willy heard the man whisper under his breath. The mayor forced a smile on his face and turned back to Willy. "Okay, Willy, do you have another letter? I do really need to get back soon."

"Well, no.... However, it is very important that I am able to return with some piece of evidence to assure the sender that I actually attempted to deliver their message. Typically, when I find the recipients have passed away or gone missing, I retrieve a family photo from their home and return it to the sender with any clues I may discover around the recipient's residence. I try to be as thorough as possible. I let the sender know if I found graves, if there were signs of struggle, if there were any notes left behind. Things of that nature. I was hoping you could tell me a little more about Hank and his passing." The mayor seemed to be considering his request, so he pushed further. "I would also like to offer my services to the people of your town. I have news of the outside world that I can share. I have information that I would be willing to trade for a hot meal and a warm bed, even for a single night. I have travelled much of the local area and I have many small villages and groups that are very appreciative of the services I provide. Maybe I could add your town to my route?"

The mayor's lips turned down. "You are obviously staying fed in your new profession. I'm not convinced yet if you are actually helping people or just taking advantage of their desperation to receive news about their lost family members and relatives."

Willy face crinkled in injury at the mayor's tone. "Well, Reverend, I will admit that it hasn't really turned out like the movie or what I envisioned when I took my job as The Postman." He sighed. "In truth, only a handful of my messages have actually reached their intended targets. The service I ultimately end up providing now is either hope or closure."

The mayor raised an eyebrow and Willy continued. "You see, many people have been separated from their families and loved ones for the last nine months. They don't know if their friends and family are alive or not and the open road is too dangerous for most people to travel without my skills. When I try to deliver a message and it fails, I always return something back to the sender. I give them closure if I find their family's bodies or graves. I give them hope if I find a note or clue that their loved one may still be alive. But even if I can find no definite clues on the recipient's whereabouts, the most important thing I always try to offer them is a picture or two. Very few people who escaped the various cities after the collapse took pictures with them as they fled the chaos. I can't even describe to you how happy they are to receive a picture of their missing loved ones…." Willy trailed off for a few moments as his hunching shoulders grew heavier. "However, I do wish that I could deliver more good news to people. I'm hoping that if I get enough towns and groups on board, I can start connecting people from the various areas and let them start communicating with each other again. I'm also willing to deliver official government business from one town to another." Willy stopped abruptly, not sure what else to say. He believed he'd covered all of his talking points. He waited.

Pastor Dan stood silent for a moment, considering Willy's words. The other men on watch stood quietly, waiting to see what the mayor would do. Finally he spoke. "Hank was on watch about two months ago when he was shot and killed during an ambush by a large raiding force from the Bradford Prison."

Willy nodded. "Yes, I'm familiar with them. They were a pretty bad lot for a while until Paul took over. He was trying to get control of them, when…well, I don't know what happened to the prison, but it was blown to kingdom come…which also doesn't make sense to me." Willy hadn't noticed but the mayor now stood silently, studying him with squinted eyes as Willy's thoughts meandered and he absently talked aloud to himself. "What is the military doing dropping bombs on a prison so far from the Green Zones? True, there was a really bad element there and they were a pretty ferocious bunch as a whole…. It just doesn't make sense why the US Government would go through the time and effort of destroying them. Heck, there are a bunch of larger and way more sadistic groups of looters that could use an airstrike, for sure. I just hope those poor girls they were holding got out of there…." Willy stopped speaking as soon as he realized that he'd been babbling again. He hadn't meant to say any of it loud.

"What did you say?" The mayor's face grew dark. "You said the leader's name was Paul. How did you know that? And how did you know about those girls?"

Willy knew that he'd slipped up and searched for the right words to explain. "Since my job requires me to travel the open roads, I make it a point to investigate any and all groups that I encounter. I study their movements, their base of operations, and the threat they may offer to me or other travelers. I have to do this if I don't want to get captured or killed while I travel."

"Studying them from a distance doesn't tell you the name of the guy who's in charge though," Dan pointed out as he crossed his arms across his chest.

"No, it doesn't," Willy admitted. "But sneaking up within ten feet of an overnight patrol and listening to the men gossip throughout the night will tell you just about anything you need to know about anything." The mayor once more looked Willy up and down, this time with a dubious look. "I told you that I have a specific skillset that keeps me alive on the open road, didn't I? Would you like me to provide an example and tell you what your forward patrolmen, the ones two miles down the road, were whispering to each other late last night?"

The mayor glanced over his shoulder at the older watch leader who was visibly upset about the possibility that this stranger had gotten so close to their patrol. With no verbal response from Victor, he turned back. "Let's hear it."

Willy reached into his cargo pocket, removed his small green notebook and thumbed through the pages, mumbling to himself until he found what he was looking for. He recited the three men's names that had been on watch the night before, the precise weapons they'd been carrying, and a short recap of their general conversations. When finished with the details, he added. "Your men were never in any danger from me. But if I may be so bold, they need some serious work on their operational security." He paused for a moment before adding, "Your guys here could use some work, too."

"Now you wait just one minute there!" Victor bellowed as he stepped forward, his chest puffed up.

The mayor turned and put a reassuring hand on Victor's shoulder. "Relax, Victor. If he'd have meant us harm, why would he be standing here talking to us?" Pastor Dan glanced back at Willy and then guided Victor a few more paces away so they could talk privately. Willy took the hint and turned around, leaning back against the hood of the car while making a show of studying the branches reaching over his head. He could still hear their low voices.

"Do you believe the things he's saying?" the mayor asked.

"Heck no!" Victor said in a harsh whisper and then continued on, quieter. "That boy is a few fries short of a happy meal." Victor sighed. "Okay, Okay. The man's obviously got some skill and a knack for travelling around without getting himself killed. Those three men he mentioned *were* on watch last night and the things he said they were discussing would be pretty hard to make up. As far as this 'Postman' stuff goes, I don't know, Mayor. I don't trust him and I don't think it would be wise to just turn him loose around town. Maybe he's a scout for another looting group or a town that's in desperate need of food. Do we really want him reporting back to them on the exact amounts and what types of crops we're growing here?"

Pastor Dan nodded his head in thought. "I really don't get the impression that he's an advanced scout for someone else. It sounds like if he wanted, he could've easily bypassed our roadblock here and snuck up to the edge of town and scouted everything out before leaving just as quietly. That story of his is pretty incredible if it's just a cover story. I'm half tempted to believe him." Willy could sense the two men's eyes as they bore holes into his back. "However, your point about him making notes on us and sharing the information to other local groups is well founded." They stood in silence for a minute while the mayor thought to himself. "I think I have an idea."

They walked back to the roadblock and Pastor Dan began, "You said that you were in contact with some of the other towns. What can you tell me about them?"

Willy knew the mayor was fishing for something, but he wasn't sure what. "Yes, I am in contact with a few other towns." His mind raced while he stalled, trying to uncover what the mayor was getting at. Willy wanted to be sure he answered correctly.

"Yes, you said that already," the mayor said with a dismissive wave of his hand. "How many towns are you in contact with?"

Willy couldn't see this being any kind of trick question, so he answered outright, "Twelve."

Pastor Dan and Victor looked at each other in surprise. Neither must have figured on so many towns surviving. "That's quite a few towns," Dan acknowledged. "How large of an area do you cover?"

"I cover most of north-central Pennsylvania, sticking to the smaller mountain towns. This is as far west as I've roamed though." Both of their eyes widened at Willy's breadth of travels.

"How is it that you haven't been killed, spending that much time alone, out on the open road?" Dan asked softly.

Willy sighed. "I've already told you. I have a specific skillset for staying hidden. Besides, not very many people travel the roadways anymore, and even less travel at night. I mostly have to be wary of the bandits and ambushes along my routes. Fortunately, I have yet to find any that can keep up with me or track me through the woods when I scramble. I also keep very good notes and detailed maps, so I don't forget which areas to avoid."

It seemed as if Pastor Dan's interest was piqued by the mention of detailed maps, but before he could bring it up, Victor asked another question. "What are some of the names of the towns you frequent? How are they faring?"

Willy thought for a moment. "I'm not going to divulge that information."

"Why is that?" Victor asked pointedly.

This time Willy didn't hesitate and looked directly into Victor's eyes. "Honestly, because I don't trust you yet." He turned back to Pastor Dan and gave him an apologetic half-smile with a small shrug of his thin shoulders. He owed the Reverend a little more of an explanation. "For all I know, there is no town of Tionesta. You could all be just a bunch of looters that have taken over an empty town. I've built relationships with the people I deliver messages for and they offer me safe refuge along my routes and help feed me. I wouldn't want to be the one responsible for them getting overrun by a large group of raiders."

"Fair Enough," Pastor Dan replied. "However, you have to realize that mistrust goes both ways." He paused for a moment before continuing. "And to be honest with you, I'm not so sure you are an entirely stable individual to bring into my town."

"Whatever do you mean, Reverend? I'm a model image of physical and mental health." To demonstrate, he flashed them another big toothy smile and with a flurry of movement, spun in a circle before deftly leaping into the air and landing in a half crouch. Willy stretched out his hands and took a deep bow.

This produced a chuckle from a couple of the men standing behind Pastor Dan and a clearly reluctant grin from Victor. He might be unstable, but he definitely had a sense of humor. "Well, Willy, we are definitely a town and not some group of looters, I can assure you that," Pastor Dan began. "In fact, I was getting ready to attend our weekly town council meeting. It's God's benevolence that you showed up today as we are going to be discussing the idea of sending out some scouting parties to make contact with other survivors in the area. Now that the Bradford Prison Gang is out of the picture, I feel it's time we start re-connecting with our neighbors and working together to rebuild. Putting together these scouting missions is a risky venture as we don't really know what's out there," Pastor Dan said as he raised his hand toward the road from the direction Willy had come.

"Willy, you could help us. With your maps and your notes, you could help my men plan their routes and avoid those dangerous areas you mentioned. I would also like to discuss sending some messages to the mayors of other towns you travel to and get a dialog started with them. I'd be happy to offer you room and board in trade for information," Dan finished with an encouraging smile.

Willy slowly turned around and was quiet for a long minute. To the others, it almost sounded like Willy was praying softly to himself. When he'd finished his mumbling, he turned back around to face the mayor. "Before we discuss the other stuff, I'd like for you to agree to take me to Hank's house so I can make some notes and take his br—I mean the sender—a picture or two. I understand if you'd like your men to come inside with me to make sure I'm not stealing anything."

The mayor nodded his head so Willy continued. "I'd be willing to trade room and board for delivering your messages to the other mayors. Normally, I'd require more of a payment for such a service, but we could offset that cost if you'd allow me to address your townspeople directly and offer my services to them as well." He looked once more to Pastor Dan questioningly.

Dan grabbed at his ear as he considered the offer. "Before I agree to that, I'd like for you to explain what you will require in the form of payment from my people for your services. They don't have much of value and I don't want to see you taking advantage of people who are desperate to receive news of loved ones."

"I don't have a set fee, Reverend. I have a general list of items that I need or would like to have. If the individual doesn't have any of those items, I am always willing to hear them out on what they could offer. I also don't take any payment until my return. Generally, I wing it," Willy admitted.

"That doesn't really answer my question," the mayor said flatly. "How about if I or another one of my council members sits in on your negotiations. That way we'll also have record of whatever is agreed upon to prevent any disagreements upon your return."

Willy shrugged. "That's fine with me."

"Okay," Dan said. "What about helping us plan the patrols we'll be sending out to look for other survivors in the area?"

Willy seemed the most uncomfortable with this particular request. "As of right now, I'm still not comfortable sharing access to my personal maps and the detailed notes I've made of the surrounding areas. I've never been asked this before." He seemed to mull it over. "I tell you what. I'd be willing to help your men plan some initial routes and show you on your own maps ambush locations and areas to avoid. I don't want to see them fall into some of the ambushes I've seen, which are fairly elaborate." Willy paused, pulling out his notebook and thumbing through its pages until he found what he was looking for. "Okay, I'm good for now on shaving cream and razors, but I could use a tube of toothpaste, an extra bar of soap, and a hundred rounds of .300 Blackout ammunition." He tapped his finger to his chin. "Yes, I think that would be fair payment for me helping your men stay alive." Willy closed the small notebook confidently, stashing it back into his cargo pocket, as if the matter was settled.

"300 Blackout?" Victor asked curiously. "I've never heard of that cartridge before. I don't even know if anyone in town would have any of that."

"It's essentially a standard military 5.56 casing necked down to .30 caliber. Do you have access to reloading equipment?"

Dan nodded his head. "Yes, we have access to reloading equipment, but we don't have extra cartridge components or powder to spare. Fifty rounds is a steep request."

"Is it worth the life of one of your men?" Willy asked.

"Of course it is," Pastor Dan answered defensively. "But at the same time, I don't even know how much information you are going to provide us. Maybe you don't even know about the areas we are going to be discussing. Maybe you just make some stuff up. How can I possibly commit to such a steep price without knowing what specific information you'll bring to the table?"

Willy considered the mayor's concerns and tried to determine the best way to reassure him that his knowledge of the surrounding areas was well worth the cost of the ammunition.

"How 'bout you let us take a look at those maps of yours to prove what you're saying?" Victor asked.

"Oh, Victor," Willy scolded with a peevish grin. "I already told you that I don't trust you yet." He turned back to Pastor Dan, "I'll tell you what. You're a Reverend, right?"

Pastor Dan exhaled a long breath in an effort to hide his irritation. "I am—or rather was—the head *pastor* of a small Lutheran Church in town before the collapse."

"So, being a preacher and all should make you a pretty honest fellow, right?" The mayor nodded his head slowly in response, not sure where Willy was taking this. "Okay then, let's agree to the terms on good faith and if you *honestly* don't feel the information I provide to your men is worth the price, then I'll agree to re-negotiate with you after the fact. Beings that you are a Reverend and all, I feel that I can trust you. Now I wouldn't agree to those terms with just anybody." He said the last with a brief glance at Victor who just shook his head and rolled his eyes in response. "That's fair, isn't it?" Willy asked Pastor Dan.

The mayor considered Willy's proposal briefly. "I'll agree to that."

Willy spat on his hand and stretched it out across the hood of the car wearing his biggest toothy smile. Pastor Dan placed his hand over his eyes, rubbing his temples. Peering between his fingers, he realized that Willy was serious and wanted him to shake the spit-covered hand. Dan let out an audible sigh and leaned forward to reciprocate Willy's tight handshake. "Okay, we have a deal!" Willy exclaimed loudly with an excited tone and a sharp clap of his hands. The suddenness of the motion took Victor off guard and he visibly flinched. "Now, about my pocket knife that young man has in his pocket…."

Chapter 5

Sean, Brody, and Randy sat idly in the front pew of the Lutheran Church that now acted as Tionesta's administrative building and central meeting facility. Several members of the town council were seated in bonded leather office chairs on the dais whispering quietly, waiting for the meeting to begin. Two of them stood at the large folding table behind the lectern, pouring over a map and having a disagreement on something Sean couldn't make out. Sean looked over at Randy who just rolled his eyes, thoroughly bored. Colonel Harris and Pastor Dan were late.

A short snore caught their attention and they turned their heads to see Brody's chin resting on his chest. "Beth Ann must not be letting him get much sleep," Randy whispered hoarsely to Sean with a wink and a grin.

"I can hear you just fine," Brody said blandly without opening his eyes or moving a muscle. Sean and Randy shared a chuckle. Brody had only been married a few weeks now and he was the constant recipient of newlywed jokes.

The oak doors at the back of the sanctuary swung open with a loud creak, and Pastor Dan strode through them followed by a man Sean had never seen before. The man was completely ordinary looking, yet at the same time walked behind Pastor Dan with jerky movements. He seemed as if he was all wound up like a spring. The man's eyes darted around the church, focusing sharply on one object before quickly moving on to something else. His stride slowed as his head turned, staring intently at the high ceiling. Sean followed his gaze but couldn't determine what the man was looking at. The man mumbled something under his breath before looking back down and realizing he had fallen behind Pastor Dan. He quickened his pace to catch up. It was almost as if the man were a well-trained puppy on Pastor Dan's heals that kept getting distracted by shiny objects. As he walked past the front pew, his head did a double take as if he recognized Brody. Brody returned the man's gaze with mild curiosity. The stranger also had a facial tic that made his right cheek flinch every few seconds. Sean was starting to become concerned about the man's sanity until he gave Brody a big-toothed smile and a wink as if they were old friends. The man then turned his attention back to his feet and shuffled them until he was in lock step with Pastor Dan's stride once more. Sean turned to his friend with an arched eyebrow. An obviously confused Brody just shrugged his shoulders in response.

"Sorry for my tardiness. Let's get this meeting started," Pastor Dan instructed loudly as he climbed the stairs of the dais. Without turning his head, Pastor Dan pointed to a lone chair off to the one side of the stage and the man made his way over to it obediently. Before sitting down, Sean watched as the man leaned the chair forward, thoroughly inspecting every aspect of the chair before sitting in it.

Pastor Dan waved Sean, Randy, and Brody up to the dais as he began. He waited for them to push in around the crowded table before he began. "Okay, at our last meeting we briefly discussed the idea of sending some scouting parties to make contact with any of the surviving locals. We've all had some time to consider the idea and I hope everyone is prepared to bring to the table any ideas or concerns." Sean took a seat across the table from the council members but couldn't stop watching the stranger out of the corner of his eye. Pastor Dan noticed Sean and some of the others casting glances at the stranger who had been mysteriously permitted to attend the town council meeting. Other members of town had been allowed to attend the meetings, but this was the first time a total stranger had been brought in. Pastor Dan addressed their curiosity. "Before we begin, I'd like to introduce someone who is going to aid us in this endeavor." He half turned and pointed to Willy. "That man's name is Willy. I believe it is purely by divine intervention that he happened to appear at our town on this precise day.

"Willy has taken it upon himself to become a mailman of sorts. He delivers messages between quite a few towns in the north central part of the state and appeared at the roadblock today with a message for Hank Keefer from...somebody." Pastor Dan paused before continuing. "While he is obviously not going to be able to deliver that message, he does have information that could be useful to us. He has been travelling these parts for many months and has detailed maps and notes about ambush locations that will aid us in putting together our scouting routes."

Sean leaned over to whisper in Randy's ear. "It sounds like the movie *The Postman.*" Randy nodded in return, familiar with the post-apocalyptic movie

Pastor Dan glanced in his direction. "Precisely." Sean was surprised that the mayor had actually heard him. Evidently, the aging man's ears were still very sharp. "While I haven't seen the movie myself, that is exactly where he derived the idea from. He will be delivering some introductory messages from me to the mayors of other towns that he frequents as well as delivering messages from our townspeople to any relatives or friends they may have along his route."

Brody raised his hand and Pastor Dan nodded to him. "I have some concerns about that, Mayor. I think you should reconsider the risks involved by giving other towns or strangers too much information about Tionesta." Even as Brody spoke, Pastor Dan was nodding his head in agreement. "We don't know their current level of survival, and we could be inadvertently opening the door to raiders from these towns coming in to steal food or other supplies."

"I agree with you a hundred percent, Brody." Pastor Dan reached up and ran his fingers through his hair. "The letters I plan on crafting will be quite general in nature and will be strictly designed to open a dialog with the other surviving towns. I agree that our food supplies will need to be kept private." Pastor Dan rubbed his hands together slowly. "At the same time, we need to start thinking about rebuilding. There are millions of people in this country that are still struggling to survive. While we can't help all of them, I believe it is our God given duty to help as many people as feasible. From our last crop report, I estimate that we could take in another two or three dozen locals while still maintaining a good buffer to make it through till next harvest. The question then becomes, how do we locate and vet the newcomers? Like I mentioned before, I think a good idea would be to have a monthly bazaar in town for the locals. We can have tables put out where people can barter and trade for goods as well as another dance and a general meet and greet. Over the course of the next three months, we can get to know some of the locals that are living in the area and approach some of them about moving their families into town before winter."

There were numerous empty houses in Tionesta, and at the previous council meeting they'd agreed to try and grow the town. Now that they had a proven system for gardening and growing crops, they had the ability to grow Tionesta. There was strength in numbers. They were already making plans to increase the size of their gardens and fields. One of the other duties of the potential scouting parties was to search for abandoned greenhouses so they could extend the growing season.

The biggest issue Tionesta faced was where to locate their new fields. The town was sandwiched between the mountains of the Allegheny Forest to the east and the Allegheny River to the west. There were no actual fields in the narrow river town, so they had been forced to turn vacant yards and oversized lots into gardening space. Currently they were utilizing part of Lighthouse Island (a small peninsula on the southern side of the town) and the baseball field off Walnut Street for their larger crops—primarily long rows of corn and potatoes. They had acquired three greenhouses during the previous winter that they reconstructed against buildings with a south facing stone or brick wall. Unfortunately, this happened to be just off the main drag through town. It was not ideal, as each time a hungry traveler was escorted through town, they walked right past greenhouses full of food. Growing their crops on Lighthouse Island wasn't ideal either. Anyone roaming the mountains overlooking the town would be able to see the long rows of food being grown, and there was always the risk of flooding during a summer storm, not uncommon to the area.

Tionesta's only option for expanding their food production was to seek farmland outside of the town's security. The East Homestead, and the original retreat property of Sean, Brody, Randy, Caleb, Andrew, and Damian, had been initially considered due to the abundance of surrounding farms and fields, but it was finally deemed too far to transport people each day with a dwindling gas supply. The East Homestead also couldn't house the town's workers without constructing a new building. The North Homestead, where Sean's extended family now resided, didn't have large enough farms around it to meet the entire town's needs. Their best and closest option was to extend the town's perimeter almost a mile to the east, where the nearest large farm was located on a ridge.

The distance from Tionesta to the farm added considerable logistical issues for transportation and for providing twenty-four-hour security over their crops. Even with ham radio communications available to a security team staying at the farmstead, it would take a full twenty to thirty minutes to muster the town's defenses and huff it almost a mile uphill. In the meantime, the security force would have to defend the crops on their own. That was a dangerous prospect for whoever was on watch if a large raiding force came through the area. They would need to get some sort of bus to shorten their response time to such an assault.

When the small detachment of Colonel Harris's soldiers had been brought to town a month prior, Pastor Dan had noticed they'd been brought on a military-green-colored school bus. One of his notes for this meeting was to ask the Colonel for use of the bus or to try bartering for it. He would also try to barter for some gas as well. As the town's gas supply stood, they'd only be able to use the bus in an emergency, but it would be nice to have the option to drive the workers to and from the field each day. This was all assuming that they would be permitted by Colonel Harris to use the bus.

The handheld ham radio on the table squawked. "This is Watch One. The Colonel and his entourage have arrived and are headed into town." Sean noticed the strange man seated at the edge of the dais quickly sit up at the word "Colonel." The man glared at the radio. Before that radio call, he'd been slumped back, looking around disinterestedly. He was now laser focused on the radio in Pastor Dan's hand.

"Copy that," Pastor Dan responded, placing the radio back down on the table. Sean watched as Willy grew more uneasy. With his back to the man, Pastor Dan hadn't noticed and continued his previous discussion. "In order to grow more food at the new farmstead like we've discussed, we're going to need more people to be trained for security details, as well as more field workers. That in turn leads to more laundry, latrines, a larger cold storage facility, and many other logistical issues. Therefore, my recommendation is to stay focused on growth and not design infrastructure that will need to be rebuilt in the future. If we need to build or create something, let's be sure we are doing it with an eye toward the future."

Pastor Dan leaned over the table to look at the local map and pointed a bony finger at the farm's location. "I think our first scouting party needs to cover this entire area here." His finger circled the length of Dutch Hill Road from the farm they were considering to a quarter of a mile farther down the road. "Going up the hill, between Tionesta and the farm, there are only three houses that we assume are vacant, but we need to check each one to be sure. Not far past the farm we want to use, right here," he paused as his finger moved along the map to the location and tapped it twice, "there's over a dozen little hunting camps set back off Ponderosa Lane and Wright Road. We need to be sure they are empty as well. Anyone living there would surely notice if we start farming nearby. From this point," he said as he dragged his finger across a thin red line, "there are another half dozen farm houses before you get to the first bend in the road, right here." His finger tapped once more on the map.

"For now, I want to be sure all these places are vacant before we start any activity up there." Pastor Dan pointed at the councilman who was in charge of taking minutes. The man's pencil was always a flurry of movement at the council meetings. "Richard, please make a note for the scouting team to also consider a new location for our east roadblock. I don't think it would make sense to have it too close to the fields where someone approaching the roadblock might be able to see our crops. At the same time, we need to be far enough back from the bend in the road here to have a good long sightline for approaching vehicles and travelers on foot."

Brody pointed to a spot on the satellite-view map near the prospective fields. "Just past these first rows of trees looks like a good spot, but it's hard to tell without actually seeing the lay of the land."

The mayor turned to Brody. "Maybe after we've cleared those houses, you could swing up there and take a look around. I'd love to get your opinion on where to put the roadblock and any other security measures you might suggest." Brody nodded his head supportively.

Pastor Dan turned his attention back to the map. "I realistically believe we can scout these areas in a day or two. Brody, do you have any recommendations on how to go about it?"

Brody's face twisted. "I've been pondering the scouting team's plan of attack for the last few days. As some of you already know, I spent a few years in Iraq as part of a Quick Reaction Force of Army Rangers. Our job was to be ready to roll at a moment's notice and go into enemy-controlled areas to capture or kill high value targets as the Army gained intel on them. I lost a few friends during that time and have some nice scars to show for my short time spent in the sand box. I have to admit, I'd almost rather go back to doing that than approach some of these farmsteads and cabins. At least in Iraq, every man was fully trained on how to handle any potential situation. You had a plan of action and you mostly knew what you were in for and how to handle the locals. If things went south, you started shooting the bad guys. It was that simple.

"But this...this is entirely different." Brody leaned back from the table and rubbed his hands together slowly. "There's no way to know the mentality of the people we may be crossing paths with. They aren't enemy combatants and while our goal is to make them an offer to help them and let them join the town, they won't know that unless they are willing to talk to us. They could be starving and desperate, or they could be thriving and super protective over their family's provisions."

Brody shifted nervously in his seat. "I think the best way to do this is to appear as least imposing as possible when approaching these houses and knocking on their doors. It's going to be vital that the men involved are very observant to their surroundings. If there is a garden or other signs of life, the situation will be extremely delicate. I would have a two-man approach team, with a third man staying at a distance with a rifle and a radio. As backup, I would have a six-man squad in a car just up the road, ready to roll in at the first call of trouble. We should also have the team watch each location from a distance for at least an hour or two before they approach so they can look for any signs of movement or evidence of people living there. The third man would stay out of view and post up with a rifle from distance as overwatch.

"When they do move forward to investigate, I'd have the two-man team slowly approach the house literally waving a white flag with their hands in the air. I would keep one man a dozen or so yards back from the front door close to a large tree or other piece of cover he could quickly get behind if needed. I'd only send one person to knock, though. Any more than that and the people inside could feel too threatened to answer. It would be important that he's unarmed, or at least appear that way. Maybe he would have an ankle holster or something. Without question, both men on approach should be wearing the body armor we secured from Mr. Andrews' bunker. The man that hangs back should have a battle rifle slung within easy reach, but not obviously holding it in his hands. His primary purpose is to provide cover for the other man's retreat should things go south." Sean watched as Richard furiously scratched at his notepad, trying to capture each of Brody's recommendations.

Brody sighed. "The only problem with that plan is every farm and cabin is different. Proper cover close to each house and the ability to have someone as overwatch are purely dependent on the lay of the land. Every approach will have to be planned specifically to what each location looks like. That's the best answer that I can really give you." Brody paused for a moment and Pastor Dan nodded soberly. "And before you even ask me, I already discussed this with Beth Ann. She all but forbade me to be any part of this endeavor outside of offering guidance. She's still pretty shook up over the attack on East Homestead and with us just getting married, well…." Sean could see him struggling for the best explanation.

Pastor Dan raised his hand. "Brody, you don't need to explain any further. We all understand." An uncomfortable Brody sighed in relief. "If you'd be willing, I'd ask you to help train some of our best men and offer them some pointers."

"Absolutely!" Brody agreed. "I'll help you in any way I can, short of being on the actual scouting team."

Pastor Dan turned to the stranger in the corner who still appeared anxious to Sean. "What are your thoughts on this, Willy? What do you do when you come across people and farmsteads on your travels?"

"I try and avoid people as much as possible," Willy responded without hesitating. "If they're on one of my regular routes, I'll watch them from a distance for an hour or two to determine if they pose a threat to me. If it just looks like a regular family and I feel it is relatively safe, I may approach them later, but not until I have lots of intel on them. It's always good to have a warm bed and roof over your head from time to time. I have a few farms along my longer routes that I stop by and offer outside information for room and board. I've become friends with most of them. That being said, I would typically advise against approaching anybody these days, but I also understand why you need to clear the areas around where you plan to farm. My biggest advice would be to take extra time studying each place from a distance…and don't get yourself killed." He nodded toward Brody. "This one here seems to be a bright lad. I'd listen to what he has to offer." Sean noticed Brody frown at the man upon being called a lad. He was clearly every bit as old as the stranger.

Pastor Dan frowned, hoping the man would have had more to offer. "Very well then. Over the course of the next week I want to get the men trained as best as possible with Brody's help. After our next meeting, I want to get started with patrols. Our first priority will be to clear each house and cabin on top of the hill. After that, I want to start the longer-range scouting patrols. We aren't going to be approaching any of the farms or houses along the way and will primarily be looking for signs of life from a distance. We'll take notes about each inhabited location and make a plan to send a smaller scouting team to spend more time watching those locations before making a determination whether or not we should approach.

"Outside of looking for people to bring into the fold, the scouting parties need to be on the lookout for anything that could be beneficial to the town. We discussed this last week, but now that we've had time to think about it, I'd like to hear ideas on additional items we should be watching for. Richard, would you mind reading back the list of items we discussed last week as a refresher?"

Richard was furiously writing something down and Sean thought for a moment that he may not have heard the mayor. "Sure, just a moment," he finally replied while he continued to scribble in his notebook. Everyone sat patiently and Sean took the opportunity to glance from his peripheral vision toward Willy. The man sat with his head lowered and totally enveloped in his hands, which periodically clenched at his raven-black hair. Sean could see his lips moving silently, talking to himself, but he was whispering at such a low volume that he couldn't hear anything other than a slight hum coming from the man's general direction. Sean lightly nudged Randy's foot under the table. When Randy looked back, he nodded ever so slightly in the man's direction. He watched Randy study the man for a moment before shaking his head at Sean in wonder.

Sean's attention was drawn to the sound of military trucks pulling up to church. Richard had finished what he had been writing and flipped back a few pages in his notebook. "Okay, we discussed being on the lookout for any grain bins in the area. Each one should be inspected for its contents and documented on the map. Since wheat and barley isn't a main crop in this area, it's unlikely that we'll actually find any grain bins containing such, but field corn or any other grains should still be logged. The locations of grain silos should also be noted in the event we are able to secure some livestock for the town.

"Second, we need to be on the lookout for any sources of gasoline. The scouting team will travel with jerry cans and check any tractors or cars within close proximity to the road, siphoning any gas they can find. We also considered the two gas stations in the area. Fritz Corners Convenience Store, ten miles south of town and the Uni-Mart, just south of Tylersburg, are the only two gas stations in the area that aren't located inside of a town." Richard looked up from his notes, "Has anyone else thought of or learned of any other gas stations in the area besides these two?" Most shook their heads and no one spoke, so Richard continued. "Okay then, Sean offered us the use of his family's crop sprayer which they've converted to pump and haul gasoline. They brought it with them on their drive up and will trade a small percentage of the gas that's brought back for its use. This seems the logical choice as it's already rigged to siphon gas from underground fuel tanks. However, our first step is to send someone down to both gas stations and check to see if there is any gas left in the tanks before we try and drive the sprayer down there. If we do find gas, we'll need a full security team in escort to—"

"Hold on a second, Richard," Pastor Dan interrupted him. He turned to the strange man in the chair who still sat hunched over, writhing in mysterious misery. "Willy?" Pastor Dan tried to get the man's attention. "Willy!" he called again much louder.

"Huh?" The man's head snapped up, his eyes wide open and his hair sticking up wildly.

"Willy, have you ever been down through the Tylersburg area?" the mayor asked.

"Uhhh, Tylersburg?" Willy seemed to roll the name over his tongue. "It doesn't ring a bell." He put his head back down into his hands.

Pastor Dan sighed. "Willy, what the heck is wrong with you?"

Willy looked up, casting a quick glance toward the congregation doors before turning back to Pastor Dan. "Nuthin," he muttered defensively.

"Would you please mind getting up and coming to look at the map so we can be sure?" Pastor Dan was having a hard time hiding his irritation at the man, which wasn't usually his nature. Sean studied the weird man as he shrugged indifferently and stood up. He trudged over to the table, shouldering his way in between Sean and Randy without even asking their pardon. Willy leaned over the map and studied where Pastor Dan pointed. Sean gave Randy another glance over the man's back. Pastor Dan seemed confident in this man's backstory, but Sean was starting to doubt if the man could be of any use at all.

Sean suddenly caught a whiff of something sweet, yet sharp at the same time. For a moment, it totally enveloped his senses. It was a smell he'd known well, yet he couldn't seem to place it. The scent dragged his mind back to when he lived in Washington State. Sean closed his eyes and stepped back in time nearly a decade. He could see the duplex on Fairchild AFB, where he and his wife had lived after they first married. It had been a great two years of their lives, growing together and feeling each other out in every way. It was a nice, newer duplex with a detached one-car garage and a fenced-in back yard where their black lab had romped and scandalously chewed the corners off their house.

It was crazy how a single scent could transport you to a totally different place in time. Suddenly it came to him. It was cologne. It was Cool Water cologne! Sean opened his eyes and looked at Willy's bent-over form. For the first time, he noticed that the man's uniform was pristinely clean and fresh. His black hair wasn't oily but had a freshly shampooed look to it. His face was clean shaven and, more incredibly, he smelled…good! That was something completely unheard of. Body odor, oily beards, and dirty, stained clothing was just something that was the norm now, nine months after the collapse. Most people had long ago run out of scented soaps, shampoo, razors, and deodorant. The man's outward appearance surely didn't fit his bearing in the least. Willy was a complete mystery--one Sean vowed to solve.

"Yes, yes, ahem." Willy cleared his throat. "Okay, Reverend, I actually do think I've been through this area before. I was travelling through the Cooks Forest area here and I believe I came through Tylersburg on Route 36. I'm confident I've travelled through this area a couple times before, though I don't remember any signs that said Tylersburg."

"You wouldn't have," one of the other council members chimed in. "It's nothing more than a couple dozen houses built around a bend in the road."

"What we are looking for are gas stations, Willy," Dan reminded him.

"Yes, I know that," Willy said, waving the mayor off dismissively. "You act as if I wasn't paying attention to you."

Sean rolled his eyes to the mayor in response to the man's tone. Sean had been sure the man wasn't paying attention the way he had been sitting there, mumbling to himself. Apparently, he had been. Maybe he was good at multitasking.

"Right here, I think." Willy gestured to the intersection of Route 36 and Route 66 on the map. Sean turned his attention back to where Willy pointed. "Without being able to cross reference my other maps and notes, I can't be sure. But if I remember correctly, there was a red gas station right here on the corner."

"The Uni-Mart," Richard said in agreement.

"Yes. Yes, that was it." Willy glanced up at him. "There was a nifty restaurant across the street with lots of various shapes and sizes of sawmill blades hanging on the walls."

"The Sawmill Restaurant," Pastor Dan said, nodding toward Sean with a "see, I told you so" look. Sean, his brother Joshua, and his father used to stop at that restaurant during their yearly fall motorcycle trip through Cooks Forest. The restaurant was sort of a landmark in the area. Perhaps this man *had* travelled throughout north central Pennsylvania.

Willy ignored Pastor Dan's interruption. "They were all so beautiful. Each of the saw blades was painted with a different country scene and had a tag on it signed by a local artist. I remember there was one big round blade over the mantle that I *particularly* liked. It must have been three feet in diameter! It was a night scene of the mountains with a wolf's silhouette howling in the breeze. Ahh-wooooooo!" Willy howled loudly, his head tilted toward the sky. It took everyone at the table completely by surprise. Willy's head came down as the note trailed off echoing off the church walls searching their expressions expectantly. Realizing that he'd startled them, he flashed his big smile in apology.

"Yes, Willy, we are all familiar with the Sawmill Restaurant," Pastor Dan said in the calm tone one would use to settle a small child. "We are more interested in the gas station across the street. Do you know if it still had any gas in the underground tanks?"

"Why would I know that?" Willy crinkled his nose as he snorted. "I haven't owned a car in the last year. I can tell you that it was incredibly rank in there. Someone had pushed over the display refrigerators and a bunch of milk cartons had busted open. The entire floor was covered in months-old rotten milk and there was thick green mold growing over everything. I do remember finding a couple packages of those pink Twinkies under one of the upended display racks though. That was a nice surprise. There wasn't an expiration date on them that I could find and they still looked and smelled good so I gave them a go…and they were excellent!" He looked around the table. "I wonder what they put in those things to make them last that long through the summer heat?"

"I don't know, Willy," the mayor said, exasperated, wiping his hand over his face. "Is there actually anything useful you can tell us about the gas station?"

Willy rubbed his chin in thought, shaking his head. "Without my other notebook…." There was a momentary pause before he continued. "I don't recall the tops being off the ground tanks though. I've seen that at other gas stations where looters have taken the lids off the underground storage tanks and left them off after they've siphoned the gas. It's really dangerous and unthoughtful of them to do that, you know? I primarily travel at night. One wrong step and 'snap!' I could break my leg in one of those holes. I don't remember seeing any open tanks there though."

"Maybe there's still gas," one of the councilmen said hopefully.

"Maybe they were kind and considerate looters and they put the lids back on when they were done siphoning it," Willy said with a shrug.

Pastor Dan palmed his face once more and sighed. "We aren't going to know for sure until someone goes down there and checks it out. Willy, if you were to get your other notebook, would you be able to offer anything else?"

"Possibly."

The doors to the congregation swung open with their characteristic un-oiled creak, and Colonel Harris strode into the room with his distinctive confident gate and a couple other soldiers in tow. "Sorry I'm late, gentlemen," he said as he approached the dais. Sean felt Willy sliding further behind him and turned to the man with a questioning look. Willy didn't even notice Sean as he stared intently in the direction of the approaching soldiers. His utter disdain for the men in uniform couldn't have been more apparent.

Chapter 6

Everyone watched as Colonel Harris climbed the dais steps and shook Pastor Dan's hand. He nodded to Sean, Randy, Brody, and the rest of the councilmen with a brief yet polite greeting, "Gentlemen."

"Hello, Colonel," Brody replied to Sean's right. Willy had currently relocated himself so he was positioned behind Sean's large frame. Willy watched Captain Whalen walk over to the chair he'd previously been sitting in and take a seat. His eyes shot toward the rear sanctuary doors for a brief moment before falling on the four other soldiers who had taken seats in the back and were now whispering quietly among themselves. Willy looked up and met Sean's eyes. He produced a small grin, but Sean could tell it was forced.

"We were just continuing our discussion from last week," Pastor Dan informed the Colonel. "We're fleshing out plans to do some scouting in the general area and see if we can find any locals who are still surviving. We plan to scout for grain bins, look for any surviving livestock, and anything else that may help the town grow moving forward."

Colonel Harris cocked his head. "Grain bins?"

"Yes. While we don't expect to find much, if any, grain that can be used for human consumption, we hope to find or acquire some livestock in the near future and we'll need it to feed them."

Colonel Harris looked at the mayor thoughtfully. "I never considered grain silos. I see them all the time, but never really gave them a second thought. The fact that you might be able to find grain to help feed your town is something you should have probably considered before. Why didn't you pursue this course of action sooner?"

Sean flashed a knowing look toward Brody, who slightly nodded. These questions were becoming more prominent by the Colonel, and the nature had them concerned. Pastor Dan deferred the question to Richard, who was the most experienced councilman on farming.

Richard cleared his throat. "Colonel, farming up here in the mountains mainly revolves around growing feed for our own livestock. The most common crop in the area is field corn followed by soy beans. The best area to grow wheat and other grains for human consumption is in the Midwest. Our summers in northern Pennsylvania are too humid and wet, which can cause various wheat diseases. Don't get me wrong, some farmers do grow wheat, but it's not one of our local staple crops and it's not the same type or quality that's grown out west. If we did manage to find a grain bin with wheat or oats, it's likely not going to be of very good quality. At the same time it would still be technically edible, which also means that most of the grain bins will probably be empty due to scavenging over the winter."

"Colonel," Sean began reluctantly, "I hate to interrupt, but I have an important question I'd like to ask." Brody glared at Sean. They had discussed this matter on the ride in, but hadn't come to terms on whether or not they were going to question the Colonel outright.

Colonel Harris raised an eyebrow expectantly, waiting on Sean who was now wondering if he should have approached this subject in private. He glanced around the table and all eyes were on him. It was too late to back out now. "I guess I'll be blunt and come right out with it. We've noticed that you've been asking a lot of questions about food the last two weeks. The nature of your questions have me…us…a little concerned. Previously, you could have cared less about food production." The Colonel's face showed no reaction to what Sean was saying.

Sean suddenly felt awkward and glanced down at the table while he continued. "Is there something we need to be aware of? Uhhh, are you having trouble with the food deliveries for your men?" He said the last in a near whisper even though every ear was now tuned in to him.

All eyes turned to the Colonel who stood with his arms crossed, staring at Sean with virtually no expression. The Colonel had planned to approach this subject with the mayor in private after the council meeting, but now found himself cornered by Sean's question. If he side-stepped the question or lied, it would make it harder to bring up later. He looked up at his men in the back of the church who were huddled together talking quietly. He was pretty sure they weren't paying attention and hadn't heard Sean's question. Colonel Harris let out a whistle causing the soldiers in the back of the room to look up. "Sergeant Timms, could you please take your squad and check in on our men stationed in town and see if they need anything? You can give me your report on the way back to Warren."

"Yes sir," Sgt. Timms answered, his deep voice bouncing off the walls of the empty church. He stood and motioned his men toward the door.

Once the doors were fully closed behind them, Colonel Harris turned a steely gaze back on Sean. "To a degree, yes." Sean's heart sank. The Colonel glanced around the table briefly before turning to Pastor Dan. "This is an item I had hoped to discuss in private with you, mayor, after the meeting, but now that it's been brought up…." He paused.

"How bad is it?" Brody asked bluntly.

Colonel Harris shrugged his shoulders. "As of now, it's not that serious. Our last couple shipments have been…." He paused again, searching for the right words. "Let's just say, they've been a bit light. I don't want to alarm you folks as I still have plenty of food to feed my men and there is no immediate emergency. However, I also want to be proactive. I want to try and become more self-sufficient as a regiment and not rely on my chain of command to keep my men fed in the future. Again, it's not a serious problem, but I want to be prepared if things get worse."

Taking Sean by surprise, Willy voice chimed in to the conversation from over his shoulder. "Running out of food, Colonel?" he sneered. "If the military is running out of food, what are you doing to feed the people you forced into the Green Zones?"

Colonel Harris placed his open palms down on the table and leaned forward. His hard look found Willy, noticing him for the first time. "And who are you?" Colonel Harris demanded. When Willy didn't respond immediately, Colonel Harris turned back to Pastor Dan and asked, "Who's that, and what's he doing here?"

"His name is Willy. He's a, well, he ahh…," Pastor Dan fumbled his words uneasily. "He travels around delivering messages to the various towns that have survived the collapse. He has a lot of experience travelling the roads throughout the area and he offered to help us plan our scouting parties. He…." The mayor was obviously caught off guard by the question and seemed unsure what he should say or shouldn't. He shot Willy a questioning look.

"That's okay, Reverend. I can speak up for myself," Willy said kindly to the mayor without taking his icy glare off the colonel. Just a few moments earlier, Willy had looked like a cornered kitten to Sean. Now he stood erect and spoke boldly, completely opposite of his previous posture.

Colonel Harris turned back to Willy with a slight curve to the edges of his lips. It wasn't a friendly smile. "What do you know about the Green Zones, *Willy*?"

"Yes, let's talk about the Green Zones," Willy said as he leaned over the table in the colonel's direction. A couple of the councilmen who flanked the colonel took a half step back, clearly not wanting to be caught in the middle. Captain Whalen, who'd been following the conversation intently from his chair, stood and came to stand behind Colonel Harris, glaring at Willy challengingly. Colonel Harris turned and softly shook his head at Whalen, motioning with his hand to go back to his seat. Captain Whalen walked back to his chair but didn't sit down. He stood next to the chair with his arms crossed, watching Willy.

"Why don't you tell these good people about what happened at the Newark Green Zone?" Willy seethed, the color in his cheeks rising to a deep red.

Colonel Harris asked quietly, "What about the Newark Green Zone?"

"You tell me about the Newark Green Zone, *Colonel*!" Willy nearly spat.

The others around the table looked to Colonel Harris, wondering where this was going. He held his hands up and shrugged. "I don't know anything specific about the Newark Green Zone. We received word that there'd been a severe outbreak of cholera and some out-of-control fires. The only reason I'm even aware of that is because the Wilmington Green Zone, where my regiment was stationed, received a sharp influx of refugees shortly after that."

Willy let out a loud snort. "There were always outbreaks of cholera and dysentery in Newark, but they were small and we quickly learned how to contain them and quarantine those infected, no thanks to the Army's medical teams. But that's not what I'm talking about. Cholera doesn't make you bleed from the nose and mouth. Cholera doesn't kill 95% of the people it infects in less than twenty-four hours. Why don't you tell the council the truth?" Willy demanded. Sean looked down to see Willy's hands balled into trembling fists. "Why don't you tell them about how none of the soldiers got sick while nearly all the civilians died? Not a single soldier!" Willy paused for a brief second, his eyes suddenly glossy. He continued quietly. "Why don't you explain to me why I had to watch my wife and my four-year-old baby girl suffer through convulsions, fever, and choking on their own vomit before they died? Explain that to me!" Willy begged, straining to get the words out. The silence in the air was thick as all eyes slowly turned to Colonel Harris.

Colonel Harris's anger toward the man had been laid to rest with Willy's account of what he'd been through. Bruce rubbed his forehead. "Willy, I'm sure you probably won't believe me, but I honestly have no idea of what you are talking about. My men were in charge of perimeter security in Wilmington, Delaware. With communications down, all I know about what's going on around the world is what my superiors tell me." Colonel Harris continued softly. "I'm sure there must be some explanation—"

"There sure is!" Willy cut him off, his outrage growing. "We were starving while the military soldiers weren't. We begged, pleaded, and petitioned *the military* for a more equitable distribution of the food NATO was delivering to the docks, but you people wouldn't listen." Bruce shook his head at Willy, not wanting people to think he was involved in that decision or knew anything about it. "People were starving to death and dying!" Willy bellowed. A tear finally trickled down his cheek and he wiped it away with a furious swipe of his hand. "We'd heard that the military was storing its food in a warehouse near the Greenville Shipyard across the river in Jersey City. Since you wouldn't listen to us, plans were made to steal some of it. But it didn't go as planned.

"It was supposed to be a silent, snatch and grab operation without any fighting, but we were discovered and things went south. Lots of my friends were killed. Only me and a few others made it out of the warehouse alive. We hid for a few days in an abandoned part of Jersey City before we could take our boat back across the river." Willy's voice was growing softer as he relived the memory. "When we did finally make it back, it was too late and most of the people in the Green Zone were already dead. The military had poisoned the well in response to some hungry people trying to steal food. Men, Women, children, infants…all dead!" Willy's voice cracked. "I was lucky enough to make it back in time to watch my wife in her final death throes. My baby girl was already dead. I didn't even get to tell her goodbye!" A deep sob escaped from his chest, but Willy forced it back down defiantly. "I actually watched the soldiers start those fires you mentioned. They were started to cover up what they'd done. I barely escaped it myself as the soldiers had set up a perimeter around the Green Zone watching for survivors trying to escape the flames." Willy paused briefly. "They couldn't let word get out about what they'd done, now could they?"

Colonel Harris stared back at Willy firmly, yet his voice was soft. "Willy, my men and I had nothing to do with that. I know nothing about what you are discussing. I highly doubt uniformed members of the military were responsible for what happened…."

"I was there!" Willy insisted fervently. "I saw it, you son of a—" Pastor Dan swiftly walked around the table to put his hand on Willy's shoulder.

The colonel's face softened. "Willy, you said that you weren't there when they poisoned the water source." Willy started to cut him off but the mayor squeezed his shoulder reassuringly and Bruce plowed forward. "I am not doubting one word of your story, Willy! What I'm saying is that I highly doubt uniformed members of the military poisoned all those people. I've served this country for over two decades. I know my men and every one of them would revolt before following an order like that as any honorable soldier should. I'm not saying that it didn't happen, or even that it didn't happen as retaliation to the raid you went on, but it likely came from somewhere else. If you say soldiers set fire to the houses afterwards, I believe you. We're instructed to burn down areas where plagues or viruses have blown through. *Obviously*, after the people are evacuated out of the area. You're putting the terrible things you have gone through on me personally and that's not fair. I've risked my command and *my life* multiple times to defy illegal orders from my superiors to help the locals here, and I'd do it again if…." Colonel Harris stopped whatever he'd been about to say. "I don't even know what else to say to you."

"He's been a great friend to our town and ridden to our rescue once already to protect us from the Bradford Prison Gang," Pastor Dan said softly to Willy. "Colonel Harris is an honorable man and I don't believe he would be involved in something like you're talking about."

"Oh really?" Willy replied shrugging the mayor's hand off his shoulder. "You said you and your men were in charge of the perimeter around Wilmington. I'm quite familiar with perimeter units around Green Zones. I've had dealings with them. You say it like you were the great shiny knights protecting the innocent people inside the Green Zones. That's a lie too. The perimeter units were in charge of rounding up the people in the suburbs and forcing them *into* the Green Zones. Just like they did with my family. We told them, 'We didn't want to go.' But we weren't given the option. Later we planned on trying to escape the horrible living conditions and head to my uncle's house up north, but we weren't allowed to leave. One of the perimeter patrols caught us sneaking out of Newark and forced us back inside the fence. If we'd been allowed to escape, my family would still be alive today. You were more jailers than protectors!"

Colonel Harris shook his head again, this was not going the way he wanted this meeting to go. He tried to stay calm. "It's complicated."

"No, it's not!" Willy insisted. "It's a simple, yes or no question. Were you, or were you not in charge of rounding up people you found and sending them into the Green Zones like lambs to the slaughter?"

Bruce stood silently, considering his answer as all eyes fell on him once more. The reaction by the councilmen around the table reminded Sean of a dog's head following a bouncing ball, swiveling in unison between the two men as they spoke. "For a short time after the collapse, yes, my Regiment was tasked with relocating civilians into the Green Zones. It seemed like the best plan at the time. Do you have any idea what kind of logistics it takes to distribute food among hundreds of thousands of people? We didn't have the resources to offer even the slightest shred of hope to people in the middle of the country. When you barely get enough food delivered to feed the people in the Green Zones, what were we supposed to do?" Bruce turned to the rest of the people around the table. His gaze searching for some understanding.

"To prevent mass chaos and violence, our only option for distributing the NATO food at the shipping docks was to register people and gave them food voucher cards to try and make the process as orderly as possible." He turned back to his accuser. "What? Do you think we should have driven military trucks full of food down the center of Brooklyn Avenue instead, tossing food off the side of the trucks like candy at a parade? How do you think that would have played out? There was zero law and order when the 31st Regiment arrived in Wilmington a month after the EMP, with neighbor killing neighbor for an apple rind. We had to restore order or it would have gotten even worse."

Bruce rubbed his temples and closed his eyes. "The powers that be decided that it would be best to keep people in centralized locations. We didn't have enough soldiers to patrol every street of every big city. We didn't have transportation sources to get people to and from the food distribution centers at the harbors each day. By keeping the populace centralized and close to the docks, we could feed them when ships arrived. Looking back, yes, it's easy to say, 'That's a terrible idea.' But who could have known that our NATO allies would have problems feeding their own people and the shipments of food would slow down so quickly? So, you ask me what

did? I followed my orders and the plan of action we had in place to feed you people!" The Colonel's voice was slowly growing louder and more defensive. "We were trying to help. I'm sorry that the whole world has turned into a crap show. I'm sorry about your wife and daughter, Willy. I truly am. I've lost family too. Every one of my men has lost someone close to them. We are out here in the middle of nowhere now, trying to help these people while their loved ones are back on base in Aberdeen. A base that is likely to get overrun soon by hungry friends of yours. It's not my damn fault there's no food! You act like the military is hoarding it all, but we're obviously not."

Pastor Dan held up a hand in Colonel Harris's direction. The mayor had a better chance of refereeing a soccer game of four-year-olds. Bruce continued, ignoring the mayor. "You stand over there and sling accusations. You ask me questions as if you're somehow better than me. So, I have a question for you, Willy. What would you have done? Let's say you were President of the United States and thousands of your citizens were dying every day from looting, rioting, starvation and sickness. What would you do? Even having the ability to look back in time, and knowing where we stand today, name one thing you would have done different than the President did. Don't get me wrong, either, and think that I'm siding with the politicians, because they are the reason we are in this mess. But what is *President Willy's* plan to organize and feed 300+ million Americans with no infrastructure to do so?"

Willy just stared down at the map, unseeing. "Come on, Willy. Put yourself in my shoes. What would you have done? What's your *expert* plan of action?" Colonel Harris wasn't letting him off the hook that easy.

Willy's head snapped back up with squinted eyes. "Well, I wouldn't have poisoned a bunch of hungry women and children!"

That seemed to push the colonel over the edge. Even Sean took a half step back from Willy as Colonel Harris leaned farther over the large table. His eyes held a murderous glint as he growled, "I wouldn't have either!"

"Okay, Okay!" Pastor Dan said, determined to intervene. His voice echoed loudly. "That's enough for now gentlemen, we aren't getting anywhere. There's enough blame to go around and then some. I wish I would have done some things different myself right after the collapse. Standing up to Mr. Andrews earlier would be chief among them. We can't change the past. The question is, where do we go moving forward? How can we work together to secure a better future for ourselves and our families?" He sighed out loud. You could cut the tension in the room with a knife. "I'm calling a fifteen minute break so everyone can cool down and gather themselves. Willy, come to my office with me, please." He didn't wait to see if Willy was following as he turned and walked down the steps of the dais. Willy held the colonel's glare for another moment before following the mayor.

As they walked down the center aisle, away from the dais, Randy turned to Sean. "This is crazy."

Chapter 7

While Pastor Dan and Willy retired to the mayor's office just outside the main doors to the sanctuary, everyone else at the council meeting retreated into smaller groups. Colonel Harris stood bristling next to Captain Whalen, the council members stayed around the table, while Sean, Randy, and Brody retreated down the steps to the front pew. Everyone was whispering among themselves and it wasn't hard to figure out what topic they were discussing.

"Wow, I really stirred the hornet's nest there, didn't I?" Sean muttered to no one in particular.

"Sean, I think that storm was already brewing," Randy replied.

"Even in death, it looks like Damian is going to be proven right," Brody added softly. The mention of Damian's death was a sobering reminder of the world they lived in, but Sean wasn't sure of Brody's meaning. At Randy's inquisitive look, Brody explained. "Damian warned us this would happen. He warned us that if the soldiers ran out of food, we could be in big trouble."

Sean leaned forward in the pew so he could make eye contact with Brody around Randy's wide shoulders. "It's a problem, but not yet a disaster, Brody. Don't forget that if Colonel Harris hadn't ridden to our rescue during the attack, we likely would have had to bury a lot more bodies next to Damian's…including yours." Brody gave his friend a sharp look, but Sean continued. "Cooperating and working with the soldiers was the right decision to make at the time. New challenges have arisen from that decision, and we'll face them like we've done with every other problem that's come up so far. I believe Colonel Harris to be a man of integrity and I don't think he intends to come riding in and confiscate our food."

"You're starting to sound like Pastor Dan," Brody muttered, rolling his eyes.

"Good!" Sean whispered harshly. "The Colonel has saved our bacon once already; it' time we repay the favor. We need to offer to help him and his men grow their own food if we can."

"I say it depends on what help they are going to ask of us," Randy said. Sean raised his eyes in surprise. It seemed Randy was siding with Brody on this.

Sean shook his head. "We'll see what he has to say in a few minutes."

"Yes, we will," Brody muttered under his breath.

Sean ignored Brody's retort and the three of them sat in silence until Pastor Dan and Willy strode back into the sanctuary. Pastor Dan didn't have to say a word. Everyone rose and resumed their positions around the table. "Well, that is enough excitement for a month's worth of council meetings," Pastor Dan said half-jokingly as he took his usual place at the head of the table. He turned to Colonel Harris. "I spoke to Willy in private and he's agreed to let the matter drop for now. Can we agree on that, Colonel? That is a conversation that needs to be finished in private. This is a city council meeting and we obviously have more pressing issues to discuss right now."

Colonel Harris nodded. "I'm fine with that, Mayor." Sean noticed that Colonel Harris hadn't so much as glanced in Willy's direction since he'd re-entered the room.

"Very well, then, we were discussing our scouting party's logistics…," Pastor Dan began.

But Brody interrupted the mayor. "Actually, mayor, we were discussing the fact that there are almost a thousand well-trained soldiers just north of us that may or may not be starving soon." He made it a point not to look at the Colonel when he spoke. "I'd like to hear some more from the Colonel."

Pastor Dan's eyes glinted. "Brody, you are out of order. I did not give you the floor to speak. Please don't forget that you three are here as guests and advisors." He scanned the three of them with his eyes as he spoke. "I'd politely ask that you don't interrupt the meeting again." Brody flushed a little, embarrassed at being admonished so bluntly by Pastor Dan who was typically soft spoken. The mayor turned to Bruce. "Sorry, Colonel." In truth, Pastor Dan had planned to bring it up himself, but not until they got back to discussing the possible use of one of Colonel Harris's buses for transportation to and from the new farm.

Colonel Harris cleared his throat. "Actually, Mayor, with your permission, I'd be happy to address what I was discussing earlier before I was interrupted."

Pastor Dan smiled back with relief. "That would be fine, Colonel. Please continue."

Colonel Harris nodded his head in thanks and began. "As I mentioned earlier, our Regiment's supply drops have been a bit short the last few weeks. I have contacted my chain of command and was assured that they will not be getting any shorter and I have no reason not to believe them. However, I also want to be prepared for whatever may come in the future. Major Samuelsson and I were discussing earlier today the option of expanding the farming and gardening that's taking place in Warren right now. When we arrived, the townspeople that were left had been doing some large-scale gardening at the hospital where we now reside. I will be honest. When most of the civilians left, my men did not maintain the gardens very well…or, I should say, we didn't maintain them at all. We were occupied with a lot of other pressing security issues as you all are familiar with.

"Looking back, as Pastor Dan mentioned earlier, I wish I would have made that more of a priority at the time, but that ship has sailed. I do have a handful of men with some minor farming experience, but none of them were professional, per say. As we speak, I have some men going through the existing garden and pulling weeds. From what I've been told, however, without watering through the hotter summer months and not keeping the weeds pulled, there isn't going to be a very abundant yield of vegetables. One of my men also reported the possibility that there was something called Powdery Mildew growing on most of the vegetables. He remembers it in his parents' garden when he was a kid, but wasn't sure what they treated it with. Oh, and I guess we have a Japanese beetle infestation, too. I was going to ask if some of your people would be willing to come up and train my men to get that garden back up and running."

Colonel Harris paused for a moment. "This is a new world we are living in, where knowing how to grow your own food is paramount to survival. I am planning to mandate that every one of my soldiers rotate through gardening duty on a weekly basis. As their commander, I want to be sure they are prepared for this new world." He had been looking around the table as he spoke, his gaze resting on Pastor Dan as he finished.

Pastor Dan didn't hesitate. "We would be very happy to help you and your men in whatever way we can," he said. He caught the eye of the Curtiss Eckley, the Gardening Team Leader at the other end of the table, who nodded his assent.

"How large of a garden is there now?" Curtiss asked.

Colonel Harris turned his head to address the councilman. "I'm ashamed to say it, but I have no idea." His gave an embarrassed smile. "I have no experience whatsoever in regard to farming and gardening. The food plot looks plenty big to me, but it's definitely less than the operations I've seen around your town here."

Curtiss couldn't hide his frown. "Colonel, the food we are growing here is for less than three hundred mouths! You've got a thousand men up there to feed through the winter!" He suddenly realized that he'd taken a strong tone with the Colonel and added a hasty, "Sir."

"Yes, councilman, I understand your concern, but you need to remember that I am still receiving food shipments every week and I have no reason to believe that will change. Right now, this is supplementary food for the provisions that are being sent. However, I wouldn't mind vastly expanding our fields. If my men can start producing our own food that will be less NATO food my men will consume and more that could be made available for our hungry countrymen." He shot a sharp glance at Willy before continuing. "I am completely serious in my intentions. I want my men and the town of Warren to become a self-sustaining town if possible."

Pastor Dan smiled. "That is a noble endeavor Colonel…teaching your men these important life skills. I would be happy to send my two best gardeners up with you to take stock of what you already have in the works. We can have them put together a gardening plan for this fall and for next spring. There are a couple items you are going to need to address, though, and one is cold storing the vegetables throughout the winter. We can also help you locate or design something that will work for that purpose."

Pastor Dan rubbed his chin in thought for a minute. "Our patrols, among other things, are going to be on the lookout for greenhouses to relocate to Tionesta and extend our growing season. Since we are so late in the season, that would be a very important item you should try and locate as well." Pastor Dan paused. "Is there any chance, you might be able to call your headquarters and see if they'll send you some greenhouses?" Pastor Dan paused for a moment before looking down at his shoes and continuing. "Maybe they could send an extra one or two for our town, as well?"

The Colonel rubbed his hand through his hair while giving Pastor Dan a forced smile. "I will approach it with headquarters and hopefully they can locate some spare greenhouses to send us. The problem is I have occasional visitors from HQ, and if they were to notice a shortage of supplies that they send me or found out I was passing them on to your town, I could get in a lot of trouble. Possibly even lose my command of the regiment. You have to understand the logistics of flying something big like that to us. I'm sure greenhouses are a valuable commodity these days and I'm guessing that if they were to send us some, they would probably be taken from somewhere else...." He trailed off for a minute. "I doubt there are any greenhouses just lying around government inventory that haven't already been put to use. Regardless, I'll still approach it with HQ." He noticed Pastor Dan's downtrodden look. "Mayor, after this meeting, I'm going to instruct all my patrols to be on the lookout for greenhouses. If we can locate some on our travels, I'd be more than happy to share with your town.

"I'll also have our patrols checking grain silos as well. My men, myself included, wouldn't know the difference between oats and wheat, but I'll have them take a sample of grain from each silo they encounter, label it, and mark its location on a map. That way we can show it to your gardening representatives the next time they're on base. Again, if we find something edible or useful, we'll be happy to share it with you."

Curtiss waved his hand until Pastor Dan acknowledged him. "Curtiss, you have the floor."

"Colonel, your men are actually going to be on the lookout for grain bins and not silos, right?" Colonel Harris gave him a blank stare so he explained. "Silos are the taller skinnier structures you typically see around here. They are constructed in a way to be airtight so the silage inside can ferment. That allows it to be digested easier by the animals its fed to. Anything that's inside a grain silo won't be any good for human consumption. Grain bins are typically shorter and fatter, made of corrugated metal. If there is any edible grain that hasn't already been looted, that is where it would be found."

Colonel Harris looked over at Capt. Whalen and gestured toward Curtiss. "Get with the councilman here after the meeting is over and take some detailed notes on what our patrols should be looking for."

"Roger that, Colonel."

Silence followed and Pastor Dan took the opportunity to wrestle back control of the meeting. "It's growing very late in the year for putting a garden in for your men, especially without having access to greenhouses. Colonel, I recommend you get started sooner than later to figure out what you've got going." He turned to Curtiss. "Curtiss, would you be available to head back with the Colonel tonight and get started on a plan of action for them?"

Curtiss flinched. "I, uh…sure…I think. I don't see where that would be a problem. I'll just need 15 minutes or so after the meeting to let the wife know and grab a change of clothes. In fact, I would like Kathy to come. She's more knowledgeable on garden diseases than I am."

"I think that would be a great idea," Pastor Dan said, turning back to Bruce. "Colonel Harris, I assume you have room in your convoy for the two of them?" Colonel Harris nodded in reply. "I also assume it wouldn't be a problem to have some of your men run them back tomorrow evening?"

"That won't be a problem, Mayor. We'll get them back to you safe and sound," Colonel Harris promised.

"Good. Moving on." Pastor Dan idly rubbed the palms of his hands across the wood grain of the table. "As Colonel Harris was arriving, we were discussing our own future patrols. We are going to make an effort to locate and pull into the fold any survivors in the immediate area, especially with skills that the town could use. We will need to be careful in our selections though as this does present a security risk. While I realize there are likely still gangs of looters around, we believe things have died down enough where we can begin focusing on the rebuilding process. Most of these locals are likely to be suspicious of our intentions, so I would like to get to know them by holding a monthly get-together. This would include providing a space where people can barter and trade for supplies or items they may need. Almost like a flea market or swap meet. I also want to make it a fun time and hold a dance and general meet and greet like we did after Brody and Beth Ann's wedding."

Pastor Dan licked his dry lips before continuing. "In order to grow the town, we will also need to expand our own gardening capacity." He caught the colonel up on the information the council had discussed before the convoy arrived. He pulled the top map on the table closer and leaned over it. "Colonel, we are looking to expand our border to the top of German Hill. There is a large farm…right here at the top of the hill." Colonel Harris leaned over the map to see where the mayor pointed. "It even has some fenced pasture we could use in the future if we are able to locate or trade for any livestock. The logistical issue we are facing with this decision, Colonel, is its distance from town."

"It doesn't look that far away to me," Colonel Harris noted.

"Technically, you are correct," Pastor Dan nodded. "In fact, it's only one mile from the edge of town to the farm. What the map doesn't show you is that there is over 600 feet of elevation gain in that one mile. It's nearly straight up the side of the mountain. Most of the people on our gardening team are elderly, or at least getting up there in years. If they were forced to climb that hill every day, they would be dropping like stones and there probably wouldn't be much work getting done after they arrived at the farm. There's only a single small farmhouse within view of the field, and there aren't any facilities big enough to house twenty or thirty people. Even if we could manage to house them up there, I doubt any of them are going to be very happy spending every weeknight away from their families back here in town.

"On top of that, the Gardening Team members aren't experienced fighters. We are going to have to expand our security forces just to maintain a small force up there. The size of force we can spare from the main town wouldn't be able to hold out very long if a big raiding party comes knocking. We risk putting too many men up there which would deplete our security forces down here. Also, in the event of the farm being attacked, we are going to be forced to quickly take the bulk of our security from town to the farm in order to defend it. That means our fighting forces will be forced to hike a mile uphill at a quick pace only to enter a gunfight when they are completely gassed from the long climb. Can you see our dilemma, Colonel?" Pastor Dan looked to Colonel Harris expectantly. The Colonel never took his eyes off the map but nodded his head in understanding.

"What we really need to accomplish this, would be a bus to transport our people to and from the farm each day and allow us to respond with a large force quickly if the farm was attacked. Do you have any suggestions, Colonel, or any way to help us out with this problem?" There it was. He finally said it. Now there was only waiting on the Colonel's response. Pastor Dan held his breath.

For a moment, the Colonel continued studying the map as all eyes were on him, waiting for his response. He finally looked up with a smile. He knew the request had been planned out, but he didn't let on. The mayor was a good man and he knew how important this need was. "That won't be a problem at all, mayor. I've got plenty of extra busses at my disposal. You are more than welcome to use one of them."

The mayor let out a sigh of relief and clapped the councilman to his left on the shoulder.

"However," Colonel Harris began. Instantly, the glint in Pastor Dan's eyes waned a bit. "I am not going to be able to spare any diesel for it. I can give it to you on a full tank, which should last you a couple weeks if you only use it two miles a day. But, I can't provide fuel for you in the long term. That is something that is about as scarce as food right now. America's fuel reserves are almost gone at this point. Getting caught letting your town use a bus is one thing, but if I was discovered providing fuel to the town, I'd be in trouble for sure."

Pastor Dan held up his hand. "Colonel, we'd never want you to do anything that could get you in trouble with your superiors. We will take it upon ourselves to locate the fuel needed to keep it running."

"Alright. I'll have one of my men drive a bus down when we bring your men back tomorrow and line you out on its use." Pastor Dan's face was radiant at the news. "One other small request would be that the bus stays parked over by where my men are billeted when it's not in use. At this point, HQ is still unaware that I am keeping a small detachment of men down here in your town. If they were to find out, it'd be best if the bus was located there and I could just say the bus was intended for their use."

"That won't be a problem, Colonel."

"Great, how have my men been behaving for you? Have they been staying out of trouble?" the colonel asked bluntly, changing the subject.

"They've been great. They've been very professional and their help keeping watch over the south bridge and the dam has been much appreciated."

"Good, I'm glad it's working out." Colonel Harris cleared his throat. "I was considering adding a couple extra squads down here, but I wanted to run it by you first. As of now, I have twenty men staying with you in town. With five men watching the bridge and five men watching the Tionesta dam, they are performing twelve-hour shifts daily." Harris ran his hair through his greying hair. "If possible, I'd like to double the men in town, to allow them some down time. I would also like to start rotating them through your Gardening Team on their off days. While we will be teaching the soldiers up in Warren the basics on gardening, maybe you could do the same for my men stationed down here."

Colonel Harris paused, looking at the men around the table before his gaze fell on Pastor Dan. "I would also like to request that the men helping on your gardening team also receive their meals on that specific day from the town's food supply as well. I could try and make the case that I am offering you manpower in trade for food, but in honesty, it would help me from having to send as much food down here each week. You'll get extra manpower in your gardens, it bolsters your town's defenses, it eases my food burden a bit, and it would reduce the long hours my men are keeping watch over your southern defenses." Colonel Harris could see the mixed expressions to his request around the table. Feeding his men was something he'd assured the mayor wouldn't be needed when he had sent the first detachment of twenty men to Tionesta a month prior.

Colonel Harris rolled his neck in a circle, stretching his tense shoulder muscles. "This is in no way a demand, Mayor. It is purely a request. Things have changed, and you're more than welcome to deny the extra men or even request that I take the current detachment back if you'd like me to. Also, this request has nothing to do with your town using one of our busses. However, if you did choose to let me station some more men down here and help me keep them fed, I could offer one more bonus. If your farm up the hill is ever attacked, I'll send half my team up there on the first bus. I'll have them work together with your security forces to set up a defensive perimeter and a strategy for defending your new farming operation. I don't want this to be considered a trade. I want this to be more of a…," Colonel Harris searched for the right words, "…a pooling of our resources together for everyone's benefit."

There was a period of silence as all eyes turned to Pastor Dan. "Well…," he began.

"If I may?" Brody interjected once more, seeking the mayor's permission to speak.

The mayor hesitated skeptically before motioning Brody to continue. "One small addition, I'd like to add to that, Colonel, assuming the council approves your request." Colonel Harris nodded back letting Brody know that he had his attention. "We are going to be sending scouting parties out to search the area for survivors and other resources the town may be able to use. After scouting, we will be approaching some of the survivors we locate, as well as clearing all the houses on top the hill near the new gardening location. While it is important that members of our town make those initial approaches, we will also need a quick response force and a medic down the road if the three men approaching the house or cabin are attacked. While we could do this ourselves, I feel it would be a huge benefit to their safety if we had access to a half-dozen trained soldiers in a bulletproof MRAP to come in and pull our men out…only if needed. As it sits now, the town will be sending in a half dozen of their security forces in a rusty pickup truck, with minimal training working together in squad tactics. Obviously, your men would be kept out of view and only come in during an emergency."

The Colonel sighed heavily glancing at Pastor Dan then back to Brody. "That is a complicated request, Brody. You are placing my men in a position, where it will *likely* lead them into an active engagement against civilians. An engagement that isn't defensive in nature since we'd be the ones approaching the civilians. Just so you're aware, if any of my men are injured or killed, I have to report it to HQ immediately and file a report. While I am willing to hide the fact that they were helping your town in my official report, we run into the issue that soldiers gossip and complain like high schoolers. If someone is injured or killed in that squad during an engagement that doesn't have anything to do with the regiment, there could be some gossip and resentment among my men. That gossip could reach my superiors on one of their visits and become a problem. I am not saying it is out of the question, I'm just going to have to wrap my mind around it for a while and figure out the best way to make it work." When Colonel Harris finished, there was a long pause at the table. Sean noticed Willy studying the colonel intently, his left hand fidgeting with his belt loop.

"Well, you've sure given us a lot to think about, Colonel," Pastor Dan finally responded. "I think we are going to need some time to discuss and vote on your proposal. Maybe you could use this opportunity to go check in on your men."

"No problem, Mayor," Colonel Harris smiled in understanding. He turned from the table. "Captain," he addressed Whalen, motioning him to follow. Captain Whalen stood up and gave Willy one more dark glare before turning and following his commander down the steps of the dais.

As soon as the rear sanctuary doors closed, Pastor Dan picked up the handheld ham radio and keyed the mic. "This is the mayor. Can whoever's near the greenhouses ask Kathy to join us in the council meeting, please?" He held the radio up, waiting for a response.

"I'll let her know," came a response over the handheld.

"Right away, please," Pastor Dan added.

"Yes, Mayor. I'm on my way over there as we speak."

"Thank you," Pastor Dan replied. He set the radio down and let out a long sigh. "Okay, who wants to start?"

Chapter 8

Sean, Randy and Brody loitered on the front steps of the church, waiting for everyone to exit the building. A weary-looking colonel finally meandered through the front door, holding it open for the mayor. As they came down the steps, Colonel Harris broke off his conversation with the mayor and shook each of their hands in turn. "It's good to see you again. Let me know if there is anything your homesteads need or any way that I can help you. I was serious in there. I want to start working together with the locals."

Brody gave the colonel a brief smile while Sean replied sincerely, "Thank you again, Colonel, for everything you've done already." Others were filing out the front doors of the church now and their little group was blocking the stairs. Sean nodded over his shoulder to the colonel who followed them a short distance away from prying ears.

"I think that we all trust each other here, at least for the most part," Sean chuckled, resulting in a small conciliatory smile from the colonel.

"Some of the things Willy brought up in there have us a bit concerned, to be honest," Brody stated flatly, cutting to the chase. The colonel nodded his understanding, but he didn't offer a reply. "That being said, we believe you that you and your Regiment didn't have anything to do with what happened to Willy's family, but it still gives us reason for pause. We realize you've already stuck your neck out for us as well as for the town here. That could create problems for us in the future. What if you were discovered and lost your regiment? Who would replace you? The state of the country doesn't look very good, especially if they are rationing the military's food supplies. If you were to be discovered and replaced with another commander that doesn't operate the strict confines of their orders, our homesteads and the entire town could be at risk."

Randy cut in. "Colonel, what we are saying is that we value the relationship we are building with you, but what guarantees can you offer us that what little food we have left won't be confiscated and that our families aren't going to be bussed off to some Green Zone in the future." Sean noticed that Randy had wisely understated the amount of food they had remaining.

"Guarantees?" the colonel responded. "I'm sorry, what's your name again?"

"Randy."

"Randy, there are no guarantees in this new world. Son, I can assure you that I have made no mention of your retreats to HQ other than my report on the ambush. In that, I just reported that a local farm was attacked but I also didn't give any specifics on your group or the location of your farm. I can promise you that I will continue to keep your two retreats and their locations a secret." He turned to Sean. "And you know I have a vested interest in keeping your location a secret since I have placed Mayor Reese with your group. Something else I have done, along those same lines, is to keep Captain Whalen in the loop. He is a good soldier and a like-minded individual that I have complete trust in. If I and Major Samuelsson were ever removed from our leadership positions over the regiment, he has sworn to give you and the town warning through Mayor Reese…uh, David." Colonel Harris used the new name the old mayor of Kane had adopted since moving in with Sean's family at the North Homestead. Colonel Harris stayed in contact with David who occasionally walked down to the main road and left messages for the Colonel at a predetermined location. David would make a mark at the location alongside the road to alert the colonel of a new message that was too sensitive to be passed on through the ham radio.

"Captain Whalen would also keep you informed of the new commander's plans. Effectively, at that time, you will have your own spy with high placement within the 31st Regiment. So, while I can't make any promises or guarantees, I have put plans in place to assist you and the town of Tionesta should something happen to me." He forced a small smile. "Let's hope for my sake it doesn't come down to that." The three men smiled back and nodded their agreement.

"Thank you for that, Colonel, and I have but one more question for you," Brody said while unconsciously twisting the new wedding ring on his finger. Colonel Harris nodded for him to continue. "Why are you still here?"

The colonel looked confused and slightly offended. "Well, the meeting just ended, and we'll be pulling out of town as soon as Curtiss and Kathy arrive with their things."

"No, Colonel, that's not what I meant," Brody snickered. "Why is your Regiment still in Warren? You told us when you arrived that you were here to destroy the Bradford prison gang and restore order to the area. The looters from the Bradford prison are all dead now. It sounds like you are talking about building some long-term gardening resources in Warren and digging in with your men for the long haul. From what David has heard from his resource in D.C., there are a lot of other massive gangs spread throughout the country. One of them up near Chicago is extremely large. Why isn't the military sending you off to fight some other warlord? Why are you still here, Colonel?" Brody reiterated his original question.

Colonel Harris's smile was gone and his face was serious now. "Brody, have you told me everything there is to know about your retreat?" He turned to Sean. "What about yours? Exactly how much food do you have remaining in Mr. Andrews's bunker?" Sean gave

Brody an uncomfortable look. "I've tried really hard to stay out of your business. I don't ask questions or pry into your homesteads or their inner workings. I would ask the same of you."

Sean shook his head uncomfortably. "The difference though, Colonel, is our homesteads aren't a threat to your Regiment. A thousand trained soldiers who may be going hungry soon is a big predicament for us. We're not asking you to tell us everything, but we also don't want to be suspicious of you or your intentions, either. Honestly, we want to continue working together for everyone's benefit like you mentioned inside. But knowing that there is something big you are intentionally keeping from us doesn't really build trust."

The Colonel nodded. "There isn't a single person outside of my Regiment that knows our other mission here: not even Pastor Dan. And there are valid reasons why." Colonel Harris saw Brody frown at his answer and he sighed in response. "What we are doing in Warren has nothing to do with you or Tionesta. It will have no effect on you or the town. You have my word on that."

Brody shifted his stance and crossed his arms, unwilling to relent. "Give me *something*, Colonel."

Sean noticed Colonel Harris clench his jaw. He didn't like the negative direction the conversation was headed, so he tried a different approach. "Just before your men arrived, we heard from the mayor of Warren that they were close to getting the electric grid up and running."

Colonel Harris snorted. "I can assure you that they were nowhere near getting electricity up and running in Warren. They made a few repairs to some of the smaller transformers throughout the town, but that was about all."

Sean continued. "We're kind of guessing that your real mission here involves the small oil refinery in Warren, but the only way for you to get that up and running would be to provide electricity for it somehow. Maybe from the Kinzua Dam...." Sean didn't phrase it in a question. He just wanted to see the colonel's reaction to what he said.

The colonel didn't react. He stood like a granite statue without batting an eyelash. A full minute passed by very uncomfortably. "Let's assume you were on to something…and I'm not saying that you are! But for the sake of argument, let's say one of you thinks that is the case and goes home and tells your wife that she will soon be able to use the dishwasher in the kitchen. Which, again, isn't the case! Your wife tells a friend of hers in town. That friend has this 'Willy character' carry a message for her to the next town over. All the while the story is changing and growing. This friend of hers, shares the news with her husband, who is friends with that town's mayor. The mayor discusses it abroad over ham radio. Pretty soon, there are hundreds of people hearing that there is electricity and gasoline in Warren…when there *clearly* isn't!" he emphasized once more. "People start showing up. Gangs start scoping us out. Maybe that big gang from Chicago you were talking about decides they enjoy the mountain air better than the slums of Chicago. Hundreds of my men and thousands of civilians could die as the result of a single, stupid rumor like that! Do you see where I am going with this, gentlemen? That rumor creates a very big problem for me, unwanted attention for both of us, and who knows how many uninvited guests suddenly hanging around the area that may or may not be friendly. All because of some pillow talk with your wife!" the colonel finished with a snap.

"We understand," Sean said, reassuringly lifting his hands defensively, "and you're absolutely right."

"I hope so," Colonel Harris grunted.

"We won't say anything, Colonel," Randy added.

"About what?" The colonel pointed his finger at Randy's chest. "You are standing there thinking I just told you something that I didn't tell you. I was just playing along with your hypothetical example and explaining how easily rumors can force us into bad places we don't want to go to. Now…are we clearly understood?"

"Yes, sir," Randy responded, followed by Brody and Sean nodding their heads.

"Good, I must be going now. I still need to speak with Pastor Dan some more and," the colonel shuddered, "barter with that mad man."

Brody and Sean both smiled at his description of Willy, resulting in the colonel smirking himself. He turned and strolled back to Pastor Dan. At the end of the meeting, the councilmen had agreed to the extra troops in town and the benefits that came along with them. When they'd moved on to discussing the patrols, Willy had factored into the discussion once more. Upon hearing mention of Willy's maps and his notes of the outlying area, the colonel had changed his demeanor a bit and softened his approach with the strange man. Willy had also developed a bit of respect for the colonel during the meeting, not that he was going to let it show. He'd continued his snappy tone, even if he did finally agree to help the colonel with his patrols in trade for some supplies to be negotiated after the meeting. When the meeting was finally over, Willy had seen enough of the town's leadership to trust them and had agreed to retrieve his maps and notes from his pack.

Willy was the last one to come out of the church and upon seeing the three of them off to one side, he angled in their direction. They watched him approach, curiously. "Hello, gentlemen," he said with a big-toothed smile. "I was just wondering if any of you had extended family in the area or a message you'd like for me to carry along my route."

"Not unless you are heading toward Pittsburgh any time soon," Sean muttered.

Willy's smile faded. "No, sir! Unfortunately, that is not on my normal postal route. You'll have to discuss that with another carrier."

Sean nodded his understanding with a polite smile. Willy knew they were aware of his backstory but he continued his charade. They all knew there weren't any other "mail carriers." What a strange man, Sean thought to himself for the fiftieth time in the last hour.

"We appreciate your help, Willy, and we'll be sure to get those hundred rounds of .300 Blackout to the mayor in the next couple days. They'll be here upon your return," Brody promised.

Willy smiled once more. "Great!" He looked over his shoulder toward where Colonel Harris and Pastor Dan stood huddled together next to one of the MRAPs. They caught him looking at them and Willy quickly turned back toward the three of them with a scowl. He sighed. "I guess it's time to go barter with the government man."

He was getting ready to turn when Sean grabbed his shirt sleeve. "Willy, I realize you've been burned before and I can't even imagine the pain you've endured, losing your family like that." Sean let go of Willy's sleeve as the man studied him intently with sharp eyes. "Like you, we don't have any faith in the government going forward and we don't have much trust for the military as a whole. That being said, Colonel Harris is a good man…an honorable man. He has helped our town tremendously in the past and has come through on his promises." Sean paused for a moment. "I'm not really sure why I'm telling you this, I just thought you should know who you are dealing with."

Willy stood silently for a moment, looking at each of them in turn. Randy was nodding his agreement to what Sean had said. Willy bowed his head toward them slightly and turned away without saying another word.

When he was a dozen paces away from them, Randy muttered, "That dude is so weird." Sean fully agreed.

Chapter 9

Several members of Sean's family stepped outside upon hearing the rusty Bronco pull through the front gate. Sean watched as Maria pushed past his father and bounded down the front steps, their infant son bouncing on her hip.

Sean couldn't stop a smile. "You better stop here, Randy." Randy caught Sean's meaning and put the Bronco in park a few feet short of the sidewalk.

Sean had no sooner stepped out of the vehicle when his wife, who'd already made it around the car, glided into his waiting arms. She didn't say anything; she just pushed her face into his chest and squeezed his waist tightly with her free arm. They stayed that way for almost a full minute, Maria never loosening her grip on him. Sean had been away from the retreat overnight before, but not for three days straight. Once Tionesta's council meeting had ended, they'd made their way back to the East Homestead to drop off Brody and inform them of the meeting's details and Colonel Harris's revelation. Sean and Randy had intended to continue on that same evening to the North Homestead, but the gathering at the original retreat had run late. There were lots of questions and before Sean knew it, dusk had arrived. Without functioning headlights on the Bronco, they'd made the decision to stay overnight and head out at first light. They radioed a message to Tionesta who relayed it on to the North Homestead.

When Maria finally released her grip, Sean could see a tear on her cheek. He smiled at her and gently wiped it away.

"Welcome home," she whispered before rising on tip toes to give him a quick kiss.

"It's good to be back," Sean replied as he turned his attention to his son and gave him a big smile and a high pitched "Hey there!" James stared back at him briefly before opening his mouth in a big toothless smile. "He smiled!" Sean exclaimed, looking at Maria.

"Yep. He's been doing that for two days now. Your brother was holding him for me while I used the restroom and he got the first smile. You know how your brother is, all goofy with him." Sean's brother Joshua was a full seven inches over six feet tall yet as gentle as a kitten with his young children. He was always playful, even with the other children in the family. Watching his brother laugh and wrestle with his boys was like watching a massive grizzly play with her cubs.

Sean could see the disappointment on his wife's face that Jacob's first smile hadn't been directed at her, even though she masked it well. "Today, he smiled at your mom, your sister, and even Uncle Nathan. You think he'd give his mother a smile too, but nooo…." She frowned as she looked down at Jacob. "All you give me are dirty diapers."

Sean chuckled as he unbuckled his battle belt, set it on the ground at his feet, and took James from her arms. He cooed and made extravagant smiles at his boy, trying to get him to smile again, but to no avail. James looked back at his mama, almost questioningly, before turning back to him. Sean was resolute on getting another smile out of his son, this time raising him high over his head while spinning in a circle. Jacob's eyes grew wide, his lip quivering. He started to wail. Sean quickly lowered his son back to his chest, rubbing his back and shushing him softly. "I'm sorry, Buddy. I won't do that again," he promised. He swayed James back in forth in a soothing manner but it had little effect on the crying infant.

Suddenly, Sean's nose caught a whiff of something awful, and he had to turn his head to the side and breathe through his mouth. He instinctively held James out in Maria's direction. "I think he has a present for you."

"What a shocker," Maria frowned as she took James from his outstretched hands.

Randy brushed past Sean, carrying his pack and a couple other duffle bags toward the cabin. "So, when are you going to learn how to change a diaper?" he asked with a wry grin, not even turning his head in Sean's direction.

"Yeah," Maria agreed forcibly. "I'd like an answer to that question as well."

Sean cringed. It was no secret around the retreat that Sean would quickly disappear or find something "important" to do at the first whiff of a dirty diaper. Sean heard Randy laugh out loud as he disappeared through the dark hole of the cabin's entryway, and he swore to get him back. Randy had surely known his question would get a rise out of Maria. "What an instigator," Sean murmured.

"I think today is as good as any to learn how to change your son's diaper," Maria said, her eyebrows raised in challenge.

"C'mon, Babe. I just got home. I've got to unpack my gear and we've got a lot of stuff to go over from the council meeting," Sean argued. Diapers were something they had not planned ahead and stored at the retreat when they'd first found out about Maria's pregnancy. Luckily, Randy's youngest daughter had been allergic to regular diapers and they had a fair amount of cloth diapers which were stretched thin with both babies using them. Unlike the East Homestead, the North Homestead had a commercial grade washer and dryer to clean their clothes, not that it helped out with the diapers. If you changed a diaper, it also meant you were forced to immediately clean it in the sink by hand and hang it up. If you didn't, it wouldn't be dry the next time you needed it. Sean couldn't believe how many times in a given day the tiny human could dirty a diaper. Over the years, he'd cleaned out a gut-shot deer on two occasions without so much as half a gag. In contrast, just looking over Maria's shoulder a few times while she changed a diaper had made him start to sweat. Sean was seriously dreading the task which was inevitable in his near future.

Maria must have read the look of distress on his face and she grinned in resignation. "Well, maybe today isn't the best day for that," she said, letting him off the hook once more.

Sean couldn't help but let out a long sigh in relief. "Well, I better get to it," he said quickly, before she changed her mind. He pecked her on the cheek, picked up his battle belt, and buckled it back onto his hips as he walked to the back of the Bronco to grab his pack. His father, Samuel, was already pulling Sean's things out and setting them on the ground. His father's work ethic was unparalleled. He still walked with a limp after fleeing the family farm with his brother and their long hike to Tionesta. Sean's father had been shot in the leg when the farm was overrun, and as of yet he hadn't achieved full recovery.

Sean shot him a grin, but his father's return smile was obviously forced. "We need to talk, son," he said in a whisper.

Sean was suddenly anxious. "What's going on?"

Samuel's eyes glanced around to the others still milling around the front of the cabin. "Let's talk when we get inside." Sean had barely heard his answer and he stared back at his father. Samuel must have seen his unease and smiled more authentically. "It's good to have you home, son."

"Thanks, dad. I'm glad to be home." He gave his dad a quick hug while giving a sidelong glance toward Maria and James as they made their way back into the house.

Samuel bent down to grab his pack. "No, you don't!" Sean said, quickly taking the heavy three-day bug out bag from his father's hands. "You don't need to be putting any extra weight on that leg yet."

"You either!" Sean flinched as his uncle, Lawrence, abruptly walked up from behind them and stood with his hand outstretched.

Sean's uncle had been a colonel in the Air Force and he was using his commander voice, which didn't leave any room for discussion or debate. "Both of you invalids just need to head inside. We'll carry your gear." Lawrence was flanked by Sean's cousin Danny who bobbed his head in greeting while trying to hide a wry smile.

"Whatever you say, Colonel," Sean responded in jest with a wink to Danny. He followed the order, trailing his limping father inside. Immediately after they walked through the large oak doors, Samuel motioned Sean to follow and led them to Mr. Andrews' wood-paneled office where he quietly closed the door behind them. Sean watched as his father walked over to the ornate wood desk and leaned against it, his fingers thrumming along the front edge of the massive desk. Sean took a seat in one of the leather chairs across from his father. He felt like he was a child again, expecting one of his father's famous "talking to's."

Samuel sighed. "We've had a visitor the last two nights." Sean raised an eyebrow as his concern mounted. "The night before last, Bug was on watch upstairs and picked up a figure outside the perimeter fence with the NVGs. He was getting ready to sound the alarm when the figure disappeared. He wrote it down in the watch log, but didn't tell the council about it until the following morning. His reasoning being, because of the distance, he figured it might have just been a deer bedded down or something. Last night, Jackson was on watch and he spotted a figure at the exact same spot at exactly the same time…two a.m. He raised the silent alarm and everyone started scrambling for positions. Before I could even get fully dressed, and without conferring with anyone, Bug ran out the back door, circling around behind the man. The only person who knew where he'd gone was Danny. He only briefly revealed what he intended as he ran out.

Jackson said the man left after scoping us out for only a couple minutes. He must have made his approach through the woods as the LP/OP didn't see anyone approach from down the lane. Bug was able to follow him a short distance but peeled off once the guy reached the main road, worried that he might get caught following him down the open road. Bug was still in his PJs and slippers." Samuel and Sean both chuckled at the detail. "He wasn't really geared up to get in a shootout. Bug said the guy headed down the road to the east." His father finished and waited as Sean stood rubbing his chin.

"Why all the whispering and secrecy?" Sean finally asked.

"Well, we haven't told the others yet," Samuel explained. "We didn't want to spook them." Sean nodded his agreement on the decision. "They know something's up though. We kept six extra men on watch the rest of the night through this morning."

"Okay, let's get the council together, discuss it and make a game plan so we can let everyone know what's going on. Not knowing what's happening is probably gonna freak them out more if we don't tell them something soon." His dad nodded in agreement. "Besides, Randy and I have a lot to discuss with you guys about the council meeting in Tionesta."

Samuel could tell by his son's face that it was something serious but wasn't about to make him go through the information twice. "I'll go get the council gathered. Everyone is pretty much ready and we were just waiting for you and Randy to get back."

"Okay. Do me a favor and grab Bug and Jackson, too. I'd like to hear a little more about what they observed."

Sean's father nodded and pushed up from his perch against the desk. "We should be able to get started in five minutes."

"Good. I'm going to go unpack and make sure my assault pack is squared away…just in case," Sean added after noticing the quizzical look on his father's grizzled face.

Sean walked through the great room and down the back staircase which led to the finished basement. It was full of Army cots and a twisting labyrinth of sheets hanging from the ceiling for some modicum of privacy for the thirty people who now called the subterranean gameroom their bedroom.

Sean pulled aside the thin black sheet that separated his family's section and almost let out a startled cry when he abruptly found himself nose to nose with his uncle. Lawrence was just as startled as he'd been, and they both chuckled.

"I set everything on your cot there." He pointed at Sean's bed. With the new baby sleeping with them, Sean and Maria were lucky to have one of the few beds in the North Homestead. It was more of a twin-sized mattress propped up on boards and plywood than a bed, but it was one heck of a lot more comfortable than the Army cots they'd been sleeping on at the East Homestead before James was born.

"Thanks," Sean smiled. "Dad's gathering everyone now for the meeting."

"Good. I'll go see if I can help."

Sean stepped aside, holding the sheet wide for his uncle to pass. "I'll be up in a few minutes. I just need to rearrange a few things."

Stepping inside his "room," Sean set his rifle and battle belt on the floor and flopped down on the edge of his bed, stretching his tight leg muscle for a few moments. He reached under the bed and slid his Condor Fuel Assault pack out beside the three-day bug-out bag that he had taken to the East Homestead. He pulled out his dirty clothes from the main compartment and carelessly tossed them into a pile to carry upstairs. Next he pulled out his summer sleeping bag and set it next to him on the bed.

Easily accessible in the side pockets of his pack, he pulled out his fire kit in its waterproof pouch, the accessory pouch, and water purification tablets, placing them in the smaller outside pocket of the assault pack. Instead of a bunch of loose items floating around in various pouches in his bag, Sean had devised a system which allowed him to transfer important items between packs quickly without leaving something important behind. He removed the large bolt knife and Silky saw from the molle webbing on the side of his three-day bag, placing them onto the bed next to his sleeping bag. Next, the three-piece Esbit cook kit, various MRE's and Mountain House meals, medical kit, single wall stainless canteen, and para cord were set next to him on the bed as well. He placed one of the MREs and a few Cliff bars into the assault pack before zipping it closed. He set the bag next to his rifle and made one more pass through each pocket of his bug-out bag to be sure he hadn't missed anything. Sean pulled out a couple loose power bar wrappers and stuffed them into his pocket to throw away later. Content that he hadn't missed anything, he slid the now-empty bag under his bed. He scooped up the loose items on the bed and stood, making his way out of the sleeping quarters.

The workout room on the opposite side of the basement had been converted into a reloading and catch-all room by his father, who spent many evenings meticulously reloading their spent ammo casings. Sean dropped the items in his arms onto the floor and bent down to release the catch on the wall mirror which smoothly swiveled open, leading into the intricate tunnel system and storage rooms that Mr. Andrews had constructed. Sean bent over with a wince, picking the items up once more and stepped into the tunnel, blackness swallowing him whole. A few feet in, he had to crouch downward to use his shoulder to flip on the light switch. A long row of LED lightbulbs that hung from the roof of the tunnel flickered to life. The solid concrete walls stretched into the distance with numerous doors down its length, leading into various storage rooms. He ambled down the tunnel to the second door on his left and once more had to set the jumble of items he clutched to his chest down on the floor. Sean pulled a ring of keys out of his pocket, found the correct key, and opened the storage room door.

Although dry, the storage room still had a slightly musty smell to it. There was a dehumidifier in each storage room, but they weren't important enough to outweigh the amount of electricity they used. He reached along the wall to his right and flicked on the light. He froze, and instantly knew he'd opened the wrong door. It was the hideous room that Mr. Andrews had used to conceal the young women from Tionesta, held hostage for his perverse enjoyment. When Sean's family had first arrived at the new retreat and scrubbed down the room, they had decided to just leave it empty. There were plenty of other storage rooms with the added bonus of shelving which his family used instead.

Sean had a sick feeling in his stomach as his mind flashed back to the day when he had first entered the room and found the young women and girls chained to the walls. He quickly shut the lights off, trying to chase away the memory, and closed the heavy metal door with a bang. He placed the padlock through the catch, slamming it home. He scooped up his gear and strode a few paces back to the door he'd intended to go through in the first place and unlocked it. The heavy metal door swung open on creaky hinges. He turned on the single light in the room and was greeted with a large storage room flanked by floor-to-ceiling shelves. The shelves were overflowing with his relatives' extra winter clothes and various other supplies and gear. Each shelving unit had a tag at the top with a different family's name to keep things organized and allow each person in the group his or her own storage space.

Sean quickly glanced over at his cousin Danny's shelf which was placed in front of the small hidden escape tunnel leading to the back of the property. Content that the shelf was tight against the wall, he dropped his gear in the middle of the room and walked over to it, inspecting the floor in front of the shelving unit. The entire storage room floor had a thick layer of dust on it but no footprints were evident other than the ones he was making. Danny and his wife must not have been down here in a while. Sean bent over and dragged his index finger across the cold concrete floor which created a line of dust that trailed behind it. He frowned. If the retreat was ever forced to escape through this tunnel, the hidden wheels under the shelving unit would surely make marks through the dust, let alone all their footprints. Those signs could give away the fact that there was something behind the cabinet. He made a mental note to have his uncle assign someone to sweep the floor in the room on a weekly basis.

Sean turned. In the center of the room was a big pile of various packs. Every member of North Homestead, including each child, had a pack in this room ready to go at a moment's notice. If they were overrun by a large raiding force, there wouldn't be time for people to scramble around the retreat and gather their belongings before they fled. Sean picked through the packs until he came across his large-sized Alice pack. With a grunt, he pulled it free from the pile and almost fell backwards. He set it down on the floor next to his sleeping bag. As he reached to open the top flap, he noticed "Sergeant" written in permanent marker on the flap. Sean sighed. He'd grabbed his father's pack by accident. His father, brother, and two of his uncles all utilized the same large-sized Alice packs. He set his father's pack aside and went back to the big pile and let out another sigh. This just wouldn't do. The big pile of packs desperately needed to be organized.

"I'm sure hearing a lot of sighing coming from in here…!"

Sean nearly jumped out of his skin as his mother stepped into the room. "Mom!" Sean exclaimed as he exhaled. "You scared the crap out of me. What are you doing down here?"

She just smiled, ignoring the question as she walked over to him and gave him a hug. "Welcome home." He snickered at himself for being jumpy and hugged her back. "I'm on the lunch team and we're out of Montreal Seasoning in the pantry upstairs. Your Aunt Sophie is in charge of the meal today and sent me down to look. I think there might be some on the top shelf in the supply room, but I can't reach it." She smiled, "And then I heard you making all this noise and, well, do you think you can give your mother a hand?"

"Of course! Lead the way," he gestured to the open door. Sean followed his mother down the tunnel in the direction of the barn entrance and came to a stop at the last door on the right which stood open. "Hey mom, help me remember to tell dad that the council needs to assign someone to come down here and clean that room and organize the packs. If we were forced to flee through the escape tunnel, that room would be a virtual mad house with everyone digging through that big pile trying to find their own pack."

She gave a noncommittal "I'll try" shrug before pointing to one of the top shelves. The concrete ceiling in the supply room was a full nine feet high with tall shelving units that ran floor to ceiling. Sean couldn't reach it either. He made another mental note to bring the small ladder from the barn down here at some point. Sean's mind was always racing and there were always things that needed done. He could never seem to get through the mental checklist in his brain. As he finished one task, three more took its place. With so many things to remember, it wasn't uncommon for him to forget things lately. Forgetting to bring a ladder down to this storage room wasn't a big deal. Unfortunately, in the new world, there had been times he'd forgotten more important items. Items that could have had bad consequences.

For decades before the collapse, Sean had watched his father every Sunday evening take a piece of paper and divide it with a pen and ruler into each day of the week. He would write out his tasks for the week and then fold it in thirds and place it in his T-shirt chest pocket alongside his reading glasses and a pen. He had always tried to convince Sean to do the same and stay more organized, but there was absolutely no way Sean was going to wear T-shirts with a chest pocket. Instead, he had settled on an app for his cell phone to set reminders and keep his tasks organized. He'd found that removing the mental clutter and ideas floating around in his brain and putting them into his phone had significantly reduced his stress level in the past. But in a world with no cell phones or electronic organizers, he was going to have to figure something else out. He remembered that he had a small waterproof notebook and space pen in his Lone Wolf pack and resolved to start carrying them in his cargo pocket. He let out a sarcastic sigh. That was, if he could remember to grab them out of his pack when he got back to what he'd been doing.

Sean placed his foot on the first shelf and tested its strength by slowly placing his weight on it. Sean wasn't sure if the shelving unit was attached to the wall or if there was just a lot of weight on its shelves, but it didn't budge. Feeling confident, he placed his hurt leg on the next shelf and with a wince slowly went up another level.

"Be careful, son," his mother said in a typical concerned parent's way.

He felt her hand on the back of his calf in support as he stepped up onto the third shelf. His head above the top shelf, he grasped the front of the shelf with one hand as he rifled through containers of various seasonings. Some of them were the same, but he was having a tough time seeing the labels on the back part of the shelf where the light from the single LED lightbulb hanging in the center of the room couldn't reach. He pulled his Surefire Titan Plus flashlight out of his pocket and shone the light with his free hand. It was a tiny yet powerful single AAA battery flashlight that he had received from his father the previous Christmas. With one hand holding the flashlight and his other holding tight to the shelf support, he didn't have a free hand to move items around. He strained his neck in one direction and then another before finally seeing a bright red label for "Montreal Steak Seasoning." He handed the flashlight down to his mother and reached into the dark where he'd last seen the large plastic bottle. He handed the bottle down to his mother and climbed back down off the shelving unit.

"This is Italian seasoning, son. I said *Montreal.* Do you need your ears checked?" his mother teased.

"What? I grabbed the Montreal Seasoning," Sean insisted.

She held out the bottle to him and clicked on her own small flashlight, shining it directly on the label for effect. She smiled in victory. There had been plenty of light in the room to read the label without the flashlight.

Sean turned back to the shelving unit with another sigh and began climbing.

"There's that sigh again." He heard his mother chastise him. He almost sighed in response but stopped himself, shaking his head. There was no point in disagreeing with her.

Sean replaced the wrong seasoning bottle and placed the small flashlight into his mouth this time. With the help of the light, he grabbed the correct container and handed it down to her. She didn't say anything, just gave him a smile and a wink and walked out. "Don't forget to close and lock the door for me," he heard her voice echo down the tunnel as she left.

"Yes, mother," he mumbled to himself with a smirk. He locked the storage room door behind him, thanking God for bringing his family back to him safely, even if they were annoying at times.

He went back to the larger storage room and finally found his pack, placing the important items where they belonged inside of it and tossing it back onto the pile. Upon leaving the room, he flipped the light off, pulled the heavy steel door closed, and locked it. Suddenly, he remembered the notepad and pen. He couldn't help himself this time. He let out a long, deep, throaty sigh, digging the keys back out of his pocket.

Chapter 10

Sean and Randy took turns before the retreat's council members, relating all the details from the meeting in Tionesta. When the council was informed of Colonel Harris' revelation on the food situation with his soldiers, their concern was evident. The council discussed the implications at length and finally came to the conclusion that there wasn't anything that could be done in the near term. They would discuss it further as more information became available. Sean's Uncle Lawrence made a point of order and they all resolved to keep the rest of the retreat members in the dark for the time being. There wasn't any reason for immediate concern and there was no point in giving the family members one more reason to worry.

The council members were still discussing the hungry soldiers when Bug and his brother Jackson sauntered in, their hands and the knees of their pants soiled from garden duty. "Hey, Bug. Hey, Jackson," Sean greeted them as they took chairs at the large barn wood dining table.

"Hey, cuz," Jackson smiled warmly.

"We were just about to discuss our, uh, *visitor*. Why don't you boys tell them what you saw," Lawrence instructed his two sons.

Jackson looked at Bug who led off. "Well, to be honest, there's not much to tell. I was on watch upstairs," he said, fingers combing through his scruffy beard in thought. “This would have been the night before last. David was up there too. He had his headphones on like usual and was monitoring one of his *secret* ham radio stations or whatever he does on that thing. A few minutes past two in the morning I picked up some movement just outside the west perimeter fence. We all know it’s not uncommon to see some small forest fauna trotting around this place at night.” Sean smiled at his cousin’s description. Bug always had a good sense of humor and knew how to lighten a mood.

“I kept an eye on it, but you also know how hard it is to pick out any detail with those Gen 2 NVG’s, especially at two hundred yards. It didn’t look very big to me and I just thought it might be a possum or raccoon. I almost lost sight of it because it stayed in the same spot for about ten minutes. When I caught movement again, I called David over to check it out but he couldn’t really make out what it was either. After another ten minutes, I saw it leave the edge of the fence and head back into the woods. That was the first time I really considered that it might be a person. The whole time I was watching it, it seemed relatively small, but when it left, I could see it was much larger than a dumpster rat. From there, I considered maybe it was just a deer which had bedded down next to the perimeter fence for a while. If it was a human, he must have been lying down.”

Bug reached in his cargo pocket and pulled out a green plastic military surplus canteen and took a long draw of water before setting it down on the table. “I made a note of it in the watch log and when I got up yesterday morning, I decided to go check out the area. Some of the high grass along the fence line was mashed down, but I couldn’t find any foot prints or any other sign of it being a human, or a deer for that matter. I knew Jackson was on duty last night, so I let him know what was up. I told my Da’ too.” He motioned with his hand toward his father.

“Then, last night, when Danny woke me up saying Jackie here had raised the silent alarm, I instantly knew why. I didn’t even change. I just grabbed my rifle, a few spare mags, and headed out. I wanted to try and get behind him before he left and see where the guy went."

"That's a dangerous stunt you pulled, Bug." Sean narrowed his eyes, causing his cousin to blush slightly and look away. "With you wandering around out there in the dark without anyone knowing, it could have resulted in you getting shot in the confusion. You know how it is after someone raises the alarm. Everyone around here is all amped up and freaking out. Somebody with an itchy trigger finger could have shot you on your return. Besides, there could have been others with the guy."

"I told Danny to tell my dad what I was doing," Bug said defensively.

"Danny told me," Uncle Lawrence added for his son's benefit. "I let everyone know to hold their fire till they were sure it wasn't Bug."

Sean crossed his arms in front of his chest. "Even still, you can't just run off into the night like that, especially without taking a radio. There's no strategy in that, Bug. There's no plan of action. There's no way to come to your rescue if we don't know where you are." Bug bowed his head in understanding so Sean let it drop. "Did you really go out there in nothing but those old striped PJs you wear?"

Bug looked up, grinning from ear to ear. "You betcha."

"You're a nut," Sean jabbed him. "All right. What happened next?"

Bug's face grew serious once more. "Well, let's see. I circled around through the woods and posted up in that thin stretch of trees that separates the neighbor's two fields. I figured he would probably head back to the road at some point. Since the LP/OP at the end of the drive hadn't radioed him passing by them the night before, I presumed he must have cut through the woods. I knew he likely wouldn't cross an open field. His only logical path was to use that tree line. Sure enough, right after I found a good hiding spot, this good ol' boy came trottin' right past me. He wasn't even trying to be sneaky. Once he passed me by, I followed him from distance. He came out to the main road about half a mile up from the crossroads with the LP/OP. When I finally reached the road, there was no sight of him. He never went past the LP/OP, so he obviously had to have gone the other way." He folded his hands and placed them on the table, signifying that he was done.

"What kind of rifle was he carrying?" Randy asked.

"Can't say for sure. I had to keep my head down because he literally ran right past me, like…within feet. I thought for sure I was busted. White jammies don't blend in to the forest right well at night." Sean smiled at his cousin again. "I don't think it was an AR, but it did have a large magazine. I don't think it was an AK either. It was a bit longer. I don't know as much about those types of guns as you two though. I couldn't really say for sure."

"But it was definitely some type of battle rifle though, right?" Randy pressed further.

Bug shrugged and Sean could see him debating his response in his mind. "All I can say is it didn't really look like your good ol' huntin' rifle. It looked more…tactical." He frowned at himself, not happy with his description, but he wasn't sure how else to describe the gun.

Sean could see he was uncomfortable, so he changed the subject. "How old do you think he was? What was he wearing?"

Bug laughed out loud. "Geez, Sean! I don't know. Somewhere between sixteen and eighty-seven. It was night time in the woods, remember?" Bug thought it over for a second before continuing. "I tried to keep my head down, so I didn't get a good look at his face, but if I were to judge by the spry way he trotted through the woods, I would guess he was more on the younger side than older." Sean slightly frowned at his answer as he wished they had more to go on. "I've watched my Da' try to run through the woods before and he definitely didn't look like that." Bug contorted his face in mock disgust. Uncle Lawrence rolled his eyes, but the edges of his lips turned up.

"Alright Bug," Lawrence responded dryly as the others tried to hold back their snickers, "I think we get the point." He turned to Jackson. "Got anything to add?"

Jackson shrugged. "Not much."

"What time did you see the guy?" Sean asked, directing his attention to Jackson.

"I logged it in at two fifteen. I first saw him in the back near the garden shed. He didn't stay long, maybe five minutes or so. I think he tried to open the lock on the shed door at one point. A few minutes later I may have seen him on the far back side of the garden, but I can't be sure. That big willow tree is in the way. I won't lie, it was a fairly close call as Danny's dad was on roaming patrol and circled around the garden shed around the same time I seen the guy reappear back there. He must've taken quick cover when he spotted Will patrolling in his general direction. Dad saw what was coming and quickly radioed Will before he got too close. He told him Aunt Eva was sick and to get back to the cabin immediately."

Lawrence cut his son off. "I was worried if I told Will the truth, the guy might overhear the radio transmission on Will's handheld and do something stupid. I felt the best plan was to just get Will out of the area as quickly as possible. Luckily, it worked."

"Will wasn't too happy about it," Sean's uncle Nathan added with a grin. "He understands why you lied to him, but said he felt like 'carp bait' after the fact." A few others smiled at that and Lawrence just shrugged.

The room was silent for a moment before Jackson continued. "I never saw the guy after that. Will's patrol must've scared him off…and that's it." Jackson recounted the event in his typical matter-of-fact way without any of the embellishment his brother had added.

"Sounds like a scout," Randy murmured. The others around the table frowned at the implication. There was likely some other group nearby that was scoping them out. "If he was just a hungry traveler, he surely would have made an attempt for some of the vegetables."

"That's what we thought as well," Uncle Lawrence offered, looking over at Sean's father.

"Well, the council is going to discuss this a little further in depth. Unless you have something else to add, you boys can head back to whatever it is you were doing beforehand," Lawrence instructed. It's not that their meetings were secret, but having too many people attend usually resulted in the discussions being pulled in too many directions. The whole point of the council was to keep focused on the important tasks at the retreat. Recently, they'd started alternating who would lead the meetings. Evidently, it was his Uncle Lawrence's duty today.

Bug and Jackson both nodded. With a screech, their wooden chairs slid back from the table. They walked toward the door, but halfway there Bug turned and tugged his beard again in thought. Sean could tell he was weighing something in his mind.

Sean's dad, Samuel, noticed his nephew still standing there. "What is it, Bug?"

Bug ran his fingers through his dark hair. "I don't know why I didn't think about this before, but what if he's from that church up the road?"

"That's right!" Jackson exclaimed, looking at his brother walking back into the room. "That would be my first bet as well." Sean knew what they were talking about. Their scouting party had come across an inhabited church, weeks before, while out on a gas scavenging trip. Both of the brothers, as well as Uncle Lawrence and Sean's own brother Joshua, had gone on that trip. Sean fumbled through his memory, trying to recount the story his brother had told them.

Running low on gas for the Bronco, four members of the retreat had ventured down their rural road in the wee hours of the morning, pulling a red Radio Flyer wagon filled with empty gas cans and a siphoning hose. A few miles up the road they were stopped by some men living in a church alongside the road. After a tense few minutes of discussion, they were allowed to proceed down the road. After finding an abandoned vehicle they could siphon gas from, they had circled through the woods around the church on their return trip.

"We also smelled a cook fire at that campground a few miles farther down the road. He might be part of that group as well," Uncle Lawrence added. "Truth be told, we just don't know."

"And we won't know unless we have a chat with our visitor," Randy said, giving Sean a knowing look. All eyes turned to Randy.

Sean shrugged. "I'm not sure that we have much choice in the matter, but who knows if the guy is even going to return."

"Really?" Randy blurted sarcastically. "The guy just scoped out our garden. Do you really believe he's not coming back?"

"No, you're probably right. I'm guessing he was just checking out the local farms the first night. Once he knew we were here, he probably reported our presence back to whoever he's staying with. Last night, he was getting a closer look but it sounds like he got scared off by Uncle Will right after he showed up. The question is whether he gathered enough information last night or not. It's possible he could come back again. Maybe even tonight," Sean agreed reluctantly.

"Yeah, he'll be back," Bug added stoically. Sean shrugged his shoulders, unconvinced. "The real question is, how many of his friends will be coming with him on the next trip?"

Sean gave a tug at his growing beard. Everyone waited for his response. While the retreat council ran the day to day operations of the retreat, they still looked to Sean and Randy on matters of security. "I think if we wait too long, we're asking for trouble. We know they are scoping us out and possibly timing our patrols. Right now, we have the upper hand because they don't know we're aware of their presence." Sean looked over at Randy. "While I'd prefer to avoid confrontation as much as possible, I think Randy is right. We need to…to have a conversation with this guy."

"I think we should set an ambush up the road a-ways and see if we can't catch him on his way in," Randy offered.

Sean frowned. "What then, Randy? So, we capture the guy, question him, and then what? Let him go? Kill him? If we just turn him loose after we question him, we are giving up our one advantage in this whole mess: the fact that we know they are watching us and possibly coming for our food."

Samuel, who was normally introspective and quiet at these meetings, spoke up. "So, if I'm reading you right, Son, our options are either to confront their scout and pray that he can be reasoned with, or to start setting up for a pitched battle and make plans to surprise them and win the fight when they arrive for our food. That's assuming they will be coming for it by force and not just looking for another group to trade with." The group of concerned men in the small room just sat there, considering Samuel's wry way of getting his point across. "Didn't you say that Tionesta was looking for local survivors to bring into the fold and possibly invite to join with the town? Why couldn't we approach a 'conversation' with the gentleman from that angle?"

Others were nodding their heads, and Sean could see the wisdom in his father's words. As usual. Lawrence suddenly noticed his sons were still in the room. He wasn't sure what else might be said, and he didn't want any further details about Tionesta and the hungry soldiers to slip out to other, more anxiety-prone family members at the North Homestead. "Thank you again, boys. You can go." Bug and Jackson left without question, closing the door behind them as they left.

Once they were gone, Uncle Nathan jumped in. "There's no reason we even need to discuss our retreat here with him. Just approach it from the stance that we're delegates from Tionesta."

"I think that ship has sailed, Nathan," Randy said as he shook his head. "They already know we're here and that we're growing food.

"I know that," Nathan said, scowling. "What I meant was, when we confront them, why don't we just pretend we're from Tionesta and feel them out first. As long as William doesn't go on the ambush, there is no reason for this guy to know we are from the farm they've been scouting the last few nights. That might put him on edge from the get-go."

Sean nodded. "That would be one way to approach it, but I don't think we should hide the fact that we've been watching them watching us. It will let them know that we keep a tight eye on our resources and make them reconsider sneaking in here and stealing food at night." He turned to his father and added. "That's assuming they are scouting us out to steal from us rather than barter. But, we aren't going to know if we don't talk to him." Sean sighed heavily. "Even then, who's to say what kind of information he'll reveal about his own group? We are taking a risk by giving up the element of surprise. We don't want to get into a cock fight with another group of locals. Once people start getting shot at, it makes it a lot harder to negotiate a truce and set up a bartering agreement. I suggest we have a talk with this guy and see what he's got to say."

Every person around the table nodded. There wouldn't be a need to vote.

Chapter 11

"Yes, sir…. I understand, sir…. I hear you loud and clear…."

Major Samuelsson winced. After another minute or two of similar responses by his commanding officer and friend, Bruce finally lowered the satphone from his ear and pressed the button to end the call. Colonel Harris slumped down in his chair and let out a long sigh.

"That didn't sound as if it went very well," Sammy muttered in empathy.

Bruce shook his head for a moment. "It could have been worse." Major Samuelsson rolled his eyes, not believing his superior after hearing Bruce's side of the conversation.

"General Duncan is going to be flying up tomorrow to check in on us."

"*Okaayyy…*," Sammy stammered. "So, explain to me how it could have gone worse?"

"He said he's going to hold off on his report to General Oates until he sees firsthand what we're dealing with."

"There were a lot more 'yes sirs' and 'roger thats' in the conversation I just heard." Sammy leaned forward and propped his chin on his fist expectantly.

Bruce nodded his head, but he wasn't about to go into depth with his XO on the tongue lashing he'd just received from the General.

Colonel Harris looked toward the office's grimy window where the last vestiges of daylight faded, casting everything in the room in a soft orange hue. With the explosion at the power facility the previous morning, the day had started off bad. After that debacle, his meetings at the Town of Tionesta and the Village of Kane had gone surprisingly well. Right now he had five of the most knowledgeable gardeners in the area going through the assorted, overgrown gardens Warren's previous occupants had left behind.

Kane had agreed to take forty of his troops as had Tionesta. That included keeping them fed in trade for his men bolstering the two towns' security details and cycling through both towns' gardening crews. It was a win-win scenario for Bruce. That would decrease the 31st Regiment's numbers in Warren by nearly ten percent. The town of Kane had only requested a few thousand rounds of 5.56 and 7.62 ammunition in trade, which Bruce had plenty of, and Tionesta had requested the use of a bus. He had four of them just sitting out in the parking lot not being used at all. They were easy trades.

Colonel Harris suddenly remembered the strange character he'd met in Tionesta. "Crap," Bruce muttered under his breath.

"What?" Sammy raised his eyebrow.

Bruce frowned. "I forgot to inquire about some supplies I'm supposed to try and acquire for Willy."

"Willy?"

"Yeah. With everything going on with the engineers, I haven't had a chance to tell you about him." Bruce chuckled as he shook his head. "He was at Tionesta's council meeting yesterday. Apparently, he just showed up at their roadblock that morning. He travels around the area delivering messages between various towns as far east as Wilkes-Barre Scranton." Bruce saw Sammy raise his eyebrows in surprise. "He calls himself 'The Postman'."

Sammy considered that for a moment. "That sounds familiar for some reason."

"Well, apparently he got the idea from some post-apocalyptic movie a few years back…I can't remember the name though."

"That's right. I think it was actually called *The Postman*," Sammy offered.

"Yeah, whatever," Bruce shrugged. "He might be a little bit crazy, but I kinda like him at the same time. He's got spunk." Bruce grinned, thinking back to the quirky way the man acted. Bruce's smile slowly morphed into a frown. He looked Sammy in the eye. "He was at the Newark Green Zone before it collapsed."

"You mean the one that had that bad outbreak of cholera?"

Bruce shook his head. "I think it may have been much worse than that. He's convinced that the entire Green Zone was poisoned in retaliation for a group of them trying to steal food from the military's food storage facility across the river."

"That's preposterous!" Sammy blurted. "You don't really believe him, do you?"

"I actually do, Sammy," Bruce said with a sigh. "You would've had to be there, but he was quite convincing and clearly shook up over the situation." Bruce's face contorted into a sad grimace. "He actually watched his wife and young daughter die right in front of him—pretty badly by the sounds of it, bleeding from the nose and mouth. He insists that every living soul inside the Green Zone died of the same thing, all within forty-eight hours. Cholera doesn't work like that."

"But still, Bruce…."

"I don't know, Sammy. We were sent to annihilate an entire town for the sake of one man's head, remember? I don't want to believe that anyone in our chain of command could do something like that, but I wouldn't put it past General Oates and whatever outfit he is running." Bruce didn't want to discuss it further, so he changed the subject. "Speaking of, have you heard anything else about him from your contact recently?" Sammy just shook his head. "I figured as much."

Sammy tilted his head. "So back to this Willy guy. Why are you so interested in him and why would you be putting through any supply requests for him directly?"

Bruce walked back from the window and reclaimed the seat behind his desk. He put his feet up on the desk unceremoniously and started clicking the pen in his hand—a nervous habit that drove Sammy bonkers. "He says he's been travelling the open roads for nearly six months straight now. You of all people know that's a pretty tall feat to accomplish these days and keep your scalp intact. He has detailed maps and notes on his travels: areas to avoid, ambush locations, surviving towns and farms, and much more. That's intel we aren't going to get unless we are willing to vastly expand our patrols and risk losing some men. Intel that may come in very useful to us in the future."

"That still doesn't explain why you would make a direct supply request with the general. What does this guy want in return?"

Bruce let out a deep, loud laugh. "Let's see…." He pulled a scrap of paper from his pocket and started listing off Willy's demands. "An electric motorcycle, four portable 200 watt solar panel kits with small battery banks to recharge the motorcycle in remote locations, a handheld FLIR monocular, a PVS-14— "

"What?" Sammy cut in. "You can't be serious!"

"I haven't even gotten to the good stuff yet." Bruce grinned. "He also wants a USPS mailman's uniform in size medium, two smoke grenades, two incendiary grenades, a pair of double-knee Carhardt carpenter pants in size 32 by 34, a Cold Steel SRK bolt knife, and a large bottle of Coco Chanel Mademoiselle perfume."

Sammy laughed out loud at the last item. "Is he crazy?"

"I told you he just might be." Bruce snickered.

"And you were going to give that list directly to the general. Are you suicidal?"

"Not exactly," Bruce said as his smile faded. "His idea about the electric motorcycles got me thinking though. You remember that detachment of Green Berets stationed in Aberdeen just before we left? They had those silent-running dirt bikes they brought back from Afghanistan. I was thinking we might be able to get our hands on a few of them for our own use...."

"...And give one of them to this Willy character," Sammy said, finishing Bruce's thought. "What if one of our visitors from headquarters realized one's missing?"

"It would be out on long-range patrol."

"I guess that would work." Sammy shrugged. "What about the other items on the list?"

Bruce held out the list to Sammy with a grin. "I'm giving it to you to handle."

Sammy took the list, shaking his head. "And where the hell am I supposed to get a bottle of...," he looked down at the list in his hand, "...Coco Chanel *Mademoiselle*?"

Bruce chuckled at the way his XO pronounced it. "I don't know, Sammy. Figure it out. Use your contact at HQ. I'm sure that wasn't something that was in high demand by looters after the collapse. I would imagine that someone could locate that at any mall near HQ."

"You're killing me, Bruce." Sammy rubbed the nape of his neck. "I can't believe you are forcing me to request a bottle of perfume with our supply list."

"Just do what you can, Sammy. I told Willy we wouldn't be able to get everything on the list, but we need to get what we can. I really want to get my hands on those maps and notebooks of his."

Sammy scowled as he folded and stuffed the paper into his own pocket. "Roger that." A moment passed before Sammy changed the subject. "I also have something I forgot to mention with all the day's activities. Our north patrol came across some sort of motorcycle gang parked along the road up near Sugar Grove this morning."

Bruce's eyes narrowed at his XO. Why hadn't Sammy led with that information the second he came through the door? "That's a heck of a thing to forget, Sammy."

Sammy nodded sheepishly. "I know. Your call with HQ had me distracted. Nothing came of it. Captain Zrucky estimated nearly a hundred motorcycles as well as a few school busses, a tanker truck, and a couple other vehicles parked at some bar. They had a dozen guys outside manning a road block in front of the building. As the two MRAPs drew close, they quickly moved the roadblock out of the way and let our men pass without a word and no signs of aggression."

"I'm sure the two fifties on the roofs of the MRAPs had a lot to do with that," Bruce muttered.

"I'm sure it did," Sammy agreed. "Since our men were so vastly outnumbered, he felt it best to just keep moving and not try to engage them in conversation."

"Probably a wise move," Bruce said, nodding his head. "You said this was up near Sugar Grove? I remember the town name, but I don't remember where it is or how close."

"It's not much of a town," Sammy offered as he watched Bruce lean back in his chair, grab a map off the shelf behind him, and slowly unroll it onto the desk. "It's more like an intersection with a bar and a gas station, like every other town out here in hillbilly central." Sammy stood and leaned over the map, searching for the right place to place his finger. "They said the bar was a quarter mile south of town on Route 69, probably in this area here."

Bruce studied the map for a moment before looking up, thoroughly pissed off now. He glared menacingly. "Sammy, that's only fifteen miles north of us!"

"I know, but do you really think a biker gang is going to face off against us?" Major Samuelsson said defensively.

"No, but they sure as hell might try their hand against Tionesta or Kane. Besides, there's no way to know if that's their entire force. Maybe they're just an advanced scouting party for a larger group."

"There is that…" Sammy conceded, embarrassed that he hadn't considered those points himself. He was getting sloppy in the relative calm of the countryside surrounding Warren. He'd just thought of the regiment and how the gang was no direct threat to them. He wasn't used to considering the fate of the two towns they'd befriended.

"Either way, we can't let this slide." Bruce looked outside and considered the waning light. "Get the men suited up and ready to roll at first light. Who is on Primary Security tomorrow?"

"Shifty with Delta Company and Bravo on standby," Sammy responded as he sat back down in his chair.

"Okay, I want Captain Spears and Alpha Company in the lead on this with Charlie Company riding support." Bruce looked at his friend with a stern gaze. "Sammy, I don't want this turning into a blood bath if we can prevent it. You hear me?" Major Samuelsson nodded back at the order. "I want this to be a fact-finding mission. I want Captain Spears to make contact with their leader and find out anything he can about this group: where they are based out of, where they are headed, what their intentions are. You know the drill."

"I'll take care of it, Colonel."

"I want them wheels up at first light," Bruce reiterated firmly. "I don't want them harassing the locals. Send a COW [Communications site On Wheels] truck up with Charlie Company. I want Spears to immediately report back to me what they're about as soon as he makes contact with them. If we need to deal forcibly with them, I want to know the details immediately. I don't want to be chasing them all over the countryside in the weeks ahead."

"You going to call it in to Duncan?" Sammy asked uncomfortably.

Bruce thought about it for a moment. "No, he's already pissed off as it is. I know General Duncan. He'd just tell us to do the same thing we're doing now. This isn't a crisis yet and there's no need to press him on anything further today. If this goes south, we can give him the details when he gets here tomorrow." Sammy bobbed his head in agreement and sat there silently.

"Well, get to it Major," Bruce instructed.

"Yes, sir," Sammy responded formally and stood, straightening his uniform before turning toward the door.

"And Sammy…." Major Samuelsson stopped and turned to face Bruce. "You'd better radio Tionesta and Kane. Give them a heads up on the details of the group. If they're on motorcycles, they may be looking for food or a place to hole up for the winter. And don't mention our plans for tomorrow over the airwaves." Sammy nodded once and left the room, closing the door quietly on his way out.

Bruce sighed as Sammy left. Sammy was growing too comfortable with their new life in Warren. When they'd been patrolling the edges of the Wilmington Green Zone, it wasn't uncommon to have skirmishes on the regular. That kept you frosty and focused. Out here, in the middle of nowhere, it was easy to grow complacent. He was going to have to call a meeting and reiterate to his team leaders to stay focused.

Bruce rolled up the map and placed it back on the wall shelf alongside a stack of other maps of the area. Sitting back down, he glared over to the stack of files on the corner of the desk and frowned. "Time to make a decision," he mumbled to no one. He needed to make a choice on the fate of the prisoners before General Duncan arrived. There were enough topics to discuss with his superior without the general finding out he'd been procrastinating a simple verdict on the fate of a couple men. The military had sent out guidelines shortly after the collapse on how to deal with looters, gangs, and captured combatants. "Combatants" is what the report labeled them. Bruce shook his head in disgust at the term. In most cases, it was nothing more than hungry and desperate people pushed to their brink, trying to get food by whatever means possible. At the same time, the men he had in his custody were all hardened and convicted criminals of various degrees. All except for one: Charlie.

Charlie Hunan was just a young man who'd been swept up by one of the Bradford Prison gang's patrols and offered food and a place to stay in trade for his services as a general handyman at the Bradford prison. With nowhere else to go, no living family, and the promise of steady food, he'd accepted. Bruce had subconsciously known for weeks what his decision on the prisoners would be. Now it was just a matter of following through. At first light tomorrow, they would be fed the best breakfast that could be mustered up and then executed…all except for Charlie.

"Private Mason!" Bruce bellowed. A flurry of footsteps could be heard in the hall before his office door flung open. His orderly rushed across the room and stopped at parade rest in front of his desk. "Private, please go down to the holding cells and have the prisoner, Charlie Hunan, escorted up to my office immediately." Bruce barely noticed the young man's salute as he raced out of the office, slamming the door in his haste. Bruce grimaced. He'd told that kid a hundred times not to slam his damn door. Oh, well. His orderly was good at almost every other task, making an occasional door slam—shut in haste to perform a task—bearable.

Bruce set the prisoners' files aside and picked up his notes from his meeting with the engineers. He frowned. There were numerous items that had been destroyed in the explosion the morning before, but one of the items on the list, which was vital to restoring electrical power, had taken HQ weeks to track down and acquire the first time around. That single item was what caused the brunt of General Duncan's anger on the phone as he wasn't sure how long it would take to locate another replacement. He stressed to Bruce how low the military's fuel supplies had grown. Duncan was under a lot of pressure from senior leadership at HQ to get Warren's oil refinery up and running as quickly as possible.

Only two days earlier the engineers had reported back to their own departments in HQ that they were close to making an attempt to fire up the old power plant just west of town. Not anymore. Now, an attempt to get the electricity flowing again was likely weeks out, or however long it took them to find the critical replacement parts and make the needed repairs. Even though Colonel Harris didn't have any direct control over how fast the engineers worked, he was still in command of the overall operation in Warren and the frustration from senior leadership was now making its way down to him in full force.

Bruce sighed and tossed the list of equipment back onto his desk. He didn't have the first clue what any of the items were anyhow. The list might as well have been written in Latin. He swiveled his chair toward the window and silently watched as the sun disappeared over the rolling hills of the horizon. He'd almost achieved a moment's worth of peace when a sharp knock came at the door. "Come in!" he shouted gruffly.

Bruce's orderly opened the door and two soldiers entered with a handcuffed Charlie Hunan in tow. The young man looked about nervously as the guards led him by the arm to stand before the colonel's desk. Charlie's eyes flittered toward the door briefly before roaming the contents of the room he was in. He avoided eye contact with Colonel Harris and eventually resigned himself to lowering his gaze to his shoes.

Bruce sat silently for a moment, taking in the man before him. Measuring him. Weighing him. "Thank you, men. Please remove his handcuffs and wait outside." The two soldiers who'd escorted Charlie exchanged a long nervous look before following the order. There was another uneasy look between the two of them and neither moved toward the door, obviously unwilling to leave an unshackled prisoner in the room with their commanding officer. "I'll be fine," Bruce said, turning his gaze to the prisoner. "You're not going to try and hurt me, are you Charlie?"

The young man suddenly realized he was being addressed. He shuffled his feet and gripped his hands behind his back, even though he was no longer cuffed. "Absolutely not…, sir."

Colonel Harris turned his attention back toward the guards. "See? There you have it. I'll be fine. Please wait outside my office until I call for you." The two men exchanged one last tentative look before saluting and exiting the room.

A few moments of awkward silence followed before Bruce began. "Take a seat, Charlie." Charlie still hadn't looked up from his feet, but he slowly took a step back and sat in the lone empty chair behind him. Another silent moment passed. "I've finally decided what I'm going to do with you."

The young man's face was a scene of pure torture, and Bruce could tell by the beads of sweat forming on Charlie's brow that he was worried. "I am going to release you," Bruce said softly. The young man's body went limp as relief washed over him and he audibly exhaled a long breath he'd been holding. "After our numerous interviews, I'm not going to hold you accountable for the atrocities committed by the Bradford Prison gang."

Bruce opened Charlie's file in front of him and flipped a few pages. "While you were captured in a vehicle a short distance from the farmstead that was attacked, you've maintained that you were told to drive the vehicle and had no knowledge of their plans to attack that farm and kill those people beforehand. You surrendered peaceably and I do not think you deserve any further disciplinary action." Bruce closed the folder and leaned back in his chair. "However, you cannot stay here as I can't spare the extra food. You've mentioned in the past that you had no living relatives in the area. Where do you plan to go?"

Charlie was still recovering from Bruce's revelation and it took him a moment to gather himself. He briefly looked at Colonel Harris with glassy eyes before lowering them back down to his feet. "I…I don't know."

"There is a small town, just south of here, called Tionesta. I am going to be sending a bus down that way tomorrow. I've heard they may be willing to take in people with certain skills. From your file here, it would seem to me that you might fit in nicely down there. What do you think?"

Bruce eyed Charlie suspiciously as he started to shift around uncomfortably in his seat. "Uh…," Charlie swallowed audibly. There was no way for Bruce to know the troubles he'd had down in Tionesta or the fact that he'd previously been part of Mr. Andrews' personal security team. "Um…, I was thinking about making my way up north. I have a cousin that has a farm just south of Syracuse. That's where I was heading when the prison gang picked me up."

Bruce shook his head. "Son, Syracuse is nowhere you want to go. You need to steer clear of the bigger cities. They're all in rough shape with large, violent gangs controlling most of them. Tionesta is a nice little town that's thriving under some good leadership. Or even the town of Kane, which is doing well. I'd be willing to make an introduction at either place if you'd like? I can't promise they'll take you in though."

Colonel Harris could see some sort of indecision taking place in Charlie. "Sir, if it's all the same to you, I think I'd still rather head up to my cousin's farm. I should check in on them. It's a good bit south of the city in a secluded area. Maybe they're still alive. They're the only family I have left."

Bruce knit his brows. "It's your funeral, Charlie. Don't say I didn't try and warn you about the threat when you get up near Syracuse." Bruce sat forward and thrummed his fingers on the desk. "I'll have the men outside take you to the mess hall for a bite. From there I'll provide you with a pack, some basic supplies you may need, and two days' worth of food. From there, you're on your own."

"Yes, sir. Thank you, sir," Charlie added sincerely, still looking down at his boots. Even upon hearing that he would be released, Charlie never expected to receive a pack with supplies. The last time he'd been released from imprisonment, he'd been thrown off the Tionesta bridge into frigid water with nothing but the clothes on his back. He'd survived that, but barely. Mike, the other member of Mr. Andrews' security team that had shared his fate, hadn't been so lucky. Charlie wondered why fate continued to smile down upon him. He surely should have been killed at least a dozen times since the world had fallen apart.

"Private!" Bruce abruptly hollered for his orderly, taking Charlie off guard. The young man nearly leaped out of his seat. No sooner had his rear end landed back on his chair when both soldiers were pushing their way through the door. They held hard looks. Bruce realized his error. His loud shout had them coming to his defense. Bruce quickly held his hand up. "It's all right, men." They seemed to relax a little bit, but not much. They both eyed Charlie with dangerous intent.

Private Mason peeked into the room, a curious expression on his face, and then disappeared from view. It reminded Bruce of the prairie dogs where he'd grown up, poking their heads out of their holes to check the surroundings. "Private Mason, get your butt in here!" Bruce bellowed. His orderly instantly swept into the room. "Type up a discharge order for Charlie here." Without even looking up, Bruce held out Charlie's personnel file in Private Mason's general direction. The file was quickly snatched out of the air and tucked under the private's arm.

"That will be all, Private." Colonel Harris's orderly snapped a quick salute, made an about face, and headed for the door. His boots were echoing down the hall when Colonel Harris yelled toward the open door: "I want that within the hour, Private Mason!" Colonel Harris's sudden booming voice had taken all three of the men in the room by surprise and they flinched.

A faint "Yes, sir," echoed from the long hall in Private Mason's sheepish voice. Bruce grinned before turning back to the two soldiers flanking Charlie. One of the men held handcuffs and arched his eyebrow questioningly to his commander.

Bruce waved his hand dismissively and the soldier stuffed them back into his belt pouch. "This man is to be released. I want you to take him down to the mess hall and let him eat as big a meal as he'd like." Bruce paused. "On second thought, have him eat somewhere private and not in front of the other men." A prisoner eating his full in the midst of hungry men who were being rationed could start some serious grumbling and rumors.

"After that, I want you to head over to supply and have them issue Charlie a pack, sleeping bag, poncho, something to start a fire with and any other basics someone might need on the road. Include three days' worth of MREs as well. After that, head back here and grab the signed discharge papers from my orderly. Make sure they have my signature or you won't get through the north checkpoint, which is where you will release this young man." Bruce looked Charlie up and down one final time. "I also want a sidearm issued to him and twenty rounds of ammunition, which you'll not present to him until he is released at the checkpoint." Twenty rounds might get Charlie out of a jam, but wouldn't be enough for him to attack some farmstead. The soldiers seemed a bit taken aback at the mention of providing a former prisoner with a weapon, but they both nodded.

Charlie looked up and met Bruce's gaze with solid determination. "Thank you, sir." Travelling the open road without a weapon was likely suicide and Charlie appreciated the Colonel's gesture.

"You're welcome," Bruce said, smiling reassuringly at the young man. It quickly faded as he added in his most commanding voice, "Now keep yourself out of trouble this time, do you hear me?"

Charlie responded with another determined nod before coming to attention and offering the colonel a crisp salute that only a former soldier could have performed. Bruce returned the salute from his chair before waving the three men out the door. The smile on Bruce's face stayed there for a short time, until Major Samuelsson returned to his office to check in one last time before heading to his quarters for the night. As Sammy took his normal seat, Bruce handed him a sealed envelope in a plastic bag. "Please have Sgt. Timms place this in its usual location on his way down to Tionesta tomorrow." Sammy covered his mouth and let out a long yawn as he reached for the letter with his other hand. He didn't ask what it was; secret letters were often passed between Colonel Harris and the former Mayor of Kane who now resided in the survivalist retreat north of Tionesta.

When Sammy finished stuffing the letter in his shirt pocket, Bruce picked up the stack of prisoner files and tossed them down on Sammy's side of the desk. Colonel Harris' face was hard as stone. "I've made my decision about these men. Give them a good breakfast and then execute them at dawn tomorrow."

Chapter 12

Sean sat with his back against a large mossy log, watching the sky turn red as the sun made its last descent through the hills to his west. He was still irritated at Maria for causing such a scene on the front stoop of the cabin. She'd stood there in full kit, hands planted firmly on her hips, loudly demanding to be allowed to be a part of the ambush team. Sean, his mother, and other family members made futile attempts to calm her, but she was defiant. It had taken ten minutes of arguing and negotiating before she finally stomped back into the cabin. Shortly after the collapse, Sean had promised to never leave her side, and she fully intended to enforce it now that she was no longer pregnant.

It was a promise Sean had intended to keep when he gave it, but things had changed with the birth of his son. The chance that both of them could be killed in a dangerous mission like this and leave the child without either of his parents was something Sean couldn't stomach. He would do anything to keep his wife and child from harm. At the same time, he still wished she was there with him now, by his side, watching his back. He sighed. He hadn't heard the last of this, and it would likely be full-scale war as soon as he walked through the front door of the retreat…IF he walked back through the door.

No. He wasn't going to allow himself to think those dark thoughts even though what they were doing was dangerous. They had no way to know if the stranger would come alone or if a dozen men would end up coming down the road with him this time. It would likely be many hours yet before they encountered the man, if he came at all, and yet Sean's heart was racing. Sean steadied his wandering mind and forced himself to remain calm. He prayed. He prayed a prayer of protection over himself and his family members, those alongside him on the ambush and those back at their new home.

Home. What a crazy concept. Thirty of his relatives living under the same roof, and most residing in the basement game room. They were living in a mansion that a sadistic man had constructed to help achieve his malicious plans. The mountains surrounding Tionesta weren't anything like the area where he'd been born and raised. This was hundreds of miles and many light years from any semblance of life that he or any of his relatives had ever known. Yet now this was their home.

Sean was hiding on an embankment at dusk, overlooking a road he was unfamiliar with, and waiting to confront a man he had no animosity toward yet he might be forced to kill if the situation turned violent. What kind of world was he living in? More importantly, what kind of world would his son be raised in? Would things improve throughout the country? In the harsh new world they now lived, it was hard to imagine a peaceful existence ever coming to pass. It was surreal.

Sean prayed again, thanking God for delivering his family and relatives to Tionesta unharmed. They had driven a tractor and hay wagon laden with supplies from the family farm all the way up to Tionesta without getting over-run by hungry and desperate people. That, in and of itself, had been a miracle. It was a trip you could have taken a hundred times and only one out of fifty would it have played out the way it did. Sean prayed for the man they would soon confront and asked that his heart be softened so that he wouldn't immediately be moved to violence. Sean prayed for his country and the town folk in Tionesta. He prayed some more. He prayed harder. Sweat rolled down his brow.

A few minutes later, Sean jerked awake when he heard rustling of leaves. He found the movement and watched as his brother left his concealment by the edge of the road and hiked up the steep embankment to where Sean was posted.

"Hey, Sean. I just received a transmission from home." The lines of Joshua's face clearly showed concern. "David just relayed a message to Tionesta from the soldiers up in Warren. One of their patrols came across a large motorcycle gang about fifteen miles north of Warren this morning. Apparently, the patrol didn't have the manpower to engage the group at the time. Sounds like around a hundred motorcycles and other vehicles in the group…and they appeared well-armed. The transmission warned that they could be looking for some place to hole up for the winter or they could possibly be a scouting party for a larger force."

Sean waited for his brother to continue, but that was all the information he had. "What are they going to do about it?" Sean asked in a harsh whisper.

Joshua just shrugged. "David said that was all the information they had at the time. What do you want to do?"

Why was everyone always asking him what to do? He knew the answer to that question; he just didn't want to make this particular decision.

"Do we continue with the ambush as planned or head back? What do I tell the others?"

Sean still didn't give an answer. His mind ran in a hundred directions with multiple outcomes for the various decisions he might make in this moment. "We might not get another chance at this. This guy surely isn't going to come back every night forever," Sean spoke his thoughts out loud. "The man's position the first night near the perimeter fence surely didn't provide him enough information about the North Homestead. Last night, Uncle Will spooked him off right after he got there and most likely before he finished his assessment of our resources. I'm hoping that's the case and he's coming back for one more look around. What do you think?"

Joshua's shoulders slumped dejectedly. "I don't know what to think about any of this stuff, Sean. This is your department. I just do what I'm told."

Sean snorted at that. Joshua's six-foot-eight frame eased itself down next to Sean. He rubbed his hands together and sat quietly, letting Sean think. A few minutes of silence passed and Sean finally made a decision. "Tell them we are going to continue with the original plan. If that group is fifteen miles north of Warren, then that puts them forty-five miles north of us. Chances of them showing up around here tonight would be extremely lucky…or unlucky, depending on how you look at it. Tell them to radio us immediately at the first sight of trouble and we'll double time it back. Tell them I want Randy in the tower helping to organize the defenses. Having the ability for us to attack from the rear would actually be beneficial if it is coordinated correctly, but also dependent on the size of force that shows up. If the entire gang shows up, they shouldn't be doing any fighting anyways, just fleeing out the tunnel and getting away. If the entire force shows up, let them know to give us a heads up and we'll meet them at the rally point. But make sure you are careful what you say and don't mention the tunnel and underground storage over the radio." Joshua was listening intently and making mental notes for his response. "I also want you to tell them that the bug out bags in the basement are…. You know what? Just let me call it in," Sean said in frustration.

Joshua handed his brother the earbud and handheld ham radio. Sean quickly keyed the mic and quietly voiced, "Come in Shire, this is Frodo."

David must have been awaiting their response. "This is the Shire. Go ahead, Frodo." The signal held a little static, but Sean could clearly hear the former mayor of Kane, who was now simply known as David. His real name was Kendall Reese. David practically manned the North Homestead's ham radio on a 24-hour basis. He even slept on the couch in the attic room, which also served as the retreat's primary watch location. Only a few people at the retreat knew his real backstory and why he'd come to live there. Aside from being the former mayor of Kane, David had also operated a nightly ham radio broadcast called "Freedom America." Sean didn't know how, but David had sources of information in high levels of government which fed him information fairly regularly following the collapse.

David had relayed that information via his broadcasts on a nightly basis to anyone who could receive his signal. His call-sign spread. Most of the information ran counter to the official government ham radio broadcasts and their narrative, which painted a much rosier picture of what was going on around the country. Because of this, someone in the government had sent a squad of Army Rangers to arrest or kill him. David had never gone into details on that, but Colonel Harris had arranged to sneak him out of Kane and arranged for him to be placed with Sean's family at the North Homestead. In trade for Sean's group taking him in, the military had used a boom truck to help install an antenna on Mr. Andrews' barn and set up their communications system. Without Colonel Harris and David's help, the retreat would never have achieved the level of communications that they had now. All they had to do now was maintain David's secret identity.

With David's sources communicating with him, the retreat was now privy to inside government information that they wouldn't have known otherwise. Not that any of it had proven useful to them personally…yet. So that's how it went. David sat in the attic all day and night with headphones on, listening to various ham radio broadcasts, some of them in code. The only thing he wasn't permitted to do was broadcast as Freedom America from their retreat. Instead, David would record a two-hour show each week into an analog tape recorder, spouting out information he had learned from his contacts and generally taking the government to task for their sloppy handling of the post-collapse America. Sean never discovered what became of those tapes.

Sean keyed the mic. "We've decided to stay on course and continue as planned. If anything comes up at the Shire, we need to know right away, including details. If a small group attacks we will be available to attack from the rear. It's vital to keep lines of communications open if that's the case. We need to prevent any accidents and make sure both hands know what the other is doing. In fact, I would prefer my brother-from-another-mother to be running the defenses in the attic if the council approves. Do you copy all that?" Sean let go of the mic button and glanced over at his brother with a wry grin. His brother smiled in return.

"We copy that, Frodo, and we understand," David's voice responded a few moments later. There must have been others in the room with him. Sean waited to be sure David wasn't going to continue.

"Okay then. If that large raiding force shows up, we need to know immediately. The Shire needs to follow the contingency plan we have in place already and inform Rohan of the situation, and we will meet you at the agreed upon location. Copy?"

Another pause before David responded. "Copy that."

Sean waited, then continued. "Okay, this last point is very important. Please talk with my mother. I told her about two projects that needed to be done when we were talking near the *spice rack*." He emphasized the location. "Both of those projects are now a priority and should be done immediately. Do you copy all of those details?"

Pause. "I copy all of the details and will discuss with your mother. What was the location of that conversation where you told her about these two projects? Over."

Sean sighed. Obviously, the term "spice rack" was getting lost in translation, but he sure wasn't going to mention "the secret underground storage facility" over the radio. "Shire, please inform my mother it was the two items we discussed when we were talking about *Montreal Steak Seasoning*." He said the last three words slowly.

"Copy that, Frodo. Please hold one." Sean rubbed his pounding temples. He was beginning to get a headache. A couple minutes passed before the handheld came alive once more. "This is the Shire. Frodo, do you copy?"

"Go ahead, Shire."

"We've discussed the seasoning you mentioned with your mother. We understand both tasks and the urgency of their completion."

Pause. "Very well, Shire. We will continue forward as planned. Over and out."

"Copy that, Frodo. Over and out." Sean had held out the radio to his brother but quickly snatched it back.

"Shire, come back," Sean said at his brother's questioning look.

"This is the Shire. Go ahead."

"Shire, did Rohan mention any plans to deal with this issue?" Sean set the radio down on his lap and waited for a response.

"No plans were mentioned by Rohan, but they did assure me that they will keep us updated on future developments."

Sean frowned at the radio and huffed. "Copy that, Shire. Over and out."

"Over and out." As David's voice died, Sean turned the radio volume down a bit and handed it back to his brother.

"Well, there you have it," Sean said quietly. "It does makes sense though. If they were planning something, they wouldn't send it out over the radio. You never know who's listening."

"That's true," Joshua agreed. They sat in silence for a while and quietly watched as the sun disappeared behind the trees. It was relaxing. Sean couldn't remember the last time he and his brother had shared a quiet moment like that together.

"You should probably get back into position," Sean said finally, even though he didn't want the peaceful moment to end. They weren't expecting the man for many hours yet, but it was important to be in position in case he came early. "I'll hike down and let Jackson and Bug know what's going on."

"No, Sean," Joshua insisted. "You need to rest that leg. I'll let them know." Sean considered arguing the point but just nodded his head. His calf *was* actually quite sore from their walk in, and he probably should give it a rest before he had to rely on it in a few hours. Joshua grunted as he stood up. He started over the embankment before pausing and turning back. He looked at Sean for a long, awkward moment before adding, "I love you, brother."

"I love you too, Joshua," Sean responded without hesitation. Joshua shot him a quick boyish grin and then disappeared over the edge of the embankment. That wasn't something they'd said out loud to each other very often while growing up, even though it was implied. Sean regretted that. He assumed his brother must be concerned with what they were about to do. Sean prayed.

Chapter 13

Sean's shoulders tensed as he watched six armed men round the bend. On the winding country road, this was the only ambush location Sean could find that allowed more than a hundred yards of visible road through the hilly terrain. He swallowed hard and fought the anxiety that welled up inside like a gushing oil rig. He concentrated on slowing his breathing and willing his heart to stop trying to pound its way out of his chest.

The previous night had gone exactly as planned, with the single spy being confronted on the dark empty road. Upon discovering that he was surrounded, the man quickly surrendered. Sean tried to be cordial and question the man in a friendly tone, but he flatly refused to give any information on where he was from or why he had been spying on their retreat. Disarmed, they brought him back to the retreat unrestrained with Sean occasionally trying to make small talk while they walked. Sean felt no need to blindfold the man since he'd already been spying on the retreat and knew exactly where it was. In his late thirties, the slightly greying man was cordial enough and engaged in Sean's small talk but was also very adept at not letting any details slip out in relation to the group he was living with. Upon arriving back at the cabin, and after Bug confirmed it was the man he'd seen the night before, he'd been locked up inside an empty feed storage room in the back corner of the barn with Sean's two cousins on watch outside the door.

It hadn't worked out the way Sean had hoped. He wasn't exactly sure what he had hoped for, but more information out of the man would have been a start. There'd been discussions about releasing the man to send him back to his group and request a parlay, but that had quickly been shot down. It would only allow the other group time to set up their own ambush. The prisoner was nothing more than a bargaining chip at this point. Their best option was to just wait for his comrades to come looking for him. It had been a long day in the hot sun. Sitting. Waiting.

And now there were six well-armed men making their way down the road studying every bush and tree along their way for clues of their missing friend's whereabouts. Sean tried to slow his racing adrenaline. The council had decided to bring a couple more family members this time, but not nearly enough. By taking that many armed men on the ambush run, they'd left their retreat fairly unprotected from the threat of the motorcycle gang nearby. The council had met and decided the best course of action was to stage everyone in the basement sleeping quarters until this new ambush was completed. If there were any signs of trouble, the family members would flee through the tunnel and meet at the rally location where they would decide on the next course of action. They were not to fight.

There were eight of Sean's family members positioned around the ambush location. Not exactly overwhelming odds. As the six men drew closer, Sean studied them intently. They were mostly country folk by the look of them, with most wearing some form of hunting camouflage. They looked relatively well-kept and not overly skinny with the dark sunken eyes that was the tell-tale sign of malnutrition these days. Everyone had lost weight since the collapse, but Sean didn't get the impression that these men were starving. Three of the men held typical scoped hunting rifles with walnut stocks, one had a break-open double barrel shotgun, and one held what appeared to be a smaller rifle with an extended magazine and a red dot optic. Sean thought it likely a Ruger 10/22 with the way the slender magazine curved. The man in the lead was an elderly gentleman who walked with a quiet grace. He seemed confident yet cautious. His shaggy white hair blew in the soft breeze and his furrowed brow gave him the look of an elder in deep thought. Sagging on his right hip was a chrome revolver in a worn western belt rig.

In no time at all, they were within twenty feet of his brother. "Why hasn't Joshua stepped out yet?" Sean thought angrily as he strained to look in his brother's direction. It was futile. Joshua was behind a large oak tree below the embankment Sean was positioned on and not in a location where Sean could see him. Did he see the men quickly approaching his location or had he fallen asleep? If he waited any longer, the men would be right on top of him and their whole plan would go south. If Joshua stood up from behind his cover when the men were too close, it would likely startle them and increase the likelihood of a gunfight. He should have been more specific with Joshua.

Suddenly the six men jerked and raised their weapons. "Don't shoot!" he heard his brother yell. "I don't mean you any harm, I just want to talk!" Joshua was only supposed to show himself for the briefest moment to get their attention and duck back behind cover before anyone had time to actually point a rifle at him. He hoped Joshua had at least followed that part of the plan.

"Come on out!" Sean heard the older man say in a gravelly voice. "We won't harm you if you show yourself." The man pointed to his left while never taking his eyes off of Joshua's location, his right hand resting on the hilt of his revolver. Two of his men rushed off in the direction he pointed. They positioned themselves behind two large trees on the opposite side of the road where Joshua hid.

Sean knew his group was quickly losing the advantage of surprise and improvised. "We don't want any trouble! We just want to talk to you!" he hollered from his concealment. The three men still on the road with the old man all swiveled their weapons upward in Sean's general direction. The old man hadn't moved since the group had stopped in the middle of the road, but his palm still rested gently, almost casually, on the hilt of the revolver.

"Listen!" Sean hollered from where he lay behind the fallen log. There was a small six-inch square area of dirt he had dug out under the log and while the three men pointed their weapons in his general direction, they still hadn't pinpointed his exact location. That would change the more he talked, but it was unavoidable at this point. His brother was just too close to them to be the lead on this now. "We don't want any trouble, we just want to talk. We outnumber you two to one and we hold the high ground. I assure you that we mean you no harm. Tell your men to lower their weapons!"

"Why would I do that?" the old man sneered. "For all I know there are only two of you."

"Well, there aren't!" Sean insisted defiantly. "If we wanted you dead, we could have killed you a dozen times already. I'm not asking your men to lay down their weapons, I'm just asking them to lower them. At which point I'll come out and we'll talk face to face."

The old man hesitated.

"You're not going to get a better offer than that," Sean insisted. "The longer you wait, the more tense this situation is going to become and the higher likelihood that something bad happens."

The old man was now laser focused on the log Sean hid behind. His hand came up and he gestured for his men to lower their weapons. They grudgingly complied. Sean slowly stood up from behind the log. He must have made quite the impression with his Ghillie Parka, plate carrier, battle belt, and his face painted a flat black. The four men eyed him warily as Sean held his AR at the low ready. He wanted to portray an image of strength but not be too threatening. "Alright, I'm going to work my way down to you so we can talk face to face. I want your men off the side of the road to come back and join your group while I do so."

"That's the only advantage I have right now. They stay where they are!" the old man responded forcibly.

"I assure you that they offer you no advantage," Sean quickly responded. "Right now, they have four rifles pointed at their backs. All they are going to do is make me nervous, as well as the men I have in position to protect me." The old man stood staring at Sean, not sure how to respond. Sean didn't wait for his answer. "What's it going to be old timer? I'm not coming down there until your men come out of hiding. I don't want their rifles pointed at my back while we talk. Like I said, if we'd wanted you dead, we could have wiped your men out in seconds when you walked into our ambush. There's no need for bloodshed at this point. Call your men out!" Sean insisted.

The old man hesitated briefly, then turned to his men in hiding and nodded. Sean saw them stand up and start to make their way back onto the road. Per their agreement, Sean slowly worked his way down the steep embankment. His mind raced between the various tasks of trying to keep his footing, keeping an eye on the six men, and focus on potential points of cover he could dive behind while he approached the small group…just in case. When Sean finally reached the road, he crossed to the other side and positioned himself about five paces from the men in a safe spot where he wouldn't find himself caught between his family members' positions and the men on the road.

"You wanted to talk…so talk," the old man said gruffly. He certainly didn't like the compromising position his men were in.

"We were just wondering where you were headed?" Sean asked with a half-smile.

"That's our business and none of yours."

"It seemed like your men were looking for something. Did you lose something?" Sean asked coyly. The men didn't respond. "Did you maybe lose…*someone*?"

The older man stared daggers at Sean, confirming his suspicions.

"Yes, we have your man," Sean said with a flippant wave of his hand. He let the information sink in for a minute. "He was disarmed, well fed, and is now being held only a short distance away. He has not been harmed in any way."

"What right do you have to kidnap a peaceful member of my group?" the man demanded.

"What right do you have to send him sneaking around our farm at night?" Sean responded evenly, trying to bring the level of the conversation down. The man didn't respond, so Sean continued. "We've been watching him watch us the last few nights. Trust me when I say that we know *everything* that goes on around our farm. We'll know the second someone steps foot onto our property. We have the defensive capability to defeat any raiding force that you'd send our way." Sean caught the man's eyes as they briefly wandered down the length of his suppressed AR. "We have let trespassers slide in the past, but you were getting just a little bit too close and a bit too curious for comfort."

"We meant you no harm," the older man said in a softer tone, "and we've never trespassed on your property before. It must have been someone else in the past."

"How are we to know that?" Sean pressed.

"Because we've never left our hole-up location until now. Just recently we decided to have a look around and see who else might be surviving in the area. At some point, we were planning to make contact with your group and—"

"But not until you knew what you were dealing with?" Sean surmised.

The man just gave a sheepish shrug in response to Sean's question.

"I understand your reasoning mister, but I don't condone your actions. By spying on us at night, you put your man at considerable risk the last few days. In fact, he unknowingly ran within a few feet of one of our men on watch. It was a nerve-racking situation for my cousin and it could have ended quite badly for your scout." Sean was trying to portray the strength of their watch detail. Even if he was exaggerating.

The older man sighed and his furrowed brow relaxed. "I realize now that it might have been a mistake, but we couldn't have known it at the time. We didn't even know anyone was living there at first. There are very few survivors in the area that we know of. I watched as Mr. Andrews built that place years ago. All we intended was to see if he was still alive or if there might be some resources there we could use if he wasn't. Now, can you please return our man to us and let Mr. Andrews know that we meant you no harm?"

Sean shook his head. "Mr. Andrews is dead. My family has taken over his premises with permission from the new mayor of Tionesta who we've developed a good working relationship with over the last few months. We also work closely with another large group of survivors in the area as well as the Army Regiment stationed up in Warren."

"Soldiers? What's the Army doing up in Warren?" The old man didn't wait for a reply. "One of the members of our group escaped from there shortly after the lights went out. He said it was getting really bad with bandits attacking regularly. When he finally decided to leave, he said the place was a virtual ghost town with only a small group of survivors held up at that juvenile detention facility north of town. He told us they weren't going to last much longer."

Sean nodded in agreement. "The Army was sent in to wipe out the large raiding force that was operating out of the Bradford Prison after Warren and some of the other local towns were attacked a few months back." It was partly true. Sean shuffled his feet trying to make himself look more casual.

"Interesting…." The old man rubbed his chin, pondering the implications.

"We stay in regular ham radio contact with them. If we are attacked, all we have to do is hold out for thirty minutes before the cavalry comes riding in. Whoever attacks us is going to have a really bad day once those MRAPs arrive." Sean emphasized the last sentence.

"I told you we were never going to attack you," the man reiterated, putting his hands up defensively. Sean bobbed his shoulders, giving the image that he was indifferent and wasn't concerned in the least on the threat of being attacked. "We've never attacked anyone: only defended ourselves. I was being honest when I told you we've never left our location since the day this all happened. It's been too dangerous up until now." Sean saw the man considering his next question. "You say you have a ham radio? Can you tell us what's going on out there? I mean, do you know how long it will be until they get power restored?"

Sean cursed himself under his breath. He shouldn't have mentioned the ham radio. "In brief, all I can really tell you is that it's really, really bad. Things are still getting worse and not better. I don't know any specifics, but you better be prepared to survive without electricity for the foreseeable future."

"The foreseeable future?" one of the other men spoke up, incredulous.

"That's right." These men obviously must have had little to no outside contact or information. Sean sighed. "America was hit by a nuclear super-EMP from North Korea, from what I've heard. Most, if not all, of the high voltage transformers in this country are fried beyond repair and they take over a year to build and be delivered from oversees. That's during normal times when the demand is low. Also, that's assuming China is even helping us at this point. Who knows how long it will take to replace them. And that doesn't take into account all the other parts of the electric grid that have been destroyed. My understanding is that it will be many, many years before power is restored to rural areas like this, or maybe longer…maybe never."

The old man let out a low whistle through his front teeth as the men behind him looked at each other in wide-eyed astonishment. "You sure about that?" one of the other men asked. Maybe he was hoping Sean would laugh it off and say it was all a joke.

Sean frowned and shrugged. "Friend, it's tough to be sure about anything these days, but I believe that is a reasonable estimate." He waited another moment while the idea sank in among the group. "How is your group fairing?" Sean finally asked, trying to be sincere.

A hint of suspicion quickly swept across the old man's face. "We're gettin' by. We're surviving." Sean was going to ask how big their group was and where they were located, but the conversation had been going well so far and he didn't want it to go the other direction. Sean believed he was a fairly good judge of character and these men seemed to be what they claimed. Just some locals trying to survive like everyone else.

Sean turned his head toward his brother and waved him forward. Joshua stepped out cautiously and strolled forward. When he arrived, Sean turned to the old man. "This is my brother, Joshua. Joshua, this is.... Sorry, I didn't get your name?"

"The name's Derrick," the old man said with a forced smile toward Joshua.

"My name's Sean," Sean added. The old man nodded an acknowledgement and started to speak, but Sean held a finger up. "One moment please, Derrick." He turned to his brother. "Can I see the radio please?" Joshua dug it out of his cargo pocket and handed it over.

Sean keyed the mic. "Hello. It's Sean in an unsecured setting, do you copy?" Sean didn't want to use any call signs in front of the other men and hoped David picked up on that.

"We copy you. What's your status?"

"We're good here. I'm speaking with a man named Derrick and a few others in his group. We're coming to an understanding and I believe things will be okay moving forward. Can you please have my cousins escort our prisoner down to our location?"

"Copy that. Hold one moment, please." Sean let the handheld fall to his side as he waited for the response. He wasn't sure what

David wanted him to hold on for. He stood patiently and noticed Derrick studying him.

Sean considered radioing back and reminding him that he was speaking in front of the other men when David's voice came back over the radio. "Can you please remind me again what *spice* you were discussing yesterday with your mother?"

Sean furrowed his brow in confusion. Why was David asking him that? He considered it for a moment and then it dawned on him. David was probably wondering if Sean was contacting them under duress. He was giving Sean an easy question with multiple answers. If Sean gave him the wrong answer to the question, David would know to send reinforcements and he'd probably contact the soldiers up in Warren, too. It was actually quite brilliant. Sean made a mental note to discuss with David a standard code word or phrase for future use.

"Montreal Steak Seasoning," Sean responded. "Everything is fine here. Go ahead and have them bring the man in the Bronco."

"Copy that, they're on their way. Over and out."

Sean handed Joshua the radio and motioned him back to his position. He didn't want anyone else joining the conversation. It would complicate matters if the wrong thing was said at the wrong time. Sean had already slipped up once.

Sean turned back to the older gentleman. He hoped the gesture of returning the prisoner would help Derrick relax and open up a bit more. "Your man should be here in a few minutes."

"Thank you, Sean," the man said sincerely.

"You're welcome, Derrick," Sean offered back, using his name in a friendly way. "I assume we won't have any more run-ins with your men in the future." Sean stated it flatly, but the old man obviously knew he wanted a reply.

"You can be sure of it."

"Good!" Sean said with a bright smile. "Now we can be friends." Any remaining tension within the group was gone now and a few of the others smiled back at him. "You mentioned that you watched Mr.

Andrews' place being built a few years ago. You must live nearby?" Sean tried to say it as casually as possible, but the old man wasn't a fool.

"Yes, Sean. I used to live not far down the road before the lights went out." Some of the softness was leaving his face now and Sean could tell he was growing suspicious again.

"Hmm," Sean remarked. He pressed further. "So, where do you all live now?"

The man rubbed his chin in thought and shook his head. "Sean, we've had a real good talk here. I'm truly appreciative that you've taken care of my friend and that you're returning him, but I'm just not comfortable enough with you yet to tell you were I live."

"You and your men know where I lay my head each night. That doesn't seem quite fair now, does it?" Sean asked it with a smile and a half chuckle. He wanted an answer, but didn't want to come across as intimidating or demanding.

The old man rubbed his hands together nervously. "It's a tough new world out here, Sean. It takes time to earn trust these days. You can't afford to just give it away or you might end up killed in your sleep over a can of beans…," Derrick trailed off.

"That's well said." Sean cut him off with a raised hand. "And understandable. However, I do think we should set up some kind of signal to communicate with each other. To stay in touch so to speak. What do you say to that?"

"I think that would make sense."

The old man seemed to lose some of the tension in his shoulders. "Do you have a suggestion?"

Sean scratched his own chin now, pretending to be in thought even though he knew exactly what he wanted. "Okay, so if you want to send us a message, come to the crossroads at the end of our street and place your message under a rock at the base of the street sign, and lean a stick up against the base of the sign so we know there's a message waiting." That would be a good location in full view of their LP/OP at the end of the drive. "If we need to send you a reply, we'll bring it here to this location and leave it…," Sean said, pausing to look around for a good spot. There was a large fallen tree just off the side of the road. "We'll skin some bark off that log over there so it stands out. If we leave a message inside the log, we'll lean a tree branch up against the skinned-up section. How does that sound?"

"Yes, I suppose that will work out just fine."

"Great. I hope we can meet up soon on better terms than this and get to know each other. Possibly do some bartering or trading in the future?"

"I would be open to some discussion on that," Derrick agreed without actually committing to the idea.

A few awkward moments passed before Sean continued. "I do have one last question I'd like to ask and I hope you will give me an answer." The man stared back at Sean without any semblance of agreement. "I was hoping you might, at least, be willing to tell me your last name. Like I mentioned before, we are on good terms with Tionesta and the new mayor there. At their last council meeting, the idea was brought up to start reaching out to some of the locals in the area. He is interested in putting together some sort of monthly market day in town where people can get together and start trading and bartering for supplies they need. It would be a good way to get to know your surviving neighbors and work together to rebuild. I'd like to mention you to Pastor Dan and let him know you and a few others are alive and well." Sean saw some confusion on Derrick's face. "He's the new mayor down there," he explained.

"Pastor Dan Glenfield of the United Lutheran Church?"

"Yep. You know him?" Sean was surprised at first, but quickly remembered that in a small town like this, everyone knew everyone. It was the real reason why he was trying to get Derrick's last name in the first place. He wanted more information about the man to discuss with Tionesta's council and see if any of the locals knew who Derrick was and verify that the man could be trusted.

"Yeah, I know him. We went to seminary together." Derrick gave one of his men a wry smile. "You mean to tell me, he's the new *mayor* in Tionesta?"

"Yessir. He was voted in earlier this summer."

"Who'd of thought? Dan Glenfield, a mayor," Derrick muttered to himself in amazement.

"So, if you guys went to seminary together, that would make you a Lutheran pastor, too?" Sean asked. The pieces were falling into place.

Derick bowed his head somberly. "I can't say I have much of a congregation left, but the Lord does as the Lord wills."

"That He does," Sean agreed solemnly. He'd lost loved ones as well. Sean waited for a while to continue, not wanting to rush his next question or seem too eager in the asking. When he decided to proceed, Sean acted as if something suddenly came to his mind, "Then…that must be your church down the road a ways. The one on the right with the bell tower?"

Derrick had that stoic look again. "I never said that."

"A couple of our men passed by there a few weeks back on their way to scavenge some gas. They were confronted as they passed, but they were allowed to continue on their way after some discussion and explanation. That was your group, wasn't it?" Sean phrased it as a question but said it as a statement of fact.

Derrick finally relented with a long sigh. "Your men never came back down the road. We were watching for them. They left their cart on the side of the road not far from the church, and we always wondered if that cart had just been the prop in a cover story to approach us and scout out our defenses. We were a good bit nervous and set double watch for a couple weeks following that meeting."

"Yep, that was our cart. They left it there and circled well around your place on their return trip. They were forced to take turns carrying some heavy gas cans through the woods and were quite late getting home. We were pretty worried ourselves. They figured one awkward meeting with your group was enough for one day. And besides, your men instructed them never to return, so...." Sean paused for a moment, then smiled at Derrick. "It sure would be nice to get that cart back."

Derrick gave him a sly grin. "In this new world, I believe that the term 'finders keepers' applies to items left by the side of the road. Wouldn't you agree?"

Sean chuckled. "Yeah, I suppose I'd have to agree with that."

One of the men behind Derick took a half step forward. "My brother and his wife live in Tionesta. Do you know if Benjamin Mellott is still alive?"

Another man quickly added, "What about Katie Sanderson?"

Sean shook his head. "Sorry, guys. I don't recognize either of the names; although, to be honest I only know a handful of people down there."

The first man pushed a bit further. "Well, how many people are still alive in town? We thought for sure it would have been overrun by now. Probably by the same group that was attacking Warren."

Sean shrugged, wishing he could give the man a better answer. "I don't have an exact head count, but I would estimate around two hundred survivors." Tionesta had been a town of nearly five hundred before the collapse. In truth, it had fared well compared to most other small towns in the country.

The man looked to Derrick who just nodded back at him with some unspoken arrangement. The awkward silence that followed was broken by the sound of the Bronco approaching, and all eyes turned to watch for it. It screeched to a halt not far from them. Bug immediately hopped out of the driver's seat with his rifle, unsure where to point it. He finally deciding to keep his muzzle pointed at the ground, mimicking everyone else standing in the road. He made a quick study of the men and the situation as a whole, looking for any signs of distress on Sean's face before turning in a circle and checking the woods around him for any sign of a threat.

Sean hollered over to his cousin. "Everything's fine, Bug! Go ahead and let him go!"

At that, Sean watched Jackson step out of the backseat, holding his father's 1911 at low ready. He studied Sean a moment before holstering it, walking around the back of the vehicle, and opening the front passenger door. Jackson leaned across the man sitting in the front seat to unbuckle his seat belt and helped him step out of the old rusty Bronco. The man's hands had been handcuffed behind his back. Sean was proud that his cousins had remembered some of the training Brody had imparted during his short stay with Sean's family before his wedding. When transporting or riding with someone who was a potential threat, it was best to have them ride in the front passenger seat while restrained and buckled in place. Someone riding in the backseat, behind the driver, could easily cover the threat with a sidearm more effectively and safer than sitting directly beside him in the backseat. They continued their approach cautiously, with Jackson holding on to the man's elbow.

Sean shook his head, muttering under his breath at them as they drew close. "I already told you everything was fine. Just release him."

Jackson made a quick scan of the men next to Sean, judging for himself before reaching into his front pocket and pulling out the handcuff key. He released the man, who rubbed his wrists as he walked forward to join the others. He nodded politely to Sean as he passed and Sean returned the gesture.

"You alright, son?" Derrick asked the man who just nodded back, embarrassed at his capture. Derrick squeezed the man's shoulder affectionately and then pulled him in for a quick hug.

"Son?" Sean thought to himself. He was suddenly impressed with how well the older man had held his cool during their conversation. Sean knew that he would have been completely irrational if his son had been captured by someone. Sean's respect for Derrick was rapidly growing the more he learned of him, and it had nothing to do with the man being a pastor.

Derrick's son moved back with the other men, who were growing anxious to be on their way. Even though the meeting had gone well, knowing that there were guns they couldn't see being pointed at them wasn't a comfortable situation for anyone.

"Thank you again, Sean, for returning my boy unharmed," Derick said sincerely. Sean gave a quick nod of his head in reply. Derrick took a couple steps forward and reached out his hand. Sean met him halfway and shook his hand firmly.

"Until we meet again?" Derrick used the informal signing off.

"Until we meet again," Sean replied with a sincere smile. It was a bonding moment, hands clasped, both men showing respect to the other. Derrick suddenly turned, motioning down the street to his men and they silently started walking away.

Sean watched them take a few steps before adding, "My name is Sean Marlin."

Derrick turned and gave him a quick smile. "Derrick Keefer." He nodded once more and then jogged to catch up with his men. Sean watched their backs as they retreated down the road. None of them looked back as they rounded the bend out of view.

"They have chickens," Joshua said as he suddenly appeared at Sean's side in the center of the road.

The curious comment took Sean by surprise. "What?"

"They have chickens," his brother repeated softly as he watched the empty space in the road where Derrick's men had just disappeared. Joshua had been part of that gas scavenging mission when they'd been confronted by Derrick's men, and he'd reported multiple chickens running around the church yard. "What I wouldn't give for some scrambled eggs," he added.

"Yeah, no kidding. I'd dance a jig over hot coals for a plate of eggs-over-easy with a side of toast…and a few crispy pieces of bacon." Sean turned to see his brother lick his lips while staring down the road. Sean couldn't help but laugh, nodding his head in full agreement.

Chapter 14

The small passenger gate area at the Bradford Regional Airport was flat-out rank. After almost a year of not being used, the combination of stale air, backed-up toilets, and mold clung to the nostrils, making Bruce nauseous. General Duncan and the 31st Regiment's bi-weekly delivery was late…again. This was the first time in months that Bruce had gone on the delivery run with his men. He wanted to be there to greet the general as he stepped off the plane. Colonel Harris stood up from the scratchy fabric chair.

Bruce's orderly suddenly appeared at his elbow. "Sir?"

"I'm waiting outside," Bruce muttered under his breath. He'd only taken one step toward the door leading out to the tarmac when Sgt. Timms stepped in his path.

Colonel Harris gave the sergeant a dark look, but he stood fast. "Sir, per our discussion earlier, I'm going to have to advise you to stay inside. There are too many hills overlooking the airport to risk some redneck taking a pot shot at—"

"Sergeant," Bruce raised his hand, cutting him off mid-sentence. "This isn't Vietnam or World War Two. I'm quite confident there are no German snipers scouting our position. We've got over a hundred men spread out across the airport right now. I doubt any local farmer is going to take a 'pot shot' at me," Bruce finished sarcastically.

Sgt. Timms shuffled his feet while garnering enough courage to continue. "I understand that, sir, but I'm in charge of your security detail today and I don't think it's a good idea." Bruce gave him a stern look in reproach. Sgt. Timms held his gaze for a moment before backing down. "If you *were* to go outside, I'm afraid I'd have to insist that you wear my jacket over your Class B's."

Bruce rolled his eyes as he glanced down at himself. This was the first time since they had arrived in Warren that he'd traded his ACU's for his Class B uniform. He conceded the point when he realized that, in fact, he did stand out from his men, making himself a target. "Very well, Sergeant." He leaned against the wall beside the glass door with a sigh. The stocky sergeant started heading in the opposite direction of his pack before Bruce realized where he was going.

"Where are you going?" Bruce demanded anyway, even though he already knew the answer to the question.

"Uh…," Timms stammered. "It's out in the truck, sir."

Bruce shook his head irritably. "Double time it, Sergeant! I want some fresh air ten minutes ago!"

"Roger that." Sgt, Timms turned back and set off at a jog, quickly disappearing around the corner.

"And grab one for the general!" Bruce hollered down the hall.

"Yes sir!" he heard the Sergeant's voice echo down the empty hall.

Bruce couldn't help but wrinkle his nose at the stench. He assumed the General would be wearing his Class B's as well. Having him throw a jacket on as he exited the plane would be a nice touch. Bruce also decided to walk him through the airport terminal. The General needed to get the full "experience" of life on the frontier and outside his comfortable, air-conditioned office at the Pentagon. A moment later, Sgt. Timms reappeared and quickly handed one of the camouflage jackets to Bruce and the other to his orderly.

Bruce was still pulling on the jacket when he burst through the door and took a long drag of fresh air through his nose. The soldiers following him doing the same. The fresh air only confirmed how bad the stench had really been indoors. Bruce frowned as tiny particles of funk must have embedded themselves inside his nostrils since he could still smell it, though not nearly as bad. A sound caught his ear and he stood still to listen. Bruce's orderly stepped next to him, raising an eyebrow. There it was! It was the unmistakable sound of a C130 on approach.

A few moments later the sound escalated as the plane appeared over the hilltops to the south and made a low pass over the airport. As customary during their bi-monthly trips to the airport, two of his Combat Controllers had taken positions the previous evening on the western hillside overlooking the small airport. They were in charge of scouting any movement at the airport throughout the night and coordinating the landing run for the bulky cargo plane. At six thousand feet, the Bradford Regional Airport's runway was plenty long enough to land a C130, but the pavement had never been designed to carry the extra weight of a cargo plane. It required special attention by his logistics officer to coordinate their shipments and spread out the delivery of heavier items.

Colonel Harris watched the plane slowly circle to make its approach when a second plane buzzed low overhead, banking to the left. With his eyes locked on the C130, Bruce hadn't heard the smaller plane's approach and its fly-by took him off guard. Luckily, he wasn't the only one. His orderly had practically jumped as the general's plane whizzed by. Bruce turned back to the C130 and watched it touch down. When it finally rolled to a stop well short of the larger runway's end, it slowly turned around and taxied back in their direction. General Duncan's plane continued to circle the airport in tight, low circles. Once the C130 was off the main runway and headed in the direction of the lone airport hangar to unload, General Duncan's plane landed.

It didn't take nearly as long for the Cessna 421 Golden Eagle to taxi ,and within a few minutes it was pulling up to the front of the terminal where Bruce and a handful of his men stood waiting. Bruce shot a quick glance over to the larger plane which was now being pulled backwards into the Bradford Airport's lone hangar. While too small to fit the entire cargo plane inside, the hangar was tall enough to pull the tail section inside and off load their supplies under roof and away from any prying eyes. The sound of the Cessna's engines shutting down grabbed Bruce's attention and he quickly turned his attention back to it.

The plane's propellers weren't even finished spinning when the door behind the left wing opened and the mechanical steps lowered to the ground by a rope. General Duncan stood in the open door with a stern look and barely waited for the steps to stop moving before bounding down them in quick succession. Bruce was suddenly nervous. He'd known General Duncan for a long time and this was his second time serving under him directly. While he was a fair and straight-talking commander, he could also be extremely harsh when pushed to anger. He looked angry. Their call the night before had not gone especially well after Bruce informed him of the explosion at the power plant. Bruce had hoped a good night's sleep would calm the general down, but apparently that wasn't the case.

Bruce's entourage approached with his orderly leading the way. Private Mason held out the camouflage jacket to the general who took it hesitantly. After noticing Bruce wearing one, General Duncan quickly donned it over his dress uniform, zipping it up tight to his neck. Bruce stepped forward with his hand outstretched to greet his superior.

"General," he said formally.

General Duncan took his hand warmly and took Bruce by surprise when the edges of his lips turned up in a small smile. "Good to see you again, Bruce." Colonel Harris let out an inward sigh. Maybe this trip wouldn't be as bad as he'd initially thought.

"How was your trip?" Bruce asked conversationally.

General Duncan rolled his eyes. "Choppy, bumpy, loud. What else could you expect from this bucket of bolts?" Bruce glanced up at the older plane with its fading paint and peeling stickers and wondered who they'd confiscated it from. It didn't matter. No civilian with an older plane like that would be able to locate the fuel to fly it. If the person had been truly wealthy, he'd likely have owned a newer plane which would've been inoperable now.

"Why don't we get you inside where it's safer," Bruce offered the general who couldn't resist glancing around at the dark hills surrounding them in response to Bruce's warning. "You never know who might be watching and eager to take a pot shot at you." Bruce risked the tiniest tilt of his lips as he glanced quickly at Sgt. Timms standing behind the general. Sgt. Timms was having a harder time hiding his smile. He knew what Bruce was up to.

They stepped inside the terminal door and the general quickly covered his nose and mouth trying to stem his gag reflex. Bruce forced himself not to smile.

"My God, it stinks in here!" General Duncan exclaimed, not able to hide his disgust.

"Yes, sir. That's what happens when sewer backs up into a structure and mold takes over. You can expect the same conditions in most structures throughout the country," Bruce offered.

"I'm well aware of these types of conditions; I just try to avoid them as often as possible." With the way his chest was heaving, Bruce was suddenly concerned that General Duncan might actually puke. "Is there somewhere else we can wait?"

"I can have them pull the trucks around, but I warn you, it will be hotter out there than in here."

"Bruce, I grew up in Arizona. Send your men for the damn trucks and let's wait outside."

"Roger that, sir." Bruce nodded to one of the other men next to Sgt. Timms, who saluted and hustled away.

They stepped back outside where the General uncovered his mouth. "Holy hell, that place stinks."

Bruce just chuckled in reply.

"When the trucks get here, why don't we head on over to the hangar. I got a couple surprises in store for you," General Duncan said, changing the subject with a sly grin. Instantly Bruce was intrigued, but just nodded. He didn't push for an explanation. They watched the pilot of the Cessna as he circled the plane with a checklist, performing the post-flight inspection. The small plane would be pulled into the hangar when they left and two squads would stay behind to protect it during the general's stay. Hopefully, it would just be an overnight stay. Although Bruce respected General Duncan, he also didn't want him poking around too much or asking too many questions.

Moving fast, an up-armored Humvee came speeding around the west side of the main terminal flanked on either side by two MRAPs with machine gun turrets on top. They screeched to a halt in the tight space between the Cessna and the people waiting outside. This provoked a disapproving frown from the pilot who wasn't very happy with how close the trucks had stopped to the wing of his plane. Colonel Harris's orderly opened the rear door for the general before racing to open the opposite door for Colonel Harris. Private Mason jumped into the passenger seat and they were off. It was only a couple-hundred-yard drive before the Humvee came to a stop in front of the hangar with the large grey plane protruding from it. They quickly dismounted, and a soldier standing guard opened the hangar's man door for them as they approached. The door opened into a dark office with only a small shuttered window letting in light. It wasn't a very neat office, but it didn't smell nearly as bad as the main airport terminal building. There must not have been any backed-up bathrooms nearby.

To Bruce, the small office reminded him of some small town's mechanic shop with greasy tools and parts lying around. A large pile of disheveled papers and instruction manuals were piled up on the two desks in the corner. There were two other doors in the dim room besides the one they'd entered through, and Bruce's orderly raced forward opening the first. It was a small closet. He quickly shut it with a smile of embarrassment and raced to open the other door into the main hangar, letting the Colonel, General Duncan, and Sgt. Timms walk through first.

Two dozen of Colonel Harris's men worked at a frantic pace to offload the supplies from the plane to the awaiting trucks. He wasn't sure if Sgt. Timms had radioed ahead to warn them the general was coming or if this was their usual pace during delivery runs. Bruce knew the plan was always to offload the delivery planes and let the C130 leave the airport as quickly as possible, but the speed in which the men moved made his head spin. The longer the plane stayed on the ground, the more time it would give locals to organize and confront them, begging for food or other supplies. Surprisingly, that had yet to happen in Bradford. In fact, ever since the destruction of the federal prison nearby, Bruce's scouts hadn't seen a living soul on their biweekly supply runs.

General Duncan strode into the orchestrated fray looking to his left and right. At one point a forklift almost backed into him forcing him to jump out of the way. Colonel Harris smacked his hand on the back of it, yelling at the soldier to pay attention to where he was going. The soldier offered a quick apology and Bruce nodded for him to continue on. When Bruce turned back, the general was gone. It took him a moment to locate the camouflaged jacket with dress pants below, and he jogged over to see what the General had found. There were three plywood crates sitting next to one another, six foot in length by three feet wide and around four to five feet in height.

A soldier carrying a heavy box was walking by and General Duncan motioned him over. The soldier rolled his eyes and changed directions, setting the heavy box down on one of the crates with a grunt.

"Wha'dja want?" he demanded. "Can't you see this is heavy?" General Duncan's eyebrows shot up in surprise at the soldier's tone. He clearly didn't remember that the jacket over his uniform hid his true identity. The soldier glanced over at Colonel Harris. Upon recognizing his commanding officer, suddenly it was his eyebrows that lifted in shock. "Colonel Harris…," he stammered, "…I…Sir…I…." When he turned back to the general and noticed the dress pants under the jacket, the blood drained from his face. He'd just given attitude directly to the visiting General. He stood there like a lemming with his jaw hanging open, not even attempting to speak.

General Duncan's voice was grave. "I need a hammer and a pry bar…now!" The poor young man didn't even remember to say "Yes sir" as he took off at a sprint.

General Duncan turned to Bruce. "Regular order getting a little slack around here?"

"No, General," Bruce said with a grinning. "You're wearing a corporal's jacket. I'm sure he didn't know who you were."

General Duncan glanced down. "Ahhhh," he said as the realization struck him.

In less than a minute the soldier came sprinting across the hangar, almost knocking over one of his comrades in his haste. He slid to a halt and saluted the General this time, holding out the tools in his left hand.

General Duncan snatched the hammer and pry bar from his hand. "Get your crap off my crate, soldier, and get out of my face!" he said in a gruff tone. The soldier snapped another quick salute, heaved his heavy box off the crate, and carried it away as quickly as he could manage. General Duncan turned to Bruce with a smile. "That will make a good story he can tell his friends." Bruce laughed openly in response.

Duncan set to work trying to pry the lid off one of the crates. Sgt. Timms stepped forward to help, but the general gave him a dark look and Timms stepped back, embarrassed. There was a creaking sound as the nails slowly gave way. General Duncan peeked inside the crate before looking up and smiling at Bruce. Colonel Harris stepped forward. Inside the crate, wrapped in clear plastic, was a black dirt bike like none he'd ever seen before.

"I introduce you to the Zero MMX," General Duncan started dramatically. "As you know, DARPA commissioned research into all-electric dirt bikes a few years back for our SOCOM boys. Unfortunately for the company Zero, they didn't get the contract. Fortunately for us, DARPA ordered four dozen of them to test and someone found them in a dusty warehouse over in Bagram Air Base, Afghanistan, before we shipped our guys out of there. Most of them, like these, hadn't even seen service. They're almost completely silent, produce very little heat signature at night, and can drive through three feet of water. They'll even go up to eighty-five miles per hour if you push them.

"The downside, and the reason they lost the contract to another company, is you can only get about two hours driving time per battery. However, you *can* swap out a spare battery in under a minute and you're getting three batteries per motorcycle. Your advanced scouts should be able to silently cover any distance they need to from here on out." General Duncan paused. "You asked for two electric motorcycles. Well, I brought you three!" The general grinned like a kid in a candy store. Bruce couldn't help himself and beamed openly.

General Duncan continued. "I brought extra FLIR monoculars, PVS-14s, and some of the newer nighttime scopes that blend FLIR and night vision so you get the best of both worlds. I know you only requested a handful of them, but I was able to acquire a dozen of each."

Bruce nodded thoughtfully to himself. He couldn't help but wonder at how easily the general had obtained such critical and in-demand hardware from logistics. Anytime he or Major Samuelsson made a request to headquarters, it was like pulling teeth to get it filled. He looked up to see the general giving him a disappointed look. He'd obviously expected a bigger reaction to the presentation.

"Wow!" Bruce exclaimed. "I…I don't know what to say. It's like…Christmas morning. Thank you!" The general just nodded back, but a smile crept onto his face at the praise.

He glanced briefly at Bruce's orderly before continuing. "I've got a couple other surprises for you, but we'll have to wait until we get back to the base to discuss them."

Colonel Harris caught his meaning. "Roger that."

General Duncan handed the hammer to Sgt. Timms and gave a brief nod to the crate. Timms quickly set to work hammering the lid back into place.

Colonel Harris caught sight of a soldier standing next to the cargo trucks holding a clipboard and making occasional marks as the trucks were loaded. "General, please excuse me for a moment," Bruce said before walking away from the small entourage. Bruce wasn't sure how to react to everything that was happening. The night before, General Duncan had been apoplectic and screaming at him over the satphone. Today he was acting as if the conversation hadn't even happened. It was quite strange. Bruce had been prepared to catch more of a tongue lashing but was completely taken off guard by the general's calm and friendly demeanor.

When Bruce drew near, the soldier holding the clipboard was talking with a corporal pulling a dolly stacked high with boxes. Bruce waited patiently as the young lieutenant finished inspecting the boxes before sending the corporal off with a nod over his shoulder at the waiting truck. Bruce grinned inside as it took the soldier a moment to register who was standing before him, then startling to attention and giving a salute.

"Colonel Harris?"

"Relax, Lieutenant. I'm just curious how things are going?"

"Uh…mmm…," the skinny LT stammered. "It's going well, sir."

"Good. How much longer till we're able to leave?"

The lieutenant ran his fingers through his scruffy hair. "Um, I would estimate another ten to fifteen minutes, sir."

"Very well," Bruce said, giving the twitchy young man a forced smile. Bruce shot a glance over his shoulder to see the general talking quietly with Sgt. Timms while gesturing toward the crate. He turned back to the lieutenant and lowered his voice slightly. "How is the shipment looking so far? Are we short again?"

"Uhhh," he said, collecting his thoughts. "That's going to be hard to say until we're finished offloading." He held up a hand at an approaching soldier carrying a large and heavy looking coil of wire over his left shoulder. The soldier stopped, irritated, as the lieutenant turned back to Colonel Harris. "If I were to guess, at this point, I would say no. It doesn't look like we're going to be short. But again, sir, I won't know for sure until—"

Bruce cut him off with a wave. "That's fine, I was just curious. Go ahead and get back to work. I'm holding up the line here." By now, there were two other soldiers standing behind the one with the heavy wire. Bruce turned and walked back toward the general, but caught a short glimpse of the confused look on the lieutenant's face before doing so.

General Duncan broke off his conversation with Sgt. Timms as he approached.

"We're on schedule," Bruce offered. "It'll likely be another fifteen minutes before the trucks are loaded." General Duncan just nodded back. Bruce couldn't hold back the question any longer. "General, what's going on with the other regiments? How are things faring throughout the rest of the country?"

General Duncan frowned. "Bruce, that's a conversation for later." He gave Bruce a "you should know better than to ask that in front of the troops" look.

It was awkward for a moment before a loud crash brought Bruce spinning around, wondering if something important had been dropped. To his relief, it was just the large metal tailgate on one of the trucks being slammed shut. Once the gate was secured, the truck quickly pulled forward and another empty truck backed into its spot.

Bruce had so many questions he wanted to ask the general—questions that had been brewing for a long time. Now the man who could answer them was standing only two feet away and he couldn't even ask them. Bruce sighed and leaned back against the wooden crate as they watched the choreographed ballet of soldiers offload the plane with well-practiced precision. At least his men were making a good impression on the general today.

Chapter 15

Colonel Harris waited for General Duncan to take a seat across from him before sitting down himself. It had been a quiet ride back to the base with occasional small talk and a few questions from the general in regard to their route and the overall security in the area. With other soldiers riding in the Humvee, they couldn't discuss anything important and Bruce was itching to get back to the base and the privacy of his office. Now that they were there, Bruce was ready to explode in anticipation for outside news. Just when the general opened his mouth to speak, Major Samuelsson, whose office was two doors down from Bruce's, walked in slowly and stood off to the side of the desk, glancing at the chair next to the general. Bruce could tell he was unsure if he was invited to join them or not. Bruce wasn't sure either.

General Duncan looked up at the Major. "How have you been, Sammy?" He didn't wait for a response, but reached down next to the chair he'd positioned himself in and pulled a soft-sided cooler onto his lap, unzipping the lid.

"I'm doing well, General. Thank you for asking." Major Samuelsson didn't have a long history with the general like Bruce and seemed surprised that the General had known his nickname.

General Duncan reached into the cooler but before he pulled his hand out, he looked intently at Sammy. "Major, how were your grilling skills before the collapse?"

"Fairly good, I guess. It's been a while now so I might be a bit rusty," Sammy admitted. Bruce had been to multiple cookouts at Sammy's house over the years and knew his friend was just being modest.

General Duncan pulled out three large T-bone steaks, each one in its own massive ziplock bag and dripping icy water onto his pants. He set them out carefully on Bruce's desk before pulling out a large can of baked beans from the bottom. "Now, I don't want you boys getting the impression that they're feeding us steak down at HQ. I had to trade a pretty penny in barter to get these this morning." Bruce's mouth was literally salivating at the sight of the steak and he leaned forward expectantly. General Duncan placed the items back into the cooler and zipped it shut. He used the sleeve of the jacket he wore to wipe the water off the edge of Bruce's desk.

"Major, could you please take this and find somewhere private to rustle up some dinner for the three of us? I want you to handle this personally, and I trust you'll keep it on the down low."

"Absolutely, sir!" Sammy couldn't keep the excitement out of his voice as the general handed over the green cooler. "Right away!" Sammy practically ran from the room, producing a chuckle from the general as the door shut behind him.

General Duncan turned back to Bruce still smiling. Bruce was salivating at the thought of steak for dinner, but it wasn't enough to overcome his need for answers. He raised an eyebrow at his boss. The smile on Duncan's face quickly turned to a frown and he sighed. "I figured I'd buy us some time to talk privately." He rolled his head around, stretching his stiff shoulder and neck muscles before standing up and tugging off Sgt. Timms' jacket. He tossed it onto the empty chair and sat back down with a dejected look on his face. Bruce felt like he was literally going to explode if the general didn't start talking soon.

General Duncan looked him in the eye. "What we discuss here has to stay in this room. You understand that, don't you?" Bruce returned a serious nod. The general paused as if searching for the right words. He finally took a long breath and began. "It's a certifiable crap show, Bruce. In just the last two weeks, we've had two more ports overrun by the locals. The whole 'Green Zone' idea that was put into place is pretty much FUBAR and UN food shipments have become almost non-existent. There's this pirate group that's formed up off the East Coast. They've intercepted two of the last ten container ships…. Poof!" He snapped his fingers in the air for effect. "Both ships have disappeared without a trace. By the time our few remaining Coast Guard Cutters made it into the area, the pirates were long gone. Whoever they are, they know what they are doing because they disable the tracking and guidance software on the cargo ships. We just don't have the manpower anymore to track them down. There are so many boats off the coast fishing for food, we can't tell who is who.

"The West Coast isn't much better. There aren't any pirates intercepting the cargo ships…yet, but we've had trouble holding the docks on more than a few occasions when they do come into port. I'm sure you were aware of the skirmish our boys had in Long Beach just before you left for Warren here?" Bruce nodded. "Well, that port totally fell apart shortly after you left, as did Seattle. The Oakland docks fell two weeks ago. After that, we've consolidated all our remaining forces on the West Coast to Portland." General Duncan sighed. "After one of their cargo ships was set fire while docked, Russia has threatened to withhold shipments until we can provide better security.

"As you know, the Green Zones are completely overflowing with starving people, and it continued to get worse after you were sent up here. The idea of positioning the Green Zones next to the docks to make it easier to distribute food to civilians has thoroughly backfired.

Every port we can effectively use for large cargo ships is now surrounded by millions of starving people and there aren't enough food shipments to keep them all fed. Just so you know, last week the President made the decision to abandon the Green Zones."

Bruce raised his eyebrow at that. "All of them?"

"All of them," General Duncan confirmed. "At this point, The UN is barely sending us enough food to feed our troops, as you're well aware.

"Our current leadership in Washington screwed up the withdrawal, too. Instead of telling the people what was going to happen and why, the President's advisors convinced him to pull out quickly and prevent any confrontation that could arise from the news. It didn't work. When the military suddenly pulled out of the Green Zones with no warning, the people panicked. They instantly attacked the warehouses at the docks and started rioting and looting. Way worse than the usual stuff we've seen. Over the course of the past week, most people have fled the Green Zones with only a handful staying behind, mainly the sick and elderly that aren't mobile. There are some nefarious gangs hanging around as well. We think they're waiting for the next cargo ship to come in. What they don't know is that's never going to happen. We hauled away what food and supplies we could when we abandoned the Green Zones and relocated it to more secure locations."

"What ports are left?" Bruce cut in, incredulous.

General Duncan shrugged. "Those locations are being kept secret and I can't tell you where they are. I know you understand, Bruce. We're going to be using a single port on the East Coast, one on the West Coast, and one down in the Gulf. All the rest are abandoned now as security has become all but impossible."

Bruce couldn't believe what he was hearing. "What about the rest of Tenth Mountain Division? Where are all our troops from the Green Zones in Baltimore, New Jersey, and Philly going to be relocated?"

General Duncan rubbed his hands together subconsciously and stared down at the floor as he spoke. "They're not, Bruce. I just received a classified directive yesterday from General Oates that said after our regiments have finished relocating all our divisional assets to the new secure location, they will be disbanded along with most of the other divisions. Anyone with immediate family will be allowed to leave along with pretty much anyone else who wants to go…for the most part. We're retaining the more elite units throughout the various branches, and those essential troops with immediate families in the area will be relocated to more secure locations and cared for. All non-essential bases will be shut down in the next few days with notice that there'll be no more supply drops sent. Not that most bases were getting regular supply drops anyhow."

General Duncan looked up and saw Bruce's mouth hanging open, his face frozen in astonishment. "I told you it was a crap show, Bruce…."

"But…. How…?" Bruce couldn't even form a complete sentence or frame a single question to ask. His brain was having a hard time processing the information and the future implications for the country as a whole.

"When I told you last week that your regiment was one of the best fed in the entire country, I wasn't kidding. You've been placed in the Tier 2 ration group, which is a good thing for you all." Bruce wondered what it took to get into Tier 1, but he didn't ask. General Duncan continued. "By the way, your previous request the other day to send a platoon to the Midwest to look for grain has been denied. We've already done that. Most of the grain that was in storage has already been used over the last year to feed civilians. The rest has been relocated to secure storage facilities.

"It's not all bad news though. These orders should make things a little better, if you can call it that. Our fighting forces will be thoroughly thinned out within the next month. We'll be lean and mean. We'll still maintain air superiority over the country and have large mobile units that can be sent wherever they are needed. The areas of the country we are relocating to will be incredibly well protected. Without trying to feed the remaining American population or entire divisions now, we should have more than enough to keep our troops fed."

Knowing the man for over a decade, Bruce couldn't believe the flippant way General Duncan dismissed even making an attempt to keep the general population fed. He must have noticed the look on Bruce's face because he quickly retorted, "Don't look at me like that, Bruce! You think I don't want to feed people? We tried. We failed. Looking back, it's easy to see how impossible of a task it was to keep everyone fed without the electric grid. But it's over now. We have to focus on what we can do and who we can feed. At this point the objective is to maintain our nation's borders and sovereignty until we can rebuild. If we can't keep the military fed and the continuity of government in place, who's going to rebuild? Right now, there are teams of people from the Department of Agriculture gearing up to start planting crops next spring in California. Once electricity for Central Valley is restored, we can get the irrigation systems back up and running."

Bruce just shook his head. "What if someone invades?"

General Duncan snorted dismissively. "You've watched too many movies, Bruce. No major country that could even pose a threat has the actual ability to invade us at this point. We're not the only country that's fallen apart. The whole world is in shambles. Besides, they'd be taking over an enormous land mass with no electric grid, operational infrastructure, or reasonable means of acquiring our natural resources. Plus, they'd be inheriting a population that is starving, desperate and whose survivors wouldn't take kindly to invading foreigners. They've seen our own struggles to maintain order. Trust me, nobody wants to step into this mess. Add on top of that, with our recent attack on North Korea, everyone has been put on notice that our nuclear capabilities haven't been diminished since the EMP."

Once again, Bruce's mouth fell open. "What? You didn't know that?" General Duncan laughed at Bruce's shock. "Well, I guess it makes sense that you wouldn't have heard about it all the way out here. In my opinion, right after they hit us with the EMP, we should have nuked them right then. With our troops from South Korea recalled, they were only able to hold their border with conventional troops for a short while. About three weeks ago, they started to get overrun and were falling back fast. We all know what Kim Junk Psychopath had planned for his southern cousins, so, the President thought it was a good time for a little retaliation…about ten months too late if you ask me. But, of course, no one's asking me for my opinion. Anyhow, we drove a sub up to their coast and dropped a dozen or so of our smaller tactical nukes on their military bases and forward positions. Unfortunately, their 'Dear Leader' made it out alive and is threatening to invade us now. It's pretty much a big joke at headquarters. Per recent reports, what's left of the North Korean Army is in tatters and it looks like South Korea is capitalizing on it and pushing northward. At this point, I'd say that 'Little Kim's' days are numbered once the South Korean army completely takes over the country."

"This is nuts. Isn't there risk of retaliation from China?" Bruce asked.

General Duncan waved his hand dismissively. "North Korea was always the red-headed stepchild to China. I think China knew we had to respond at some point. There are rumors that Beijing actually gave the President the go ahead, but I don't know that for sure. Either way, China is busy themselves. Their economy crashed when we stopped buying their crap and they're having a hard time keeping their own people fed." Bruce continued shaking his head in disbelief as General Duncan continued. "Oh yeah, Russia officially annexed the Ukraine and is eyeing some of the other Baltic states. Israel has been under attack for months. They closed their borders up tight and seem to have things well in hand. Short of nuclear weapons being deployed, I think they'll be okay for now. The European Union completely fell apart last month. It's still meeting, but most of the bigger countries have left and are focusing on their own problems." He grew quiet for a moment. "I'm sure I'm forgetting a bunch of stuff, but in a nutshell, the whole world has gone to hell in a handbasket since we got hit."

"This is nuts," Bruce reiterated. General Duncan bobbed his head in agreement.

"Our biggest security threats right now are CONUS." Bruce gave him a questioning look. "Well, for one there is a large raiding force out of Chicago that's been wreaking havoc up north. I guess I should call it an army. We estimate their number to be around four thousand." General Duncan stopped and chuckled at Bruce's expression. "Bruce, if you keep dropping your jaw like that, you're going to get TMJ."

Bruce snapped his mouth closed. "You're telling me there's an army of looters—four thousand strong—in Chicago?" he asked, astounded at the figure.

"That's right," General Duncan confirmed. "Complete with military hardware. We guess they are responsible for the raid on the Rock River Arsenal in Davenport a few months back. By the time we were able to mount a response team and get air support to the battalion stationed there, the looters made off with a bunch of weaponry that they ferried across the river. They disappeared and hid the stuff somewhere in the city and then slowly squirreled it out of Davenport to Chicago. We're not sure how. Things were still a bit crazy back then and the Chicago group wasn't very large or high on our priority list at the time. There were other bigger groups back then. One in LA; one from Spokane, Washington, that was raiding survivalist bunkers in the northwest; two factions near St. Louis almost a thousand strong before they destroyed each other in a head-on clash. There were others, but the big ones all fell apart over the summer as food became almost impossible to find and keeping their men fed was unsustainable. Most of them disbanded into smaller groups that now just fight each other for the remaining resources. In contrast though, the Chicago group has continued to grow somehow. We now have a drone over their forces pretty much 24-7 tracking their movements. They'll be dealt with when the time is right."

"Why don't we just hit them with a bombing run?" Bruce countered.

"It's not that simple. We estimate their actual fighting force is closer to two thousand. The other two thousand are women, children and support personnel. They made a run a few months ago to the Midwest and cleaned out some of the remaining grain storage facilities. One of those larger facilities had a platoon of troops guarding it, but they weren't prepared to fight over a thousand well-armed looters, so they abandoned the compound. You should see the pictures of the tractor trailer convoy they brought back to Chicago. It was nearly a mile long. That raid is actually what put them on our radar. They keep their food under cover of various warehouses while bunking a lot of the women and children in the same facilities." General Duncan frowned. "It's likely some of them aren't really 'willing' accomplices. It makes it hard to hit them from the air without significant collateral damage."

Bruce considered bringing up the fact that General Oates surely wouldn't have had a problem with it, but decided to leave that subject alone for the time being. Instead, he stated the obvious. "A fighting force of four thousand up in Chicago is going to be tough to take on if we disband most of our fighting forces."

General Duncan wobbled his head. "We're not looking for a toe-to-toe fight, and for the most part they've avoided any fighting with uniformed military forces. Other than their attack on the Rock River Arsenal, they've only been raiding abandoned military facilities. When they do encounter one of our security forces, they always give them the option to leave without a fight like they did at the grain facility. I've heard that General Oates has been organizing a bunch of reconnaissance and infiltration type operations into the group for months. We're trying to find the best course of action to proceed while minimizing civilian casualties. We don't even know who's leading the group, but I'm sure as soon as we discover that, he or she will be our number one target."

He continued. "On a side note, Bruce, disbanding our forces might not have been the best description of what we are doing. We are…thinning the herd. Probably by half. We're keeping our best and most combat experienced fighting forces mostly in-tact, but support groups and most of our non-essential personnel like paper-pushers and office fobbits are being released. I've had to get my own coffee for a week now." Duncan snickered. "Of the remaining fighting forces, some will be granted leave based on individual circumstances, but none of the elite groups. Even HQ is cleaning house and releasing some of the lower brass."

"All of this information I am giving you leads me to the main point: We need this refinery up and running immediately. Our country's fuel reserves are almost completely depleted. If you don't get this thing operational soon, we're going to have serious OPSEC issues."

Bruce sighed. "I'm trying, but I don't know what these circuit brains do from day-to-day and I'm—"

General Duncan raised his hand. "I know you're trying, Bruce. Everyone at HQ knows your're trying." He sighed. "But I can't continue to protect you if more accidents, like the one the other day, keep happening. I was sent here to get a first-hand account of the situation on the ground and try and light a fire under the engineers in charge of the repairs. It sounds like HQ is going to be sending a couple more experts up here in the coming days to help out."

Bruce huffed audibly. "That's all I need is more *experts* to throw into the mix. Those engineers already argue like a bunch of schoolgirls on the playground, and their reports might as well be written in French. It sounds to me like what they're trying to do has never been done before and there are a lot of moving parts, issues to overcome, too many chiefs, and too few Indians doing the actual work. For the most part, I've just tried to stay out of their way and accommodate anything they request or need. Those *were* my orders, sir."

"And I'm not second guessing anything you've done up to this point," General Duncan reassured him. "All I'm saying is that HQ is willing to pull out all the stops and get you whatever you need to finish the task at hand. Ever since our last call, there's literally been a small army of people at HQ working day and night to track down every item on the list you sent. We've actually located and acquired everything, except for one item. Unfortunately, that particular part has to come straight from China. As I was boarding the plane to fly up here, I got word that Beijing was contacted directly by the President himself and they're sending us a replacement right away. Likely, you will receive everything that was requested on your list within the next few days."

"The President…?"

"Yes, Bruce. The President of the United States of America called Beijing directly on your behalf. I was sent here to talk to the engineering team and make sure they understand the gravity of the situation and have every resource they need. We'll be sending another small team of the very best and brightest electric grid engineers to oversee the rest of the project and double check the work that's already been done before they attempt to fire it up again. In addition, HQ is putting together a separate team of engineers to send up here and inspect the refinery. Even though there's no power to it yet, they're going to bring extra generators up and run diagnostics on the refinery's control systems. So that's what our country needs us to do, and that's what we're gonna do." General Duncan sat up and looked him in the eye. "You with me on this, Bruce?"

"Of course, I am!" Bruce said defensively.

"Good. I knew you would be. So, with that said, is there anything else that your Regiment needs to speed this process up?"

"You mean like food? You know, that stuff every soldier needs to keep their bodies and minds functioning at a high level?" Bruce said irritably.

It was General Duncan's turn to be defensive. "I'm working on that, Bruce. Have you not been listening? The directive to thin our forces will be going into effect in literally days. At that point, I promise, you will get every cookie calorie you request and more." He held out his hands as if to say, "What else do you want from me?"

Bruce leaned back a little in his chair. "How is this disbandment notice going to affect my regiment?"

"It's not going to have any effect on the 31st. None at all," General Duncan said reassuringly. Unfortunately, that wasn't the response Bruce was hoping for.

"I've had forty soldiers go AWOL since I've been up here. Most of that happening in the last two months since the food shipments have grown thin. I was already considering a request to do some thinning myself."

General Duncan's face contorted. "I don't think you want to do that Bruce. That army we discussed up in Cleveland could present a problem."

"Cleveland? You said they were in Chicago!" Bruce exclaimed, leaning forward at the news.

General Duncan grimaced. "I said they were 'from' Chicago. You interrupted me earlier with one of your questions and I hadn't finished my story yet. They swept up to Detroit a month ago, and recently settled down in Cleveland."

"So, what you are saying is that I've got a fighting force, twice my size, parked only 200 miles away and they are headed this direction?" Bruce asked.

"No," Duncan responded. "What I'm telling you is that you have an army, potentially three times your size, 159 miles away and we have no idea where they are headed. However, we have no reason to believe they're heading your way or that they even know you exist."

"Oh yeah?" Bruce countered. "Let me guess. They use a motorcycle gang and a couple of RV's to scout ahead?"

General Duncan squinted. "That's right… How'd you know that?"

"Oh, a little birdie told me," Bruce said sarcastically. The General didn't look amused and Bruce realized he might be treading on his superior's good graces. "One of our patrols ran into them a couple days ago. They were outmanned so, following protocol, they just passed them by and didn't confront the group."

General Duncan tried to dismiss his concern. "Bruce, we do a pretty good job of tracking their movements most of the time. We don't even know for sure if we are talking about the same group. So let's not jump to conclusions just yet."

"Really, sir?" Bruce asked trying to bite back the sarcasm. "What do you think the chances are that it's a *different* motorcycle gang cruising around the area with an RV and a convoy of support vehicles?"

General Duncan shrugged his shoulders and sighed. He clearly wasn't going to admit out loud the overwhelming coincidence. "Okay then, where did your men last see them?"

Bruce's frown deepened. "A few miles north of here."

General Duncan sighed and closed his eyes while his head fell back to rest on the chair's back. He was quiet for a long moment and if Bruce didn't know better, he might have assumed that he'd fallen asleep. When he finally did speak, it was quiet and serious. "Bruce, before that steak is finished, I'm going to need to use your satphone."

Chapter 16

Sean casually handed a pair of binoculars to Randy who turned them over in his hands, inspecting them before placing them up to his eyes and looking down the length of Main Street.

"Vortex sure puts some nice glass in their stuff," Randy said to no one in particular.

Sean just grunted as Randy handed them back and picked something else off the table to study. Sean looked through the binoculars once more before lowering them and tapping them thoughtfully against his left palm. He turned to see the heavily bearded vendor studying him. The man sat with his nylon folding chair reclined precariously against an old rusty Jeep. He was a heavier-set man, but clearly not as large as he'd once been, his dirty shirt hanging off his shoulders like a barber's cape. Still, he was heavy enough to fill up the chair and make its thin legs bow in protest to the man's mass. He watched the man take a brief glance at Randy before turning back to him.

The vendor licked his lips and gave Sean a wary smile. "So whatcha thinkin', mister? You interested?"

Sean gave him a half shrug. "We've already got a good set back at the farm."

The man's chair pitched forward, its front two legs digging into the soft soil with a thump. "Not like them uns," the man insisted. "Them are Vortex Razor HD bi-nocu-lars, over fifteen hundred bucks new."

Sean knew they were expensive, but he doubted they'd cost that much. His rationale was based on the man's appearance. There was no way he could have afforded those binoculars if that had been how much they'd cost. Then again, you couldn't judge people by their appearance anymore. Everyone was dirty and scruffy these days. Heck, the vendor could have been a millionaire a year ago. Not that it mattered; this guy wouldn't take a hundred thousand dollars in cash now, even if Sean had it to give. This was a bartering duel and Sean wasn't sure where to begin. With a twelve powered zoom and 50mm objective lenses, these binoculars were far better than the generic eight power binoculars they currently kept at the LP/OP. They would be nice addition to the watch if he could walk away with them cheap.

"What are looking to get for them?" Sean asked politely.

"Whatcha got?" the man asked without hesitating.

"Whatcha need?" Sean replied just as quickly.

The man leaned forward, scratching vigorously into his long reddish beard. Sean tried to hide his grimace. He likely had fleas or worse yet, lice. Randy set down an old kerosene lamp with faded blue-grey paint that he'd been inspecting and turned to watch the two of them barter. It had been an interesting morning so far, wandering around the various tables and bartering with people he'd never met for items with no price tag and a value completely determined by one's need.

The man glanced at Randy before turning his attention back to Sean. "Yinz got any food? Any rice?"

"Yeh, I've got a little left," Sean mumbled. "Not sure how much food I'd be willing to part with though." In truth, that was one item the retreat had a lot of and one of the things the North Homestead's council had agreed to allow Sean and Randy to trade if they found something the retreat really needed. "How much rice are you thinking?"

The man's grubby fingers gave a short tug to his beard before they began to dig for the imperceptible offenders once more. A moment later the stocky vendor came to a decision. "I'm gonna have to git three buckets of yer rice for 'em." Randy snorted at the offer and Sean shook his head, frowning. "Them 'ere are fifteen hundred bucks new!" the man insisted, this time defensively.

"I'm sorry friend," Sean smiled. "That's just too steep for me." Sean gently placed the binoculars back down onto the table among the man's other wares and turned to leave. Sean heard the chair creak in protest and he turned back as the man stood with a grunt and stepped forward, leaning over the table. "Okay, mister. I could take as little as two buckets a yer rice. But that there is my final offer."

Sean glanced at Randy who responded with a slight shake of his head. Sean smiled consolingly toward the man. "That's still too steep a price for us. While those are a nice set of binoculars and I'd like to have them, I couldn't trade that much for an item I already have." The man huffed out loud and turned back to his chair without another retort. Sean gave the vendor a consolatory nod before turning and walking away, Randy at his side.

Randy stopped at the next table when something caught his eye. Sean stopped next to his best friend but couldn't help staring down Tionesta's Main Street. Tables lined both sides of three entire blocks. It'd been almost a month since the first "market day" Tionesta put together, and this one was ten times the size. The first one only had about ten tables, most of them manned by Tionesta's own citizens and a couple from up near Warren. It was a local affair with only a handful of strangers risking the trip into town from some of the outlying homesteads that had been approached in recent weeks.

The local outreach effort had turned out both good and bad. With the aid of Willy and his notes on the nearby areas, a security team from Tionesta had been trained by Brody. For weeks, they'd only run intel and observed the outlying homes and farms from a distance. Over two dozen families and groups had been found still alive and thriving to one extent or another. After internal discussions with the town's council about each location, most were approached and introductions made as well as invitation to the town's upcoming market day. While most were extremely cautious and untrusting, the interactions went fairly well with only a couple occasions of the town's representatives being run-off at gunpoint. It was understandable and there were no hard feelings toward the suspicious homesteaders.

It all came to an end after three weeks of scouting. One of the homes they approached opened fire as soon as the two representatives set foot onto the rickety front porch of a run-down farmhouse. One of the townsmen was shot; a bullet missed his plate carrier and entered his chest at an angle, hitting both of his lungs. In an effort to pull the wounded man out and retreat, the security team from down the road had rushed in and provided heavy cover fire while the man was dragged to the safety of the nearby woods. Chest seals were applied and he was rushed back to Tionesta, but, unfortunately, he didn't survive the return trip.

The man's death had been taken very hard by the town council, especially Pastor Dan who'd personally assigned the man to the detail. All future outreach was halted, with over a half-dozen homes that hadn't been approached yet. Brody informed Sean that there was no timetable to do so. One of the most surprising revelations of the situation was that Pastor Dan, defying the strict forbiddance by the town's council, had led another team the following day to the same farmhouse and didn't permit anyone to approach the house with him. He'd told Brody that he wanted to personally apologize to the family for the confrontation. Upon approach, he found a very malnourished woman and her young child digging a grave in the side yard. When the security team had rushed in to retrieve the injured townsman, their heavy cover fire had killed her husband.

Brody was choked up while telling Sean about Pastor Dan's emotional interaction and how he'd helped her bury her dead husband all the while apologizing profusely. Apparently, she was in complete shock, and Pastor Dan wasn't even sure if she capable of speaking or understanding what he was telling her. Fearing for the safety of both mother and child, he'd instructed the team to return to Tionesta and bring some women to help convince her to move into town and recover, at least temporarily. The woman never spoke to anyone or agreed, but she also didn't stop the women from assisting her and her child into the awaiting vehicle. Brody said they were both still on a regimented diet until their health could be restored. The woman still hadn't spoken to anyone, but the young child was coming around and starting to interact with some of the other children in the village.

The scouting groups struck out on gasoline runs, as well. Neither of the local gas stations that had been sought out had any remaining fuel left. The underground fuel tanks had been looted by the locals, probably in the first few months following the collapse.

So while maybe a dozen of the people shopping around were from the outskirts of town, the majority of the credit for the amazing growth was due entirely to Willy. He'd not only delivered Pastor Dan's introduction letters to the other towns he frequented throughout the mountains of North Central Pennsylvania, but he'd also put in a good word on the town's behalf. This time, most of the tables were manned by people Sean had never met.

One of the tables was manned by a delegation from the town of Canton, nearly two hundred miles east of Tionesta. Upon arrival the night before, they'd met with Pastor Dan privately, as had the other delegations from the few remaining mountain towns that were still thriving. Pastor Dan and Tionesta's council would meet tonight with everyone as a group in the church to have an open discussion time. Brody told Sean that the town of Brockway, fifty miles to their southeast, had even offered to host the next market day. It was a more centralized location so the other towns wouldn't have to travel as far.

They insisted their town would also provide the best possible security for future events.

After the first attack by the Bradford prison gang, the townspeople of Brockway had moved into the Little Toby Coal Mine on the outskirts of town. A third of the men from town worked at the mine and knew every nook and cranny of its vast network of tunnels. They'd fortified the main entrance and easily beaten back the prison gang the next time they were attacked. The townspeople, although vastly outgunned, where able to pop in and out of the ground from numerous locations, fire a few precise shots with their deer rifles and quickly disappear once more. Supposedly, they'd inflicted such a high casualty rate on the gang that it had never attempted an assault on their town again.

Brody had been in town since the day before, helping to organize the town's security before everyone arrived, and had been the only one from the two homesteads at the various meetings the previous night. He had recounted everything he'd heard from the meetings to Sean when they arrived early that morning. Sean inquired how the town of Brockway managed to garden and farm being stuck underground like that and how the townspeople had stayed fed. Brody had only shrugged his shoulders and said that they'd brought a whole trailer full of oats with them. "Maybe they had some big grain storage bins in the area that they confiscated. I don't know," he finished.

Sean turned his thoughts back to the table of various items that Randy was picking through and gave it a quick once over. Nothing caught his eye. He remembered back to when he was in junior high and how he used to go with his grandmother to various "flea markets." Back then, old TV's, VHS and cassette tape vendors, and people selling home-made furniture and knick-knacks dominated the majority of the tables. Most of the tables this day didn't hold items that were of any great value, except to the right person who might need something specific. It was almost surreal to hear people bartering fiercely over such mundane items as toilet paper, honey, a garden hoe, or a half-full box of hunting ammunition. Simple everyday items that were taken for granted a year ago were now traded with the utmost passion based on of the rawest of human needs...and everyone had different needs now.

A similar scene from the television series *The Walking Dead* popped into Sean's head and he smiled. Hollywood's depiction of post-apocalyptic America couldn't have been further from the truth. Nobody around him was wearing clothes without at least a few stains. Nobody's hair was cut or combed neatly, and most people's clothes hung off their bodies showing severe weight loss over the hard year without electricity. Not a single woman wore a speck of make-up. Everything was dirty. The summer grass had grown knee high along the sides of the street and bits of paper trash dotted the roadway. It wasn't a pretty and organized scene like the TV show had depicted. It was chaos. But it was a familiar and comforting chaos all the same, and now there was finally some optimism emerging on most people's faces. They had survived the worst and it was time to move forward. What that looked like was yet to be seen, but at least there was hope for a better tomorrow.

Sean felt Randy brush past him and they moved on to the next set of tables. An elderly gentleman glanced up at them with a nod and smile. "Let me know if there is something you fancy or something I can help you boys with," he said in a thick British accent. He sat on a wooden stool hunkered over a leather belt with a hole punch, drilling some new holes into the thick leather. There was a six-inch section of leather on the asphalt between his feet that'd been removed from the end of the belt.

Sean looked to the man waiting patiently to his left, holding onto the waistband of his oversized trousers with one hand. He gave Sean an embarrassed grin. Sean recognized the man from Tionesta but couldn't remember his name, so he just gave him a warm smile in return. The man's wife stood quietly next to him, holding an armload of what appeared to be new clothing from the vendor's table. Next to her, a young girl stared up at Sean while maintaining a firm grip around her mother's leg. When Sean offered the little girl a smile, she instantly shrank back, wrapping her mother's long skirt around herself until only her eyes peered from their depths. The mother noticed the exchange and tried to encourage her daughter to say "Hi," but the little girl only shook her head and turned to look down the street in the opposite direction. The woman gave Sean an apologetic look.

"It's all right. I seem to have that effect on most children," Sean chuckled.

"Here we are, sir," the elderly vendor said, interrupting their small talk. He stood from his small work station, handing the belt forward.

"Thank you," the man said.

"Again, no charge for the belt. It was nothing. Now if you want to get those pants taken in by the misses, just bring them back a little later after you get a chance to change. We'll work something out." The older man's charm came naturally.

"We'll see," the townsman said evasively. "I thank you again for fixing my belt."

The vendor waved away the man's thanks jovially, but Sean could tell the wheels were spinning in the old man's head. He was probably questioning his benevolence. Now that the man's belt was fixed, he'd probably pass on bartering to have his pants taken in. The man turned, placed his muscular arm around his wife's shoulders, and walked away. The little girl turned back to Sean as they left and gave him a gapped-tooth smile before squinting her eyes and sticking out her tongue. Sean chuckled and waved farewell. She giggled shyly and turned to race away in the opposite direction. Her mother caught her tiny wrist with a deftness every mother possesses, reminding her to stay close and not run through the market.

Sean was still smiling when he turned back to the old man who was taking in Sean's reasonably well-kept clothing, his gaze ending on Sean's belt. Sean smiled, sticking his thumbs behind his belt's buckle, showing the man that he'd already drilled new holes into it.

The man nodded his head approvingly. "Only two notches, eh? You've done fairly well for yourself then." Sean's shoulders tensed and he suddenly felt defensive, wondering if he'd given something away.

"Don't see too many two-notchers these days," the man said heartily, not noticing Sean's reaction. "How can I help you lads? Me and the misses can take in clothing, repair worn out knees, and perform any other clothing repairs you may need." He gestured toward the elderly woman who was bent over a pedal-powered sewing machine. She risked a quick glance up and a friendly smile. "We also have a full line of newer clothing for sale." He gestured down the length of the table where men's and women's clothing of various shapes and sizes were stacked both on top of and underneath the table. "Some are new and some are repairs. If you find something that suits you and we don't have your size, the misses can fix it right up for you."

"I'm not sure that I need any repairs right now. We're just browsing around. What about you, Randy?"

"No, I think I'm good for now. Where you from?" Randy asked with a friendly smile.

The old man wobbled his head back and forth. "Ahh…, we've been living in a small town a good bit east of here. You've probably never heard of it." Old habits die hard, and while everyone was being neighborly for the most part, there was still a thick veil of distrust that hung over every conversation. People were still being cautious about how much and what type of personal information they shared. It was to be expected and most people were smart enough not to pry.

Randy chuckled. "No, I meant where are you *from*? …Your accent?"

The old man laughed out loud at the misunderstanding. "Oh, ya mean the wee tone of my voice," he said dramatically, exaggerating his accent. "We're from across the pond, don't cha know. The land o' the Scotts." Randy smiled at the man's theatrics. The joker leaned forward and whispered loudly in a conspiratorial tone, "After a decade of beggin' and pleadin' by the missus, I finally gave in and took her on her 'dream vacation to the States' here. We sure picked the wrong dates to visit, I'll tell ya." The man chuckled. "Now we're stuck over here with you Yanks and the misses is getting thick legs pedalin' that machine all day."

Sean and Randy both laughed out loud and ducked as a plastic cup whizzed past their heads from the wife's direction. "Why don't you put a cork in it, Walter, and do something productive."

"Yes, Mum," he replied quickly.

"And go get me cup, y'old beggar," she added. Randy quickly retrieved the cup from the middle of the street and handed it over the table to the man. He took it and rushed it back over to his wife. She'd never even stopped pedaling. She didn't make a move to take it from him, so he slowly set it down on the stool next to her. "There's no water in that cup, Walter!" she demanded. He just nodded with a grin and disappeared behind their box trailer to fetch her some. She looked up and winked at Sean and Randy with a vicious grin. Randy clapped Sean on the shoulder. They both laughed once more and continued on down the road.

Chapter 17

Sean and Randy meandered through the tables at a casual pace. One table had a man who must have owned a cobbler shop; he was busy repairing a pair of old boots. He cussed under his breath as he struggled to get the sole off the boot in front of him, the worn sole held by the largest pair of vice-grips he'd ever seen. The veins in the man's neck bulged and his face grew crimson as he struggled to pull at the heel of the boot. The vice-grips gave way suddenly and the boot tumbled off his work table. He took in a long breath and Sean heard him mutter another curse. The cobbler looked up in frustration just as Sean and Randy strode past and gave them a questioning look. Randy just nodded politely and they continued moving, the cobbler bending over to retrieve the boot out of the high grass.

The table after the cobbler was covered in small paper bags full of various types, shapes, and sizes of gardening seed. A woman Sean didn't recognize was haggling with the vendor who barely offered the two of them a look as they passed by. She was wholly focused on the potential customer in front of her who held a hefty pile of the paper bags, her arms wrapped around them possessively. Sean was a little concerned for the customer. Harvesting seeds was a learned skill. If you didn't dry and remove just the right amount of moisture from them, they wouldn't last long in storage and you risked putting effort into your garden for seeds that wouldn't grow. While the East Homestead had a big self-sufficient lifestyle library, including a book with instructions on harvesting your own seeds, it was something the group had discussed thoroughly before the collapse. Compared to most other preparedness purchases, gardening seed was so incredibly cheap that it made no sense to Sean why some preppers only bought a small amount. Why would you want to go through all the extra work of harvesting your own seeds each year with the potential that they wouldn't be dried or stored properly for the next year's growing season? Damian had agreed, and the East Homestead had easily bought ten years' worth of various gardening seeds to store at the retreat.

Sean's feet were beginning to grow sore. Sean, Randy, David, and Sean's uncle Nathan had spent half the night walking into Tionesta since they were almost out of gas at the North retreat. The East Homestead was in the same predicament and it had been weeks since either group had visited the other. Any ounce of gas was now being saved for springtime to use in the tractors for tilling up the four acres of ground behind the North Homestead. Sean couldn't imagine how they were going to be able to achieve that the next year if more gas wasn't acquired. They might be forced to use handheld garden implements.

Sean wondered how Caleb and the others at the East Homestead were making out. He remembered back to his visit the previous month and how depressing it had been to be there without Damian or Andrew. It must be tough to live with every building riddled with bullet holes providing a daily reminder to the battle that had been fought and the precious lives lost. With all their discussion regarding the previous night's happenings, Brody hadn't even discussed the East Homestead and Sean hadn't thought to ask. He promised himself to remedy that when they reconnected later that evening.

The biggest revelation from Brody was when he recounted how a man on a motorcycle had shown up across the bridge on the west side of town early that very morning. He'd waved a white flag as he approached the concrete barriers blocking entrance onto the bridge and requested to speak with the person in charge of the town. Pastor Dan was fetched and Brody had joined him at the chain link gate next to the roadblock. The man told them he was part of a small fighting force that was just travelling through the area and willing to trade guns and ammo for gasoline. Pastor Dan firmly informed him that the town was nearly out of gas themselves and had none to spare, even for precious guns and ammunition. The man insisted they were just passing through, but he added that his group was looking for a town that may need help with security in trade for room and board over the coming winter. Pastor Dan motioned toward some of the Army soldiers who guarded the bridge and said, "We have our own soldiers. Real ones."

Brody said the man had been friendly and not in the least bit threatening or demanding. However, upon leaving he'd said, "Mayor, I'm glad to see your town doing so well. Maybe I'll check back in a couple weeks and see if you change your mind." Pastor Dan had tried to refuse the offer, but the man insisted that they only had the best intentions. The biker then shared a sad story of how the group had come together after their small town had been destroyed by a large raiding force. His group only desired to help other towns survive a similar demise, and they were looking for a new place to call home. He reassured Pastor Dan that they meant no harm and finally left when Pastor Dan reiterated to him that the town didn't need any additional security. Brody said the man was relatively well-kept and seemed friendly enough. The thought of a "fighting force" in the area was still a disturbing prospect even if they were friendly. There'd also been some discussion amongst the council on whether it could be the same group Colonel Harris had warned them of a month earlier. As a precaution, security at both homesteads was going to be increased for the time being.

Sean looked up from his musings and saw Derrick sitting behind the next table. They locked eyes at the same time. "Derrick!" Sean called out.

Their neighbor stood up with a smile and shook each of their hands. "Hey, Sean. Hey, Randy," he said in greeting.

Sean looked down to see a cardboard box full of baby chicks skittering about in fresh sawdust. "Derrick, you've been holding out on us!" Sean joked.

"These were just hatched this week. Haven't seen you since. Besides, don't you owe us some rabbits?" The edges of Derrick's mouth were turned up.

"We weaned the first litter a little later than normal, but they're almost ready for you guys," Randy replied.

Derrick's group had grown closer with Sean and the North Homestead over the last three weeks. After a few meetings to get to know each other better, they'd begun bartering and trading…to a degree. Both groups still held most of their cards to their chest, but the fact that Derrick's group had chickens and Sean's group had rabbits wasn't really a secret to either group. At their last meetup, they'd finally agreed to a trade the next time Sean's group had a new kit of rabbits.

David, who brought the rabbits with him a few months ago when he left Kane, had been instructing the North Homestead on how to breed and raise them. The rabbits were bred on a very tight and regimented schedule to maximize production. He'd brought six rabbits with him, five does and a buck. After 30 days, the five does had delivered thirty-six kits made up of sixteen bucks and twenty females. Only needing to keep 1 buck as a backup to the one he'd brought, the retreat could start butchering the remaining bucks at ten weeks old. In six months' time, the twenty does would be ready to breed as well. By breeding 25 does every 7 weeks, it would give the North Homestead a steady supply of meat year-round. Within seven months, it would meet their entire group's protein needs and make up about 30% of the entire retreat's caloric needs. They'd just bred the original five does again the previous week (at seven weeks) and were hoping for another large litter in twenty-one days. While they had planned to butcher most, if not all of the next litter, the North Homestead's council had voted to give four of the does from the original litter and one of the bucks to Derrick's group in trade for some chickens and replace those four does with some from the next litter. The idea of having eggs for breakfast in the near future was highly anticipated from every member of Sean's family. The biggest problem they faced now was trying to acquire enough fencing to build out the rabbit enclosures to house more than a hundred rabbits of varying ages in the coming months.

Someone else wandered up to the table and Randy nodded toward them to Derrick. He didn't want to interrupt a potential trade. Derrick turned his attention to the newcomer and struck up a friendly conversation. Sean and Randy stood by, watching the exchange, when Randy abruptly tapped Sean on the shoulder and pointed. It was David walking in their direction. David saw Randy waving him down and turned toward them. When he reached Derrick's table, Sean was astonished at what he held in his hands.

"Is that…an elephant ear?" Randy asked, eyes as wide as saucers.

"Mmm, hmm!" David responded, his mouth full and his lips coated with powdered sugar.

"Give me a bite!" Randy insisted, reaching for an edge of the pastry that hung limply off the side of the foam plate.

David quickly spun the plate out of his reach. "Keep your grubby paws off of it, Randy! Go get your own!"

Sean couldn't believe that someone had wasted the ingredients in making such a delicacy, not that he knew what ingredients were in an elephant ear, but surely the powdered sugar alone was something that was in high demand these days. Unlike the ones Sean had bought at the county fair before the collapse, this one had a fraction of sugar sprinkled on it, but it still made his mouth water.

"Where'd you get that?" Sean asked him, envious.

"Down at the end there," David answered, nodding over his shoulder while shoving another oily bite into his mouth. "It's the table with the fresh bread sign and the big line." His last words came out jumbled as the pastry stuck to the roof of his mouth.

"What did you trade?" Randy asked as he looked down the row of tables longingly.

David chewed a couple more times and swallowed the bite before answering. "My pocket knife."

"You're pocket knife!" Sean exclaimed.

"Dude, you traded your pocket knife for an elephant ear?" Randy laughed. It was more of a ribbing than a question.

"Don't knock it until you've tried it," David said as he tore off another bite and shoved it in his mouth, rolling his eyes back in ecstasy. "Besides,"he continued after he chewed the bite a few times. "I've got another knife back at the homestead. The same one, actually."

"But still…," Sean said in disbelief. He looked down at the end of the street and noticed one of the tables near the end was developing quite a line. Sean had to concede that it was the little things in life that were important now. People might barter and argue over a box of ammunition, but offer them an elephant ear with powdered sugar on top and you just might get their first-born son. Well, maybe not that. Sean suddenly had a huge longing to hold his son in his arms, and he wondered if he'd ever get the chance to introduce him to the taste of an elephant ear. The little poop machine had grown on Sean immensely in the last couple weeks. Maria was sure going to be pissed when she heard about how big the market day was this time and the fact that there were elephant ears for sale. Maybe he'd just skip that small detail. Sean had anticipated that there might be a few more tables and vendors than last month's market day, but he'd never expected this!

"I can't see where you're talking about?" Randy pleaded while holding his hand over his eyes and peering down the long row of tables.

David turned and pointed. "Right there, Randy. The one with the big line of people." David turned back just in time to once again rescue the edge of his elephant ear from Randy's outstretched fingers. "Damn you, Randy! I swear I'll break your fingers if you touch it!" Sean wasn't sure if David was seriously getting angry or kidding around, but Sean and Randy both doubled over laughing.

When they finally regained their composure, Randy muttered, "I think I have an extra pocket knife in my pack…."

"Seriously, Randy?" Sean chuckled, not believing his friend was actually serious.

David shoved the last bite into his mouth. "Trust me, Sean. It's well worth the trade." Sean just shook his head. He'd have to wrack his brain about what he had to trade, but it surely wouldn't be his beloved Kershaw Camber pocket knife.

"I'm going down there to check it out," Randy finally said with determination.

"Alright, let's go," Sean chuckled. They started to turn away, but Sean stopped them with a hand on Randy's forearm. "Hold up a sec, guys." Sean stepped up to Derrick's table and heard him discussing the weather with the potential buyer. Throughout the afternoon, Sean had noticed it was customary to get to know the person you would be bartering with and feel them out. Since the two of them hadn't entered into the bartering side of things yet, Sean interjected himself into the conversation. "Excuse me one second, mister," he said to the stranger standing beside him before turning to Derrick. "Hey, we're going to continue on down the road, but I'll swing back by later, alright?"

"Sounds good, Sean."

"Oh, yeah," Sean said as a thought popped into head, "are we still on for poker night this Friday?"

Derrick smiled. "Yes. I spoke to the group and they agreed to have you guys over for dinner on Friday night. It will be fun for the guys to play cards while the wives get to know each other."

"Great!" Sean agreed. "Well, I'll let you get back to it." Derrick waved him off and turned his attention back to his customer as Sean joined the others. Randy was rocking back and forth on his toes, obviously antsy to trade his knife for a single elephant ear.

They started down the street and halfway to the end of the tables, Sean saw a vendor with boxes upon boxes of ammunition on one table and an entire reloading kit set up on a different table where the vendor was carefully lining up a rifle case before lowering the machine's press.

"Hold up," Sean said, veering off in the man's direction.

"C'mon, Sean!" Randy protested. "He'll still be there in bit!"

Sean snickered. "Go ahead, Randy. I'm not your babysitter! I'll catch up to you in a few."

"Fine," Randy sulked. He turned to David. "You comin'?"

David grimaced. "I don't think so, Randy. I'm going to stay here with Sean. If I go down there and smell those things again, I might end up selling my soul to the devil for another."

"Alright. I'll be back in a few minutes," Randy said.

Sean motioned to the expansive line that had formed in only a few minutes. "You'll be longer than that," he said. "I hope they have some left by the time you get there." Without another word, Randy jogged off down the street.

David grinned at Sean and they stepped up to the table with the ammunition. The man at the reloading bench looked up. "Be with yinz in a sec," he said. He finished maneuvering the next cartridge into place and pulled the lever once more. Placing the finished rifle shell into a large ammo can, he stood and sauntered up with a genuine smile.

"How can I help you? Do you have any specific ammunition needs? I carry a large variety of various calibers and I have the ability to reload most other calibers if you bring your own spent casings."

"To be honest, we are just browsing for the most part. We have our own reloading equipment at the farm but we're running low on powder." Sean didn't put it into question form, but his statement was obvious.

"So, you're looking to trade for some powder," the man said, tilting his head to the side. "That's the first request I've received for that. I do have plenty of powder to trade…for the right price." And so, the bartering commenced. No small talk from this vendor. "What type of powder are you looking for?"

Sean shrugged his shoulders looking to David for help. David just shrugged. Sean turned back to the man hopelessly. "I don't actually do any of the reloading at the farm, short of helping my father a few times, and even then I was just doing what I was told. All I know is that we're getting low on powder."

"Uh, huh," the man sympathized. "That's going to make it hard for me to make a recommendation then. There are numerous types and brands of gun powder. What type of ammunition are you reloading?"

"Mostly 5.56, .308, 9mm, and some .45."

"Well for the 5.56, I've got some Varget, Ramshot, CFE, and AR-Comp powders I could trade. The .308 is harder because it depends on what type of bullet you're loading. The 9mm and .45…." He trailed off as he saw Sean's blank look. "What are the chances your father might come by to barter?"

Sean sighed. "Not very good. We don't live in town."

The conversation wasn't going very well and the man was obviously worried about losing a possible trade. "Do you know what type of reloading equipment your father is using?"

Sean shook his head, again. "I just know it's green."

"RCBS then."

"Yeah, that sounds right," Sean agreed.

He scowled. "I'm in need of a few dies that I seem to be missing. But, unfortunately, my kit isn't compatible with your dad's."

Sean perked. "I know we've got a bunch of different reloading kits and various equipment to go with them. My dad said he uses the green one because that's his own personal kit he used before the collapse and he's most comfortable with it. I know there's at least two other types of kits with various parts in storage. I think one of them is red."

"Really?" the man asked with an arched eyebrow. "How did you end up with so many different kits?"

"How'd you end up with so much powder?"

The man just chuckled. "Probably the same way you did."

"Are you coming to the town's next market day?" Sean asked.

"I plan to," the man answered before leaning over and whispering. "I do have to tell you that there are rumors floating around that the next one is going to be in Brockway."

Sean smiled knowingly. "Yes, we've heard that, too. I tell you what. Make me a list of everything you want or need and I'll run it past my father when I get back to the farm. We'll dig up what we can and bring it with us, wherever the next market day ends up. As of now, I know we aren't completely out of powder, we're just getting low."

"That sounds like a plan," the man answered. He stuck his hand out. "I'm Cameron."

Sean shook his hand firmly. "Sean. It's a pleasure to meet you, Cameron." Sean scanned through the ammo once more. "What about box ammunition? I notice you mostly have standard calibers here. We've got an assortment of ammunition of various calibers at the farm that we don't need. We also have a bunch of hunting rifles and some revolvers we could part with. It seems to me that selling guns would go hand-in-hand with what you're trading here." When Sean's family had taken in Kenneth and Brian, the owners of his hometown Duke's Sporting Goods store, just after the collapse and, by default, most of their store's inventory, they had acquired a lot of ammunition and various guns that their group wasn't utilizing.

"I have a couple guys in town that could use some extra 44 magnum and some .270 rifle ammunition. I've reloaded the same twenty rounds for them three times now and those cases are reaching the end of their life span. I could also use some 6.8 Grendel that I'm not set up to reload. Do you think you have any of that lying around?"

"We might," Sean nodded.

"I'll take all of what you got in those calibers, then. As far as the guns, it depends on what make, model, and type of guns you're talkin'. I'd have to ask around back home and see what people may need or want. And at that point, I assume we've moved past trading for some extra reloading powder."

"Yes, we'll have moved past that," Sean agreed. "For now, just get me the list of what you need personally and I'll swing back by later and pick it up." Suddenly an idea popped into Sean's head. "Do you happen to know Willy? He calls himself the Postman?"

Cameron rolled his eyes. "Sure. Everybody knows Willy. He's been frequenting our town for most of the year. He's a wacky one, but good at what he does. In fact, he's the one who provided our delegation the maps on how to get here and bypass any danger areas."

"Well, once you get back to your town and ask around, make up a list of the guns and ammo your town may need and send it on with Willy on one of his runs. If we have what you need, we'll be sure to bring it to the next market day."

Cameron nodded, then pursed his lips and sighed. "That's a good idea…, but you do realize that he charges an arm and a leg to deliver messages, right?"

"I didn't know that," Sean said. "I've never used him before."

"Me neither," Cameron admitted. "I've just heard it from others who have. Then again, they were asking him to go look for missing family members. Maybe us townsfolk could beat him down to start delivering normal mail between the towns."

"Maybe we can get him to deliver small packages as well," Sean added.

"Like a couple dies for my reloading kit." Cameron was clearly more interested in the idea now.

"Yeah, they're small enough. I'll discuss it with him when I see him."

"Me too," Cameron said.

They talked for a few more minutes and shook hands before Sean and David moved on. Looking down the row of tables, Sean spotted Randy. He was still at the end of the line at the baked goods table and the line was moving slow. He was speaking with the person in line next to him, a man Sean didn't recognize. There was something special about the market day. People weren't scared. They were still suspicious of each other, but there was an overall calm demeanor to most in attendance.

"We should probably discuss trading those extra guns with your father and the rest of the council," David suggested.

"I was going to," Sean said a bit defensively. "I was just starting a dialog with a prospective buyer."

"No, no," David said, raising his hands in surrender. "I wasn't implying that you weren't going to. I was just thinking that maybe we should man our own table at the next market day. There's only so much black powder a man needs. We might be able to trade those extra guns and ammo for something the retreat really needs."

Sean stopped and turned to David, suddenly embarrassed about being defensive. "That's a great idea, David. With the growth between this market day and the last, I'm really curious to see what shows up at the next one." David nodded his agreement.

"Mayor Reese!" a voice from behind them shouted. David locked eyes with Sean and froze.

Chapter 18

David spun around to find the Postman striding in their direction. Willy's awkward lope reminded Sean of some creature out of a science fiction movie. David's eyes shot to the various bystanders in their vicinity, obviously checking to see if anyone recognized the name Willy had just hollered out.

David gave Willy a forceful "Shhhh!" before gripping his arm and steering him away from the crowded street. Sean followed the two of them as they wound their way between several tables. One of the vendors shot them a warning look when Willy bumped into one of the tables, knocking over a display of colorful handkerchiefs. Sean just smiled and shrugged apologetically at the vendor as he tried to keep up with the other two. The vendor quickly stood up from his chair and followed them as they walked past his old Chevy Astro van. He eyed them suspiciously, making sure they didn't sneak into his vehicle and steal any of his goods. Sean watched as Willy tried to pull his arm away, but David's grasp held firm. They worked their way down one of Tionesta's short side streets. When it dead-ended at the river, David looked around the empty roads before moving them down into the high weeds of the embankment and to the river's edge.

"You can't use my name here, Willy!" David said forcibly, releasing Willy's arm.

"Sorry about that, ahhh…," Willy apologized, uncertain what name to use.

"It's just David now."

"Okay." Willy didn't say anything else, but he gave David a questioning nod in Sean's direction.

"It's alright. Sean knows everything."

"Yes," Willy said, looking Sean up and down before cocking his head to the side and commenting. "It seems Sean here knows a little bit of everything about everyone."

Sean wasn't quite sure how to respond to the odd comment. He was saved from making a generic response when Willy quickly turned his attention back to David. "I began to worry for my old friend after my last visit to Kane. Nobody knew where you'd gone and the new mayor wouldn't give me any information on your whereabouts."

"Good," David said, relieved that his secret was being kept.

"Not for me," Willy said with a snort. "I've got more information that I'd like to get out there," he said as he flung his arms wide, gesturing to the world at large, "and my megaphone has disappeared."

"Well, now you've found it," David said with a small smile, starting to relax.

"You still hidin' from the Boogey Man?" Willy asked pointedly.

David shook his head. "The Boogey Man is dead. But yes, I'm still in hiding. I don't think The Boss will ever stop looking for me until he has my head on a pike adorning his office at the White House." Most people wouldn't have understood whom David meant, but Sean was very familiar with David's code words. The Boogey Man was the term David used to refer to Lt. Jenkins, who had led the Ranger team to assassinate him four months earlier. The Boss was the name he used in his broadcasts for General Oates. Sean never heard David while he was recording his messages, but the entire retreat—those not on watch duty—always gathered on Tuesday nights to listen to the broadcast transmitted from an unknown location by the Rangers. It was kind of strange as no one in Sean's family ever recognized David's voice and if they did, they'd never brought it up.

"Oh, so you haven't heard about the White House then?" Willy said, leaning in conspiratorially. David and Sean waited for Willy to continue, but he just stood there with a triumphant look on his face.

"Okay Willy, you have my attention," David sighed. "Spit it out."

Willy took a step back and struck a pose like he was getting ready to make an announcement. "The White House and Capitol Hill have finally been abandoned," he said triumphantly before relaxing his posture again.

"I heard rumors of that a few weeks ago, but nothing's been confirmed by my sources."

Willy sneezed and wiped his hand on his trousers. "I'm confirming it now. Did your source tell you where they were going?" David shook his head. "The President and Congress have been moved to the underground Raven Rock complex just two hundred miles south of here."

"And you know this how?" David asked, his tone showing he was unconvinced.

"A little birdy told me," Willy answered with a wave of his hand.

David stood with his arms crossed. "You know how this works, Willy. I'm not going to put my reputation on the line for the Brockway rumor mill and whisperings on the wind."

Willy pretended to be aghast. "Have I ever steered you wrong?" David responded by shooting him an icy glare. "Okay, okay! There was the one instance." Willy gave Sean a sheepish grin and added with a low mumble, "The information seemed reliable at the time."

"Well, it wasn't," David said.

"What about all the information I gave you about the Green Zones? That was all accurate," Willy pointed out.

"It was," David conceded. "And broadcasting it almost got me killed. I was forced to flee everything and everyone I'd ever known."

Willy held his hands out apologetically, but his reply had an adamant tone to it. "The American people deserved to know what they were walking into."

David sighed. "Yes…, they did." A light bulb went off in Sean's head. This was one of David's sources. One of the main reasons General Oates had sent a kill squad after David was the fact that he was broadcasting the horrible and deadly living conditions inside the Green Zones and pushing back on the government narrative that there was plenty of food, water, and medical attention at those locations. Those details must have come from Willy who'd lived in one of the Green Zones before his wife and daughter were killed. It all made sense now, and Sean wondered how long the two of them had known each other and how long Willy had been travelling to Kane before approaching Tionesta. He made a mental note to ask David later.

"But now you're telling me that the President and Congress have moved into Raven Rock. That seems like highly classified information that only a handful of people would know about. I wasn't even told that, and my sources know everything that's going on down there. Sorry if I'm skeptical. It's one thing to know that D.C. has been abandoned; it's another thing to know about the secret facility where they're being moved to. It sounds like another rumor to me." David began to nervously rub his hands together. "If I'm going to poke the bear, I want to make sure it's a sharp stick." David obviously wasn't convinced the story was real and needed evidence before broadcasting the information. He'd told Sean on multiple occasions that he would do whatever it took to take down those involved in trying to kill him, but he was also adamant on maintaining his reputation of broadcasting reliable information.

Willy's face couldn't hide its irritation over his information being brought into question. "I can assure you it's no rumor. It came to me from a firsthand witness. The problem is, if the nature of how I learned this information is leaked, it could put a young family's lives at risk."

"You know that I never leak my sources!" David protested.

"I know that," Willy said, raising his hands defensively. "I didn't say you would do it intentionally and I haven't said that I wouldn't tell you. It's just that you have to keep any of the details to yourself on this one." Willy turned to Sean. "That goes for you, too."

"Who am I going to tell?" Sean asked sarcastically.

"Just spit it out," David pressed.

"Oh, alright," Willy relented. "Two nights ago, I was staying in one of the other towns I frequent south of here. A relative of one of the townspeople showed up at the gates in the middle of the night. They'd been living down in Blue Ridge Summit, Pennsylvania, and their farmstead was just a short distance from the Raven Rock complex. They said that the complex had been quiet the last year and then all of a sudden there's been an enormous amount of activity over the last two weeks. Their farm's watch location overlooks the road leading into Raven Rock and they reported a steady convoy of military and civilian trucks rolling in and out, day and night, for two weeks straight. The man was outside in his field a couple days ago and he's adamant that he saw Marine One flying very low overhead…straight toward the Raven Rock helipad.

"In addition to that, their one surviving neighbor was a woman who'd been sleeping with some of the soldiers in the complex in trade for food. One of her patrons told her the surviving Congressmen, their immediate families, and even the President himself was being moved into the complex. She was told that the security at the facility was being bolstered and the perimeter line would soon be re-drawn. True to what she'd told them, the very next day their family farm was approached by a full platoon of soldiers and they were told they had twenty-four hours to pack up and leave. After pleading with the soldiers, they were permitted to stay an extra day and harvest some of his crops that were ready. The soldiers were even instructed to offer him an old M1008 military pickup so he and his family could relocate. Apparently, the soldiers had been aware of the family the entire year and had been keeping an eye on them. Since they'd never poked around the complex, their commander had let them stay in place undisturbed…but not any longer. The soldiers refused to tell them what had changed and why they were being asked to leave after so long, and the man was smart enough not to ask about the President and Congress or let on that he knew about them."

David cut in. "Okay, so if you figure in the neighbor woman's account and how her warning about them getting kicked out came true the next day, and then add in the fact that he personally saw Marine One flying to the complex and the sudden influx of trucks and equipment getting delivered to the site…, all happening at the same time that D.C. is being abandoned, then I'll admit the story has merit. I could probably run with that."

"But you see the dilemma here?" Willy added. "As far as this family knows, they were the last survivors within miles of the complex, not counting the neighbor woman. If you give out any details about how you know the President and Congress are at Raven Rock, it's not going to be hard for The Boss to figure out who's spilling the beans. They're an innocent family and I don't want to see anything bad happen to them."

"I understand," David acknowledged. "The Boss has to know by now that I have a high-level mole in the White House feeding me intel. I'll just leave out the details and they'll likely assume I heard it from my source." He paused for a moment and cocked his head to the side inquisitively. "Willy, I'm just curious, why is the information on the new location of the President so important for you to get out there? I'll admit that it's a good nugget and I'm happy to broadcast it, but why do you care?"

Willy's face grew hard. "Because the President is a coward and he's hiding from the mess he created. His people are starving to death while he runs off and hides under a rock. Eventually those people in the Green Zones are going to start working together and forming groups. I want them to know where they can go to get the retribution they deserve." By the time he finished speaking, his words were dripping with venom.

"Very well. That's a good enough reason for me," David said, satisfied with the answer and unwilling to probe further.

"There's more," Willy added. His serious face was suddenly replaced by his big gap-toothed smile. Sean was always amazed at how fast Willy's moods could switch. Sean also started considering the fact that Willy seemed a lot less crazy today than he had in the past. He wondered if maybe Willy wasn't crazy at all and it was just an act. Almost in response to Sean's thought, Willy started hopping up and down clapping his hands like a three-year-old waiting to be handed a slice of cake. "This bit is sooooo exciting!" Willy exclaimed.

Nope. He's definitely crazy, Sean thought to himself.

"Alright now, Willy," David said, chuckling. "Simmer down and tell me what's got you so wound up." He handled Willy like a parent would handle an overly-excited child. Sean guessed that David had been dealing with Willy for quite some time and knew how to keep him focused—something Sean, Pastor Dan, and the other townspeople in Tionesta were still figuring out. Willy seemed to calm down a bit, but not much.

"They have electricity in Warren!" Willy blurted out.

Suddenly it was Sean's turn to have his interest piqued. He butted in to the conversation. "What's this? Where'd you hear that?"

Willy's lean body leaned forward conspiratorially. "Ahhh! So the great Sean doesn't know everything then, does he?" Sean just frowned back at him, not wanting to get goaded into one of Willy's confusing verbal tennis matches he loved to start. "And it's not a rumor. I saw it for myself." Willy rubbed at his left knee before continuing. "I must admit that it was one of the more difficult and risky things I've attempted to date. I wanted to find out for myself why they'd pushed Warren's security perimeter so far away from the edge of town, so I had to get close."

Sean wasn't sure how he felt about Willy spying on Colonel Harris. Sean had thought that Willy and the Colonel had come to some sort of mutual understanding since their initial interaction, which had clearly been filled with fireworks. Sean couldn't blame Willy for his deep resentment to all things government after the murder of his wife and child, and Sean even shared his resentment to a certain degree. However, Sean's allegiance was definitely planted more on Colonel Harris's side than this new figure who was more than a little bit crazy. Colonel Harris had shown himself to be a man of honor and had saved the lives of those at the East Homestead…most of them, anyway. Sean was still skeptical of the government for the most part, but he felt that the Colonel had earned his trust multiple times over.

"What did you see and who else have you told about this?" Sean asked, thinking back to the Colonel's warning about the larger public finding out about the electric grid becoming operational in Warren.

"It's not what I seen. It's what I heard!" Willy planted his hands on his hips but didn't continue.

David glanced toward Sean and he could see the irritation in his look. "Okay, Willy. What did you hear?" David caved to Willy and finally asked the question outright.

"I heard, and saw, the United Refinery in Warren up and running. I saw a long row of tanker trucks waiting to be filled. There was a full military escort of soldiers surrounding the trucks and they weren't Army. They were Marines. Gentlemen, I believe Colonel Harris is holding out on us. Boys, there's gas in Warren!" Willy looked from David to Sean and then back to David, trying to judge their reactions. He frowned when he realized they weren't nearly as excited as he thought they'd be. To no avail, Willy had tried to help the town of Tionesta locate gas stations, ones with some fuel remaining in their underground tanks. He knew that the town was critically low on fuel and likely suspected that Sean's group was as well.

"Interesting," Sean noted. And it was interesting. Sean now understood why Tionesta's gardening team hadn't been invited back to Warren the last few weeks. Pastor Dan had continued to offer their knowledge and assistance to help train the soldiers in gardening, but his offer had been brushed off by Colonel Harris. Everyone assumed it was because the military's rations had recently been increased to previous levels, but Sean was curious why the Colonel wasn't continuing the soldier's education. Surely the new increase of food could always drop off again in the future. Now there were new soldiers in Warren.

Sean looked directly at David. "You can't broadcast that," he said flatly.

David looked confused and a little annoyed at being told what he could and couldn't do. "And why not?"

"Because it could bring trouble for Colonel Harris and all of us," Sean said. David and Willy both seemed uncertain. "Look…. Let's assume you broadcast that the town of Warren has electricity and a refinery operating. As far as we know, this may be the only town in the country where the electricity has been restored. How do you think the survivors out there are going to react to the news? We could face an influx of tens of thousands, if not hundreds of thousands of starving and desperate people into the immediate area. They'd likely think that electricity and food go hand in hand. When the electricity stopped, the food infrastructure stopped. Naturally, they'd probably assume the opposite would be true."

Sean clasped his hands behind his back and started to pace back and forth in the tall grass along the river's edge. It was a habit he'd inherited from his father when in deep thought. "It's obvious now that the refinery in Warren was the main reason the Army was sent here. I'm guessing the newer and bigger refineries down in the Gulf of Mexico can't be brought online. I have no idea what kind of fuel reserves our country has but I'm sure it's not infinite. I'm also sure that they will defend that resource with force, if needed. We'd be putting Colonel Harris in a very tough position. We'd likely get some of his men killed in the fighting, not to mention the civilians that would be killed trying to get into Warren.

"And what about our own towns? Where do you think all these hungry people are going to hole up and position themselves? What are they going to eat after they've been turned away in Warren? Will they have enough food to get back to where they came from? Guys, it's been relatively quiet around here the last few months. We're starting to grow as a community and I don't just mean Tionesta. Do we really want to do anything that could bring a huge influx of outsiders into our area? People we don't know…people we won't be able to trust at first?" Sean shook his head. "We need to be extremely careful with this information."

Sean looked up to see both of them nodding at their feet as they considered his words. "So, I'll ask you again, Willy. Who else have you given this information to besides us?"

Willy's head snapped up. "No one, actually."

"You sure?" Sean demanded. This seemed too good of a secret for Willy to have held on to for long.

"No, Sean. I'm not sure," Willy quipped. "I just can't seem to remember these days who I talk to and what words come out of my mouth."

"Okay, Okay. I just had to be sure," Sean said in his defense. "It's really good intel that you've acquired and I'm surprised you were able to get through the military's lines up in Warren," Sean commended him. Willy's face beamed at the praise. "We need to be sure we approach Colonel Harris carefully with this information. Hopefully, we can work out a way to get some fuel from them without putting him into a compromising situation. None of us have much love for the way the government has handled this whole debacle, but I think we all can agree that Colonel Harris has been a good neighbor so far. Let's not risk getting him in trouble with his superiors or risk having him replaced with a new commander that may not be willing to bend the rules like Colonel Harris has been willing to do." Sean regurgitated the same points Colonel Harris had expressed weeks earlier. Points that Sean agreed with.

"I agree, Sean," David nodded. "Willy, can you promise not to share this with anyone else until we have a chance to discuss it with Colonel Harris and see how he'd like to handle it?"

Willy frowned. "I suppose. At the same time, that's a privately-owned refinery that they've seized and nationalized. It's only fair that they share the resource with the local people."

Sean sighed. "Willy, I don't think you can say that it's been seized or nationalized. It was a non-functional, abandoned, and useless resource as it sat. By repairing the electric grid in Warren and making repairs to the refinery, that surely entitles the military to make use of it." Willy frowned at Sean's defense of the government. "And don't give me that look like I'm taking the government's side against the people," Sean scolded. "I agree that they should share a portion of it to help the locals, but we need more details first and we need to approach that conversation carefully. Picketing the facility with signs isn't going to get us what we want."

Willy huffed and kicked at a rock under foot. It came loose and he bent over, picked it up, and tossed it across the river. Sean watched the flat rock skip once, twice, three, four, five times before sinking under the murky water of the Allegheny River. Willy turned back to Sean with a smile. "I like you, Sean."

Sean was taken aback and chuckled. "I like you too, Willy."

There was a moment of uncomfortable silence before David spoke up. "Do you think we should take this to Pastor Dan privately and bring him into the potential negotiation with Colonel Harris?" Sean rubbed his scruffy chin hairs in thought. "Obviously, it would be something we'd have to insist that he not discuss with the town council for the time being. But having Tionesta with us at the negotiation table could throw some weight behind our request."

"Would he be willing to intentionally keep them out of the loop, though, and negotiate on the town's behalf without their knowledge of the situation?" Sean asked rhetorically. "I wonder if he'd have a hard time with that."

"You know him better than we do," David answered with a glance at Willy. "I'm just thinking that if the North Homestead suddenly has access to gas, Pastor Dan is going to wonder where we got it."

Sean had an idea. "I wonder if the Colonel would agree to deliver a truckload of gas down to the Uni-Mart south of town once or twice a year. We could go and get it the next day. It would eliminate any outside questions from the townspeople as no one would know it hadn't always been there. Maybe the scouting party we sent just missed one of the tanks. I don't think any of the townspeople would know exactly how much gas an underground tank at a gas station holds. I know I don't."

"Most older mom and pop gas stations have two 8,000-12,000 gallon tanks, whereas most of the newer and bigger gas stations have at least two 20,000 gallon tanks. That allows them to buy when fuel prices are low and store it longer," Willy offered.

Sean and David both stared at him shaking their heads. "Willy, you never cease to amaze me. I don't even want to know where you learned that useless piece of information," David said with a snicker.

"Good," Willy smiled back. "Because I wasn't going to tell you anyway."

Sean steered the conversation back on track. "Okay, so I'd have to assume even filling one of the 8,000 gallon tanks once a year would be more than enough fuel for the town and our retreats."

"Retreats? Don't you mean retreat?" Willy asked with a knowing smile.

Sean panicked a little at the slip but did a manageable job at maintaining his composure. "That's what I said—'at our retreat.'"

"Noooo," Willy countered. "You clearly said 'retreats'…plural."

"Huh, did I?" Sean said, looking over to David.

"I just heard you say 'retreat.'" David came to his defense. "What are you getting at, Willy?"

"Me?" Willy asked with a wry grin. "Nothing. I must have just heard you wrong. Sorry, Sean," he apologized, but there was still a conspiratorial twinkle in his eye.

Sean was quick to change the subject. "Randy is probably going to come looking for us soon. David, we should wrap this up and head back."

David turned to Willy. "Do you have anything else?"

Willy flashed his ridiculous smile. "I've always got more."

David sighed. "Anything relevant? Anything important?"

"Everything I say is important," Willy insisted.

David just shook his head. "Whatever." David's attention was distracted and he looked up, studying the dark fast-moving clouds. "Willy, I think we're going to be spending the night in town. It looks like it's going to really start coming down in a bit." Willy looked up at the sky and studied it closely, nodding his agreement.

"Why don't we connect after tonight's big meeting? And if you think of anything else I should know about from your travels over the last two months, we can discuss it then," David offered.

"And I've got an idea I want to run by you as well," Sean added. "An official Postal Service type of idea," Sean said, playing up Willy's alter ego. Willy seemed interested and started to open his mouth to speak, but Sean held up his hand. "Not now. We'll discuss it later. David and I need to get back."

David didn't wait for Willy to answer. "See you later," he called as he turned to lead the way back up the river's steep embankment.

"I can't be long though," Willy said to their backs.

"Huh?" David asked, stopping mid-stride and turning back to Willy.

"I've got a recon run up to Pleasantville tonight for some poor family in Brockway whose son is missing." He shook his head sadly. "I planned to head out around two a.m. so I could be back before daybreak, and I'll need to get a few hours of beauty sleep before I leave."

"Trust me. I'd be happy to keep it short." It was clear that while David wanted Willy's information, he obviously didn't enjoy his circular conversations. "Don't forget to take a rain coat," David muttered, turning once more and scrambling up the bank.

Sean could tell by the way Willy's shoulders slumped that his feelings might have been hurt by the comment, but he didn't say anything. Willy looked up to sky once more and studied the clouds. Sean could hear Willy muttering softly to himself, but as usual, he had a hard time picking out the exact words. Sean thought he heard Willy saying something about "angels" again, but he couldn't be sure. A strange scent suddenly caught Sean's attention. He couldn't be sure, but it was almost if he could smell perfume. Willy was always one to wear fresh, clean clothes and he maintained his personal hygiene better than anyone Sean had met since the collapse. The first time he'd met Willy, he'd clearly smelled Cool Water cologne which Sean used to wear himself during his military days. But this smell was different. It was crisper. It almost smelled like a woman's perfume. Sean leaned a little closer.

Willy looked down to see Sean still standing close and his cheeks reddened a little at being caught mumbling to himself. "I think Mayor…errr, David, is right about a storm coming," Willy said. "Heading up to Pleasantville in the pouring rain sure won't be very…pleasant," he smiled, proud of his comment. But Sean didn't even catch the play on words as another lightbulb went off in his head.

"Wait a second! You said you're heading to Pleasantville at two in the morning but plan to be back before daybreak?" Sean questioned.

"No, I just said that I was going to Pleasantville tomorrow night on account of this storm that's brewing," Willy deflected.

"No, that's not what I mean." Sean shook his head. "Earlier, you said you were going to leave at 2am and planned to be back before daybreak. How's that long of a trip even possible on foot?"

Willy grinned suspiciously. "It's a secret." Sean stood there pondering it over in his head. Sean knew that Willy preferred to travel in the middle of the night when most people were sleeping. Willy had also insisted that he'd never use a vehicle because they were too noisy and drew too much attention. He'd even gone so far as to give Sean and his family members grief for using the Bronco to travel the short distance between the North Homestead and Tionesta. "If you don't use them legs, you're gonna get fat!" he had insisted.

Willy let Sean ponder for a moment before adding, "Sean, you can't know everything."

Sean was about to respond when he heard David grunt. He turned to see David standing at the top of the hill. "You comin'?"

Sean nodded but turned back to Willy to get his answer, but Willy was already ten paces away, picking his way along the rocks at the river's edge. Sean shook his head at the strange man before turning and scrambling his way up to David.

Chapter 19

Sean restlessly turned over in bed, trying to make his movements slow and deliberate. The last thing he wanted to do was wake up the baby who slept between him and Maria and had turned out to be a light sleeper. He carefully readjusted his pillow, turning it over once more to try and find a cool spot. What he wouldn't give for his soft bed and feather pillow in Pittsburgh. His retreat pillow was a cheap synthetic, and it seemed to capture every BTU of heat that Sean's head emitted throughout the night, radiating it straight back into his skull. He hated trying to sleep when he was hot. He finally found a reasonably comfortable position and breathed a long sigh.

Sean felt a small movement in the bed and he froze, praying that he hadn't awakened the baby…again. Maria had already giving him an earful an hour ago and threatened to kick him out of the bed for the night if he didn't stop squirming. James made a few more movements behind him before Sean heard a soft suckling sound as his son found what he was looking for. It was a peaceful and soothing sound, but not enough to help him fall asleep. He let his mind wander over the events of the previous day.

Randy, David, Uncle Nathan, and he had walked to the North Homestead early that morning. It was a long walk, but it wasn't necessarily a difficult hike as the road was mostly level, winding its way along the river's edge. That was until you got to the turn off and had to hike the last grueling mile and a half winding up the face of the mountain ridge. It had been significantly easier on the walk downhill to Tionesta.

The group meeting the night before, with all the visiting delegations from the surviving towns in North Central Pennsylvania, had gone extraordinarily well. There were a few representatives that kept their towns' resources and abilities under wraps, but most were openly bartering and trading quickly after the meeting ended.

Pastor Dan and the council had finalized a great deal with the town of Emporium. Tionesta had produced a bumper crop of high calorie potatoes, more than the town could come close to eating over the winter. In fact, the town could thank Mr. Andrews for that development. Shortly after taking over the town, he'd given a coffee can size container of potato seeds to the Gardening Team's leader, Curtiss Eckley. These were actual True Potato Seeds (TPS) from a company named Bejos, not cut up tubers kept from the previous year's crop or purchased at a local store. He'd insisted that the small amount of tiny potato seeds in the container would feed the town for a dozen years. He might have been underestimating. Tionesta was able to grow four acres of potatoes from only four ounces of seeds, and a separate container had been found in one of his underground storage rooms after Mr. Andrews' death. They had enough seeds for the town to produce potatoes for decades.

Now a city councilman, Mr. Eckley had thoroughly reviewed the literature Mr. Andrews included and had set to work planting the unusual seed that spring. Finding great early results, Eckley even had the foresight to plant a second late season crop which was just coming on. Unlike regular seedling potatoes that rot after a year in storage, TPS seeds would easily last over ten years with proper storage, maybe longer. And unlike the multigenerational cloned seed potatoes most commercial and residential gardeners use, there is no carryover of disease inside of a seed. The Bejos seeds showed an unbelievable vigor and not a single plant experienced any kind of disease.

On the flipside, Emporium had recently discovered Ring Rot in their stored potatoes. While the delegation hoped they had sorted out and disposed of all the infected potatoes, they were worried that they would run out mid-winter. That's assuming the infestation didn't spread. Sean had listened intently as Curtiss gave the representative his opinion on how to deal with the problem. He'd insisted that the town only plant Tionesta's more disease-resistant first generation Bejos seed potatoes the next year and do so in an entirely separate field from where the infected potatoes had been planted. He also advised that they make a second pass through the old field and make sure all the offending tubers had been removed and disposed of so they didn't infect future crops. Every piece of equipment, down to the knives used for cutting the tubers, would need to be thoroughly cleansed with bleach water. Any storage bags and their current storage location must be thoroughly scrubbed down or replaced, if possible. Sean made mental notes while the representative took notes on paper.

Luckily, Emporium had found over five tons of iodized salt in a canning facility just outside their town limits, and it didn't take long for Pastor Dan to negotiate a trade. Salt was an essential preservative in a time without refrigeration, helped provide electrolytes, and made a useful flavoring for monotonous and bland food choices. In fact, with their massive amount of salt for trade, their delegates were very busy after the meeting negotiating with almost every town in attendance.

Potatoes were a very easily grown and calorie-rich vegetable. Nutrient density per acre of potato production is four times higher than corn and ten times higher than wheat. But as with any vegetable, diseases were much harder to control now that you couldn't run to the garden supply store and buy Neem oil and other sprays used to control the various diseases. Tionesta's ability to grow from TPS seeds prevented them from having those problems.

But even potatoes grown from TPS are susceptible to insect damage. So, one of the jobs given to the smaller children in Tionesta was to literally go row by row and inspect the fields every single morning, physically removing any worms, caterpillars or other insects found on the leaves. In late June, field and crop inspections had been increased to twice a day when Japanese Beetles emerged from the ground. Each child held a small bucket of water and walked the various rows of crops and vegetables, pulling the bugs off the plants one by one and dropping them in the water. Some of the children were initially scared of the little squirming bugs with their prickly legs. With a little practice, most quickly got over it once they discovered the beetles couldn't actually bite them.

Sean hadn't been present when Pastor Dan negotiated with the town of Abbot, but Brody filled him in on the negotiations later that evening when they met to spend the night in Beth Ann's now-vacant house. Apparently, Abbot wasn't so much of a town as a handful of houses and farms clustered around an untraveled intersection in the middle of the Allegheny Mountains. Their saving grace when the collapse occurred had been a large pig farm with over three thousand pigs. Unfortunately, their group, consisting of only forty men, women, and children, had a very hard time keeping the pigs fed in the commercial facility once the stored grain ran low. Brody said that they literally released over two thousand of them into the wild instead of watching them starve in captivity. There were already discussions from other town delegates on travelling to Abbot to trap any surviving pigs wandering around the neighboring forest.

Brody told Sean that Pastor Dan and the council hadn't negotiated for the pigs for their meat alone. Tionesta's rabbit operation was expanding and in another month would be in full swing. The pigs were going to be raised and butchered with an eye for the forty to fifty pounds of cooking lard each pig would produce. There were other ways to produce cooking oil, but most were labor intensive and required special machines like the Piteba oil press for rendering oil from nuts. Tionesta also considered trying to obtain some cows for churning their own butter but didn't have the equipment to do it on a large scale for the entire town. On a smaller scale, it was still a possibility. Cooking oil was a vital resource now and finding a self-replenishing oil resource was on the top of the town's list of needs. Sean wished that he'd known of Abbot's pig problem. He definitely would have tried to negotiate for a couple pigs for the North Homestead. Now they'd have to wait for the Brockway market day. While it was originally planned for the following month, the unanimous consent among the delegates was to schedule it only two weeks out. This way the agreed upon trades could be finalized and more trading could occur. Most of the delegations were starting to realize that by working together and each town focusing on what they were good at, life could become a lot easier for everyone.

Lying in the dark and listening to the breathy sleep of family members around him, Sean's head was spinning with ideas. His thoughts finally turned to transportation. Sean hoped that he and David could convince Colonel Harris to give them some fuel. The thought of walking to and from Tionesta on any regular basis was discouraging. Sean spent a few minutes thinking over ways that he might be able to convince Colonel Harris to help them out by providing some fuel from the refinery. It would be tricky and he'd have to be careful not to overplay their hand.

Just before dinner, David had written a message to Colonel Harris, requesting a meeting. The message had included new intel he'd received earlier in the day from his source in Washington D.C.. He'd never told Sean who it was, and Sean had never asked. But whoever the mole was, he or she seemed to be extremely close to the President's inner circle of advisors. Apparently, the government was abandoning the Green Zones. It would leave the American people to fend for themselves and most people had no idea how to do that. Sean knew that a lot of those people were going to starve to death because of the decision, even more than had died off the first winter. The East

Homestead, where Sean had lived for the first few months, was well tucked away and their group had avoided interactions with most people. He knew that, by having a plan in place, they had been spared the horrific living conditions of the big cities. Even still, when clearing the local farms around Mr. Andrews' retreat the week following his family's arrival, he'd seen enough bloated dead bodies to last a lifetime. Some had been chewed on by rats or other small animals that had made their way into the dead people's homes. It had been an awful experience. David said that his source had informed him the decision wasn't made lightly, but the logistics of feeding millions of starving people in the coastal cities had proven to be impossible.

The news made Sean angry. Anyone with a radio after the collapse had heard the President's voice over the last year: "Come to your local Green Zone if you need food or medical assistance." People had believed those messages. Desperate, they "needed" to believe in those messages! It was really horrific to think about how those people were fairing now, and Sean thanked God that his family was well away from those conditions. Now the President and Congress had fled D.C. to some underground bunker called Raven Rock and were planning to just ride out the storm. Sean couldn't say he was surprised—important government people and their families, eating well, hidden away in some fully-stocked bunker. He'd never expected to hear anything different. But having it confirmed by Willy made Sean furious. The "important and protected class of people" survived in relative ease, while the general population starved to death in a slow and painful way.

While in town for the market day, Sean had only caught a quick glance of the woman that had been brought in from the neighboring farm after the shootout with the Tionesta's scouting party. She was rail thin, and Sean thought she could have been one of the actresses from *Schindler's List*. That movie had made an impact on his innocent teenage mind. He couldn't understand how someone's body could continue to function when it looked like a breeze would blow it right over. He hadn't seen the woman's child, but Brody had assured him that the boy, while malnourished and thin, was in a lot better health than his mother, who would need months to recover. It wasn't hard to fathom where most of the family's precious calories had been going.

The country was in a weird place now. Some starving person might kill you over a bag of hard pretzels, yet not eat a single one of them. Average, everyday people committed horrible acts of violence toward each other, and most of it was committed out of love for someone else, such as to feed a starving family member. It was a strange dichotomy.

It hadn't just been city people that had been affected. The small town country folk had become just as vicious and deadly when they began to starve. The night before, when Willy had stopped by Beth Ann's house in town to talk to David some more, he had been asked by Brody for stories on things he'd seen during his travels. Willy's face grew somber at the question, but he eventually relented to Brody's desire for more information on the outside world. Sean wished that he hadn't listened in to the stories.

Just a month prior, Willy had approached a man who was camped out along the side of the road. Typically, Willy always avoided such people, but the older man had been crying profusely as Willy watched him from a distance. Out of an intense curiosity about the man, he had made his silent approach and taken the man by surprise. After a few uncomfortable minutes of extreme suspicion on both sides, the man finally opened up when Willy offered him some vegetables from his pack. The man was clearly starving to death, but had been lucky enough to kill a raccoon which hung on a spit over the open fire. After an hour of general conversation, the man shared his story.

The man and his family had been on vacation and visiting his brother's family in Albuquerque, New Mexico, when the EMP hit. With the city's infrastructure quickly shutting down, and knowing that survival in the desert was nearly impossible, he'd convinced his immediate family to flee back to Vermont where they had some extra canned food in their basement. His brother and sister-in-law had insisted that it would all blow over and they were going to stay in Albuquerque where "there were more resources." They were likely long dead by then, the man surmised. Over the last winter, his family had been taken in by two different groups on their hike back home to Vermont. Both of the groups had eventually been over-run by larger groups and his wife had been killed by a stray bullet in the last attack. He and his son had continued on, desperately trying to make it home.

Mid-summer, his son had somehow scratched his leg and the wound grew infected. Malnourished and sick already, the boy hadn't stood a chance. The man told how he'd held his son along the side of the road while he died. After retelling the story, the man began to cry uncontrollably again. When he'd finally been able to speak, he confessed to Willy that it wasn't a raccoon on the spit. It was their family dog that had recently grown sick and he suspected worms were the culprit. Nearly starved to death himself, the man couldn't stomach watching his dog die the slow death any longer. He'd been carrying it for two days and just didn't have any strength left. His dog was the last piece of his family and he'd killed it just before Willy arrived. The man was totally broken. Willy told the man that he might be able to get him to a safe location if the man was willing to work for food, but the man flatly refused. All he kept saying was that he "needed to get back home." Willy spoke with the man for a short time longer, but when the man walked to the edge of the woods to relieve himself, Willy snuck away. Willy said he'd left the man most of his food.

That wasn't even the worst or most graphic story Willy had told, but it had been the one that stuck out the most in Sean's mind…probably because the man had a wife and son. That could have easily been his own family in different circumstances. Sean was glad that he'd read the signs before the collapse and prepared with his friends as best they could. At the same time, he also knew their survival had more to do with God's protection over the last year than his own preparations beforehand. Sean tried to think back to how many gunfights he'd been in over the last eleven months and how many bullets had been fired in his direction. It really was a miracle that he, his family, and most of his relatives were still alive today.

Willy told them stories of a dozen small farmsteads that he'd befriended on his various routes. Sean was surprised to hear about how few had made it through the winter. Willy snorted at Sean's surprise. "All the country people thought they could survive because they grew a garden each year and kept a few chickens, but they were wrong. Very few of them had the real knowledge and experience to make it without prior provisions," Willy had stated flatly. Their "country skills" still needed electricity and supplies bought from stores to function. Only a few of the 'real' homesteaders had made it through and not been found or overrun by the golden horde of refugees fleeing the big cities in the months following the collapse. At one point, Brody asked how many homesteads were still thriving. "Thirty-seven," Willy answered without hesitating, though most of them he only observed from a distance. Most were actively starving and he knew he couldn't trust desperate people.

"Wait. Only thirty-seven farms in all of north central, PA?" Brody had asked, shocked.

Willy only shook his head. He feared that most wouldn't make it through the next winter without serious outside help. A lot of them had grown crops by hand, but not nearly enough to make it through a long winter. They just didn't understand how much food they actually ate on a daily basis. He anticipated that a lot of people would be down to eating nothing but potatoes by February. Fortunately for them, there were now small towns or groups of people in the area that might be able to take them in and help them if things grew dire over a long winter. When asked of the towns, Willy told them that he only knew of three small towns that had survived the winter: Kane, Tionesta, and Brockway.

"Hold on," Sean had cut in. "Weren't there representatives from at least eight or nine towns there tonight?"

Willy shook his head again. "Most of those groups don't live in the actual towns; that's just the nearest village that they identify with." Other than the three towns he'd mentioned and Abbot, if you could even call that a town, all the mountain towns had failed to pull through. Sure, there might be a starving family or two still hidden away somewhere in each town, but they were barely hanging on in most cases. Willy did offer one positive point when he shared how the roads had grown safer over the last couple months. With very little refugee traffic anymore, the locals relying on ambushes for survival had either starved to death or moved out of the area to busier thoroughfares that might have more travelers. That was his theory at least. "Don't get me wrong," he'd said. "The road is still plenty treacherous and there are still groups laying ambush out there, but luckily those same groups like to sleep as well, and only a couple operate at night." Willy mentioned that he'd given the ambush locations he knew of to Colonel Harris, who'd promise to deal with the offenders in due time. Sean wondered when Willy had spoken with the Colonel and what they'd discussed. The last time he'd seen them together, the day Willy had shown up in town, there had been serious fireworks between the two of them.

"Sean…."

Sean's whole body jolted at his name being whispered in the darkness. James immediately let out a whimper which in turn was likely going to wake Maria. *Crap!* he thought to himself. Sean looked around the tight enclosure of hanging sheets that made up their room. Had he imagined someone whispering his name? He *had* been half asleep.

"Sean!" This time he was sure he heard it and it was said with more urgency. His cousin Danny was on the other side of the sheet that acted as a door to their portion.

"Yeah, come on in," Sean whispered back. He wasn't sure if Danny had heard him or not over Jacob's fussing. It was pitch black; Sean sensed more than saw his cousin pull the sheet aside.

"Sean, the LP/OP just radioed. Three men on bicycles are headed in this direction. What do you want me to do?" his cousin whispered.

Sean leapt out of bed, climbing unceremoniously over his startled wife and child. James was crying loudly now.

"What's going on?" Maria asked in a groggy voice, wiping sleep from her eyes with one hand and rubbing Jacob's chest with the other, trying unsuccessfully to console him.

"Get everyone up!" Sean instructed his cousin in a sharp whisper. "You know the drill."

"But it's just three guys," Danny responded. "We don't even know if they're headed here for sure yet."

"When's the last time we've seen refugees travelling through the area? Let alone down our actual street? Where else would they be going? Hurry up!" Sean insisted. He fumbled around on the floor for his flashlight which he'd knocked off the nightstand in his haste to grab it. "Hurry up!" Sean said turning to Maria, who scrambled out of their bed into the darkness. A light flicked on somewhere else in the basement, giving Sean just enough illumination to find his flashlight which had rolled halfway under the bed. He clicked it on and set it back on the nightstand pointed at the ceiling. Sean could hear Danny's voice saying "Code Orange, Code Orange!" as he wound his way through the corridors of hanging sheets in the basement. He could hear the others quickly hustling out of bed and getting dressed. Sean pulled his pants on and threw his plate carrier over his head not even bothering to clip it. He slung his Assault pack over his shoulder and quickly slid his newer Bravo Company AR out from under the bed. He grabbed a full magazine from the cluttered nightstand and drove it home into the mag well. He would wait to chamber the weapon until he reached the stairs to the attic watch location.

"Wait for me!" Maria whispered harshly as Sean made to leave.

"I can't, Babe. Finish getting dressed and give James to my mom like before. Help get everyone organized and meet me upstairs when you're done."

Sean saw Maria frown in the dim light reflecting off the ten-foot ceiling in the basement. "They know what to do," she insisted. "Once I get James dressed and give him to your mother, I'm coming with you."

"Fine," Sean said, not having time to argue. He turned again but Maria grabbed him by the arm this time.

"You better be there when I get up there," she whispered forcibly. "Don't go running off anywhere without me. We're a team, remember?"

Sean looked down at his son, crying on the bed, before turning back to Maria and giving her a nod. She gave a tug on his arm and he bent down, giving her a quick kiss. He turned and hustled out of the basement. As he reached the top of the basement stairwell, he clicked off his flashlight and slowed his pace, working his way through the dark main floor by feeling. It was vital to maintain light and sound discipline with possible threats approaching the cabin. It shouldn't be long before the women and children, as well as a few of the men, were holed up in the underground storage room with their bug out packs. Under a Code Orange, they would just wait there until further notice. In a worst-case scenario, they could flee through the long escape tunnel that Sean and Brody had explored when they first moved in. The escape tunnel ended in a small room with some extra supplies and exited into the woods outside the homestead's perimeter fence. Some fast-growing Dawn Redwood trees had been strategically planted by Mr. Andrews around the escape hatch which allowed someone to come up above ground and not be seen from the cabin.

"What's going on?" Sean heard his Uncle Lawrence whisper from somewhere in the darkness off to his right.

"Code Orange," Sean whispered back, while maintaining his slow movements toward the steps leading upstairs. "LP/OP radioed three men approaching on bicycles."

"Okay," Uncle Lawrence said calmly. Sean heard his soft footsteps headed back down the dark hallway leading to the first-floor bedroom he shared with his two sons, Jackson and Bug.

Sean hurried up the two flights of stairs to the third floor where he found his older sister, Faith, and her husband on watch. His sister held one of the PVS-14s to her eye studying the front gate, while Sean's brother-in-law, Tyler, slowly moved about the large attic space, checking the other three directions.

"Anything?" Sean asked as he entered.

"No sign of them yet," Tyler whispered.

"Shouldn't they have been to the gate by now?" his sister added in a concerned whisper, not taking her eye off the night vision monocular.

"They're probably out there," Sean suspected. "I'm guessing they are watching you, watching out for them." That was the one big drawback to night vision devices. If you stayed still, you were hard to see at a distance. Sean bent down and approached his sister's position at the open window, gently tapping her on the shoulder. "Hey, Sis. You need to back away from the window. Any of the ambient light from the moon, even when overcast, is going to highlight you that close to the open window. If you stay back a few feet, you'll be harder to see." Sean frowned to himself. That was something he had shared with most of the others, but he must not have shared it with his own sister.

"Who's on roving patrol?" Sean asked to no one in particular.

"Randy is," Tyler answered.

"I assume you let him know about the threat?"

"Yeah, Danny radioed him before he went down to wake you," Faith answered her brother while she tried to find an effective body position to see the front gate with the PVS-14 after backing away from the window a few feet.

"Good. Do you know where Randy went or what he's planning?"

"He said he is going to circle around to the north and take a peek at the neighboring farm to see if they stop there," Danny answered as he entered the attic room and came up behind Sean. "He said to let him know if anyone approached the gates and he'd work his way back toward us so we have someone at their back." Danny walked over to Tyler and took the small binoculars from him. Tyler made his way toward the steps downstairs, passing Sean's father on his way up. As usual, David sat at the radio desk in the corner of the attic room, his blankets strewn about him on the floor. Likely he'd jumped out of his bed at the first sound of trouble. He would typically sit at the desk all day with his headphones on, but the headphones were lying on the desk now and he was fiddling with the scanner. A handheld radio sitting nearby was set to "Scan." David used all three to hopefully pick up any radio transmissions of looters nearby before they were on the retreat's doorstep. Any bit of advanced warning to a threat approaching them was vital.

Sean whispered to David. "Have you radioed Warren yet?"

"Yes," David whispered back. "I gave them a Code Orange and let them know we will update as things progress."

"Okay," Sean said.

There were two short clicks over the radio in Danny's hand. He quickly passed it over to Sean as he moved from the east window to the west window, scanning for the approaching threats. Sean's father had taken position at the south window now. Sean pressed the mic key on the radio twice in response.

A garbled message came over the walkie, but Sean couldn't understand what had been said. Randy was obviously trying to whisper into his handheld's microphone. Sean was about to respond with a "repeat" request, but he looked to David first. David just shrugged his shoulders and raised a finger at him to "wait." He rifled through a desk drawer, pulled out an adapter and plugged his large ham radio headphones into the small handheld on his desk. He motioned for Sean to continue.

Sean keyed the mic and spoke slowly into the radio. "Repeat…last."

There was a pause and then another garbled message. Sean was reluctant to turn the speaker up too high on the handheld for fear that the sound might escape through the open windows. "Where are the damn earbuds that were supposed to be kept with this radio?" he cursed, looking around in the dark. Sean saw David's dark figure wave him over and he approached, bending his ear down close to David's face.

"Randy said, 'There's no sign of them at the farm,'" David whispered.

"Okay," Sean answered, rubbing his chin. He keyed the mic once more. "Roger. Sit tight for now." Two clicks of the mic quickly followed.

"Someone is coming down the street toward the gate," Faith whispered sharply.

Sean hustled over to her position. She handed him the PVS-14 and backed away from the window. He suddenly remembered that with all the conversation, he hadn't chambered a round into his rifle. He slowly pulled the charging handle back and then let it gently slide forward. Wedging the rifle between his knees and holding the PVS-14 to his eye, he slightly pulled back on the charging handle, ensuring there was a round was in the chamber. Sean slowly and quietly rode the charging handle home with a click. He gave a tap to the forward assist to ensure the rifle was fully in battery. Last, he ensured his safety was on before attaching the night vision monocular to the quad rail behind his Aimpoint PRO red dot.

Sean raised the rifle and peered through the green haze of the night vision monocular. The red dot was glaring back at him through the PVS-14, so he quickly reached up, turning it down as low as it would go. It took him a moment before he caught the movement on the road. A man was pushing a bicycle with his right hand and holding a stick with his left. At the end of the stick, an improvised white flag bobbed back and forth in tune with his steady stride. Sean slowly turned the focus knob on the night vision monocular trying to pick out more details, but at over 100 yards that was asking a lot from the second generation device. Sean couldn't be sure, but he was fairly confident the man had a battle rifle of some sort slung across his chest.

Sean followed the man's approach while whispering to the others. "He's holding a white flag and heading straight for the gate. David, radio Randy and let him know we have one bogey approaching the gate and two unaccounted for. He should probably start making his way back in this direction. But, be sure to tell him to keep an eye out for the two we can't put eyes on."

"Okay," David answered.

"Faith, can you head downstairs and let the others know what's going on? Upgrade to Code Red and make sure everyone is taking their proper positions." His sister didn't respond, but Sean heard her soft slippered steps as she made her way down the stairs. Sean could hear her whispering to someone in the stairwell and a moment later Sean heard more feet, this time coming up the steps. The upstairs attic room was growing crowded.

Uncle Lawrence's voice came from behind him. "Bug and Jackson are covering the front and back doors. Your brother is in the tunnel watching the stairs leading up to the barn entrance. Nathan is moving throughout the first floor ensuring all the windows are closed and locked. Where would you like me?" his uncle asked.

"What weapon do you have on you now?" Sean asked, not taking his eye off the man who had almost reached the gate now.

"Both," his uncle responded. "I have my deer rifle and my AR."

"Good," Sean responded. "For now, take the east or west window, whichever one Danny isn't at. We're trying to locate his two friends." He sighed. "I have a feeling I'm going to have to go down and talk to that guy in person. Uncle Lawrence, I want you and your .270 watching my back."

"You got it," his uncle responded over Sean's left shoulder as he made his way to the west window.

Sean watched as the man reached the front gate and slowly leaned his bicycle against the chain link fence. He continued to hold and wave the flag in his one hand, keeping his movements slow. He obviously knew they were inside and was trying to portray himself as non-threatening. "Could this be someone from town?" Sean wondered. Surely, they would have followed protocol and radioed ahead first. It surely didn't look like anyone from Derrick's group down the road. His clothing and stance looked much more…militaristic. And the three of them had ridden bicycles from the opposite direction as Derrick's group. "It couldn't be soldiers from Warren. Could it?" Sean's mind worked through the scenario. No, Colonel Harris would have definitely radioed ahead to let them know they were coming. Sean wracked his brain trying to think of anyone else who might know where their retreat was located and still be a friend. The man waited patiently for a moment before reaching up and smacking the chain link fence in a knocking fashion. In the perfectly quiet night, the fence's rattle seemed extraordinarily loud.

"Crap," Sean muttered. "I'm going to have to go down there and talk to this guy." Sean glanced around the attic behind him. Maria still hadn't joined them in the attic.

Chapter 20

Lieutenant Colonel Harris fumbled groggily through his dark office when his big toe decided that he needed to know exactly where the corner of his filing cabinet was located. Bruce cursed as he scrambled and reached for the nearest chair. His knee found the chair before his hand. He cursed again, grabbing at his knee this time. Bruce flopped down on one of the upholstered chairs in his office, rubbing his bruised knee and throbbing toe in turns. He let out a long yawn, trying to clear the cobwebs from his sleepy brain. Leaning forward in the chair, he reached for the lantern that he kept on the front corner of his desk. It wasn't there. He continued to rub his knee as he cursed his orderly. "How many times have I told tell him not to clean my desk?" Bruce stood and leaned over his desk, feeling around for the old kerosene lantern. He kept his movements slow so that he wouldn't bump into it and tip it over.

When he finally determined the lamp wasn't anywhere on his desk, Bruce sat back down in the same chair and reached around the floor for his boots that he'd dropped upon stubbing his toe. His hands felt the smooth black leather of the well-polished Bates boots; he snatched them up and pulled them onto his feet. He didn't tie them, but instead tucked the laces down inside the boots, making a slightly uncomfortable bulge against his ankle bone. He wasn't going to wander around in the dark anymore without the boots…even if he hadn't put pants on yet.

Bruce walked back the long hallway toward his room. The Warren State Hospital was everything that typified what he imagined a psychological-hospital-turned-juvenile-detention facility would look like—white walls and floors with nary a picture or decoration to be found in the building. Luckily, the whiteness provided a small semblance of ambient light, allowing one to walk the halls in near darkness and not run into anything. Bruce made a right turn at the end of the hall. One, two, three doors on his right and Bruce opened the heavy, high-security latch of his windowless room, stepping into pitch black once more. One, two paces and Bruce reached down to find the edge of his bed. He followed the bed to his nightstand where he'd left his flashlight earlier, not wanting to use its precious batteries needlessly, and not expecting his office lantern to come up missing.

Colonel Harris clicked the tail cap. The super bright light emitted caused him to turn his head to the side and squint his eyes. He quickly clicked the tail cap four more times until the flashlight was on its lowest mode, then hurried back to his office. When he walked in the door, his left hand instinctively reached out and flicked on the light switch. The rectangular fluorescent light on the ceiling flickered a few times before springing to life. Bruce couldn't help himself as he started to laugh, nearly hysterical.

It was the middle of the night and he was out of his routine. He typically awoke at daybreak when there wasn't a need to use his office lights. His brain had automatically followed its new post-EMP routine. But…, electricity! It was a surreal and almost magical experience to be able to flip a switch and have light flood an entire room. A few months ago, the idea of doing that would have seemed a million years away. Bruce walked over and sat at his desk. He rubbed his eyes once and gave his head a good shake. "Okay, what am I doing?" Bruce said aloud to himself as he looked up at the wall clock. It was three in the morning.

Colonel Harris had been awakened by one of his radio men when he'd received a coded radio transmission from Mayor Reese. The radio man didn't know what it meant; he only knew that if he ever received the specific code word, he was to report it to the Colonel immediately. It wasn't exactly an emergency, but it meant that there would be an urgent message for Bruce hidden in the usual spot off Rt. 62 from the mayor who now lived incognito as "David." Bruce had immediately dispatched Sgt. Timms on one of the new electric motorcycles to retrieve the message. Too curious about the message's contents to be able to fall back asleep, Bruce would wait in his office for Sgt. Timms' return. It shouldn't take him long to run down there and back. Bruce clicked his pen anxiously.

Electricity in Warren had finally been restored three weeks prior, and the United Refinery facility had been operational for a full week as it hadn't been nearly as difficult to get it operational as they'd expected. It was an older facility and had not been fully modernized like the bigger refining facilities along the Gulf Coast. The part of the operation that had proven the most time consuming was tracing the origin of the pipeline leading into the facility and restoring electricity to the various pumping stations along the pipeline's length. Even now, Bruce could hear the low thrum of the refinery through the closed window in his office that had been painted with numerous coats of thick black paint. For now, the facility had been repaired to strictly produce standard diesel fuel. They needed to replenish the American military force's diminished fuel reserves first. His engineers had informed him they would soon begin producing a small amount of regular gasoline with the possibility of producing jet fuel in the future. The United States, if you could even refer to it as that anymore, was relying on NATO fuel deliveries to keep the American planes in the air. While there wasn't a need for the more volatile fuel in the near term, headquarters wanted to have the ability to produce it CONUS if a break in the supply chain ever occurred. Another team of "experts" would be arriving in the next day or two to see if jet fuel would be possible at the small refinery.

General Duncan's trip had been a relative success and, as promised, Bruce's food deliveries had recently grown even larger than before the cutback. Fulfilling his mission to produce electricity and fuel in Warren had seemed to open the floodgates from Headquarters. They flew him everything that he wanted for his men, and more. Even everyday creature comforts like coffee had started arriving in the last delivery without Bruce requesting it. In the past three weeks, Bruce hadn't lost a single man to desertion. It had been a long time since that had happened. Three square meals a day wasn't something his men were going to leave behind. Before being stationed here, they had worked the Green Zones and knew what awaited them outside of Warren.

Bruce wondered if he'd shared too much with General Duncan during his stay. He hadn't told the general anything specific, but he'd shared some of his concerns and doubts about the long-term stability and viability of the government and what that could mean for his troops if food shipments started to slow again. Bruce regretted that conversation until two men from the Penn State Agricultural Extension had shown up on the last cargo plane. The men had been sent to replace the help they'd been getting from Tionesta and Kane's gardening teams. With the electricity and refinery functioning now, there was no way to bring in the gardening experts from the two neighboring towns and risk word escaping of electricity and fuel in Warren. While General Duncan had said that he didn't fully understand the need himself, he knew that Bruce wanted to train his men to become more self-sufficient for the future. Duncan had sent the men in secret with a letter to Bruce not to mention the gesture on any of their calls. He'd also included a cryptic message that he was doing some digging on the person that Bruce had asked about during his stay. Bruce could only assume that he meant General Oates, but anytime he had brought up the mysterious general or tried to ferret out any details about his knowledge on the general's background, he had been told firmly to "Let it be!" and "Don't make waves!" Now General Duncan was "doing some digging" into the general and Bruce couldn't be sure if that was a good thing or a bad thing. Either way, it was risky.

One of the things Bruce hadn't discussed with General Duncan was his desire to build on and improve relationships with the neighboring towns. With word on how dysfunctional the government had grown, it served to reinforce Bruce's skepticism about the long-term continuity of the government and his desire to make the 31st Regiment self-sufficient. If he were to accomplish that, he would eventually need cooperation from the local towns. With the rugged individualist temperament of the locals in these small mountain towns and their suspicion of anything government, he would need to develop strong bonds with them long before ever seeking their aid in the future. Aside from that, Bruce also knew that he and Sammy might be forced to flee at some point if General Oates ever sniffed out what had become of Lt. Jenkins. With the cache of supplies they had put together in town, they would have enough food to stay hidden for a while, but eventually they would need someone to take them in.

Bruce also thought back to his meeting with Willy a few days before the electricity had been restored in Warren. It had been a long meeting, and by the end Bruce felt as if he'd rucked twenty miles. The meeting had started out quite strained with Willy still very suspicious of the Colonel. Even though they'd parted the Tionesta council meeting on relatively good terms, the friction between them during that meeting had clearly carried over. Even though Bruce had acquired everything on Willy's list of demands, the distrusting man was still very hesitant to share the information and intel he'd gathered over the course of his travels the past year. Willy had spent the first hour grilling Bruce over his motives and intentions for seeking the information. He'd obviously developed some deep bonds with the small towns he visited and was concerned for their safety.

Bruce shared his desire to help the small towns and groups by offering to clear out the remaining groups that were threatening or attacking them. While most of the towns were quite distant and too far for a quick response force, Bruce still offered aid in the future. He explained that there would need to be further discussions directly with the towns' mayors on the logistics. He couldn't just blindly send his men into a gunfight with no idea who was friend or foe. In the meantime, Bruce had offered to show his willingness to help Willy by clearing some of the ambush locations along his route. In the last three weeks, Bruce's men had utterly destroyed two ambush groups and forced another one completely out of the area.

Once Bruce had gained a certain level of the strange man's trust during their meeting, Willy had produced four notebooks and various maps of the surrounding areas. Most of his maps and notes used codes so anyone stumbling across them wouldn't be able to read or decipher his markings. Bruce had been surprised at the use of cyphers and the level of detailed notes Willy kept. He even had notes on abandoned homes and farms along his route. The man was so quirky and couldn't seem to focus on a single item longer than a few minutes, yet he kept detailed notes and coded maps. By the end, Bruce knew that he'd clearly underestimated the man on their first meeting. The one item Willy wouldn't share was the precise location of the surviving groups he knew, and Bruce didn't push the point. Willy eventually drove away on his new electric motorcycle, leaving a faint trail of lady's perfume behind him. Bruce couldn't help but smile over the memory.

Bruce also had a good conversation with Tionesta's mayor the previous day over the radio, who told him how successful the town's market day had been. If Bruce had known how many people and towns would show up, he would have made it a priority to attend. He'd also learned that the next town gathering was to be held in a village called Brockway. Bruce politely offered Pastor Dan the use of their busses and an armed escort for their trip. His only request had been permission to meet with the rest of the mayors after the Brockway swap meet as Pastor Dan's guest, and the mayor had gladly accepted. Bruce even offered his men to provide security around the town during the market day if Brockway requested it. If not, he would gladly station his men a few miles from the town until the Tionestans were ready to return. He was glad to see the various survivors in the area starting to work together, and he realized that it likely wouldn't have happened without Willy's assistance. Now, if only Bruce could offer the locals his aid in some other way and earn more of their trust.

Bruce stood and stretched his legs, yawning. He wandered over to a small, walnut-stained table in the corner of his office and cracked the lid on the small plastic tub of Folgers, drawing in a long whiff. He grabbed the gallon-milk-carton-turned-water-jug and filled the coffee pot's reservoir until it held four cups. Sgt. Timms should be returning shortly and Bruce was sure he would appreciate a cup. The faded white coffee pot was clearly quite old, bearing brown coffee stains down both of its sides, but Bruce didn't care what it looked like. The thing brewed a good cup of joe and had been another gift from General Duncan when the first shipment of coffee had arrived.

Bruce tapped his fingers on the top of the brewer as the coffee's aroma filled the room. He willed it to brew faster. While he waited, Bruce considered the newest arrivals to Warren the day before. A team of Navy Seals had suddenly shown up at the gates in two up-armored Humvees. They arrived with no warning or any kind of "heads up" from Headquarters. At the checkpoint, they had requested to immediately speak with Colonel Harris by name. Normally he would have sent Sammy or Shifty to find out what was going on, but Bruce had been glad to cancel the laborious mid-afternoon meeting he'd been having with the engineers.

Upon reaching the checkpoint, Bruce had been introduced to a tall and lanky lieutenant who'd been waiting patiently while leaning against the brush guard of the lead Humvee. His Multicam pants were covered in dirt and grime and his battle shirt was thoroughly covered with powdery white streaks of dried sweat. Bruce approached the LT who stood and gave Bruce a short salute before handing over a letter he pulled from beneath his plate carrier.

While Bruce unfolded the wrinkled and sweat-stained paper, the man introduced himself in a deep baritone voice. "Hello, Colonel Harris. My name is Lieutenant Baier, Second Platoon, Team Four, Navy Special Warfare Group. You'll find those orders instruct you to aid us on our mission and offer resupply before we head back out."

Bruce didn't respond. He scanned down the letter, finding it a properly formatted set of orders from headquarters. Before reading it in its entirety, his eyes slid down to the signature block, signed by none other than one "General Norman Oates." Bruce had nearly sworn out loud at seeing General Oates' name but forced himself to keep his emotions in check. He had carefully read down through the orders looking for anything out of the ordinary or for any specific details on what "type" of aid he was required to give these men. He hadn't found any. It was short and to the point. Colonel Harris was once again supposed to give aid and assistance to someone he'd never met, someone who was most likely a spy or agent working directly for General Oates. Bruce's stomach churned at the thought, and he felt an invisible noose tightening around his neck.

Bruce's orders from General Duncan had been crystal clear: no one, not even uniformed military personnel, were to be permitted anywhere near Warren. Headquarters insisted that the electricity and refinery operation in Warren were to be kept secret. Direct orders from headquarters would be needed to get through their checkpoints, which had been moved further out from town now that the noisy refinery was in operation.

"What's your mission, Soldier?" Bruce asked in his most commanding voice yet keeping the edge from it.

"I'm sorry, sir. I can't discuss that with you," the Lieutenant responded bluntly.

Bruce thought through his options for a few moments before responding. "I'm sorry, but this is a highly secure facility, and I have very specific orders not to let anyone into the town for any reason. I would be happy to offer aid and resupply you and your men if you give me a list of things you need."

Lt. Baier let out a short sigh and then smiled. "Sir, I am well aware of your mission here. I know all about the electricity and oil refinery you are operating. I have specific orders to follow. My men and I need to be bunked in one of the houses in town well away from where your own men are billeted. Preferably, we could use a place with a secure basement and electricity. Hot showers would be appreciated as well. We won't be staying for more than a few days and we'll keep to ourselves. We'll need privacy during our stay while we plan our next mission. Other than that, some food rations and a couple other small resupply items will be requested."

Bruce studied the LT, wondering how deep in General Oates' pocket the man was. He clearly had the bearing of a bona fide soldier, unlike Lt. Jenkins who'd looked and acted out of place in a military uniform. The LT held Bruce's intense gaze confidently, but not disrespectfully. He obviously wasn't one to be pushed around by Bruce's seniority.

"Very well," Bruce agreed. This wasn't a fight he was going to win. If he pushed his luck, General Oates would surely hear of it and grow even more suspicious of Bruce. He didn't need that. "We can find a private house to put you up in with a basement. Unfortunately, none of the houses in town have functioning electricity yet, but I can provide you the use of a generator if you like.

Lt. Baier frowned but nodded his head in understanding. "No generator needed, sir. We won't be here that long."

"Very well then," Bruce responded. "Just follow us."

"Thank you, Colonel," the lieutenant answered with another perfunctory salute before scrambling into his vehicle as if he were in a hurry to be somewhere. The convoy took them across the river via the Hickory Street Bridge; the south side of Warren was seldom entered by Bruce's men and only on their periodical patrols through the residential areas. Bruce took the Seal Team to a large nursing home off the tree-lined Pleasant Drive; the sign hanging askew by one nail announced "Warren Manor." When the 31st Regiment had first entered Warren, Bruce had ordered a team to thoroughly clean out the facility. He'd planned to eventually house some of his men there, but as of yet, it hadn't been put to use. After pulling under the porte-cochere of the historic building, Bruce offered to show the lieutenant around the building and help get his men situated. Lt. Baier politely refused.

"We'll figure it out," he said.

"Very well," Bruce answered. "If you need anything, please let the guards at the Hickory Bridge checkpoint know what you need and they'll radio me." One of the other reasons for bringing the Seal Team across the river was that they were forced to cross over one of the bridges to get to Bruce and his men would be able to give him a heads up.

The lieutenant just gave him a dismissive nod and turned to his men, signaling for them to dismount the two vehicles. Bruce climbed back into the passenger seat of his own vehicle and tapped on the metal dash twice. His driver navigated through the small parking lot full of dirty, abandoned vehicles. As they passed by the front entrance, Bruce had caught a glimpse of Lt. Baier's men dragging a bound and hooded man out of the lead Humvee.

Three shrill beeps from the coffee pot brought Bruce's attention back to the present, and he quickly poured himself a cup, adding the luxury of a little sugar and powdered creamer. He strode to his desk and sat down, fully awake now. He couldn't help but wonder who the Seals had captured and what they planned to do with the man. Bruce shook his head, not wanting to consider the interrogation methods that they might be employing. At the end of the day, Bruce decided that since he couldn't do anything about it, he couldn't afford to care. As long as General Oates' men stayed on their side of the river and didn't bother him or his men, they could do whatever they wanted. Bruce leaned back in his office chair, taking a long, slow drag of the hot liquid. He sighed in contentment.

The sound of boots hurrying up the steps outside his office made Bruce sit up in anticipation. After a light knock at his office door, Bruce set his coffee cup on his desk and said "Enter!" Sgt. Timms walked in stiffly, visibly shivering. He apparently hadn't dressed appropriately for the early morning ride. Bruce watched as the sergeant repeatedly flexed and balled his hands as he walked to the front of Bruce's desk and placed two ziplock baggies onto his desk. "He clearly didn't wear gloves either," Bruce thought to himself. Sgt. Timms took a step back, standing at parade rest.

"Relax Sergeant," Bruce offered. "How was your ride?"

Sgt. Timms wobbled his head. "It was alright, sir. It took a little bit of getting used to the torquey engine and riding a motorcycle that you can barely hear. It was a lot different than my old Soft Tail."

"I bet," Bruce chuckled. It had been a long time since Bruce had owned a motorcycle of his own. It was an old Honda CB900 with plenty of dings and dents, but on nice fall days, Bruce missed the exhilaration of driving the old country roads where he'd grown up. He decided to make it a point to give one of the new motorcycles a spin around town. "It looks like you might have been a little underdressed for the ride."

Sgt. Timms couldn't hide the embarrassment on his wind-reddened cheeks. "A little bit," he agreed with a humble smirk.

Bruce chuckled. "Well, I appreciate you heading down there for me on such short notice…in the middle of the night." Bruce pointed to the corner. "Would you care for a cup of coffee?"

Sgt. Timms turned to where Colonel Harris was pointing. "Honestly, sir, I could murder one."

"Good," Bruce said. "Grab any cup there except the red one and go to town. There's powdered creamer, as well, and sugar in the brown paper bag."

"Thank you again, sir," Sgt. Timms said as he set about pouring himself a cup.

"No problem. Once you're done, I'd like you to go wake up Major Samuelsson and ask him to meet me at my office immediately. Then I want you to hit the sack and get some sleep."

"Roger that, sir," Sgt. Timms said, stirring in some creamer before turning back to his commanding officer.

"That's all, Sergeant. Dismissed." Sgt. Timms turned for the door, both hands wrapped tightly around the warm ceramic coffee cup.

"And be sure to bring my mug back later," Bruce added with fake gruffness.

Sgt. Timms raised the mug toward the Colonel in acknowledgement before quietly pulling the door shut behind him. Bruce picked up his own cup and took another swallow. The sergeant was getting a little too comfortable with Colonel Harris lately. He hadn't even saluted on his way out. "Oh well," Bruce said to himself, turning back to the messages.

Bruce grabbed the two baggies and opened the one with the small piece of red tape on it. His eyes scanned the short note. "Sgt. Timms!" he hollered. "Get back here!"

Chapter 21

The tall man standing at the front gate that barred access to the North Homestead offered a polite, "Hey Sean," as Sean and Maria drew close. After discussing it among those in the attic watch room, a unanimous decision was made to meet with the man at the gate in person. They couldn't just leave him there all night, banging away at the chain link fence. He obviously wasn't going away. Sean had encountered Maria on his way down the steps and their long-standing disagreement of her putting herself in harm's way was rehashed in front of everyone. Maria insisted on joining him, and "no" wasn't having any effect on her.

Sean finally relented, and she donned one of the ceramic plate carriers found in the hidden storage room at the end of the escape tunnel. Jackson, who'd been wearing it while guarding the front door, had graciously passed it over upon request, knowing the danger they faced once they stepped through the front door. Sean tried to adjust it all the way down to fit her small build, but it still flopped on her as they made their way to the front gate. Per their discussion before walking out the front door, Maria followed Sean to a specific point, a few feet off to the right side of the man. This allowed his Uncle Lawrence a clear shot from the attic window if needed. Maria scanned the darkness in the direction of the road, and Sean turned his attention to man.

Even though they were only a few yards away now, Sean still hadn't answered the man's greeting. He studied the figure intently. The man was decked head-to-toe in Multicam with a Shemagh scarf draped around his neck, the front of it covered by a long beard. His sweat-stained khaki ball cap was pulled down tight, shadowing the man's face from the light of the moon. Most surprisingly, he stood almost a head taller than Sean's six feet, four inches. He looked the poster boy for a Special Operations soldier. An M4 with an Eotech optic hung low over top of his plate carrier and the rifle had been rattle-canned a Flat Dark Earth color. It bore numerous scrapes and scratches across its surface which were visible even in the dim light. That M4 had been well-used. Even though the stranger had used Sean's name in greeting, Sean was quite certain he'd never met the man before. This was clearly a dangerous man and Sean would have remembered meeting him.

The man turned his gaze up to the third-floor window of the attic, allowing the moonlight to briefly highlight his face. The matte black camo paint absorbed the light, making his facial features seem flat, almost two-dimensional. Only the whites of his eyes were readily visible. Sean was suddenly concerned for his wife. Where were the other two men that had travelled with him?

The man took his eyes off the window and turned back to Sean as he stopped his approach two paces away, his hand clenched around the grip of his Glock 19. "You don't know me, but I'm a friend of David's," the man began.

"We," Sean corrected him.

The man raised a blackened eyebrow at Sean questioningly.

"I know that you have two other men back there somewhere," Sean nodded toward the road.

The man sneered. He didn't seem near as anxious as Sean felt, and he didn't give any other outward response to Sean's revelation that he knew the man wasn't alone.

"Son, I've got a lot more than two men back there," he said with a smile. "You guys really need to consider changing the privacy code you're using on your handhelds. We heard you talking to your man watching the farmstead up the road." The man's own revelation shocked Sean, and he tried to remain as calm as he could. He probably wasn't doing a very good job. It was beginning to feel like a competition to see who knew more intel than the other.

The stranger seemed to read Sean's thoughts. "My men and I don't mean any harm to you or your family. I just need—" he broke off suddenly, raising his finger and pressing it to his ear. He was getting a radio transmission from one of his other men, Sean surmised. The man let go of his earpiece and keyed a mic on his lapel. "Copy that." He gave a long audible sigh and turned to Sean. "Please, radio your man down the road and tell him to stop approaching us from the rear. I really don't like having guns pointed at my back."

Sean was sure he didn't hide the surprise and concern from his face that time. They had spotted Randy and likely had him in their crosshairs. Spotting Randy was no small feat. He was nearly as accomplished as Sean at moving quietly through the woods at night.

"Seriously, Sean. I'm here with an urgent message for Mayor Reese and, by default, your family. I need to speak with him immediately, but not before you radio your man to stop his approach." His tone held a note of urgency to it.

Sean slowly pulled the radio from his pocket and keyed the mic. "Randy, hold tight and take cover. You've been spotted. Everyone else beware, they are listening in on our frequency." Sean said the last defiantly as he looked the man dead in the eye. The man nodded at Sean reassuringly. "Randy did you copy that?" Sean radioed once more. Randy didn't answer but Sean's handheld clicked twice in response.

"Very well," the man said as he nodded. Sean hadn't explained to him what the two clicks meant. He'd just seemed to know. The man's confidence was evidence that he knew he was in control of the situation. "Now, can you please ask David to come down here?"

"There's no David living here, mister. I think you're—"

"Really?" the man cut him off with sarcasm. "Then who's that?" he asked, poking his gloved finger through the chain link fence and pointing over Sean's shoulder.

Sean turned to look where the man was pointing. "What the hell?" he thought to himself as he watched David walking briskly toward them. They stood in silence while David approached them at a brisk walk. Sean stole a glance in Maria's direction. She stood resolute, and didn't look near as nervous as Sean felt.

David strode directly up to the fence and reached through the gap between the gate's edge and the metal pole next to it, shaking the man's hand. "Good thing I asked to take a peek through the night vision monocular. I wasn't quite sure until Sean stood next to you, and then I thought to myself, 'Hey—I know that monstrosity of a man!'" David joked, producing a quick flash of a smile from the man. His white teeth stood out prominently in contrast to his blackened face. David motioned for the handheld in Sean's left hand and he gave it over without hesitation.

"Everyone can relax," he said through the radio, making no attempt to keep his voice low. "I know the men and they are friends of mine. Randy, you can make your way back to the front gate. Please use the road and don't confront any of our other friends that might be out there watching you. Lawrence, you can let those with you know to return to normal watch duties. Everyone else can get back to bed."

"Copy that," Randy's voice responded, followed by Lawrence. David handed the radio back to Sean.

"Good to see you, Mayor," the man offered in a deep gravelly voice.

"You, too, Lieutenant Aguilar. I was starting to worry about you guys after not hearing my broadcast last week." Sean suddenly knew who the man was. It was the leader of the Ranger team that had been sent out early that spring with Lt. Jenkins to kill David. It had been the first attempt on his life for transmitting his Freedom America broadcasts in opposition to the government's narrative while he was still acting Mayor for the nearby town of Kane. After working with Colonel Harris, and with the disappearance of Lt. Jenkins, this man and his platoon of Army Rangers had taken it upon themselves to travel around the nearby areas and find locations where they could still transmit David's pre-recorded Freedom America broadcasts each week.

"Yeah," the lieutenant began, "about that. We've kind of hit a snag there. A month ago, we found one of our broadcasting locations destroyed. Whoever it was, pulled down the tower and cut the antenna up into two-foot lengths. We were concerned but moved on to the second location and broadcasted. Shortly after that, we found that second location torn down as well. That only left us with three broadcasting locations left, and one of them involved a friendly family of survivors living at the location. We obviously had someone tailing us and we weren't going to lead them back there. So that left us with two locations. We figured, if whoever's tracking us has the ability to triangulate the exact broadcast location during one of your short thirty-minute recordings, we might have a serious problem on our hands. So, three weeks ago, we broadcast from location three and then watched over it for three days. No one showed up so we moved on. When we arrived at the fourth location last week, the tower there was destroyed as well. This time they left a note." He handed a small piece of paper through the fence.

David unfolded the piece of paper while Sean pulled out his small 20-lumen keychain light from his pocket and shined it over his shoulder. "To: Mayor Kendall Reese. Hello. You can run, but you cannot hide. It's just a matter of time until my dogs sniff you out from the dank hole you're hiding in and run you down. Run, rabbit, run!" It was signed, "The Boss."

"I see General Oates has finally adopted my nickname," David said dryly.

Lt. Aguilar shuffled his feet. "We're thinking it's probably about time to pack up and move on to another area altogether. The area that we've been patrolling down south of here is starting to get boring anyway. We've dealt with all the local threats and it's too quiet. We thought maybe we'd head a little north for a few weeks, and then we'd like to go somewhere warm before winter hits." The lieutenant smiled. "Somewhere with sandy beaches, Mai Tais, and girls in grass skirts." David nodded his understanding of what Lt. Aguilar was actually saying. "We'll swing by in another week and pick up any recordings you have then. We'll likely only get back here once or twice in November before heading south. So, if you want to let your listeners know your broadcast schedule is going to be bumped to once a month, that would be good, I guess." The Lieutenant seemed genuinely regretful about the situation. "I wanted to come in person and tell you the news myself."

David wore a look of dejection on his face. "Thank you for everything you've done for me and I understand why you need to leave. It just really sucks! Things around the country seem to be ramping up and I've got so much important intel to get out to the American people. Especially the news I just received yesterday." David briefly shared the news from his mole about the Green Zones being abandoned.

The lieutenant's eyes widened. "I'm not sure what to tell you, mayor. Continuing these broadcasts is getting too dangerous for my men. After our meeting with Colonel Harris, it sounds as if General Oates is more than willing to call in an airstrike against us instead of meeting us face-to-face. And based on that note he left you, they obviously believe it's you out there wandering around making the transmissions. That's good for both of us: your cover here is solid, and they don't know that we're still in the area. I'd be willing to put out one more brief transmission for you at location three to let your listeners know what's going on. That's assuming they haven't doubled back and destroyed that one since we left. After that, we need to let things die down a bit and relocate. If we are only broadcasting once a month, and from further out, it will take them more time to pinpoint our new location. In order to triangulate our signal, they need to have some personnel in the local area while we're actually broadcasting. By the time they figure it out, we'll have moved down south. We're still willing to transmit for you, but we need to hold off for a while, I think."

"Yeah, I understand." David rubbed his hands together. "But if you could transmit one last broadcast for—"

"Just a second," Sean cut it. "So, you've got someone, probably some serious bad guys sent by this General Oates, triangulating your transmissions. How do you know you didn't just lead them straight to us?"

Lt. Aguilar gave a small snort. "Sean, they're not tracking us. They're tracking the signal. As long as we aren't at a broadcast location when they show up, we're good. Even before this we only stayed at a location long enough to hook up the ham, play the broadcast, and get out of the area as soon as it was over. We've always assumed they would track the signal at some point." David nodded his head in agreement, affirming they'd discussed it in the past. "Besides, have a little faith in my men. We know how 'not' to be found." Sean frowned but nodded his acquiescence.

"But that also leads me to my next reason for stopping by in person, instead of just grabbing the tapes on our way through. We wanted to give you a heads up that we discovered a fairly sizeable motorcycle gang camped out alongside the road not far from here. Last week when we discovered the note at the broadcasting location, we immediately headed south, out of the area. We've been slowly working our way around in a big circle and came down past Titusville last night. We just wanted to be sure no one was following us." He gave a pointed look toward Sean before continuing. "The motorcycle gang doesn't seem to be trying to hide. They had multiple large campfires blazing like a Boys Scout's summer camp. We scoped them out for most of the night and throughout the next day. We estimate they've been camped there for at least a few days now. There's probably around two hundred of them. They keep regular patrols and have smaller groups that come and go at random times of the day and night. They're well-armed and well-provisioned with plenty of food and supplies. They're a rough lot, not too friendly looking." The Lieutenant seemed to consider his last comment before shrugging his shoulders and adding, "Then again, nobody's very friendly these days."

David looked to Sean. "You think that guy who showed up at the bridge in Tionesta is part of that group?"

"It would be a coincidence of gigantic proportions if he wasn't. That also flies in the face of him being part of a small group of men from a nearby town that was overrun."

"I should probably contact Colonel Harris. It's likely the same group he's been looking for the last couple weeks," David said to no one in particular. Sean wondered when he'd spoken to Colonel Harris about it and just assumed it must have been one of the messages they regularly sent to each other via a secret location at the bottom of the hill.

"I left my men to keep eyes on them for now. I just brought two of my men down here to give you a heads up. There's too many of them, and with those motorcycles, they're too mobile for us to engage. Maybe the Colonel can sort them out."

A jolt of panic stabbed Sean in the gut. "Wait a minute! You just said you came down through Titusville. Where exactly are these men camped out at?"

The tall figure returned Sean's concerned look. "Just outside of Pleasantville, off Rt. 27. Why?"

"What time is it?" Sean asked in panic, pulling his small flashlight from his pocket and shining it onto his watch. "Holy hell! It's 2:00

a.m.!" Sean turned to David. "We've gotta radio Tionesta and warn them to stop Willy!"

David cursed and turned back toward the cabin at a dead run, calling out over his shoulder as he ran. "Don't leave! I'm going to need more details from you and I need you to drop off a message for me at the bottom of the road!"

Randy suddenly appeared out of the dark behind the lieutenant. "What's all the shouting for?" he asked anxiously. Sean and Maria both jumped in surprise at Randy's large figure suddenly appearing in the darkness behind the lieutenant. Aguilar didn't budge, as if he knew Randy was walking up on them the entire time.

"We just heard about a large motorcycle gang camped out in Pleasantville," Maria answered. Sean reached into his pocket and grabbed his keys. He unlocked the gate and it swung on a wide creaking arc until it slammed into the grass with a jingly clank. Lt. Aguilar stepped through the gate on Randy's heals.

"Wow! Isn't that where Willy was heading tonight?" Randy exclaimed.

"Yeah," Maria answered. "David just went back to radio Tionesta and see if they can stop him before he leaves."

"Wait a second," Lt. Aguilar interjected. "Are you talking about Willy the 'Postman'?"

Sean looked at him, aghast. "You know him?"

Lt. Aguilar just chuckled. "I guess you could say that. We've had a few run-ins with him. It's turned into a bit of a game to see who spies who first." He shook his head. "Crazy old coot."

Randy snorted. "He certainly gets around."

Chapter 22

"I want ten MRAPs from First Platoon, led by Lt. LaPierre, to blow straight through any roadblock they may have in place. Per our last run in with this group, they'll likely let you pass right by. I don't expect them to start a fight and they'll likely assume we're just passing through like we did last time. Lieutenant, I want you to instruct your men not to fire unless they are fired upon." Colonel Harris leaned over the table in the conference room which had been covered with several different maps of the area. Across the table from him stood nearly a dozen officers and NCOs from Alpha and Charlie Companies. "If shots are fired, then by all means feel free to light them up. But I want your convoy to keep moving and continue heading north on route 36. When you reach the first intersection past their encampment, I want you to set up a roadblock similar to how you handled the farm assault earlier this spring. Your primary objective is to keep anyone from escaping the main assault force."

Bruce turned his attention to Captain Spears, who stood with his arms crossed and a serious look on his face. It was game time and Spears was obviously ready to smack someone. "Captain Spears, you and the rest of Alpha Company will be following a mile behind Lt. LaPierre's advance. As soon as you receive the radio transmission from LaPierre that their last truck is past the encampment, you're to haul ass in there and secure the area. I have no idea what the terrain will look like or what the situation on the ground will be, so I'm leaving it up to you to use your best judgement on how to proceed once you get there. Preferably, I'd like this to happen without shots fired. Use the loudspeaker on the lead truck and let this gang know that if they hold their fire, they won't be fired upon. I want intel on who they are and where they're from. That's going to be hard to do with a bunch of corpses. Be sure your men are clear on this point. Understood?"

Captain Spears frowned visibly but nodded his head.

"Okay then. Once you set up a secure perimeter around their encampment, Captain Zrucky will handle negotiations and disarm their group in an orderly fashion."

Captain Spears shook his head. "I can—"

"No!" Bruce interjected. "There's no discussion here, Spears. I want you strictly focused on internal and perimeter security."

Spears was obviously irritated at the news but nodded anyway with a "Yessir." He didn't so much as glance in Captain Zrucky's direction.

Bruce sighed. "Captain Zrucky, once the area is secure, you are to locate their leader and put him on the radio with me. I want to talk with this guy," Bruce said in an ominous tone.

There was a rap at the conference door. "Come in!" Bruce barked. He'd left specific instructions to his orderly that they weren't to be interrupted.

His orderly leaned his head into the room. "Sir, I'm sorry to disturb you, but you've got a call from HQ and they say it's urgent." When Colonel Harris didn't respond immediately, he continued. "I tried to take a message for you but they insisted."

Bruce clenched his jaw and turned back to his men. "Alright, everyone, take five. I'll be back shortly." He turned from the table and motioned for Sammy to follow. They walked briskly through the labyrinth of white hallways. Even though they'd spent a whole summer there, the halls all looked alike to Bruce. His orderly opened his office door and pointed to the satellite phone sitting on the center of his desk. As Bruce walked to the phone, he pointed to the wall locker in the corner of the room where his safe was located. Major Samuelsson went to the cabinet, opened it, and entered the combination. Bruce heard the latch-click of his office door announce the exit of his orderly.

Bruce stood staring at the phone for a few seconds before picking it up, sighing, and finally holding it to his ear. "This is Colonel Harris," he stated flatly.

"Please verify fourteen."

"Hold one." Bruce turned to Sammy. Only the bottom half of his body was visible. The upper third of his torso was bent forward, leaning into the wall locker. Bruce heard the snick of the locked safe being opened and Sammy rushed over to the desk, holding out a small yellow notecard. Bruce scrolled down the card until he found the fourteenth number.

"Charlie Echo Foxtrot Zulu Zulu."

"Copy that. Please hold a moment for General Oates." Bruce shook his head and silently mouthed "Oates" to Sammy, who frowned in response. Bruce took a seat behind his desk and Sammy followed suit, sitting down in his usual spot across from him.

"Colonel Harris?" The general didn't sound happy. Then again, Bruce couldn't remember a single time he'd actually seen or heard the general in a good mood.

"Yes, sir."

"Just what the hell do you think you're doing?"

"Sorry, sir?" Bruce asked, honestly unsure what the general was getting at.

"I didn't ask for a character reference, Colonel." Bruce rolled his eyes at the childish insult. The general continued. "How come every time something goes bump in the night, you feel the need to run off and get your men into a gunfight?"

Bruce wasn't sure what he should say or how he should respond to the rhetorical question. There were a few short moments of awkward silence before the general continued. "Well, Colonel? Let's have it!"

"I'm not trying to get my men into a fight, sir. I'm—"

"Of course you are!" General Oates retorted. "Why else would you radio General Duncan requesting permission to send an entire company of your men forty miles away to deal with a couple dozen bikers that haven't threatened you or your men in the least?" Again, Bruce didn't answer. "What is your mission there, Colonel Harris?"

"To secure the town of Warren and…"

"…and get the refinery up and running," General Oates finished for him. This was typical of how Bruce's conversations with the general would go: lots of rhetorical questions and consistently being cut off mid-sentence. Major Samuelsson could clearly see Bruce's blood starting to boil and Sammy gave him a questioning look. Bruce just shook his head.

"A motorcycle gang in Pleasantville has nothing to do with either of your missions!"

"I beg to differ, sir." It was Bruce who cut the general off this time. He was officially fed up with being talked over and constantly talked down to, regardless of the general's rank. "They're only thirty-six miles away from our current location. If—"

"Don't interrupt me again, Colonel!" The General's tone was ice and Bruce winced. "If you were to intercept that group of men, you risk one of them escaping and sending word back to…wherever, and spreading the word that there are soldiers stationed near Warren. People might start wondering what you're doing there. Whatever group they are a part of may send more scouts to the area to get answers. We don't need that problem. Thirty-six miles away might as well be thirty-six light years away in the scheme of things. They hold no immediate threat to your current mission."

Something the General had said earlier in the conversation sprung into his mind. "Sir, how can you be sure there are only a couple dozen men there? We believe there may be a lot more." Bruce hadn't given General Duncan any specific numbers on his earlier call when informing him of the situation. General Oates sure seemed to know more about this group of bikers than he was letting on.

"I'm confident in their numbers, Colonel," the General continued. "We've been tracking that group for quite some time now."

"General, if they aren't a threat, then why are you wasting resources tracking them? You seem to think they're part of a bigger group. Why would you assume they'd tell someone else about us? How do you know they aren't working alone?" General Oates didn't respond immediately, so Bruce continued. "And if I may be so bold, sir. Why wasn't I informed of this group before now if you've been tracking them? Hell, a month ago, they popped up only two miles north of Warren." Bruce saw Sammy palm his face and shake his head at Bruce's tone.

"You may not be so bold!" General Oates snapped. "I'll tell you what you need to know, when you need to know it. Those men have moved out of your area now and they aren't currently a threat to your mission. That's the end of it. You will not proceed with your plans to intercept them. Am I clear?"

"Crystal," Bruce replied coldly.

"If they get within your five-mile perimeter, then and only then, may you intercept them." The satphone was quiet for a long moment before the general continued. "And another thing. Your standard patrol is five miles. How exactly did you find out about this group thirty-six miles away?"

Bruce hadn't been prepared to answer that question. "We intercepted a radio transmission from Tionesta discussing the threat." Sammy looked shocked at Bruce's mention of Tionesta.

"I see." There was another long pause. "In the near future, you and I are going to have a discussion on the transmissions you are intercepting from the nearby towns." Bruce cringed at the thought. "For now, I've got a busy day and I have to go. I'm officially ordering you and your men to stand down and steer clear of this motorcycle gang. Do you copy that?"

"Roger that, sir."

"Very well. That's all I have." The satphone in Bruce's hand beeped once, signaling the end of the call.

"Hello?" Bruce called into the phone. "Hello?" There was no response. "Not much of a sign-off," Bruce thought to himself. He made sure to power down the satellite phone completely before turning to Sammy.

"So?" Sammy asked.

"So, we stand down," Bruce said bluntly with a shrug of his shoulders.

"How did General Oates even find out about your call with Duncan?"

"The hell if I know."

"You don't think General Duncan...." Sammy let the thought hang.

Bruce sighed. "I don't know." He thought about it for a moment. "No, Sammy, I don't think Duncan has anything to do with this. Maybe someone on his staff." Bruce shrugged his shoulders. He stood and stretched slowly. It was growing stuffy in the room. He walked over to the window and cracked the blackened window pane open slowly. The sun was coming up over the edge of the hillside to the east now and bathing the mostly abandoned town in an orange glow. Bruce opened both the windows wide and positioned a box fan in front to blow some fresh morning air into the room.

Sammy waited patiently in his chair until Bruce was done. "What now?" he asked when Bruce flopped back down into his chair.

"Now? Nothing," Bruce answered. "He gave me a direct order to keep clear of them. I'm going to need you to head back down to the conference room and cancel the op. Send everyone back to what they were doing."

Sammy stood, stretching himself. They'd both been up since the wee hours of the morning. Sammy yawned into his fist. "I'll let them know. At least we can go back to bed now."

Bruce let out a light snort in disagreement. He leaned back in the office chair as Sammy quietly shut the door behind him. After a few minutes, Bruce began to nod off and the office chair started to tip backwards. Bruce slammed awake as he grabbed his desk to stop his fall. The office chair pitched back and then violently forward with a hard thud of protest from the plastic wheels. He'd nearly fallen out of his chair. Bruce shook his head at his foolishness. In his haste to stop his fall, he'd knocked some of the papers off his desk and onto the floor. As he picked them up, he came across a sealed ziplok baggie. In his haste to muster his men after reading the first message from Mayor Reese, the one marked with the red "urgent" tape, he'd totally forgotten about the other message. Bruce turned the message over in his hands, trying to find the free edge of the clear tape. He eventually grew frustrated and pulled out his pocket knife to open it. Bruce started to read the letter which looked to have been hastily written.

Intel on Subject Zero (SZ) from a reliable source:

SZ was a college roommate of the President during their senior year of undergraduate at Yale. SZ wrote his senior thesis on human population planning which called for a universal one child per family limit and called for government-funded research grants to study the viability of forced sterilization in certain third world countries. Most of SZ's military records are sealed. SZ was promoted heavily during the Clinton administration. After retirement from active military in early 2006, SZ was hired by and worked at no less than four organizations under the Open Society Policy Center run by George Soros. SZ eventually settled in on the board of directors for the Brookings Institution (a far left lobbying firm in D.C. pushing for global governance among other very progressive ideologies). Two weeks before the EMP attack, the President tapped SZ to take over as director of the NSA and serve as Director of US Cyber Security. Note: this is not to imply any relativity between the two. On an unrelated note, apparently the President and Congress have been relocated to the Raven Rock complex in south central PA per a reliable source. Reports are that Congress is officially at a standstill and no one can agree on the best way forward, so the country is still operating under martial law.

Intel on Subject Zero from the rumor mill:

There's a rumor that SZ was forced to retire under previous administration for unknown reasons. Supposedly, both the President and SZ were Bonesmen at Yale's elite Skull and Bones society during their senior year. SZ and the President reportedly stayed close and maintained contact throughout their careers. SZ was allegedly a close advisor to the President early on in his political career during his bid for the New York Senate seat. While SZ's military records are sealed, where he was stationed and his exact position is fuzzy after gaining the second star. Some say he was often seen in D.C. with other high brass in military R&D circles but, nothing concrete. It's no secret that the President has severely reduced the number of close advisors surrounding him. Some are saying that SZ is running most cabinet meetings at this point when the President can't attend. Some are insinuating that the President's health is failing but nobody can confirm this, either. There are rumors that SZ is working on an operation to infiltrate and undermine the largest looting force in the US. Apparently, it is more of a private army than a group of looters with potentially thousands of members in the Chicago area. There is some serious concern in D.C. over this group and SZ is the person the President put in charge of handling it."

Bruce stared down at the message in his hands. Where the hell was Mayor Reese getting all this information? Sammy's secret contact down at HQ hadn't produced a tenth of this information in three months' time. Bruce stuffed the message into his cargo pocket. It was past time for a face-to-face with Mayor Reese!

Chapter 23

With the assault on the motorcycle gang cancelled, Bruce retreated to his room to catch a few more hours of sleep. The second message from Mayor Reese was bothering him more than the report of the nearby gang. Bruce tossed and turned in his rack and eventually gave up on the prospect of more sleep. He stood and stretched, then decided to go for a jog to clear his head. Leaving through the main gate at a brisk walk, he picked up his pace and followed his normal 2.6 mile route which circled the Warren State Hospital. The relatively flat and tree-lined road wound its way along the west side of the Conewango Creek before dumping out onto the main drag through town. He silently jogged past vacant houses and empty, shuttered storefronts for Mom-and-Pop type shops that had sprung up around the juvenile detention facility over the years. As he neared the end of the loop, directly across from the front gates to the facility, there sat a large shopping plaza. It was predominately taken up by a Walmart and Lowe's building supply. Shortly after arriving in Warren, the Lowe's was cleaned out and now housed most of the Regiment's vehicles and supplies.

Bruce slowed his jog to a quick walk for the last hundred meters and noticed that someone had taken the liberty to pilfer some of the letters off the Walmart sign and combine them with the Lowe's signage to spell "alamO" over the front entrance. Bruce chuckled and wondered how long it had been like that. The men had been calling that position "The Alamo" for months. It now made sense to him, and he couldn't believe it took him so long to have noticed it. Bruce shook his head with a smirk; probably some bored privates. There were sandbags stacked high on the four corners of the Lowe's roof with light machine guns mounted at each position. Bruce could see multiple helmets bobbing along the edge of the roof as his men walked the perimeter. The non-functioning cars that had been abandoned in the two parking lots after the EMP had been stacked in a makeshift barrier, three vehicles high and twenty feet out from the building. There was only a single entry point near the tall doors of the contractor entrance and the makeshift vehicle barrier surrounded the entire building with razor wire running along the top. The facility looked like something out of a post-apocalyptic movie. Bruce realized he was actually living one of those movies now.

Bruce turned away from the Alamo and walked down the front drive to the Warren State Hospital. He wound his way through the zig-zagged concrete barriers, which would slow any vehicles trying to rush the main entrance. The two men stationed in the makeshift guard shack at the last barrier stepped outside and saluted him as he passed. He returned the salute and grabbed his canteen and towel which he'd set on the last concrete barrier at the beginning of his run. Bruce unceremoniously splashed his face with water from his canteen and wiped the sweat from his brow before slinging the towel over his right shoulder. He passed through the narrow space between the two MRAPs guarding the front gate. As he did so, a soldier, manning a 50-caliber machine gun atop one of the vehicles, nodded at him and he gave the man a cursory wave in return.

Bruce had missed breakfast earlier with all the morning's commotion, and he now found himself thoroughly famished. He knew that if he went back to his office and sent his orderly for food, it would mean an extra half hour, at least, before he ate. Bruce glanced down at his watch and cursed. It wasn't even 11:00 a.m. The officer's mess wouldn't be serving lunch for another hour. "Screw it," Bruce muttered to himself and deviated course toward the enlisted's chow. "This ought to be interesting," he thought. It was a long-standing tradition that officers rarely ate with enlisted unless they were in the field or other extenuating circumstances. Bruce figured that the majority of the soldiers probably wouldn't even recognize him outside of uniform; he would likely blend in. He was wrong.

All in all, it worked out fine. He'd eaten at a table with four junior enlisted from Bravo Company. They were full of questions, yet perceptive and respectful in how they asked them. Not surprisingly, most of the questions had to do with their desire for news from the outside world. Bruce tried to be as forthcoming as he could but found himself misdirecting their questions more often than not. He wished he could have been more honest with them, but he also knew that whatever he told these men would metastasize into something entirely different by the third telling. Outside of his frustration for misleading his men, Bruce enjoyed his short foray into enlisted life and was happy to see that most of the men entering and leaving the dining facility seemed to be in good spirits—none of the long-faced hungry stares that had been commonplace only a few weeks prior when his men had been on reduced rations. It was amazing what a little bit of food could accomplish. It was also heartbreaking to consider how the rest of the country's once civil society had literally fallen apart without it.

When finished, Bruce walked his tray to the kitchen and worked his way back to the main office complex where his sleeping quarters were located. After nearly a year of cold showers, he was looking forward to a nice, long, hot shower now that they had power at the hospital. Hot showers was another luxury he had taken for granted before the electric gird came down. But first, he needed to grab his uniform and shave kit from his office.

Bruce opened his office door to find Sammy lounging in his normal spot with his back to the door. But it wasn't Sammy! Bruce paused and realized that he was at a loss for words. In the past, no one had ever intruded into his office space uninvited. He wasn't sure if he should call his orderly and give him a tongue lashing for letting the man into his locked office, or if he should call security.

The man's head slowly swiveled in his direction. "Afternoon, Colonel."

Bruce panicked. It was Lt. Baier. Bruce wracked his brain, wondering if there was any incriminating evidence in his office. His eyes came to rest on his uniform, dangling from a hanger on the side of the wall cabinet. More precisely, his studied the left cargo pocket. Had his uniform been moved? He couldn't tell. If the lieutenant had found the note from Mayor Reese, he was in a world of—

"Sorry for letting myself in uninvited. I seem to have a problem getting clearance to cross over the bridge." He looked at Bruce with a raised eyebrow.

Bruce snapped out of his bewildered and panicked state and quickly answered. "I apologize for that. My men were instructed to let me know if you needed anything and inform me immediately if you wanted to meet. Although, I never told them to prevent you from crossing the bridge." It was a lie, but Bruce delivered it smoothly. "I'll have a chat with their XO." Bruce walked over to his uniform and draped it over his arm, trying to feel the letter inside the cargo pocket without being obvious. He couldn't tell. He grabbed his shave kit which was sitting next to the coffee pot and turned back to the lieutenant.

Bruce tried to give his voice a little edge. "With that being said, Lt. Baier, it is entirely inappropriate for you to enter my office without my permission. I'm curious how you managed to convince my orderly to let you in here when he knows better."

"Again, I apologize for the intrusion, Colonel. It was urgent." He glanced at the open door. "And before you crucify that young orderly of yours, he doesn't even know I'm in here." He leaned forward placing a solitary, silver key onto the center of Bruce's desk. "You'll likely want to return this to him and tell him not to keep it in his top drawer."

"I see," Bruce said darkly. "And how exactly did you manage to get through the front gate?"

The man shrugged nonchalantly. "I didn't come through the front gate." He rubbed his hand through his hair, smoothing the dark silky strands off his forehead and pushing them off to the side. He was acting as if he hadn't just snuck into a highly classified facility and broken into the commander's office.

Bruce was at a loss for words. It then dawned on him that this man had very powerful friends at HQ. He was measuring his response when a light knock on the doorframe behind Bruce startled him. It was his orderly; he must have heard Bruce come in and was checking to see if he needed anything. His eyes suddenly fell on the tall man in the chair and his eyes opened wide. Bruce could tell he was trying to put the pieces together, as well as trying to gauge whether or not he was in trouble.

"I asked Lt. Baier to stop by," Bruce offered. He still wasn't sure how to handle the situation, but delaying a call of alarm seemed the best tactic. "We have some things to discuss." Bruce could tell his orderly was also contemplating his current state of dress with his uniform draped haphazardly over his arm. Bruce was always a stickler for his appearance, especially when meeting with anyone not named Sammy. "It's fine, private. I lost track of time on my run. Please close the door." He forced the corners of his lips to turn upward.

That seemed to convince the private and he muttered a grateful "Yessir" as he closed the door behind him.

Bruce casually strolled over to his desk. He wanted to portray an aura of confidence, even though his stomach was churning at the entire situation he found himself in. Bruce set the brown leather shave kit down on the front corner of his desk. After that, he draped his uniform over the desk and pretended to straighten it and smooth out the wrinkles. He tried to appear casual while feeling for the ziplok baggie holding Mayor Reese's letter in the cargo pocket. Lt. Baier casually watched him with a disinterested nature. It was still there! The next question was whether or not it had been read and replaced back into the pocket. For now, Bruce would proceed as if it hadn't.

He calmly took a seat across from the lieutenant who was watching him closely now. "Okay. So you somehow bypassed our perimeter security before stealing a key to my office. I think I'll give you about sixty seconds to explain yourself before I call for security and have your ass thrown in the brig."

"Fair enough," Lt. Baier said calmly. He adjusted himself in the chair and leaned back, interlacing his fingers across his chest. He seemed to be pondering his next words.

Bruce raised his left arm in front of his face with an overt look at his watch. "Fifty-two seconds."

The lieutenant remained calm, studying Bruce for a full thirty seconds. It was a challenging gaze and Bruce returned it without flinching. "I'd like to discuss General Oates with you."

"What about him?" Bruce quickly answered without emotion. Inside, his heart was pounding.

"What can you tell me about him?"

Bruce's mind raced. He wondered if the lieutenant was testing him. "I've only met the general once." Bruce turned the question around. "You're the one who works for him. What are you asking me for?"

Lt. Baier sighed, scratching at his rough-shaven chin. "Before two weeks ago, I'd never worked for him either, or even heard of him for that matter. Technically, I still don't work for him. I work for SOCOM."

There was a long pause. "Okay?" Bruce said slowly, breaking the silence. However, he sure wasn't going to offer up any information. Lt. Jenkins, or whoever he'd been, had been quite crafty and able to maintain his disarming persona throughout his time around Colonel Harris. Bruce wasn't going to let his guard down with Lt. Baier.

"I guess I'm just trying to figure out what sort of man he is."

Another open-ended statement phrased as if it was a question. Bruce wasn't going to take the bait. He just shrugged his shoulders in response. "Like I said, I only met the man the one time."

Another long pause from Lt. Baier. Bruce could tell the lieutenant was growing frustrated, though he hid it well.

Bruce looked at his watch and leaned forward as if to stand. "Alright, son. Your time is up. Enjoy your time in the brig because I can assure you that you'll likely be facing a court martial soon."

Lt. Baier didn't flinch at the threat as held his hand up to Bruce, motioning his request for more time. Bruce relaxed back into his chair, more out of curiosity than in response to the lieutenant's silent plea. "So…, minutes before we left base on our current mission, I had a very unusual conversation with my CO." Bruce cocked his head to the side, intrigued. "He pulled me aside after our final briefing with General Oates and told me that he shared my concern over some of the more…'unusual' aspects of our orders. He'd done some asking around and was told by others at HQ that you're an honorable man and a patriot. He said that you could be trusted." He stopped talking waiting, for a reply from Bruce which never came. "These are confusing times…and it's hard to know who to trust," he said, almost as if he was talking to himself.

Bruce nodded his head slowly. "I'll agree to that. Continue."

"You see, sir. My CO is also an honorable man and a patriot. As am I…." For the first time since they met, Lt. Baier seemed unsure of himself. "Our orders from General Oates are…complicated. The problem I'm having is that there's a plane landing tomorrow to pick up a report I'm putting together for General Oates. And, well, I'm having some serious problems finalizing the report." His head lowered and he studied his boots in a completely uncharacteristic way for the bold and dangerous persona he'd portrayed earlier.

So far, Bruce had forced himself to stay as calm as possible throughout the conversation, but now his stomach was turning into knots. General Oates was sending a plane here? Was he going to be on it? Oates had told him on their call earlier that he wanted to talk with Bruce more about his intel report from Tionesta. Was that why Lt. Baier was really in Warren? His mind raced. Was the report Lt. Baier putting together about him? Bruce realized that he should say something in response. "Well, son, I would tell you to do the right thing. The honorable thing."

Lt. Baier didn't take his eyes off the floor as he nodded. Another pause, and then he looked up. "Colonel, this is a highly classified mission I'm on. I'm not supposed to be discussing it with anyone, for any reason. However, I feel strongly compelled to discuss my current situation with someone I can trust, like my CO, but I can't. He was adamant that I wasn't to contact him via satphone for any reason during this mission. He wouldn't tell me why." Lt. Baier once more wiped his fingers through his hair. "On past missions we've always maintained lines of communication. I've always had a satphone on me. For this mission, it was taken from me during our briefing and I was ordered to report to General Oates in person after our mission. That is a first for me and my unit. My CO told me privately that if something serious came up, which it has, I could discuss it with you." He stood and walked over to Bruce's open window and stood for a long minute, staring off into the distance.

Bruce was starting to believe that this had nothing to do with him. He broke the silence. "How about a cup of coffee?"

Lt. Baier nodded without turning his gaze away from the window. Bruce walked over to the small table in the corner of his office and started a fresh pot. He felt a trickle run down his temple and over his cheek, and he realized he was sweating. It had been a long time since he'd been this nervous. He grabbed the corner of the towel that still hung over his shoulder and wiped at his face. General Oates might be showing up at his office tomorrow to question him about Tionesta. What should he tell him? What should he tell Lt. Baier? Bruce stood silently, staring at the coffee pot as it made puttering noises and began to fill the room with its rich aroma. He considered having his orderly get Sammy so he'd have a witness to the conversation but quickly dismissed that idea. If this went south, he wanted his friend well clear of the consequences.

Bruce's mind raced in multiple directions as he pondered what to say to the young Lieutenant who was obviously dealing with his own inner struggles. Hopefully, the young soldier would just continue talking and Bruce wouldn't have to say anything. Bruce risked a quick glance in the man's direction. Lt. Baier still stood by the window, gazing off into the distance, almost in a trance. The tall soldier stood rock solid and still had a dangerous air about him, but there was also a genuine hint of uneasiness to his bearing. If he was acting, he deserved an Oscar. Bruce surmised that the young man's brain was doing the same somersaults as his own: "What should I say?" "What shouldn't I say?" Bruce felt another bead of sweat forming on his brow and he quickly wiped it away. He cursed to himself. He needed to stop sweating. It would be an obvious sign that he was nervous, which he was.

They both stood separated by silence for several long minutes, Bruce watching the coffee pot and Lt. Baier staring out the window. Bruce's senses were heightened in his current state of anxiety; he could hear birds chirping outside and the quiet thuds of someone's boots walking down the hallway past his office. Three beeps from the brewer brought him back to reality and announced the completion of the coffee pot's cycle. Bruce looked over his shoulder. "Cream? Sugar?"

Lt. Baier turned his head slightly to Bruce and gave him a tentative smile. "Yes. Both, please."

In that moment, Bruce was confident the lieutenant was about to share with him whatever was on his mind. He doctored up both cups of coffee and walked over to the window, handing one to Lt. Baier.

"Thank you," the LT said. "It's been months since I've had a cup."

Bruce just nodded and motioned to the guest chair, inviting the Lieutenant back to the desk. They both took their seats and slowly sipped at their cups, savoring the small luxury. After another minute of silence, Bruce gave the lieutenant a small reassuring smile and said, "So what's your problem, lieutenant, and how can I help?" He tried to give his best portrayal of a senior officer lending guidance to a junior officer.

Lt. Baier took a long sip and placed the half empty cup on the edge of Bruce's desk. He leaned back in his chair and took a deep breath, and then a stream of words tumbled out. "In short, I'm concerned about the legality of what I've been ordered to do. I'm also concerned about my men and what the consequences to them may be if we try to back out or don't continue on with this mission. I'm truly worried about how General Oates will respond if we don't follow through on his orders."

Bruce waited for the lieutenant to continue, but he was obviously waiting on Bruce to say something in response. Bruce slowly bobbed his head. He cupped his coffee with both hands, leaned further back in his chair, and rested it on his chest. He continued to hold eye contact with the man and realized that if he didn't contribute to the conversation, the lieutenant would likely grow uncomfortable and eventually clam up. *Be careful what you say*, he thought to himself. "My understanding of General Oates is that he's not a man to cross. I've heard that he's got very powerful contacts in high places. If you're considering disobeying your orders from him, then I think your concerns are quite valid." Lt. Baier nodded slightly and seemed to wait for Bruce to continue. Bruce wondered if he'd already said too much.

Bruce sighed. This was all or nothing for both of them. "Son, you're going to have to give me more information and tell me what your problem is if you want my advice on how to handle it."

Chapter 24

Lt. Baier exhaled slowly. "Screw it," he muttered. Sitting forward, he grasped his coffee mug, drinking the rest of its contents in two gulps before reclining back into his chair again. "I'm probably going to end up hanging from a rope regardless of what I do or say, so…." Bruce leaned forward, giving the man his full attention. "Have you heard of the civilian army that started up in Chicago this spring?" Bruce nodded. "Well, it's grown incredibly large. Apparently, the brass are growing concerned about it with the recent downsizing of our military forces. Per our briefing, Oates was Johnny-on-the-spot months ago at the first sign they were going to be a threat and had some undercover agent infiltrate the group. He said they stayed in contact over the summer until a few weeks ago, when he stopped receiving updates from the man. We were sent in to locate him and get an update on where things stood."

"Is that the man you pulled from the back of the truck yesterday when we dropped you off?" Bruce asked. If the lieutenant was surprised at the question, he didn't let on. Bruce was growing concerned that there might be another Lt. Jenkins held captive in his town, right under his nose. With General Oates or one of his operatives showing up tomorrow, that could go bad regardless of whether he was directly involved or not.

"No," Lt. Baier said dismissively, waving away Bruce's concern. "We'll get to that later." Bruce raised his hand apologetically and motioned for him to continue. "Our mission was three-fold: infiltrate the enemy camp, locate and make contact with the undercover agent, and glean as much intel on the enemy encampment and its layout as possible, all without raising anyone's suspicions."

Lt. Baier leaned forward in his chair as he spoke, wrapping his giant hand around the small coffee cup. He had it halfway to his mouth before realizing that it was empty. The sheer disappointment on the man's face was clearly evident. Bruce pointed to the coffee pot, "Please. Feel free to grab another." He realized that he probably should have brewed more than the four cups. This meeting might take a while.

Lt. Baier nodded his thanks and continued talking as he made his way to the small table in the corner. "Before leaving base, our intel on the enemy encampment was light to say the least. We weren't really sure what to expect when we arrived. All we knew was they'd taken over the Cleveland airport and were using the main terminal as a central operating base for their numerous recon and scavenging parties. When we arrived, we discovered their perimeter security was surprisingly tight for such a large group of looters. Even still, it didn't take my team long to find a way in. We wore civvy's and, once inside, we didn't have much problem blending in. To say that we were surprised by what we found inside the airport would be an understatement." Bruce gave him a questioning look as he returned to his seat, fresh cup in hand.

"Colonel, we've been doing this type of thing for a while now. Typically, when we investigate or take out a looting group or warlord, it's total chaos and near anarchy inside the camp. They live in squalor and spend as much time fighting among themselves as they do raiding towns and villages. This was a completely different atmosphere. This was organized. It's hard to put into words without you being there to actually see it. Nobody was fighting. It was clean. Each person and family seemed to have their own cordoned off section of space with nobody encroaching into the central walking areas. There were vendor areas everywhere. Their tables were aligned in perfectly straight rows down the center of specific terminals and kept away from the quieter sleeping areas. There was a solid policing force that patrolled the terminals. They weren't heavy handed or intrusive, and nobody seemed to mind their presence or even notice they were there. It was incredible. In fact, it rivaled most military encampments I've seen over the years.

"We set to work and split up, sniffing around a bit and getting the lay of the land. We talked to vendors and other people with friendly faces. We needed to locate our contact yet be careful in our questions so the people there wouldn't suspect we were outsiders. It took us most of the first day to get enough intel. What we discovered in those conversations, and from the person you saw us pulling from the Humvee which, again, I'll get back to, is that the original group started in Chicago under a man named Keith Bronson.

"At first, Bronson banded together with some of the neighbors on his suburban block for protection. They quickly ran out of food and were unable able to hold out very long against larger and better armed gangs of looters from the inner city, so they were forced to flee. They become refugees just like everyone else on the open road. At some point, soon after the collapse, his wife was killed. This group of regular, everyday people was 'forced' into a life of looting throughout the Illinois countryside to keep themselves and their families fed. It's the typical story we've seen a thousand times over the course of the last year." He waived his hand dismissively and Bruce nodded his head in agreement. Shortly after the grid came down, the 31st Regiment had numerous run-ins with similar groups while in charge of patrolling and providing perimeter security for the Green Zones in Baltimore and Wilmington. It was just a fact of life now that everyday people had been pushed to commit violent acts they never would have dreamed of before society fell apart.

Lt. Baier continued. "Over time, Bronson's raiding party grew, joining forces with some other groups over the winter. In a bold move, they apparently raided some military base and acquired all sorts of weaponry and military vehicles which they put to efficient use in the rural areas south of Chicago. Early this spring, he developed an assault strategy and they ran roughshod over Chicago. They either destroyed or absorbed every warlord and looting group they encountered in the city. A couple weeks after Chicago, they cleaned out Detroit. Being former military, Bronson ran a tight ship but he didn't rule with an iron fist, which is why a lot of people were drawn to him in the first place. However, as his group grew, he started having trouble maintaining order, mostly due to overwhelming logistics. He organized committees to run different aspects of the camp so he could focus on their operational security and their strategy for invading Cleveland. Overseeing those committees still took up a bunch of his time, so he eventually formed a head committee to oversee the other committees. The leaders in those committees quickly grew proficient in their duties and in short order the camp was running smoothly again."

"So they have formed their own government," Bruce said, completely transfixed at the information, but also wondering how the lieutenant and his men could glean so much information on the history of the group in a single day's time. Surely the vendors and everyday people in the camp couldn't have known so many details.

Baier nodded. "As time progressed, Bronson began to recognize that his army had grown too large. Even with hundreds of men sent out on regular raids, he was soon going to have problems keeping everyone fed. It happened sooner than he'd planned. They ran out of food in Detroit and were forced to move on to Cleveland. This time, instead of fighting his way through the city, he set up shop at the airport and made the various warlords and other surviving groups come to him to pay homage. The word had spread from Chicago and Detroit before he even arrived and they knew fighting him was pointless. They were required to pay a tax in the form of food and supplies or it would be taken by force. While all this was happening, his oversight committee was implementing more and more strict rules on how the camp was run. They formed their own civilian police force to patrol the camp, and after making examples of a few men, raping, stealing, fighting, and other depraved behavior was quickly met with swift justice.

"Bronson's fighting force, which included a lot of unsavory types, weren't real happy with this turn of events. They'd been with him since the beginning and had done a lot of his dirty work. Now here was some '*committee*' of refugees they'd captured or absorbed into their group telling '*them*' what they could and couldn't do and how to behave. A serious resentment between the fighting forces and the rest of the encampment was mounting. While Bronson may have overseen and had his guys do some terrible stuff over the year, he was also realizing that he would eventually run out of cities to raid or the military was going to step in and take him out. He knew their encampment would need to evolve into some type of orderly and self-sustaining society or it would collapse. He also needed to keep his fighters happy; he was going to continue to need them to protect the refugees. If the fighting forces grew too bitter and restless, they might just mutiny and take over the entire camp. So, about a month ago, he started sending the worst of them out on extended raids throughout the nearby countryside to locate small towns and surviving groups where they might acquire more food. This got the fighters out from under the thumb of the committee and it gave them their freedom back. Who was to say what they could and couldn't do while they were out on the open road?"

Lt. Baier took a sip of coffee and cleared his throat. "While this was happening, the bulk of his fighting forces out of the way, the head committee grew emboldened and started to butt heads with Bronson. They wanted to pursue a more realistic and long-term approach to feeding the group. They wanted to move the camp to a permanent location, one with a warmer climate and longer growing seasons.

Possibly start some large-scale farming operation. Bronson agreed with that, but he also wanted to continue acquiring their food by force until they could locate a suitable location and get the farming infrastructure set up and producing food. In contrast, the committee had discovered via a ham radio broadcast that a large group in Missouri had formed and was already producing a lot of their own food. The committee wanted to immediately pull up stakes and head there. They were coordinating and organizing passage using some old steam trains that could haul the majority of their encampment by rail.

"A rumor began to spread that the committee wanted to leave the more nefarious segments of the fighting forces behind and just take their internal policing forces and some of the tamer elements of the fighting force. Now these were just rumors, but you can imagine the reaction from Bronson's fighters about being left behind when they were the whole reason the group had been formed in the first place. Apparently, Bronson and the committee argued this point for days before he finally relented and gave in. He agreed to send the bulk of his forces, the more illicit and immoral men, off on a big looting engagement to Youngstown, Ohio, with the instructions they would be gathering food for the group's journey to Missouri. Some of the more honorable fighters, the ex-military types, and those who were more easily controlled were to stay back at the camp. The plan was to leave Cleveland while the bulk of the fighting force was raiding Youngstown. Unfortunately, the bad element of fighters caught wind of the plan. That meeting happened only two weeks before we showed up."

Lt. Baier had grown more and more animated as he told the story. He took another long sip of coffee before continuing. "So here is where it gets interesting. The morning after Bronson gave in to the committees demands to leave the bulk of the fighting forces behind, and mind you these were very secret closed door meetings, Bronson was found stripped naked, beaten to death, and hanging from a noose off the air traffic control tower. The tower had been his center of operations for the fighting forces. It was a secure location where he and his closest group of advisors slept and kept watch over the entire encampment. Those responsible didn't even try to hide the fact that they were the ones who'd killed him. They were sending the committee and everyone else a message. The committee was quickly informed that Bronson's second in command, a man named Skyler Benningfield, had taken over as leader of the fighting forces and was to be the new leader of the entire group."

Lt. Baier rubbed his hands together conspiratorially. "I'll give you three chances to guess the name of our undercover contact in the encampment."

Bruce whistled through his teeth and raised his eyebrows as it sunk in. "Wow...." He hadn't expected that twist.

"Exactly!" Baier agreed. "Skyler demanded that the committee officially recognize him as their new leader and, in trade, he would permit them to continue running the day-to-day operations of the camp. What could they do? Their measly policing forces wouldn't stand a chance against the bulk of the fighting forces. They were forced to capitulate."

Bruce was frowning at the direction the story was going. "Earlier, you mentioned that this Skyler character hadn't made contact with Oates in the past few weeks."

"That's right. Not since he'd taken over as the big dog in the kennel."

"That's your problem, isn't it?" Bruce surmised. "If you try to approach him directly and he's decided that he doesn't need Oates anymore since he's king of his own little country now, well, you and your men are probably going to disappear."

Lt. Baier grimaced. "Errr..., not exactly. You see, most of that information, especially the information about the inner workings in the committees, the camp's history, and how everything progressed and came down, comes from the prisoner we took when we left. Going into this mission, we assumed the original leader, Bronson, was just your typical, run of the mill, psycho warlord like we'd encountered dozens of times in the past. From our conversations with the vendors and the general public on the day we arrived, we only knew the basics. We only knew that there was tension between the committee and the new leader who'd only been in power for a few weeks. Nobody in the main part of the camp really knew much about him except his name and boy weren't we shocked when we found out who it was. At that time, with the limited information we had, we just assumed that he was following some contingency plan from General Oates that we weren't privy to in our briefing. In truth, our briefing from General Oates had been rather vague on Skyler's overall objective. We knew that he was supposed to infiltrate the camp, gain rank and favor with the leader and try to get close to him while providing intel back to Oates so they could develop a plan to deal with the group. Without all the other details, we just assumed he'd gone the extra mile and gained complete control of the camp when he saw the opportunity."

Lt. Baier briefly paused and glanced at Bruce's hands. Bruce suddenly realized that he'd begun clicking his pen while he was listening. Bruce set the pen down and interlaced his fingers on his chest to prevent himself from unconsciously picking it up again. The lieutenant continued. "There was virtually zero chance of us getting close to him up in the air traffic control tower. It was guarded like Fort Knox. So, we sent him a message for a meeting which included a code word that General Oates had given us. We had no idea the dangerous position we'd put ourselves in at the time and if I knew then what I know now, we never would've tried to meet with him. Surprisingly, he met with us. He told us that the encrypted satphone he'd been using to contact Oates had stopped working and he knew that eventually Oates would send someone to him directly. He put on a brave face and bragged about how he was running the committees now; how everyone in the camp respected him; how they were happy with his leadership, etcetera, etcetera. We now know that's not exactly true. He's already had one committee member killed. The most outspoken member on the panel chewed him out in public the day after he took power and was found dead in his bed the next morning. Now there's no proof he did it, but everyone on the committee knows that if they speak out against him, they'll end up dead. Again, this is all intel we didn't have at the time, so I took what he said at face value. He seemed a nice enough guy and we didn't have any reason not to believe him.

"He took us to a party that night on 'his' side of the encampment where we got to see how his fighting forces lived. It was closer to the other groups we've dealt with in the past: rough men, lewd women, and lots of alcohol each night. After Skyler left us for the night, I ordered my men to split up. We had a few drinks and made our way around the party talking to some of the other men and doing some digging. They were a mixed lot—ex-military guys, gangbangers, hillbillies, the gambit. Later, when we had reconvened for the night, we started piecing together bits of conversation and information we'd gleaned.

"Earlier in the day, Skyler had told us they were planning to camp in Cleveland throughout the winter. But his men told us that they were pulling out on trains within the coming days to assault the Missouri group and set up a new home base before coming back and bringing the rest of the group to the new location. It just seemed odd that he'd lie to us about overwintering in Cleveland when we'd obviously find out from his men that they were leaving. It was the first big inconsistency that made us start to wonder if something else was at play.

"The majority of the more reprehensible types seemed wholly confident in Skyler's leadership and the direction he was taking them. They hadn't been happy about Bronson's softening style, him giving so much control over to the committees, and the rumors that he was going to leave them behind while the rest of the group headed off to utopia. They were mostly happy with the new leadership.

"In contrast, the more respectable elements of fighters had been happy with the direction Bronson had been taking them. Most were looking forward to less fighting and possibly settling down into some semblance of normal life again. We heard from one man that Skyler had risen in the ranks because he was a cold-blooded killer. Everyone was either scared of him or held him in awe. He'd turned out to be an extremely effective captain over one of the more cantankerous squads of fighters who were known for their butchery. He led them with an iron fist, keeping them in check. More importantly, with his amazing tactics and assault planning, not a single one of his guys had been killed for months. His raiding successes were ultimately what earned him a spot on Bronson's inner council of advisors.

"There were other smaller rumors and items we picked up. You know how drunk soldiers love to talk! But in the end, we all held the same view. Something was very off with Skyler's story. He'd been so nice and cordial when he'd met with us, yet many of the stories we heard painted the picture of a seriously demented and sadistic monster. Now, I know that heroic war stories have a tendency to get embellished over time, but some of the specifics had to have some origin in fact.

"This last bit of information kind of sealed the deal. When he'd left us for the night, we'd watched him enter a small office building attached to the hanger where the party was held. Turns out it was a brothel. There were other brothels in the main camp as well, but this one was different. The brothels in the main camp were strictly overseen by a committee, and they were voluntary. The women that worked at them lived better than most anyone else in the camp with what they made. It's the oldest profession in the world, eh?" Lt. Baier asked with a chuckle.

When Bruce didn't return a smile, he cleared his throat and continued, his face reddening slightly. "So, come to find out, the committee's rules didn't apply in the fighter's camp. The brothel they ran wasn't exactly…voluntary. They were prisoners that had been acquired from their various raiding parties throughout the year." The lieutenant cleared his throat and drank down the last of his coffee. Bruce realized that he hadn't even taken a sip of his own coffee since Lt. Baier had begun speaking. He picked up the cup and looked down into the murky pool of liquid and instantly got a sick feeling in his stomach. A mental image of the poor abused women his men had rescued from the Bradford Prison flashed into Bruce's head. He couldn't help but think about the horrible conditions those girls, maybe even boys, were living in inside that brothel. He set his cup back down on the desk.

"Come to find out, Bronson had been dating a girl he'd met a month earlier. They'd grown close and she lived with him in the tower. The night Bronson was killed, she was taken hostage. We heard she was being held in the brothel, where apparently Skyler had been an avid customer since he'd joined the camp. She was kept there specifically for his use and no one else was allowed to bed her. The fighter who'd shared this news with me wasn't real happy. Apparently she was quite gorgeous and I think the guy had a bit of infatuation with her."

Lt. Baier sighed and held his hands out questioningly. "So, what to do? My men were adamant on rescuing the girl before we left, but I absolutely forbid it." Lt. Baier diverted his eyes down to his boots for the first time since he'd started and his tone grew softer. "Colonel, you have to realize, with all the missions my team has been on over the past year, I've seen some shit. This wasn't anything new." He paused again and Bruce nodded his understanding. "There were a lot of moving parts, numerous twists and turns, and we needed to get clear of it all and discuss it with General Oates to find out what we were supposed to do next. Nothing had turned out like we'd expected. Even though the brothel wasn't guarded well, the risk of rescuing her and getting caught could jeopardize the whole mission. My personal stance was, we had urgent intel with an extremely short timeline that we needed to get back to headquarters. If we didn't succeed, no one would know what was really going on inside that camp. So, at first light the following morning, we left. We had breakfast with Skyler and he graciously walked us to the front gate and gave us a letter to help us get through the various checkpoints in the area."

Lt. Baier shuffled his feet. "We hiked out to where we'd stashed the Humvees and hit the road. With urgent intel, my plan was to head here instead of going all the way back to…where we originated…and use your encrypted satphone to radio General Oates, to find out what he wanted us to do." Bruce caught the misdirection, but he let it pass. He made a mental note to possibly bring it up later if the opportunity presented itself. He was curious where this Seal Team called home base.

"We didn't make it a mile down the road from the airport. I just couldn't do it. The security at the brothel was just so lax. We couldn't save them all, but at least we could get one of them out. Besides, after living with Bronson for months, she'd probably have some good intel as well. Skyler had walked us out the front gate and watched us leave. He'd likely guess it was one of the degenerates in his camp that took her.

"So, we turned back. In the early hours the following morning, we snuck back in through the airport's perimeter security and were able to rescue her. We made a clean getaway and arrived here yesterday afternoon."

"That was Bronson's girlfriend under that hood you pulled from the back of the truck," Bruce said aloud to himself. "You boys were a bit rough with her, forcibly dragging her out of the back of the Humvee if I remember correctly?" Bruce asked with a reproachful glare.

Lt. Baier sighed. "Yes, that was her. Yes, we had her hooded. We were bringing her into a highly classified location, so it was for her own benefit that we hooded her. We couldn't have her seeing the refinery up and running, now could we? As far as the last, we knew you and your men were watching us as you left. We surmised your guards at the gate had also seen we had a prisoner. We felt as if we needed to make it look authentic, and we didn't want you to know our prisoner was a woman…for various reasons." He rubbed his hands together. "Well, after speaking with her most of the night, my thought process on this whole situation has changed considerably. My men's opinion on our mission has changed as well. The only thing left to do was to speak with General Oates, make our report, and see what he says."

Bruce sighed. "So, the point of this whole story is to gain access to my satphone to make your report?"

"Nope," Lt. Baier said, looking Bruce directly in the eye. "I've already done that."

Bruce looked down at his bottom left desk drawer, the one with the lock. It stood slightly ajar and he hadn't even noticed it. He yanked the drawer open and the satphone slid from the back of the drawer, slamming into its wooden face. Bruce looked up furiously. "You couldn't have! It's encrypted and you'd need to know my pin!" He hadn't even finished the sentence before he knew the truth. General Oates had given Lt. Baier his pin code.

"I watched you leave through the front gate on your jog this morning. I was planning to be in and out before you returned, but—"

"You…, you…." Bruce was so pissed, he was stammering. Even if he could talk he wasn't sure what he would say. He was sweating again.

"Let's just say the call didn't go so well," Lt. Baier added.

"What do you mean, 'the call didn't go well'?" Bruce demanded loudly. That's all he needed was some lone wolf using *his own* personal satphone to call General Oates and piss him off.

Lt. Baier studied him with an intense gaze. "I mean, the-call-didn't-go-well." He said it slowly as if Bruce were hard of hearing. "Please keep your voice down, Colonel. This was a mission contingency I'd been given by General Oates in case I had urgent news to relay that couldn't wait. He's currently under the impression that I followed orders and snuck in here, used your phone to report, and snuck back out again." He paused for a minute. "Yet, here I sit." Lt. Baier roughly rubbed his face with both hands. "Let's keep this conversation quiet as I don't think we want word getting out that we're having a private conversation in your office. Right?"

Bruce had been so singularly focused on this being a trap by Lt. Baier working on behalf of General Oates that he'd never even considered he'd end up on the other side. All of a sudden, he was in a different type of trap. If the lieutenant and his men went off the radar now and Oates found out he'd met with Lt. Baier after his call, there likely wouldn't be a trial. He'd probably have an accident falling down some stairs or having a heart attack while he slept. He'd never get to tell his side of the story or what he knew of General Oates. Sweat was pouring down Bruce's face and he wiped it with the towel on his shoulder.

Lt. Baier noticed his anxiety. "I'm not trying to jam you up here, Colonel. I'll leave the same way I came in. If you can keep your orderly quiet, there's no reason for anyone to ever know we met." While a nice gesture, it wasn't entirely reassuring to Bruce.

Lt. Baier continued. "So anyway, I spelled out the entire scenario to General Oates that I just told you minus a few details. He is sending someone up at first light tomorrow with a new satphone for Skyler. Bronson's girlfriend, Catalina, is to be flown back to HQ for 'debriefing.'" He said the last in air quotes.

"We are to give his agent my full written report and head out the second we have the replacement phone in our hands and deliver it to Skyler as quickly as possible so Oates can be properly briefed from his agent. From that point, our orders are to stay there and assist him in whatever he needs. We're to help him solidify his control over the entire camp, even if that includes killing every single member of the committee." Lt. Baier's voice had grown hard. "I tried to tell the General that I didn't feel the man was still reliable or even completely mentally stable. But the prick kept cutting me off. I'm to receive written orders with various contingency plans tomorrow morning by whoever he's sending up here."

Lt. Baier stood and walked over to the open window again. Bruce was still speechless. "Just so you're aware, I…myself and my men, have discussed it, and we have no intention of turning Catalina over to General Oates for *'debriefing.'*" His voice grew softer, almost imperceptible. "That poor girl has been through enough shit for a hundred lifetimes." He stood quietly for a few moments. "I'm starting to have a very hard time believing that the people who are running our government are standing behind a guy like General Oates. I just don't want to believe that. I'll admit that my men and I have walked a fine line on ethics at various times over the past year. In fact, I'm sure we've likely crossed it a few times. I have no doubts I'll need to answer for some of the things I've done when I meet my maker," he said solemnly.

More silence. "I guess what I'm saying, Colonel, is I'm done killing people just because I'm told to. You weren't there and you didn't see it, but I swear to God, those people in that camp had hope in their eyes. That's something I haven't seen for a very long time. I think that group has a good chance of making it through this, with the right leadership and a little bit of help from, I don't know, somebody. I'll be damned if I'm going to go there and help that psycho put those people back into chains of despair."

A long time passed before anything was said. Bruce's mind was racing. He was trying to see all the angles and cover all the bases, but the wires in his brain were sparking without making any contact. He knew if he had time to sit down and process everything he could figure out a way forward. That's what he was good at—processing information, making plans, being decisive, delegating and finding a way to succeed. Bruce couldn't even see past the first row of hedges on this one.

Bruce shook his head. "Why are you telling me this? It seems as if you've already made up your mind on what you're going to do. Why involve me at this point?" It was hard not to sound petulant.

Lt. Baier turned back from the window and held his gaze. The man's strong and decisive bearing had returned. Apparently, he just needed to get some stuff off his chest. Unfortunately, his baggage had landed on Bruce…fallen onto him from a mile above his head. "I'm telling you, Colonel Harris, in case what my men and I have planned, fails. If that happens, we're likely dead. Someone needs to hear this story. I don't know who that is, but someone does." He looked at Bruce and gave him a slight smile. "Besides, I trust you."

Bruce snorted and then laughed out loud in incredulity. That's the only emotion he had left. "Why do you trust me? You don't even know me."

Lt. Baier smiled back. "Yes, I do." His eyes departed from Bruce's gaze and moved down to his coffee mug. Nope, he wasn't looking at his coffee; he was looking at the cargo pocket of Bruce's uniform.

"You sneaky son of a bitch…!" Bruce instantly felt new sweat flowing. A moment later he couldn't help himself. He was laughing again.

Chapter 25

Sean held Maria's tiny hand as half the members of the North Homestead walked a slow pace along their deserted country road. He watched as Joshua and his wife, Leah, rounded the hill in front of them and disappeared from view. Randy and Jackson had volunteered to lead point this time and preceded the procession by a few hundred yards. They walked in pairs, keeping at least fifty yards between each couple and paying close attention to their surroundings.

It was likely overkill as a fire squad from North Homestead periodically swept the surrounding farms for anyone that may have moved into the area. They'd not found a single survivor living nearby since moving into Mr. Andrews' retreat, and Sean had always wondered if Mr. Andrews' men had cleared the area directly after the EMP. Maybe the locals had died off or just fled on their own. Either way, he was thankful that the surrounding area was quiet. In fact, their LP/OP at the end of the lane hadn't seen a single refugee travelling their tiny country road in months. Most of the refugees fleeing the major cities had done so the first couple months following the loss of the electric grid, and most survivors remaining throughout the country probably had kept their heads down and focused on surviving in place. For the first year following the collapse, travelling away from your home location was just asking for unwanted trouble. Sean couldn't be sure if refugees still travelled the major highways and main roads, but the country roads sure had grown quiet. Now that the Green Zones were abandoned, he worried there might be an increase in desperate refugees. They would have to wait and see while not allowing their quiet surroundings to loll them into complacency. They'd need to stay disciplined on their perimeter security around the North Homestead.

Sean had never travelled this far down their road, and from Joshua's description of their previous foray for fuel, he thought they should be getting close to their destination. He couldn't help but be a little excited at the prospect of their first large get-together with Derrick Keefer's group. He wondered how they had survived the winter when so many of the other locals had perished. The church was situation directly beside the road and likely couldn't have withstood any large looting force that stumbled upon them. What had they eaten the first six months to get by until they could grow their own food? Sean had lots of unanswered questions regarding the group and reminded himself to be patient with Derrick. While most of his desire for more information from the man was born strictly out of curiosity, if he asked too many questions too soon, it could come across as probing.

Per their full group meeting before leaving the North Homestead, everyone had been advised by the council not to reveal any information regarding the North Homestead's food, supplies, or defenses. The last few weeks, Sean, Randy, Lawrence, and Sean's father had met a few times with Derrick and his son in centralized locations to discuss bartering and get to know each other better. But this was their first big get-together between the two groups. It almost seemed like a mini vacation to Sean as they were finally able to leave the all too familiar walls of the North Homestead and see a new place with new faces.

The day after their first run-in with the group, Sean had asked Pastor Dan if he knew Derrick Keefer. Dan only had great things to say about his former college buddy. They'd drifted apart ten years ago when Derrick left the Lutheran Church and started a small nondenominational bible church in the area. It wasn't intentional on either person's part and there was no animosity between the two, they just didn't see each other as often after that.

When they reached the small knoll, Sean reached into his cargo pocket and pulled out the handheld Baofeng ham radio. "Shire, this is Frodo. Do you read me? Come back," Sean said, testing the strength of their connection.

"This is the Shire. You're a little distorted, but I can still make you out fine. How about on your end?" David replied.

"I read you loud and clear," Sean answered. The 100 watt base station and antenna tower at the retreat would have no problem sending a signal to them, but with the smaller 5 watt handheld ham, there was no way to know if they would be able to maintain comms all the way to Derrick's Church. There was only one way to find out. "I think we are almost to our destination. I'll try again when we get there."

"Copy that," David responded. "Over and out."

"Over and out," Sean echoed. Maria gave his hand a small squeeze and Sean looked down at his wife. He surmised that she might be even more excited about getting away from the North Homestead and getting a short break from Jacob. She was still sore about not going to the last market day in Tionesta, especially after the elephant ear secret had leaked out. Sean guessed Randy had been the culprit.

Not much farther down the road, they walked into a Norman Rockwell painting. The small, two-story white church featured arching stained glass windows, a quaint picket fence encircling the front yard, and a sturdy bell tower, which now held a man on watch. Sean and Maria had been in the center of their procession; they all waited at the edge of the road for the last of their group to arrive.

Pastor Derrick was standing at the front wooden gate talking quietly to Uncle Nathan when Sean walked up. They greeted each other warmly. Sean suddenly caught a whiff of something cooking; it smelled like meat! Derrick must have read Sean's expression and said,

"We bagged a buck last night standing right there in the middle of the church yard." He pointed off to his right. "It's roasting on a spit out back. God's own benevolence." Sean and his family had packed enough food for their own members to eat, not wanting Derrick's group to be compelled to feed the extra twenty people from their own food stores. But the idea of fresh meat was mouth-watering. Sean hadn't had venison, or any other red meat for that matter, since Brody's wedding. The hunting crew in Tionesta had shot two deer the night before the wedding, yet they'd only been able to kill a handful of deer in the months since. Sean was starting to wonder if God was sending them a message about his support for working together with other groups and towns going forward. It was just too much of a coincidence.

With pleasantries exchanged and all of Sean's family accounted for, Derrick gave them a short tour of the small church. The main sanctuary was typical of an old country church except half of the pews in the rear had been removed and replaced with mattresses, wardrobes, and dressers, which partitioned off square, wall-less bedrooms. There was a small office and a nursery on opposite sides of the front double doors which had also been converted to bedrooms as well. A small balcony above the front rooms, with pews removed, served as a sleeping area during the winter, as it was too hot to sleep there during the summer. After that, Derrick took them downstairs to a large finished basement under the sanctuary. There was a small kitchen on the left at the base of the stairs and two bathrooms to the right. The rest of the basement was finished into one large room. There were three rows of folding tables down the center with some prepared food already preset. Sean noted the stacked mattresses that lined the one wall and he surmised that most of their group had been sleeping in the cooler basement during the summer months. In all, there were twenty adults and six children living in the church.

Both groups combined their food and soon they were all sitting down to eat. It reminded Sean of the family reunions, holidays, and birthday parties his own family had enjoyed in the similar basement area of his parent's church growing up. They intentionally spread out and sat among each other. Throughout the meal, a steady buzz of conversation echoed off the painted cement block walls. When the meal was finished and the plates cleared, the women from Sean's family were invited by the women in Derrick's group to join them upstairs to the sanctuary, leaving the men behind. The organic and natural way it came about, with no words or instructions given, implied this must be their group's evening routine.

Sean found his way over to where Derrick sat in deep conversation with another member of his group. "That was fantastic!" he offered in praise when there was a break in their conversation. "I can't thank you enough for sharing your harvest with my family. This will surely be a day to remember."

"Thank you, Sean," Derrick said with sincerity. "We were more than happy to share. We haven't seen a deer in almost a month. We assume you haven't either?"

"Nope, it's been a couple months for us since our family has had venison, though we don't send hunting parties out like Tionesta does. Even though we haven't encountered strangers for quite a while, we feel it's still too risky."

"We feel the same," Derrick agreed.

"The last two times we've met, I keep forgetting to ask you a question on that subject."

"What? Deer?"

Sean chuckled. "No. About others living nearby. When we came through here looking for gas a while back, our guys reported smelling smoke from a campground a bit farther up the road. Do you know if there are other survivors in the area?"

Derrick shrugged. "Like I said before, we've kept to ourselves and haven't travelled around the surrounding areas." He frowned. "That was until, going against our specific instructions that no one was to travel outside our perimeter, my son decided to sneak out one night to check out Mr. Andrews' farm to see if there was anyone still alive down there." He gave his son a dark look. "I'd watched that place being built years ago, and we always wondered whether there might be some resources we could acquire if it was abandoned or maybe barter for if Mr. Andrews was still there. He'd always been generous to our church in the past." Sean raised an eyebrow at that. "While he didn't attend regularly, he made a large, unexpected donation last year to help us put a new roof on the sanctuary."

Sean desperately wanted to chime in and set the record straight on exactly what type of man Mr. Andrews had been, but he decided it was a conversation for another time. He wanted to hear more about the locals.

"As far as the folk still living at the campground, we've had a few run-ins with them over the past year. We're not sure how many of them are left, but I don't think they're doing very well." Derrick sighed. "In fact, we ran one guy off just the other day. He shot one of our chickens with a BB gun and tried to make off with it. We heard the poor thing carrying on and we were able to intercept him before he made it too far. Poor guy was skinnier than any living person I've ever seen. He barely had the strength to walk, let alone run. It reminded me of World War II movies I've see—the ones with the Nazi concentration camps. We let the guy go with a warning, told him to stay away and inform the others in his group the same." There was a long pause before he continued, his face somber. "I wish we had the extra food to help them."

Derrick didn't seem to imply it was a big deal, but Sean thought otherwise. If whoever was staying at the campground was that hungry and desperate, Sean feared they'd likely be returning. "Don't you worry about them coming back?"

Derrick shrugged. "We'll deal with it when the time comes. No use worrying over something you can't do anything about."

"Don't you have anyone that was prior military, or a security team you could send up to scope them out?" Sean asked with concern. Derrick was clearly underestimating the threat they faced.

"Nope, though Craig was a police officer up in Erie for twenty years before retiring." One of the men standing off to one side of their table tipped his hat to Sean as Derrick spoke, and Sean gave him a friendly nod back. "My younger boy here was in ROTC in college and thinking about a military career." He stopped and let out a long breath. "My wife and I thank God every day that he was home on break when the electricity went out. He was studying business administration at the University of Virginia and likely would have had a tough time of it getting home." His son, a scrawny young man sitting across from Sean, smiled sheepishly. "We've mostly survived on God's miraculous benevolence ever since."

"On top of that, I figure our location is pretty unique. There's not much reason for any travelers to come down this road. There was never much traffic on our road even before things fell apart, just those of us who live nearby and those visiting the campground. Anyone that needed to flee north or south would take Route 36 to our west or Route 127 to the east of us to keep from having to walk over the big hill down past your place. Heck, this road doesn't even show up on most maps."

"That makes sense" Sean said, picturing the roads in his head. It also explained the complete lack of refugee travelers they'd seen since moving into Mr. Andrews' compound.

"The first few weeks after the outage, we did have more people pass by, mostly those leaving the campground and making an attempt to walk home, but there were only a few of us holed-up here at the church then. Most of the others didn't trickle in for a month or so. We did get the occasional refugees travelling through over the winter from time to time. But just like we dealt with your guys a couple months ago, we found that being stern yet still accommodating to their passage past the church seemed to be the best approach."

"And you've never been forced to face down a larger group of looters or refugees trying to attack you for food or supplies?" Sean asked thoroughly surprised.

Derrick shook his head. "Has that been a problem for you guys?" he asked. Sean snorted in response. Derrick's question was clearly a result of their mostly unchallenged out-of-the-way location, combined with their lack of outside information.

Sean recalled the handful of bullet holes in the front of the church he'd noticed on their arrival but didn't push for an answer on that. "It didn't take long for most of the big cities to deteriorate into warring factions and gangs. Once they'd gone house to house in the city scavenging for supplies, they spread out and went road by road through the countryside. Unless you were well off the beaten path, most survivors have had to face off against a looting group at least a time or two."

"Well, off the beaten path describes us here perfectly," Derrick said. "While we've never encountered any large looting groups like you describe, we did have a few run-ins with some locals earlier in the year. They didn't want to cooperate or work together and decided they would simply steal our food one night. We were forced to defend ourselves…," he said and then cleared his throat. "We buried them in the cemetery behind the church alongside two of our own. Sean, it's not really something I'd care to relive or get into the details on," he said.

Sean felt bad for the old man, but he also felt compelled to help him at the same time. "I'm sorry to hear about the loss of your friends. We've lost a few of our own family members to looters as well. I don't want to say your group has been lucky because I also believe your limited engagements have been a result of God's hand of protection over your group. But, Derrick, your church sits right up next to the road. You're well aware that Tionesta was approached a few days ago by a biker who said he was part of a bigger group in the area. If a group like that one comes through here and decides to take advantage of your kindly approach to dealing with travelers, you might lose a lot more than two people next time."

"Are you sayin' we should just kill people travelling through?" Derrick's eldest son asked with a hint of disgust.

"No!" Sean said defensively, looking up at him. "All I'm trying to get at is that your defenses here and your group's tactics could use some work." Derrick looked back at Sean with a raised eyebrow. Sean gave him a simple example without getting into the more complicated reasons why their perimeter was set up too close to the church. "Take for instance the first time we met. The six of you walked directly into our ambush. With only five guys, three of which you never even saw, we were easily able to neutralize your bigger numbers. If you'd opened fire at the outset, the gunfight would have been over before it began, and my guys would have walked away without a scratch."

Derrick's son cut in. "Well, that's the whole point of an ambush, isn't it? You don't see it until you're surrounded."

"Yes and no," Sean agreed. "If you and your men had been walking in a line with fifty yards between each other, we couldn't have surrounded you. As soon as we confronted the lead guy in your line, the others in your group could have swung around and came at us from behind. It's not really a foolproof tactic, and you're still likely to take casualties, but at least you're engaging in a fair fight. Walking all bunched up in a single group makes taking out the lot of you just like shooting fish in a barrel. It's a similar technique that was used in the thick forests during Vietnam. You need to keep your men spread out." Both Derrick and his son were nodding their heads in understanding now. Craig had walked over to their table to listen in, as had a couple other men from their group.

"Look. I realize we're still feeling each other out, and like you said the first time we met, 'It's a tough new world and it takes time to earn trust.' I agree with that. I'm just hoping that at some point in the future, you might let us help you secure your perimeter a little better and let us offer you some help on your tactics. I know a thing or two about setting up a perimeter, but I'm no expert on the subject, either. Another member of our group that's not here today used to be an Army Ranger, and he's worked with our retreat and also helped set up Tionesta's perimeter security. Someday, maybe we can get him to take a look at your security plan and offer you some pointers."

"We've already got a lot of secret security stuff we've set up around here. Stuff that you just ain't seein'," Derrick's younger boy said confidently. He was cut off by his father's outstretched hand on his arm.

"I'm sure you do, and I'm definitely not going to ask about them," Sean replied, raising his hands and smiling. "I'm just offering some advice from an expert if you're willing to receive it."

"Thank you for your generous offer, Sean," Derrick said calmly and coolly. "We will discuss it among our group after you leave. We'll let you know what we decide."

There was a long awkward silence, which Craig broke by suggesting, "Let's play some dang cards, ya'll!" Laughter erupted and the tension quickly melted from the room. They stood, rearranged the tables, and split everyone into five tables of five players each. Sean stayed at Derrick's table with Randy, Derrick's eldest son, and Craig. They played for kernels of field corn, and before long, Derrick had a decisively large lead in their game.

"Pastor Derrick! You, sir, are not supposed to be this proficient at a sinner's profession!" Randy joked as he lost his final hand and went out of the game.

Derrick wore a large grin on his face. "How do you think I paid my way through seminary?"

Sean and Randy both gave him a shocked look and Derrick let out a hearty laugh. "I'm only kidding. I was blessed that my parents were able to pay my tuition. *However*, there *was* a big rumor on campus of a high stakes poker game every Saturday night between our professors. I can neither confirm nor deny that I used to play in that game while I was down there. Dan doesn't even know about that." Randy stood from the table and squeezed Derrick's shoulder in a friendly manner as he passed by to refill his water glass. Derrick swiveled his head to follow him. "Besides, Randy, your tell is really easy to spot. Every time you have a good hand, you get all serious and every time you're bluffing, you start joking around."

Randy shrugged. "Maybe I was just bluffing the whole time and planning to take you for everything you have the next time we played."

There was no hesitation from Derrick who'd since turned back to his cards to study his next hand. "Nope," he said confidently with a wry grin. "Son, this really isn't your game. Maybe you should go upstairs with the children and give checkers a try." Sean almost spit out his drink at Derrick's taunt and began laughing out loud at the look on Randy's face. For once his best friend was speechless. What does one say when a preacher decides to insult you?

Not long after, Derrick won the table and the winners of the five different tables were joined in the final showdown. In order to be back to the North Homestead before dusk, it was decided to raise the ante significantly for the final game. Only Sean's uncle Nathan was left to uphold the honor of the North Retreat and he didn't do very well at it. He was the first to exit the game. Sean was starting to surmise that Poker Night was likely a regular thing in Derrick's group. It had been an entertaining afternoon and Sean thought it might be fun to start having their own poker night at the North Homestead. The final game was winding down and it was almost time to leave when Sean went upstairs to see how Maria was faring.

Upon entering the sanctuary, Sean was greeted with sounds of multiple women's conversations all happening at once. He quickly spotted the back of Maria's head in the front pew. When Sean drew close, he noticed his wife was…*was she crocheting?* She sat with a ball of yarn on her lap and a plastic needle in her right hand, threading it through the small square she was working on. Maria was surrounded by three other grey-haired women whose fingers all blurred with a similar motion, but with pointedly more deftness at the task. A fourth woman, who sat in a chair in front of Maria, was guiding her through the process.

Maria looked up to see the shocked look on her husband's face. She beamed. "I'm making a hat for Jacob!" she said excitedly.

Sean didn't think the small blue square of woven yarn looked like much of a hat. Evidently, it was a work in progress. In nearly two decades of marriage, he would have never guessed that his wife would take an interest in crochet. He smiled back at her warmly. "Nice!" Sean sat down across from his wife on the steps leading up to the dais. The woman who was teaching Maria scooted her chair to the side a little so Sean could watch the process.

"They're wrapping up downstairs and it's almost time to go," he offered after a few minutes of watching her work. She seemed to be learning the process quickly, though he didn't know the first thing about needlework.

"Okay," she answered, not looking up.

The woman helping his wife gave Sean a friendly smile and reached her hand out. "Hi, there. My name is Martha." She was a middle-aged woman with serious eyes and a lock of silver running down from her temple.

"Hello," Sean said in return, shaking her cold, bony hand.

"Your wife is picking this up really fast," she said. Maria blushed at the praise. "She'll be a pro in no time." Sean continued to watch Maria's fingers move through the process.

"Oops," Martha abruptly said, pointing. "See what you did there? You'll need to—"

She was cut off by a loud bang coming from outside, followed by silence. Everybody froze and Sean cocked his head to the left, listening intently.

"Was that a gunshot?" one of the women to his right asked no one in particular. A few seconds later, all hell broke loose. Sean's rifle was downstairs.

Chapter 26

Sammy was sitting in his usual chair going through a detailed report on their latest supply shipment. Annoyed, he let out a long sigh. "You're going to ruin that pen."

"Sorry," Bruce muttered, tossing the pen onto his desk.

"Seriously, Bruce. What is going on with you? You've been off in La-La land all day."

Bruce just shook his head dismissively. He stood and walking to the window, peering outside.

Sammy wasn't going to be satisfied with Bruce's dismissal. "I've known you for a long time Bruce. I don't know that I've ever seen you this nervous. What's going on?"

Bruce had made a decision not to tell Sammy about his meeting with Lt. Baier the previous day; there wasn't any reason to get Sammy involved. "General Duncan's going to be visiting us soon," he finally offered, changing the subject.

"And that's a bad thing?" Sammy asked with a muddled look.

"No," Bruce admitted. "I don't know. Maybe."

Sammy chuckled. He stood, set the stack of papers from his lap onto the desk, and walked over to join Bruce at the window. "You do realize that you're kinda freaking me out, don't you? If there's something coming down the pike at us, I'd like to know what it is."

Bruce turned to his friend, looking him in the eye. "No. No, you don't, Sammy. There've been some developments on the General Oates front. Some big developments. I'm not going to tell you what they are because if things go bad it's way better for you if you're not involved."

"I've been involved up to this point," Sammy pointed out, crossing his arms across his chest. When Bruce didn't reply, he asked, "Is that why General Duncan is coming?"

Bruce gave his friend a flat look. "Seriously, I can't talk about it. General Duncan is coming up here to evaluate my plans to work with the local towns and improve security in the area."

They were interrupted by a knock at the door. Bruce's orderly stuck his head in. "Sir, I've just been informed that a Cessna is on approach for landing."

"Well that was quick," Sammy said suspiciously.

"It's probably not General Duncan," Bruce offered as he walked over to his desk and pulled his uniform shirt off the back of the chair. Bruce had been expecting the plane with the General Oates's man all morning and it was now almost dark.

"Who would it be then? I didn't get a report of a plane scheduled for today."

"Me neither," Bruce muttered.

"What the hell is going on, Bruce?" Sammy demanded loudly.

Bruce ignored the question as he fastened the last button on his shirt. He headed toward the door. "I'll talk to you later, Sammy."

Sammy snorted stubbornly as Bruce shut the door behind him.

The Cessna landed at the Warren Airpark, a tiny, single airstrip just west of town that they didn't utilize very often. Nearly every plane to Warren was a transport plane and needed the longer and heavier duty runways at the Bradford Regional Airport. Bruce was surprised when General Duncan was the first to step off the plane. When he'd spoken with him the previous day, he'd slipped a code phrase into the beginning of the call so Duncan knew it was urgent. Then, when Bruce requested that he make a trip up to Warren at his soonest possible convenience to discuss setting up official lines of communication with the local towns, General Duncan hadn't put up any resistance to making the trip. If Bruce hadn't slipped in the code word, General Duncan surely would have pitched a fit about making the trip. It was no secret Duncan didn't like to fly. He'd told Bruce he would make arrangements to come on the next supply run, yet here he was. Bruce's feigned urgency on the call had obviously impressed on the General that Bruce needed to speak with him on an urgent matter. They greeted each other warmly.

A second man in an expensive looking pinstriped suit and dark sunglasses stepped off the plane after Duncan. "Who would wear those things anymore if they didn't have to?" Bruce thought, eyeing the man's suit. Not to mention that it was overcast and the man was still wearing sunglasses. Bruce also noticed the man's shiny black leather shoes which didn't seem to have a single scuff on them. Either this guy was important or he was trying to portray an image of importance. General Duncan introduced the man as Horace Singleton, General Oates's personal secretary. The man frowned at General Duncan's description of his job title but remained silent. With introductions made, the three of them, the pilot, and Bruce's security team for the day, all quickly boarded the row of Humvees and headed back into town.

Bruce rode up front and as soon as they pulled off the noisy gravel driveway to the airstrip and onto the paved road he turned backwards in his seat toward Duncan. "How was your flight?" he asked with a snicker.

"C'mon, Bruce, you know now much I hate to fly! There is no way that tin can should have received clearance to even taxi down a runway. Half the instrumentation in that plane doesn't even work. Can you believe that crazy pilot flew us here without a functioning artificial horizon? Twice we had to fly fifty feet off the deck to stay below the clouds. It was horrifying."

Bruce chuckled in reply. Apparently they were supposed to have arrived early that morning, but the thunder storms that had blown through the area earlier prevented them from keeping their departure time. Bruce knew if a pilot tried to fly through heavy clouds without an artificial horizon, he'd quickly lose spatial awareness and wouldn't know which way was up and which way was down. Even a good pilot would eventually drive a plane straight into the ground without it. "It's only a four-mile trip back to town. We'll get you situated somewhere comfortable and you can relax. We can catch up over breakfast."

Horace spoke up loudly from directly behind Bruce's seat. "I'm sorry, Colonel. I'm going to need you to take me to where your visitors are staying. The ones that arrived a few days ago." He gave General Duncan a purposeful, sideways glance.

Bruce caught the meaning. "Wouldn't it be better if we dropped the general off first and let him get situated? It's not far out of our way."

"No, sir. I'm under strict orders to meet with them immediately upon landing."

Bruce shrugged. He leaned over to his driver and was informing him of their new destination when he felt a tap on his shoulder. He craned his neck to find the suited man holding out an envelope in his direction.

"What's this?" Bruce asked taking the letter.

"I'm not sure, Colonel. I was told to give it to you as soon as we landed."

Bruce opened the letter. It was obviously a hastily handwritten note from General Oates.

"Colonel Harris, due to a string of heavy storms this morning in D.C., and only having this one aircraft available at the time (which can't be operated in inclement weather), a very critical mission has been placed behind schedule. You are to provide Horace anything he needs or requests with no delays. There is also a package of utmost importance which he is to deliver. Since Horace will be forced to stay overnight and return in the morning, you are to assist him in keeping the package in a private, safe, and secure location. That means away from your men. You are not to ask any questions of Horace in regard to the package and you will personally assist him in loading it onto the plane for the return trip tomorrow.

I also just became aware that General Duncan will be flying up there on the same flight. He is not permitted to accompany Horace and the package on the return flight. Another return transport for General Duncan will need to be arranged. You will not discuss any details you may or may not think you know about this particular mission with him, either. I will be expecting a full report from you on your meeting with General Duncan and the nature of your dealings with the town of Tionesta or any other correspondence or intel you may have gathered on any of the other towns or groups in the area during your stay in Warren. No detail is too small.

Whatever you do, Colonel Harris, do not screw this up or interfere with this mission in any way!"

It was signed, "General Norman Oates."

Bruce read down through it again.

"What is it?" General Duncan asked.

Bruce handed him the letter with a sideways glance at Horace. General Duncan's eyes took on a sharp glint as he read his colleague's words and he blew out his cheeks in a huff as he finished. When he tried to hand the letter back to Bruce, Horace reached out to intercept it. Duncan quickly snatched it away from his reach. "I will break your fingers if you try that again!" General Duncan scolded him. The man rolled his eyes and leaned back in his seat, turning his head to look out the hazy, sand-blasted window of the Humvee. Bruce was trying not to laugh at the exchange as Duncan handed him back the letter. "Chatty Cathy over there barely said a single word the entire ride up here. Now he wants to get involved in everyone else's business!" He shot a glare at the back of the man's head. Horace never turned to acknowledge the insult. Colonel Harris couldn't help but smile.

Colonel Harris and General Duncan sat in the Humvee, waiting for Horace to return from the Warren Manor building where Bruce had billeted the Seal Team. They were both forbidden to accompany the man, and neither of them argued the point. This would give Bruce a few minutes to coordinate with Duncan without getting into too many details. As soon as Horace had walked through the front doors of the building, Bruce told his driver to go take a smoke break. Bruce had never seen the private smoking, but the perceptive soldier caught on to his commander's request for privacy. He jumped out of the vehicle and shut the door behind him.

Bruce was about to speak when Duncan held a finger to his lips. He pointed at Horace's briefcase which was positioned, suspiciously, directly between them. Bruce hadn't noticed it, and General Oates's assistant must have placed it there when he exited the vehicle. Bruce gave the general a look of incredulity. General Duncan just raised his hands and shrugged. Bruce nodded his silent agreement. While it was dubious that there was a recording device in the briefcase, it wasn't worth the risk.

Bruce motioned the general to lean forward and whispered in his ear. "I'll meet you in your room tonight at 0200. Don't lock your door." General Duncan nodded and sat back into his seat.

Bruce shifted to find a more comfortable position, not sure how long their wait would be. However, it was only minutes later when Horace came barreling out of the building's double glass doors. Bruce's driver caught the clue and jumped into the truck with a questioning eyebrow raised to Bruce. He nodded back and the young man settled into his seat and fastened his seat belt. Bruce was shocked when Horace opened Bruce's door instead of his own.

"Where are they?" he demanded loudly.

"What are you talking about? They're not there?" Bruce constructed his best confused face.

"No! Dammit! They're not there!"

"How should I know?" Bruce demanded. "I haven't seen them since—"

Horace held out an urgent hand to stop Bruce from continuing whatever he was about to say. He glanced in Duncan's direction briefly. "I need you to take me back to your office and I need to use your satphone immediately!"

"We're waiting on you, chief. Are you going to get in?" Bruce bellowed sarcastically over the roar of the Humvee's engine as his driver started the vehicle. Horace slammed the heavy door and climbed in behind Bruce. Again, Bruce couldn't help himself; he let out a long laugh barely concealed by the roar of the diesel engine as they pulled out and headed back to his office building.

As soon as the three of them stepped foot into Bruce's office, Horace demanded that he punch in his passcode on the satphone and then shooed them both into the hallway, closing the door in their faces.

Bruce now stood with his ear pressed tightly to his own office door.

"This is ridiculous," Bruce heard Duncan whisper from behind him. "I feel like we're in second grade, listening in to the principal's office."

"Shhh," Bruce said softly in response. He was trying to listen to the conversation, but all he could hear were snippets. "I know, sir." "Yes, sir, I understand." Then a short silence followed by, "That's not really what I do—" Bruce heard the poor man try to speak or explain himself on more than one occasion only to be cut off by the person on the other end of the line. It was very likely an agitated and pissed off General Oates. Bruce was glad to learn it wasn't just him that couldn't get a word in edgewise when talking to Oates on the phone. Bruce heard the creak of a chair and the approaching clack-clack of dress shoes. He scrambled back from the door, leaned against the wall next to General Duncan, and tried his best to look disinterested. The door opened.

A forlorn Horace held the phone out to Bruce. "He wants to speak with you."

"Who?" Bruce asked in mock surprise.

"You know who!" Horace hissed while covering the mouthpiece with his palm. Bruce sighed and took the phone. The man had the audacity to put his hand on Bruce's back and gently steer him into the office, shutting the door behind them. Bruce ignored Horace's impertinence…for now.

"This is Colonel Harris," Bruce said in to the phone.

"Colonel Harris! What in the holy hell is going on up there?" Bruce's suspicion was confirmed. It *was* a very pissed off General Oates on the other end of the line. "You have a very uncanny way of screwing up important missions of mine!"

"Excuse me, sir! I've done nothing of the sort!" Bruce said defensively. General Oates tried to cut back in, but Bruce just raised his voice and talked over him. "I followed your orders to the T. I put your men up in a private part of town well away from my own. When they provided a list for resupply yesterday morning, I instructed my men to get them everything on their list, no questions asked. I never even looked at their damn list! Other than that, I have not seen nor spoken to a single one of your men since they arrived. I have no idea when they left. You instructed me to stay out of their way, and that's exactly what I did. If you needed someone to babysit your men, then you should have told me to do so!" By the end he was practically yelling into the phone…at a four star general. He realized that Horace was standing next to him with his mouth gaping. Bruce shot Oates's lackey an icy glare and waited for the tongue lashing he knew was forthcoming.

Colonel Harris was bewildered when there was a long pause before the general spoke, his voice surprisingly calm. "Very well, Colonel. It was not your responsibility to keep tabs on those men.

However, I'm now making it your responsibility to help track them down. Horace is clearly not cut out for this line of work. I want that list of supplies they requested. Maybe that will tell us where they've gone. I also want the both of you to thoroughly scavenge through the rooms those men were staying in."

"Yes, sir," Bruce responded as calmly as he could. If General Oates was willing to take the conversation down a notch, he wasn't going to poke the bear. "I'll do what I can," he added.

"I want you to call me back as soon as you've searched their rooms and spoken with your men who were on perimeter security. I want to know where they've gone!"

"Yes, sir."

"I'll be waiting for your call…later tonight," General Oates added.

"Yes, sir," Bruce repeated once more as the phone beeped vociferously in his ear. General Oates was never one for a lengthy sign off. Bruce set the phone down on his desk and bellowed for his orderly.

"What's going on?" Horace asked him.

Bruce ignored the man's question, stepping around him and walking to the door. He'd no sooner turned the handle when his orderly appeared in the door opening. "Run downstairs and grab Sgt. Timms for me," Bruce ordered.

Horace started to say something and Bruce held his finger out, motioning him to silence without even looking at him. Bruce faced General Duncan who leaned casually against the wall trying to hide a grin. "I apologize for all the commotion and the inconvenience, General. I seem to have just sent my orderly away. When he returns, he'll show you to your room for the night and retrieve your luggage for you. I assume you're hungry, so once you're settled he can take you over to the officer's mess for something to eat." Bruce glanced down at his watch. "They'll be closing in a half hour, so you'll have to make it quick."

"What's going on, Colonel?" General Duncan inquired.

Bruce sighed. "Unfortunately, sir, General Oates instructed me not to discuss the matter with you."

"Is that so?" Duncan said. He turned an icy glare toward the suited man in the open doorway behind Bruce. "Well if that's what the General ordered, then I guess you need to do as he says."

There was a moment of awkward silence before Bruce continued. "Sir, why don't you go ahead and get some rest. Apparently, I'm going to have a busy evening ahead of me. We can meet in my office at 0900 for breakfast and discuss my plans we were talking about on the phone."

Sgt. Timms bounded up the steps from Bruce's left with his orderly trailing a few paces behind. Horace tried once more to say something, and once again Bruce held up a finger in his direction. Bruce was starting to enjoy this. While he could never get away with treating General Oates this way, antagonizing his personal assistant was a rewarding substitute.

Sgt. Timms came to attention. "Sir."

"I want you to go talk with Major Samuelsson and find out who was on perimeter security the last two days. I want to know where and when a convoy of four up-armored Humvees with non-31st Regiment troops left the base and which direction they were headed. I want every soldier at that location who spoke with the convoy as they left brought to my office in exactly one hour. This is to be kept quiet and done discretely, understood?"

"Roger that, Colonel," Sgt. Timms answered with a nod, glancing down at his own watch to check the time.

"You can go," Bruce said and Sgt. Timms sped down the hallway. Bruce hollered after him, "And tell the rest of the security detail, we are wheels up in 1 minute!"

Sgt. Timms had stopped halfway down the steps with only his head visible above the landing. "Yes, sir!" he hollered back before his head disappeared from view.

"Private Mason, please get General Duncan's bags from the back of the truck downstairs and show him to his room, ASAP. After that I want you to personally take him down and show him where the officer's mess hall is located. Make yourself available to him this evening in case he needs anything else."

"At once, sir," he said, scurrying off.

"Colonel Harris," Horace said, finally finding an opening to interject himself, "we need to hurry back to…." He trailed off with a quick glance at General Duncan.

"I know where we need to go!" Bruce said indignantly. "And General Duncan's not an idiot, you know." Bruce rolled his eyes at Duncan who smiled back. They might be overstepping their bounds a little with Oates's man, but his peevish nature and fancy clothes made it difficult for them not to give the guy a hard time. He was severely out of place on a military base.

"Alright, General. I'll talk to you tomorrow morning," Bruce said.

"Enjoy your evening," Duncan replied with a coy smile.

Bruce turned away with Horace following on his heels. "Oh, yeah. It will be all gumdrops and fairy tales tonight," he muttered under his breath.

Horace took a couple quick steps forward until he was even with Bruce. "What was that? I didn't hear what you said."

"I wasn't talking to you," Bruce said flatly. Though Horace was nowhere near as competent or formidable, the way Horace followed him down the hallway made Bruce think back to the day he'd met Lt. Jenkins after his first mission briefing with General Oates. At least Jenkins had known when to shut up and quit asking questions.

Chapter 27

Colonel Harris awoke to his alarm clock blaring static. There were no radio stations anymore, but waking to the static was far better than the annoying buzzer on his bedside clock. With sleepy motions, he rolled over and smacked the oversized "off" button on the small plastic clock through the t-shirt he'd placed over it. The LCD screen was only partially functional and flickered incessantly which necessitated covering it if he were to achieve any sleep. Bruce lifted the edge of the t-shirt. 2 a.m. He felt as if he'd gone through a spin cycle and been put away wet. He'd hardly slept at all the last few nights. Bruce groaned as he sat up.

Per his instructions from General Oates, Bruce had taken Horace back to Warren Manor to inspect the rooms previously occupied by the Seal Team. They found a worn envelope addressed to General Oates sitting in the center of Lt. Baier's perfectly made bed. Bruce couldn't help himself as he scolded Horace for not seeing the note earlier when he'd first come in to find the Seal Team gone. Bruce was conspicuous in how he immediately handed the letter over to Horace as if he didn't care to know what was in it. Besides, he already knew its contents.

Lt. Baier had instructed Bruce he would leave a note for General Oates telling him they were not going to turn over Catalina and insisting that he was making a monumental mistake in trusting Skyler. They also informed him that it was a mistake he and his men weren't going to take part in. Bruce had watched Horace's face grow pained as he read through it, and Bruce was glad he wasn't going to be the one to read it to General Oates over the phone. Upon returning to his office, Bruce had interviewed his men in front of Horace and found out the Seal Team had left through the southeastern checkpoint headed down Route 6 into the Allegheny National Forest. No words had been spoken as the men manning the checkpoint weren't accustomed to stopping a row of Humvees leaving town. Their orders were to challenge anyone trying to enter Warren, not leaving. One of the men had observed what he thought was a female riding in the passenger seat of the second Humvee and he'd found it odd, but not important enough to report. Bruce thanked them for the information and asked for their discretion in not discussing it or the overall nature of their meeting with their peers. Bruce dismissed his men.

Last, Bruce took Horace over to The Alamo where they spoke to Captain Whitmar, the officer in charge of supply. He'd quickly located the handwritten supply and equipment list the Seals had turned over to the men guarding the Hickory Street bridge. Capt. Whitmar seemed concerned by the attendance of the man in the suit and kept giving Horace sidelong glances as they walked. His commanding officer's presence requesting the list was fairly odd as well, since Bruce had not stepped foot into the man's office since arriving in Warren. Captain Whitmar apprehensively reminded Colonel Harris that it was he, personally, that had instructed him to fulfill any request by the visiting soldiers staying down in the Warren Manor with no questions asked. Bruce set the man at ease. "Captain, this is just a cursory follow up. You've done nothing wrong." Once they were back in Bruce's office, they poured through the list to find the Seal Team had requested enough provisions to last them for two months.

Horace had literally been in a near state of panic by the time he was ready to call General Oates and give him the bad news. All indications were that the Seal Team had defied their orders and gone AWOL. Bruce had to admit he didn't want to be in Horace's shoes on that call. When Horace had worked up enough courage to make the call, he'd politely requested that Bruce leave the room. Bruce complied graciously this time, beginning to feel a little empathy for the man. After the call, Bruce was surprised that the general hadn't requested to speak with him again. A sullen Horace had emerged from his office after only two minutes and informed Bruce that General Oates wanted him to keep his eyes open for the missing men and report back to him directly at the first sight of them. Bruce nodded in reply and instructed his orderly to take Horace to his room and arrange for food to be brought to him. By then the main chow facility was closed. Horace issued Bruce a sincere "Thanks" before disappearing down the hall after Private Mason.

The ruse he'd constructed with Lt. Baier had worked so far. Only Bruce knew their real objective. He stepped back into his office and locked the door before pulling a thick envelope out of his right cargo pocket. Per their plan, the note had been hidden inside the ceiling vent of the restroom down the hall from the Seals' bedrooms. During their search of the rooms, Bruce had excused himself from Horace on the pretense of taking a piss and retrieved it. Inside was an officially formatted and detailed report by Lt. Baier on their entire mission, his findings, the intel on Skyler and the encampment in Cleveland, and a sharp condemnation of General Oates's handling of the entire mission. He'd left it to Bruce to put it in the right hands. Bruce was still unsure of who that might be. He hoped General Duncan could assist him in making a recommendation.

Upon finally dragging his weary body from bed, Bruce didn't bother to dress and just wore his PT outfit. He slung a towel over his shoulder for appearances as he left his room. Two doors down, he knocked on his orderly's door and the groggy-eyed young private answered, plainly surprised to find Colonel Harris standing there in the middle of the night.

"Private Mason, I know you're probably tired right now. The last few days have been long and hectic. But I have a very important task for you and I need your help. I'm sure you've noticed a lot of strange things happening today and it's very important I am able to have a private meeting with General Duncan without any chance of somebody listening in." Bruce gave his orderly a slight grimace. "I'm going to need you to walk this hallway from end to end until I am done meeting with General Duncan inside his room. If you see anyone enter this hallway, for any reason, you're to loudly, but casually, ask them if they need anything. No need to confront them or take it any further. This will let us know someone is approaching. Do you understand what I am asking of you?" His orderly rubbed his eyes and nodded. "This meeting, like my meeting yesterday with Lt. Baier, is to be kept completely secret. If word leaks out about these meetings, it could be very bad for me and the Regiment as a whole. I—"

Private Mason actually had the audacity to cut him off. "Colonel Harris, you don't need to say anything else or explain anything. I understand what you need me to do and I don't need any more details. No one will ever hear anything about it from me." There was a short pause before he added, "Sir."

Bruce smiled. "Thank you, Mason. I knew I could count on you."

Bruce left the private's doorway and walked past Sammy's room to the last door on the left. He knocked softly. Motion to his left caught Bruce's eye, and in the dark he could make out his orderly's silhouette as he took a seat on the floor with his back to the wall, lacing up his sneakers for his mid-night patrol. Bruce was getting ready to knock again, when the door pivoted open slightly, spilling lamplight into the dark hallway. General Duncan was still in uniform and Bruce could see an open book resting in the center of his bed.

"I couldn't sleep," General Duncan offered as he opened the door the rest of the way. Duncan peeked his head into the hallway and looked both directions before closing the door. "I assume you know that your orderly is sitting in the hallway?"

"Yeah," Bruce replied. "He's going to patrol while we talk and give us a heads up if anyone comes down the hall."

"Good idea," Duncan agreed. He walked over and sat on the edge of his bed, leaving Bruce the lone chair in the room. He placed a bookmark in his novel and set it aside.

Bruce sighed. "It's been a long night. Besides dealing with Horace and General Oates, one of the small groups of survivalists I've come to know down near Tionesta was attacked tonight."

General Duncan looked back, his forehead wrinkled in concern. "And?"

"They only lost one man in the fighting. One wounded. One of their attackers was a woman in serious need of medical attention or she was going to die."

"A woman?" Duncan asked, a little surprised.

"I guess. I sent a platoon down with our surgeon to see if he could help." He watched General Duncan to see his reaction on sending his men down to help.

General Duncan nodded but didn't condemn his actions. "I hope it all works out for them," he said sincerely. General Duncan fidgeted with the book on his nightstand briefly before asking. "So, what's really going on here, Bruce? I assume something important is happening."

Bruce didn't hold back. He'd spent considerable time the previous day pondering what to tell his commanding officer and what to hold back. But once he started down the path, he realized that he was going to tell Duncan everything. And he did.

Bruce started with their original mission briefing from General Oates and his concern over the legality of their orders to take out the AWOL Ranger unit. He told him of his dealings with Lt. Jenkins and how he discovered the truth behind the Rangers' mission from Mayor Reese. He even shared the details surrounding Lt. Jenkins' ultimate demise. He told Duncan how Mayor Reese was also a pirate ham radio broadcaster with contacts inside the highest levels of government, and how Bruce had helped relocate the mayor in a nearby area to protect him from General Oates in the future. The precise location he didn't share as there was no reason for the general to know the specifics. He conveyed that they'd maintained contact over the last few months and how David had provided to him more information on General Oates background, going so far as to show Duncan the actual message he'd received from the former mayor a few days prior. He also shared his interaction with Willy at Tionesta's council meeting and his suspicion of General Oates being behind the mass murder of the entire Newark Green Zone. Bruce insinuated that it fit with General Oates's MO for dealing with hard situations like that and how he couldn't envision one of their fellow commanders acting alone in such a situation. General Duncan nodded his agreement with that point.

Last, he shared with him the details of his secret meeting with Lt. Baier and more details on what had happened with Horace the previous evening. When he'd finished, he handed General Duncan Lt. Baier's report and leaned back in his chair. His voice was almost hoarse and he wished he'd brought his canteen with him. Duncan pulled a pair of small reading glasses from the nightstand drawer and placed them on his nose, bending over into the light of the small bedside lamp. He read the report slowly. Bruce waited patiently, nervous as to what his commanding officer's response was going to be. At the same time, he was relieved to have everything off his chest.

When General Duncan finished the report, he slowly folded it, placed it back into in the thick envelop, and slowly tapped the heavy wad of paper on his open palm. He sighed and looked up at Bruce with a troubled gaze but still didn't say anything.

"We've got to tell someone," Bruce said uneasily. "I don't know what game General Oates is playing at, but he's clearly off the reservation. I was hoping you might be able to help me make contact with someone in Congress or someone who can do something about this."

General Duncan snorted at that. "Your message from the former mayor of Kane is surprisingly accurate and backs up the information I've dug up on General Oates over the last few weeks. So accurate, in fact, that I'm quite curious who his contact is. General Oates is without a doubt the most powerful man in the country right now and likely the most dangerous. Everyone at headquarters knows he's running the show for the most part, and no one there is willing to cross him." Bruce groaned at the confirmation of his misgivings on getting someone at HQ to help them. "To be honest Bruce, I don't want to cross him either. I have a family…." He trailed off and began to restlessly tap the envelope on his palm once more. "This is very disturbing information and I agree it needs to be shared with someone, but I just don't know if…." He trailed off again. "I don't know who would have the power at this point to stand up to General Oates or if they'd even have the ability to do anything about it."

"What about someone in Congress?" Bruce proposed.

General Duncan slowly shook his head. "Congress is a joke. They're completely clueless on how to handle the situation, and they seem content to just let the President continue fumbling his way through the mess using his authority under martial law. Every remaining Congressman has a different opinion on how to handle the situation and there's no unity of purpose and no reigning majority behind any of the proposals. I think the last thing they tried to vote on a few months back received something like ten percent support. The chance of them actually passing something these days is pretty slim. Heck, half of the Democrats want to use the situation to strip the Constitution and redraw it to 'meet the challenges of the new world.' Half of the Republicans continue to play politics and work harder at condemning the President's actions than trying to help him through this." He sighed. "There are still some good men there, but I just don't know what they could do about this." He waved the letter in front of Bruce.

"Besides, while there's a lot of circumstantial evidence here, there is nothing concrete. Who knows what General Oates is playing at? While I find his willingness to destroy an entire town to take out one person operating a ham radio to be quite disturbing, he didn't actually succeed in doing so. The best thing would be to have solid evidence placing him behind the orders to poison the insurgent Green Zone. But as of now, all we have are suspicions and I don't have the first clue how we would go about proving his involvement."

General Duncan tapped his finger on his chin. "I seem to remember discussing the Newark Green Zone with General Owens a few months ago. He'd told me that there'd been a horrendous outbreak of some fast spreading disease that had devastated his Green Zone; it was unlike anything he could have imagined. I remember him being very disturbed over it and worried that it might still spread among his men who'd been quarantined at the time. He'd shared with me how he'd been ordered to burn the place afterwards, but that's standard operating procedure for something like that. I've known General Owens for many years and I'm confident he wouldn't have been involved with poisoning those people. I agree with you that General Oates would likely be the culprit and it's quite possible that he used one of his agents to poison their water supply. But we have no way to prove that."

"What if we could?" Bruce jumped in, intensity growing in his voice. "Get proof, I mean." General Duncan raised his eyebrows questioningly. Bruce's epiphany was taking shape in his head as he spoke, and he leaned forward intently. "From Willy's description of what happened, I truly believe that a nerve agent or biological weapon was used. That stuff is a highly controlled substance and it would take someone at the highest levels of government to access it. There would have to be some sort of paper trail involved." Bruce was starting to speak faster as the idea took shape. "All we'd have to do is get a sample from the water source inside the Newark Green Zone and have it tested. Once we have proof, it would just be a matter of following the trail to its current storage location and find out who checked it out of the lab. If I could acquire a sample of infected water for you, could you arrange to get it tested at a facility that handles this kind of stuff?"

General Duncan held up his hand. "Bruce, Bruce, slow down!" He sighed. "I only know of one location where they keep this stuff. From my understanding, that facility is still operating and guarded better than headquarters. We can't be letting that stuff fall into civilian hands now, can we? If a chemical agent or biological weapon was used, it likely would have come from this facility. That said, what do you want me to do? Walk up to the front gates and tell them the water bottles I'm holding potentially contain a dangerous chemical that I'd like them to test for me? Even if I could convince them I'm not completely off my rocker, who do you think they are going to call to get permission for me to enter the facility? If they don't reach out to Oates personally, they'll still be calling their own commander at headquarters. I know it's something we haven't discussed yet, but I believe General Oates has men that are somehow intercepting and monitoring Sat calls through the Pentagon. He seems to know about my calls before my orderly even passes me my messages."

"I suspected as much," Bruce said. "Especially after the other day, when he knew specific details about our call only an hour beforehand." Bruce smiled. "To be honest, I was a little concerned at first that you might be passing him information."

"C'mon, Bruce." Duncan admonished him for even considering it.

"But then I thought you might have a leak in your office. Maybe your orderly?"

"No way!" General Duncan said definitively. "I'd trust my orderly with my life. I know I can't prove it to you, but I know for a fact he's not leaking intel. It has to be through interception of the satphone system because there are others at headquarters having the same issue." He gave Bruce a knowing look but didn't elaborate with more details.

"But to get back on point, Bruce, I don't have the clearance to get into a facility like that. I surely wouldn't want to ask the two people I do know that have the kind of clearance needed. You have to surmise that General Oates will know the second someone enters there and starts asking questions about missing nerve agents and offering a canteen of water for testing. I don't think that person is going to have a long and fulfilling life after that. Besides, you're missing an obvious problem. Who are you going to send down to Newark to retrieve the samples? It would be a suicide mission for one of your guys. Out of uniform, they're a target for an ambush. In uniform, they'd likely be picked up by some patrol who'd assume they're AWOL. Even if they could find where the Green Zone had been located inside the city, how would they go about finding a sample if they'd never been down there before or understood how that specific Green Zone's food and water distribution operated? Surely if Oates were behind this, he'd have cleaned up his tracks and destroyed the original water source by now. Who would you be willing to send in there, knowing that it's likely a death sentence?"

Bruce smiled. "I actually have the perfect person in mind."

"Who?" General Duncan asked, skeptical.

"The same guy who lived in the Newark Green Zone and helplessly watched his wife and daughter asphyxiate on their own blood and vomit. I have a feeling Willy would be willing to make the trip if it could bring down the man responsible for their deaths. And he actually has the skills needed to survive the open road to get down there and back."

"But didn't you say this Willy guy was crazy?"

Bruce snickered. "I said he's half-crazy. The other half might be genius."

"Even so," General Duncan muttered.

"Even so, what? What? Why are you…?" Bruce pleaded angrily. He sensed General Duncan's obvious reluctance to get involved. Could he blame the man?

"Bruce, I have a family," General Duncan reminded Bruce once more. "I realize you have bad history with General Oates and I'm with you that the man needs to get *disappeared.* But whoever takes on this plan of yours to bring down the most powerful man in our country is likely to end up disappearing themselves. I can't do that to my wife and baby girls. I'll help you however I can, but you're asking too much of me to lead this battle charge." It was General Duncan who was pleading with Bruce now.

Bruce gave the general a frustrated smile. "I understand, sir." They sat silently for a few moments. "Is there someone else you could recommend? Is there someone in Congress that I might be able to speak with? Maybe someone who's vocally opposed to General Oates?"

General Duncan rubbed his temples as he thought hard. "Most of the Republicans are vocally opposed to the President and General Oates at this point. What you'd need is someone with the clearance and authority to get into the facility that houses this stuff. I think your best point of contact is going to be Trent Epstein who sits on the Intelligence Committee. He's a former Navy Admiral, as well, if my memory serves me correctly."

Bruce was feeling his determination starting to grow again. This was going to work. It had too. "Good. So all I need now are the samples from Newark's water supply. The next question is how do I get into Raven Rock to meet with Senator Epstein?"

"Leave that to me," General Duncan offered. "I'll have to wrap my head around an effective pretense to give you access to him, but I'll figure it out." He paused. "Bruce, I'm sorry but this is the most I can offer you." Bruce bowed his head in acknowledgment. "I also have to warn you that this may not go the way you want. Senator Epstein may not want to get involved. Maybe the samples will come back negative. There are lots of ways that this may go south on you. You need to realize that if that happens, your life will be in immediate danger. You need to have a back-up plan in place to get out of dodge. I'd start working on that now, if I were you."

Bruce nodded. "Yeah, that's probably a good idea." He stood slowly and stretched. "Let's push back breakfast to 0930. We can discuss what I've got going on with the local towns before you fly back. Sounds like you get to fly back with Horace after all." Bruce smiled and General Duncan rolled his eyes in disgust.

Bruce went back to his room after relieving a tired-looking Private Mason and thanking him for his help. He put his uniform on and made his way across campus to the COW communications trailer. He knocked once and pulled the door open stepping inside. The young soldier sitting at the radio panel almost fell out of his chair at Colonel Harris's sudden appearance in the wee small hours. "Sir?" Was all he could muster.

"I need to send an urgent message to Tionesta."

"Yessir. What would you like me to send?" The soldier placed a set of headphones over his ears and began turning various knobs on the large desktop radio.

"Let them know that I need to speak with the Postman immediately and that I'm requesting his whereabouts. Let them know it's of the utmost urgency."

The soldier flicked a couple more switches, then began speaking into the microphone in front of him. "Shire, this is Rohan. Come back." There was a lengthy pause. Bruce realized that even if Tionesta was replying, he wasn't going to be able to hear their response since the man was wearing his headphones. He walked over to the radio and pulled the headphone jack from the display. The soldier looked up with an embarrassed smile and reached over to turn up the external speaker volume. "Shire, this is Rohan. Come back," he repeated into the mic.

Just when Bruce was wondering if they were going to get a response, he heard, "This is the Shire. Go ahead Rohan."

"The king has an urgent message for the Postman and needs to speak with him immediately. Do you know his current location?"

There was a slight pause. "I believe so, but I'm not sure. I can check."

Bruce leaned over to the radio man. "If he's there, have him ask the Postman what is the absolute earliest time we could arrange a meeting at the southwest checkpoint."

The radio man nodded and thought about it briefly before transmitting. "Yes, please. This is of an urgent nature and can't wait. If you can locate him, please have him provide the earliest possible time that he could travel to Rohan and meet with the king at the southwest checkpoint."

"Roger that, Rohan. I will see if I can locate him and radio back his response."

"Copy that, Shire. Thank you. We'll await your reply." The radio man turned a couple more knobs before turning to Bruce with a questioning look.

"Good," Bruce said. "As soon as you get a reply, please come and inform me directly. I'll either be in my office or my room. I don't mind being awakened as this is urgent."

"Yes, sir. As soon as I get a response, I'll let you know immediately."

"Thank you, Private." Bruce left the communications trailer and went back to his office. Although his body was worn out and tired, his mind was wide awake. He sat at his desk for a while thinking through everything that had happened with General Oates. There were so many things to remember. He retrieved a notebook from his desk drawer and began to write out a full report of everything he knew or suspected on the man. Bruce knew that General Duncan's warning was well founded and there was a good chance he would wind up dead over this. If that were the case, he wanted a written record that could be passed on to someone else. Who would keep this report and where it would go were yet to be determined, but at least there would be a record. Bruce began to write and without realizing it, was soon bent over his desk, fast asleep.

Chapter 28

When the smoke finally cleared, six men, two women, and a teenaged boy lost their lives following the gunfight at the Mount Shiloh Bible Church. At least two of their attackers had escaped and fled through the quickly darkening forest, leaving a trail of blood behind. Randy and Sean forbade Craig from following as he would likely be walking into more gunfire from the wounded men. That's assuming they could even track them in the dark. Derrick expressed his desire to help the wounded men, but Sean insisted they were on their own now.

Sean held a compression bandage to the midsection of one of the wounded attackers, a woman. She lay bleeding from the two gunshot wounds, one in her side, and one up near her collar bone. The second wasn't bleeding as badly as the first. Her dirty hair was matted down across her face with sweat, and her rotting clothes hung from her famished body.

"My babies!" she croaked. "Someone needs to get my babies!"

"Stop squirming!" Sean scolded her gently as she writhed under his hand that was holding tight pressure to the bandage on her side. "Where are your babies?" he asked with concern.

"Please…get…my babies," she said. This time the words were faint, barely a whisper. A moment later, she was unconscious. Sean swore under his breath feeling for a pulse. It was faint, but it was still there.

Sean looked around the front yard of the church; it was pure chaos. People from both of their groups were rushing around on various tasks but some were just standing around, not sure what to do. Sean noticed the woman who'd been teaching Maria to crochet standing just outside the front doors of the church staring blankly at the bodies strewn about the yard.

"Martha," Sean called to her. She didn't respond. "Martha!" he yelled this time, breaking her out of her trance. "I need you!"

She hesitated briefly, but eventually started walking in his direction. "Hurry!" he insisted, spurring her on to a jog, her long skirt swishing around her legs. She approached the last few steps tentatively. "Hold pressure on this bandage for me," he instructed.

"I…I…don't think…," she stammered, clearly in shock at the sight of blood puddled around the woman's torso as she lay motionless on the ground before them.

"Martha, get down here and hold pressure on this bandage. Right now!" he insisted firmly. She knelt down and reached her hands forward hesitantly. Sean released the bandage and grabbed her wrists with both of his bloody hands, pushing them down onto the squishy bandage. She turned her head squeamishly. Sean pulled the Celox Syringe from his trauma kit on his battle belt and moved her hands aside, inserting the plunger into the wound. He hesitated briefly, not completely confident of what he was doing, before depressing the plunger halfway and forcing the blood clotting granules deep into the wound. Sean wasn't certain how much he should use and decided to save the other half in case someone else needed it. The small bullet hole was still leaking blood and Sean he didn't know how long it would take to stop the bleeding.

He grabbed Martha's hand, the one that held the bloody bandage, and pushed it back onto the wound. She still had her head turned to the side and her eyes were closed. "Martha, pay attention. Keep pressure on this wound until I tell you to stop, okay?" Martha glanced down at her bloody hands, repositioning them over the wound before turning her head again.

Sean pulled the Celox impregnated gauze from his trauma kit and laid it next to the woman's head. He stuck his finger into the bloody hole in the front of the woman's t-shirt, just below her collar bone, and tore the fabric open. There was a small bullet wound, but it wasn't bleeding excessively. He grabbed the woman's shoulder and tilted her onto her side. "Keep pressure," he reminded Martha once more. Sean inspected the back of the wound and it was small as well, not larger than a quarter inch. It was a through and through, likely from one of the full metal jacket rounds from his or Randy's AR. He lifted the back of her t-shirt and found the exit wound on her side. The bleeding had stemmed, though it was obvious that this was the wound she'd lost most of the blood from. Sean tore open the Celox gauze wrapper and cut the gauze in half with his knife, poking it into the wound with his pinky finger and following suit with the other half of the gauze on the wound near her shoulder. Sean laid her back down and looked closely at her chest while feeling for a pulse. She was still alive.

"Martha, keep pressure on that wound until someone comes to relieve you. Do you understand?" Her head was still turned in the opposite direction, but Sean caught the brief nod of her head. Without another word, he stood and rushed back toward the church. When he entered, he found that one of the folding tables from the basement had been brought up and one of Derrick's men lay on it, moaning loudly. Half a dozen people stood around the table helping to hold the man down. Sean found a woman holding pressure on his thigh with a dishtowel.

"Randy!" Sean yelled loudly, startling the two men he was standing behind at the table. A moment later, Randy came rushing through the front doors of the church. "Do you still have your battle dressing?" Sean asked. Randy nodded and pushed his way to the table. He unclipped the flap of the HSGI Bleeder Pouch on his battle belt and pulled the D-ring, spilling its contents out and onto the table.

Sean grabbed his own EMT shears, tucked behind his half-empty trauma pouch, and quickly set to work cutting the man's pant leg off just above the wound. When he was finished, he pulled the bloody nitrile gloves he wore off his hands replacing them with the clean pair from Randy's pouch. Sean motioned to the woman holding pressure on the man's leg. "Let me have a look." She complied, stepping back and unconsciously wiping her bloody hands on the front of her dress. Sean removed the rag and slid the man's pant leg down over the wound. He let out a cry and kicked his leg free from the man holding onto his foot. "Hold him still!" Sean demanded. As soon as the rag was removed, blood began pouring from the wound. It wasn't squirting and Sean surmised that, while serious, it hadn't hit the man's femoral artery.

The wound staring up at Sean was jagged and open with meaty flesh hanging out. This was obviously the exit wound from a high-powered rifle. Randy tore open the wrapper on his Quick Clot gauze and held it out toward Sean. Sean cut a small piece off the end with his shears and pushing the bulk of the gauze down into the wound. The man kicked and bucked, but this time the others were ready for it and they held him down, mostly. When Sean was done, he reached around the back of the man's leg, finding the small entrance wound and pushing the smaller piece of clotting gauze into it. Randy stood ready with his H-fold pressure bandage and held the open top of the package facing in his direction. Sean pulled it from its packaging and tightly wrapped the man's leg, placing the thick absorbent pad on the larger wound and knotting the bandage directly over top of it. After that, he rewrapped the wound again with the bloody dishtowel, this time tying the knot on the back of the man's leg over the entrance wound.

He turned to the man holding tightly to the injured guy's foot. "Take that boot off and keep an eye on his toes until we can get him to a doctor. I put that bandage on tight. If you notice his toes turning purple, you'll need to loosen this bandage. Do you understand?" The man nodded as he set to work untying the blood-covered boot.

Sean turned, looking for Derrick, and found him sitting a few yards away on the end of a long wooden pew. He'd been watching Sean work and his lips were moving silently. He appeared to be praying.

Derrick looked up at him with a blank stare. "He was manning the smoker out back when they came. I'm the one that asked him to check on it."

"Have you seen anyone else injured?" Sean asked, ignoring the information.

Derrick shook his head. "The others?" he asked, bobbing his head toward the front door.

"You mean the ones that attacked us?" Sean asked roughly. Derrick nodded slightly. "All dead, except for one woman who I don't think is going to live very long without a surgeon." Derrick bowed his head, placing it down into his open hands.

Sean was irritated with the man. He'd almost gotten Sean killed during the firefight not to mention himself.

As soon as the shooting began, Sean had yelled for everyone in the sanctuary to get down and had raced for the steps to retrieve his rifle. Randy was just rounding the top of the stairs and he practically threw Sean's rifle at him. They had both moved toward the wide-open front doors of the church where most of the shots could be heard. As they approached, they could make out half a dozen people making their way across the road at a walk, firing haphazardly toward the church.

They took positions on each side of the six-foot wide doorway and opened fire. Firing in controlled bursts of two and three rounds, they had quickly dropped two of the men, causing the others to race forward toward the only concealment available to them. But they clearly didn't understand the difference between cover and concealment as every one of them ducked down behind the white picket fence. Sean and Randy emptied their magazines through the thin wooden spindles and quickly performed mag changes. They could only see the attackers' shadows through the pickets but continued shooting through the fence until they couldn't see any further motion.

A splinter of wood had exploded from the door frame next to Sean's head and he fell backwards in surprise. It was then that his brain decided to register Derick's voice from behind where Sean lay sprawled out on the floor. Derrick had been yelling "Stop shooting!" at the top of his lungs since the firefight began. At the break in the action, Derrick stepped over Sean and into the open doorway, yelling and pleading with their attackers to "Stop shooting!" Sean jumped up and grabbed Derrick by the back of the collar, roughly yanking him back into the church's foyer as another bullet zipped through the air past Sean's head. Randy leaned to his left and started shooting, providing cover fire.

"Changing!" Randy hollered out.

Sean took position standing over Randy who knelt on the right side of the doorway. Sean transitioned his rifle to his left shoulder and leaned out, firing sporadically into the wood pile fifty yards to their right. Another bullet whizzed by and this time Sean saw the muzzle blast, but his magazine had run dry again.

He ducked back inside. "Changing!" Sean dropped the empty magazine which bounced harmlessly off Randy's head. Randy leaned out and started firing again in a slow steady rhythm. "He's to the right of the wood pile!" Sean hollered to him over the steady ring of gunfire. With a fresh mag inserted, he slapped the bolt catch and leaned out. Injured and completely overwhelmed, the man was limping his way into the woods while, dragging his scoped deer rifle behind him by the sling. Randy and Sean held their fire.

Shots could still be heard coming from behind the church and Randy nodded toward him. "Go! I'll stay here."

Sean leaped over Derrick's body which was curled up in the fetal position just inside in the foyer. He'd still not recovered from where Sean had roughly thrown him down. In the sanctuary, there were huddled bodies everywhere. "Maria, are you okay?" Sean screamed, not seeing his wife anywhere.

"I'm here!" she yelled. Sean found her bent down below the large stained-glass window behind the pulpit. She was just finishing a magazine change.

"Stay down!" he screamed at her as he rushed forward.

Jackson was shooting through a smashed-out lower section of the window next to her and ducked down as Sean made it to their position. "Changing!" he yelled out. Sean stood overtop him as he changed the empty magazine and scanned the edge of the woods thirty yards behind the church. He noticed a pair of dirty sneakers sticking out of the tall weeds, their toes pointed toward the sky and unmoving.

"I think he's down," Jackson said. "I think I got him," he reiterated as he slapped the bolt catch on his rifle.

Minutes later, they would discover that it had been a teenaged boy the attackers sent around the back of the church. He'd been sent to fend for himself and he was now dead. Shortly after the collapse, Sean had been forced to take a boy's life in self-defense and it still haunted his dreams to this day. In the weeks following the shootout at the church, Sean would try to offer his cousin what comfort and advice he could, but taking a young man's life was something hard to live with.

The whole gunfight had lasted less than three minutes. When the shooting stopped, Derrick's man behind the church had begun calling out for help and screaming that he'd been shot. In a rush, half a dozen of Derrick's people raced out the front doors of the church to help the man. Randy and Sean both yelled for them to stop, but they continued anyway. Sean, Randy, Jackson, and Maria, the only ones with battle rifles, covered them as best they could while the group carried the injured man inside. Sean had then moved back to the front doors where Randy still knelt, rifle swiveling back and forth through the door opening, scanning for any further threats. He coughed sharply as he tried to catch his breath. His adrenaline was still racing and his heart was pounding.

Kneeling at the door frame, his breathing beginning to slow and the blood thrumming in his ears lessening, Sean started to hear a man crying. Not crying like a small child would after getting hurt, but a deep guttural sobbing. The man was weeping openly and Sean found his movement through the slats of the picket fence. The man was dragging himself back out onto the road, away from the church. Even though these people had been shooting at them, with no regard to the women and children inside the building, Sean's heart broke at the sound. Randy looked at Sean with a similar look of dismay. Derrick appeared between them and walked past Sean, heading for the man.

"Wait!" Randy insisted. "We don't know if it's clear yet!"

Derrick ignored Randy's plea and strode into the dim church yard. "Dammit!" Sean swore.

Randy stood and gave Sean a knowing look. "Let's go. I'll go right."

Sean nodded and Randy stepped out, turning right toward the wood pile. Sean covered his friend as he moved quickly across the church's front yard. Once his friend was behind the woodpile, he turned back to Sean and gave him a quick thumbs-up. Sean stepped out and made for a sprawling oak tree in the front yard. He moved to the far side of it and swiveled his red dot in a slow arc around the entire tree line to their west. When he was certain there weren't any threats, he signaled for Randy to stay where he was and in one quick motion, hopped the short picket fence. Sean raced to the middle of the road where the crying man lay in a large, rapidly growing puddle of dark blood. Derrick knelt next to him with his hand on the man's chest. The man was no longer crying and was making more of a whimpering sound now. Sean took a knee next to them and scanned the woods opposite the road. A single body was half visible in the tall weeds but it didn't seem to be moving. It was a woman in a dress.

Sean looked back to Pastor Derrick and was surprised to see him staring up at Sean.

"Help him," he pleaded softly.

Sean looked down at the man. It was hard to look at. Nearly his entire emaciated body was covered in blood. His body was riddled with bullet wounds and Sean couldn't believe the man was even alive. That's when Sean noticed the man's outstretched hand. His fingers were pulling at the gravel as if the motion could propel him forward. Sean suddenly realized he was trying to get to the woman in the dress. Before Sean knew what was happening, a tear ran down his cheek and a sob escaped from his chest, but he forced himself to hold it together. There could still be others willing to take a pot shot at them as they knelt in the open roadway. He scanned the tree line again, but his eyes kept being pulled back to the woman in the grass.

"Help him, please." Another soft plea from Derick.

Sean didn't look down this time as he stood. "He's not going to make it, Derrick." It's all he could muster. Sean quickly moved to the woods and inspected the blonde-haired woman clutching a pump-action shotgun to her chest. She was dead. She'd taken a single round to the center of her forehead. Her dead eyes seemed to look directly into Sean's. He reached down and slowly slid his fingers over her face, forcing her eyelids closed. Another sob, and he let the silent tears flow while he turned to scan the perimeter around the church. He noticed a thick trail of blood crossing the road off to his left and he warily moved in that direction, his rifle raised and safety off. When he reached the location where the trail entered the forest, he forced his breathing to slow and peered deep into the woods. Even in the deeply shadowed forest, the glistening blood trail was still visible in the underbrush and continued as far back into the trees as he could see. He wasn't about to follow an armed and wounded man into the woods. Besides, with the amount of blood loss Sean was seeing, he wasn't going to make it far.

"I think this woman's still alive!" Sean heard a man's urgent voice say from behind him.

The entire gunfight had begun and ended so fast that Sean was still trying to recover from the shock of it all. It had been fifteen minutes since the first shot had been fired. Sean surmised the attackers were likely the same starving group from the campground that he'd been discussing with Derrick only an hour before. He could only assume that they'd been periodically checking in on Derrick's group and the sight and smell of a deer on a spit must have been too overwhelming for them to ignore. It was pure luck that Derick's church been attacked the same day Sean's family was visiting. Good luck that is. The only thing that could be considered a battle rifle in Derrick's group was an old SKS that his eldest son had clung to tightly during the firefight. Sean didn't think Derrick's men had fired a single round throughout the entire engagement. If Sean and his family hadn't been there, Derrick's group would surely have suffered more casualties than a single man with a wounded leg.

Sean stood looking down at Derrick, who now sat before him on the church pew with his head in his hands, praying for his injured friend who lay on a table only a few feet away. The man's desire to prevent the inevitable shootout had nearly gotten him killed, let alone Sean, who had to pull him back from outside and nearly took a round to the head. Sean couldn't stay irritated at the man, though; he just didn't understand tactics.

"Derrick," Sean said softly, jostling the man's shoulder. Derrick looked up with red rimmed eyes and wet cheeks. "If we don't get that woman help soon, she's not going to make it. I also worry that your friend here might not last long either, without proper medical attention."

"Dick."

"What's that?" Sean said, surprised. He was taken aback at the Pastor's harsh use of the word toward him. He was only trying to help.

Derrick looked up at the man on the table, who was still moaning softly but not squirming around any longer. "His name's Dick."

"Oh," Sean said, embarrassed that he'd assumed Derrick had insulted him. Derrick didn't seem to notice the misunderstanding and just sat there staring at his friend. Sean shook his shoulder a little rougher this time, trying to pull him out of his trance. "Derrick, if we're going to help Dick, I think we need to call the military up in Warren. They have medics and surgeons that are trained to treat gunshot wounds. There's a doctor down near Tionesta who treated a gunshot wound in our group before, but he's just a general practitioner and I don't think could save that woman…if that's even possible." The woman likely only weighed seventy or eighty pounds. Her body was malnourished and Sean wondered how much trauma it would be able to take. "Can you show me how to get up to the bell tower so I can try and radio home?"

Derrick nodded and stood, taking Sean up into the balcony where an extension ladder had been placed to get up into the bell tower. Derrick held the bottom of the ladder steady as Sean climbed. The further he climbed, the more the ladder seemed to flex and shake. Sean wasn't necessarily scared of heights, but climbing up thirty feet over the sanctuary floor caused Sean to falter a little. He slowed his pace.

"Be careful, Sean!" He heard his wife call out from somewhere beneath him. He fought the urge to look down.

At the top of the ladder, he reached the hatch opening into the bell tower and pushed on it with his hand. It didn't budge. He called down to Derrick who stood with one foot on the bottom rung of the ladder, holding it steady. "Is there a lock here somewhere that I'm not seeing?"

"No," Derick answered flatly. "Just push on it. If it's not moving, it's because Tommy's standing on it. Try knocking."

Sean gave two sharp raps on the thick plywood hatch, but there wasn't any movement or scuffling of feet from above. He took another step up the ladder, putting his back to the hatch and lifting with his legs. The plywood door felt much too heavy as it lifted up a quarter of an inch. Sean saw a trickle of blood start to pour through the opening. He let the hatch drop closed. He took one more step up for better leverage and heaved against the door. Tommy's limp body was lifted as Sean forced his torso into the opening, awkwardly pushing the man's lifeless body off the hatch.

"Tommy!" Sean heard a concerned call from Derrick. "Tommy?"

Sean's upper body was in the bell tower now with Tommy's body wrapped awkwardly around the hatch in the tight confines. Sean reached out to feel for a pulse. He quickly pulled his hand back. Half of Tommy's head was missing. Sean sighed and took two steps down the ladder, letting the hatch slam shut.

"Tommy!" Derrick called again. Sean didn't answer. He hustled down the ladder at a reckless pace. "Sean, where's Tommy?" Derrick asked, his voice cracking as Sean made it to the bottom rung. Sean stepped off the last rung slowly and fought for the right words to say.

He settled on, "I'm sorry, Derrick." Sean wrapped his arms around the trembling man as he'd finally had enough and began to weep. Sean heard rapid footsteps ascending the narrow stairwell up to the balcony. It was Martha.

"Tommy?" She cried out. "Where's my husband?" She had come out of her shock straight into panic, running for the ladder. Sean released Derrick and swiftly grabbed her around the waist. She struggled against him and he slowly released her down to the floor as her legs gave out. "Tommy!" she screamed an ear-piercing cry, her eyes flashing up toward the hatch above them. In seconds, other women arrived in the balcony and Sean stood back, letting them get to her. Derrick looked on in utter defeat, tears still streaming down his face.

"Don't let her up there," Sean said to him, drawing closer. "In fact, it's best if you take her downstairs." Derrick nodded slightly, but didn't say anything as he continued to cry. Sean snapped. He grabbed the front of Derrick's shirt, yanked him up onto his toes, and forced his face close. Derrick's eyes grew wide. "Snap out of it!" Sean said in a hiss. "Your family needs your leadership right now! There will be time to grieve later, but for now we need to try and save those still living. In order to do that, I need to go back up there and use my radio." Sean paused before continuing. Derick was visibly trying to shake himself out of his stupor. Sean released the front of his shirt. "Now, I need you to get Martha downstairs immediately." Sean leaned forward and whispered harshly into his ear. "You can't let her see him!" Sean stepped back, staring into his eyes purposefully. "Not even later. Do you understand what I am telling you?"

Derrick sucked in a sob as his eyes welled once more. He coughed into his hand, trying to control his emotions. "I understand," he croaked. Sean waited for him to do as he'd asked, but he just stood there clearing his throat heavily three or four times as he sobbed between each, attempting to contain himself. Sean watched a dam break in the man and he his knees buckled. He cried openly, doubled over on the floor. Sean rested his hand on Derrick's head. He was asking too much of the man in that moment. He rubbed the Derrick's back consolingly.

"Craig!" Sean called out over the balcony railing. "I need you! Randy, Jackson, Maria, I need you too!" The four of them came up the stairs swiftly and Sean caught Craig's eye, nodding toward Derrick and motioning to the stairs. Craig understood and helped Derrick back to his feet. Sean turned his attention back to the other three. "Maria, I need you to get these women down to the basement immediately." She turned her face toward the pile of weeping women on the floor and nodded somberly.

"I need to get up there and radio home. We have to get word to Colonel Harris. Maybe he can send a surgeon. I don't think that woman is going to last very long, and Dick down there is going to need some attention as well." Sean leaned in close between Randy and his cousin, lowering his voice to a whisper. "I'm going to need help with that body once the women are gone. It was a headshot. It's not a pretty sight." Jackson grimaced, and they both nodded.

Sean sighed, looking at Maria who was trying to get one of the sobbing women to a standing position with limited success. "It's going to be a long night," Sean muttered.

Sean reclined back in the open hatch of the MRAP, his finger absently poking in and out of the hole in his t-shirt. He hadn't even realized it until an hour before, when he had removed his battle belt. A bullet had passed right through the fabric of his shirt, just above his right hip. It didn't make any sense. There was an entrance hole and an exit hole nearly two inches apart, yet no bullet had pierced his skin. How was that even possible? He could only assume that the shirt must have bunched up and billowed out above his Brokos battle belt during the gunfight. He'd been that close to being shot, again.

Sean was exhausted. It was the wee hours of the morning and his adrenaline had been pumping for hours. All he wanted to do was sleep, but he was still waiting for news on whether the two injured people could be saved. Dick's wound was more serious than Sean had first thought; the man had gone into shock and passed out not long after Sean had radioed back to the North Homestead. They'd heard the gun battle and David was obviously distressed upon first hearing from Sean. After explaining the situation to him, David radioed Warren for medical aid which Colonel Harris had dispatched immediately.

An entire platoon of soldiers, acting as escort to their medical team, arrived at the church within a half hour of receiving the request for aid. While the medics quickly went to work on the two wounded, two squads cleared the surrounding woods around the church and set up a perimeter. Both of the injured attackers, the ones that had fled, had been found…dead from their wounds. Overhearing the ham radio transmissions between the North Homestead and the soldiers up in Warren, Tionesta had graciously volunteered to send the bus on loan from Colonel Harris, and most of Sean's group had been ferried back to the North Homestead. The entire night had become a blur of activity.

Sean looked over at Maria where she slept next to him on the inclined metal ramp of the MRAP, her small body curled up onto her side. Sean was proud of her and the way she'd handled herself during the ordeal. As soon as the shooting had started, she'd grabbed her rifle and, without hesitation, had taken position surveying the yard behind the church. No one had told her what to do and she'd done it on her own as Sean ran to get his rifle. Most of the men and women in Derrick's group had huddled together and hidden in the pews while his wife ran into the fray to defend them.

Sean's head was spinning; there was no way he was going to be able to sleep. He pulled himself up to a sitting position, stretched, and quietly stood with his rifle, leaving his battle belt lying on the ground next to his wife. As he rounded the MRAP, a soldier leaning against the side of it nodded to him as he walked by. Sean walked through the double doors of the church, which still stood open, and found two more soldiers seated just inside. They were whispering to each other softly and didn't spare him more than a glance as he entered. It was dim inside the church with only two small battery-operated lights on tripods set up near the two tables where Dick and the woman lay motionless. They were covered to their necks in white sheets and next to each table was an IV stand with a half empty bag hanging from it. Major Samuelsson stood in between the two tables, talking softly to one of the medics. He looked up as Sean entered the room. Sean scanned the rest of the church sanctuary; the floor was covered with sleeping bodies, which he was forced to step over in his effort to reach the major.

Major Samuelsson noticed him heading in his direction and signaled for him to stay where he was. He said a couple more words to the uniformed soldier with a white, blood-soaked apron hanging from his neck before turning and picking his way through the sleeping bodies to Sean. Without saying anything, he motioned to the front doors and Sean followed him outside. Major Samuelsson had been a blur of motion since the moment they arrived, taking charge of the scene. Not wanting to interrupt him earlier, this was the first chance Sean had found to speak with him.

"You guys were lucky by the looks of things," Major Samuelsson said quietly as they walked down the front steps of the church and away from those trying to sleep inside.

"There's a lot of dead people piled up over there," Sean said somberly, motioning toward the stack of shiny black body bags near the front of the dirty MRAP where Maria slept. "I'm not sure how lucky we were," he muttered.

"Yes, well, only one of those bodies was yours," the major pointed out. "It could have been much worse. This place isn't very defensible with a close tree line on three sides like that. You guys did a good job defending it."

Sean shrugged. "It wasn't much of a fair fight. They just wandered out of the woods walking forward with no real strategy and no cover. They were shooting wildly. It was like shooting fish in a barrel."

"Still," the major maintained. They stopped by the gate in the bullet-riddled picket fence and stood quietly for a while. The steady stream of peaceful nighttime sounds contrasted starkly to the nightmarish scene that had unfolded only hours before.

"How are they doing?" Sean asked finally, breaking the silence. "Any updates?"

Major Samuelsson shook his head. "Nothing new, I'm afraid. Dick should recover okay, though he'll likely never dance again. The woman…." He shrugged his shoulders. "We'll know better if she makes it through till morning. She lost a lot of blood and there's a big risk of infection with a gut wound like that." He turned to Sean and cocked his head to the side. "You saved her life, you know? The surgeon said she never would have lasted until we got here if you hadn't used that clotting plunger."

Sean nodded his head. He'd assumed as much. They stood silently for another long minute.

"Do you know where they came from? Do you expect retribution or any more trouble from their group?"

"That's the reason I came to speak with you." Sean sighed and exhaled a long breath before continuing. "The woman, when I first reached her side, she was crying for her children. Her 'babies' actually. She kept saying that someone needed to go get them," Sean said dismally.

"Oh, man," Major Samuelsson exclaimed softly. "Any ideas where they might be holed up?"

"We assume they're part of a group of people living in the campground about a mile up the road. Derrick told me they had tried to sneak in and steal food a time or two in the past. Derrick's men never scouted out the campground, though. Who knows how many people are living there."

"I see," Major Samuelsson said.

"I've been thinking on it the last couple hours," Sean said. Major Samuelsson looked at him attentively. "If they were a big group, I assume they would have attacked the church for their food long before now. They're obviously not eating well or producing much food by the looks of them. Tonight, there was a deer roasting on a spit out back for the first time in months. I'm just guessing here, but maybe the sight and smell of that deer cooking out in the open was just too much temptation for them to resist. If they were finally making a move on Derrick's group, I'd have to assume they brought every able body to the fight."

Major Samuelsson nodded his head in agreement. "That sounds like a reasonable assessment."

Sean frowned. "That also makes me worry about the woman's kids. If all the adults came today, who's watching over the children back at the campground? You might assume they'd have left an adult behind, but the fact that they even brought that young teenaged boy to the fight, well, it gives me pause." Sean turned to look directly into the major's eyes. "I'm thinking we should probably make a trip up to the campground tomorrow morning and check it out." Sean phrased it such a way that it wasn't really a demand, but it wasn't a question either. "If that woman's children are there unattended…." Sean let the thought hang. They both knew they wouldn't last long.

Major Samuelsson thought on it briefly. "I'll need to radio Colonel Harris and get clearance, but knowing him, he'll likely approve it."

"Thank you," Sean said, relieved. "If you weren't able to do it, I was going to attempt it myself with some help from Derrick. I think there'd be a lot less risk involved if you guys rolled into the campground heavy. You're a lot better equipped to handle an ambush than we are."

"We'll see. I'm going to request some back up since we don't know what we're walking into. I'll likely send in a two-man team of scout snipers first to scope out the situation and the lay of the land. We'll see what they report. Colonel Harris has had a lot on his plate the last couple days, so I'm going to let him sleep tonight. I'll reach out to him about this first thing in the morning. It shouldn't take long to get some extra troops sent this way. Have you ever been to this campground before or have any other intel on it that you can share?"

Sean shook his head slowly. "Nothing. You'll have to talk with Derrick and the others in his group on that."

Major Samuelsson studied Sean intently for a few moments. He must have read the distress on Sean's face. "How are you holding up Sean?"

Sean shrugged again and gazed down the road into the darkness. "I hate this stuff. I hate killing people like this. I hate the dreams I have because of the things I've done. I hate watching my friends get shot up and killed. Overall, I hate that the world has gone crazy. I keep thinking that things are starting to settle down and maybe we can move on and I can just raise my family in peace, and then something like this happens. I wonder if there's ever going to come a time when I can lay my rifle down and truly relax."

Major Samuelsson's face grew even more solemn, if that was possible. "I feel for you, Sean, but don't think you're alone in that regard. Every one of us in the 31st Regiment feel the same way you do. We've all found ourselves in tough positions over the last year. If we ever hope to get there, we need to continue working together to rebuild." He turned back to Sean, his face silhouetted by the full moon behind him. "While we can't do anything about the rest of the country, I can assure you that Colonel Harris and I have your back. Off the record, I can tell you that we've been discussing different ways that we can help the locals without getting caught by command. If there's anything your group needs to make your lives easier, be sure to ask us. I can't promise we'll be able to get it for you, but we'll certainly try to help where we can. We've been encouraged by the recent development of the local towns starting to work together, and we want to foster that and help where we can."

"Thank you, Major," Sean said sincerely. "You guys have already bailed us out a couple times now. Be sure to relay our thanks to Colonel Harris as well."

"Will do," Major Samuelsson promised.

Sean was getting ready to walk away when something else crossed his mind. Images of babies swaddled in dirty rags, alone and hungry in some campground tent, kept invading the forefront of his mind. "Major, what if you do find those children or other survivors at the campground? I think you may want to consider reaching out to Pastor Dan and seeing if Tionesta can take them in."

Major Samuelsson gave Sean a small smile. "I'll reach out tomorrow. We'll find a home for them. I promise."

"Okay, be sure to let us know if you don't." Sean looked back toward the MRAP where his wife slept. "Goodnight, Major."

"Goodnight, Sean."

Chapter 29

At breakfast the following morning, Bruce recapped the night's events at the church with General Duncan. It provided him with a perfect transition to explain his desire to start helping the locals and build mutually-beneficial working relationships with them. At first, Duncan seemed skeptical and quite concerned that doing so could eventually lead to the news of electricity in Warren leaking out. Bruce acknowledged the risk but countered that it was still possible while also keeping the electricity and refinery in Warren a secret.

After discussing it for quite a while, Duncan saw the wisdom in what Bruce was trying to achieve, but said he didn't have the ultimate authority to let Bruce move forward with his plans. He said that he could make the request up the chain of command, but warned that it would likely end up on General Oates' desk for final approval. With Bruce working on gathering evidence against Oates, General Duncan recommended that it would be wise to keep his head down and not do anything that might turn General Oates' attention back toward Warren. By the end of breakfast, Bruce agreed that he'd wait until later to pursue better working relationships with the surviving groups and towns in the area. However, he still intended to grow the relationships with or without Duncan's approval; he would just have to be careful and keep it under the radar.

Just before noon, Bruce escorted General Duncan and Horace to their plane, even though he was cutting it tight for his noon meeting with Willy at the southwest checkpoint. Bruce was surprised when the general actually gave him a short hug just before boarding. "Good luck," he said stoically. Bruce surmised that General Duncan didn't have much faith he was going to succeed and maybe even felt like it would be the last time he saw Bruce. It was a nice gesture though, and it reaffirmed Bruce's decision to trust his senior and confide in him. Perhaps due to the overall feeling of the moment, Bruce offered his hand to Horace as he boarded. The twitchy man took it with a warm smile and shook the colonel's hand firmly.

"Take care of yourself down there," Bruce offered. "And don't let anyone give you too much crap." He added the last with a smile and a nod toward the plane where General Duncan sat looking down at them.

"Okay," Horace agreed half-heartedly.

Bruce didn't even wait for the plane to lift off. He quickly mounted the Humvee with his security detail and set off for the southwest checkpoint. Upon arrival, his men reported that no one had approached the gate all morning. Apparently, Willy was running late also. However, within a minute of his arrival, Willy emerged from the tree line a hundred yards south of the checkpoint and trotted in their direction. It was now obvious that Willy hadn't been late. He had been waiting on Bruce to arrive before emerging from his concealment.

Bruce didn't wait for Willy to reach them and walked down the road in his direction. This conversation would certainly need to be kept private from his men. After only a few steps, he realized his security detail was trailing him. He dismissed them with an irritated wave of his hand. They seemed a little reluctant but obeyed his directive, taking up position at the front edge of the checkpoint and watching him closely.

When they convened, Bruce held out his hand and Willy took it in his typical, guarded way. "How was your trip?" Bruce asked, breaking the ice.

"Uneventful," Willy said. "Why don't we meet in your office, where you can feed me?"

"I…," Bruce began, but his brain failed him. He couldn't believe that he hadn't anticipated such a simple question. Willy watched him closely, waiting for an answer. "It's a conversation that needs to stay private."

"What? Did you remove the locks from your office door?"

Again, the bluntness of the question befuddled Bruce. "No, it's just that…." He trailed off again as his mind raced for a rational answer. Willy waited with his arms crossed, smirking at him.

"Forget it," Willy said with a wave of his hand. "What's so urgent and what do you want from me?"

Straight to the point, as usual. "I believe I may know who poisoned your family," Bruce started and watched Willy's face as it turned dark.

"Who?" he demanded.

"There's a man named General Oates who's the President's closest advisor. I have reason to believe he was behind what happened in the Newark Green Zone, but I don't have proof yet."

"I already know it was General Oates. What else have you got?"

"You knew?" Bruce couldn't hide the surprise in his voice.

"Well, suspected anyway," Willy corrected himself.

Bruce was curious about where he received the information implicating Oates and what he knew, but it wasn't the time for asking questions from him just yet. "I'd like to get proof he was involved and actually do something about it."

Willy studied Bruce for a long moment. "And what do you want from me?"

"How would you feel about returning to Newark on a scavenging mission?" Bruce waited for a reply but Willy just stood there staring at him blankly, arms still crossed. "I'd like you to go down there and poke around the ashes. I'm hoping you might be able to locate a sealed drinking container or bottle in the rubble: whatever people were using to transport the drinking water they received on ration from the main source. I believe that whoever did this would likely have covered their tracks and destroyed the source where the poisoned water originated. But, if you were able to get some samples from a few different sources, I have a contact that could get it tested at a lab. From your description of how fast this thing killed everyone, and from other eyewitness testimony I've heard about, it's very likely that a highly classified and controlled substance may have been used. There's sure to be a paper trail at the facility it was removed from. If our suspicions are confirmed, which I believe they will be, I'll be able to take this directly to Congress. We can have him put on trial."

"A trial? Yeah, I'm really sure that's going to pan out," Willy said sarcastically. "More likely anybody with information or willing to testify against him will be dead long before the trial even starts." His visage suddenly grew dark. He looked up at the clouds for a moment and Bruce thought he heard Willy mutter an apology before turning back. "No, thanks. I've got other plans for General Oates."

It was Bruce's turn to snort. "You plan on killing him yourself, don't you? Seriously? You'd have a better chance of killing the President." Willy seemed to consider that for a moment as if he hadn't considered that possibility before. Bruce continued. "They're both held up in a heavily fortified bunker and you wouldn't get within half a mile of either one of them."

"I'm fully aware of where he's hiding," Willy said with a smile.

His mood changes made Bruce's head spin. He raised one eyebrow questioningly.

Willy sighed as if the information he was about to impart was common knowledge. "General Oates is down there in that Raven Rock complex, just outside of Blue Ridge Summit, PA, along with the

President and what's left of Congress. He splits his time between there and the Pentagon."

Bruce couldn't hide the shock from his face. "Well, if you suspect that, then you know what I said is true. You won't be able to get anywhere near him. You plan to just ride down to the front gate and knock on the door? You think they'll just let you in to meet with the most powerful man in the country?"

Willy shrugged. "Maybe. We'll see. Whatever my plans entail, I'm definitely not going to share them with you."

"C'mon, Willy. Don't be ridiculous. In the end, I want the same thing that you do."

"I highly doubt it."

"Even so," Bruce continued, "I want to get rid of him for my own reasons. This is our best option for the time being. I can't send one of my troops down to Newark because it would be highly suspicious if he were seen. Not to mention he wouldn't even know where you were living, the lay of the land, how the water was distributed in the Green Zone, or anything else. And to be honest, I'd be putting one of my men's lives at risk for our own personal vendettas. You've shown that you know how to stay alive out on the open road. The best option we have is for you to go."

"That's the best option for you. It's my neck on the line Colonel." Willy paused for a few moments. "If I were to agree to this, what would you offer in return?"

"Nothing!" Bruce shot back angrily, irritated that Willy would even try to barter over something like this. "I only offer you the chance to see General Oates get the punishment he deserves."

"And what does that punishment look like? A slap on the wrist?" Willy asked skeptically. "If I wanted him to get the justice he deserves, I'd put a bullet in the man's skull."

**Bruce sighed. "In truth, if it were up to the President, maybe he'd only get a slap on the wrist. But I intend to put this and a lot of other incriminating evidence that I've gathered before some reliable members of Congress. While I've never cared for politicians, there are still some good people down there. General Oates sending a kill squad after someone is one thing, but poisoning thousands of innocent and starving people in retribution for them trying to steal some food is inexcusable. How many women and children died a horrific death when they had nothing to do with what you and your men did? I fully expect him to receive serious retribution, if not a death sentence, for crimes against humanity. I'm also going to put the stipulation on the Congressmen that if Oates isn't dealt with and removed from power, I will send my report and evidence to the international community. While they haven't been able to supply much food lately, the UN is still operating and I don't think they'll take lightly to the man next to the President poisoning the same people they are sacrificing to feed. I'm not sure if I would follow through on that, because it could cut off the food supply to my own men, but the threat should be enough to get them to act." Bruce finished speaking and waited patiently on Willy's response. Willy's head twitched in multiple directions, evidence of the struggle going on inside his thoughts.

"I already have a sample," Willy muttered under his breath, almost too softly to hear.

"What!" Bruce said, incredulous. "How?"

Willy suddenly seemed to fold into himself. It was another long while before he spoke, but Bruce waited patiently. Willy turned from Bruce and paced to the edge of the road a few times before continuing. "After finding my…family and the rest of the neighborhood dead, I had my suspicions as to what had happened. When I awoke the next morning, I intended to drink the contents in the stainless water bottle next to my wife's bed, but I was a coward. I…I…couldn't." Willy shifted his weight back and forth, choking back tears.

"I'm so sorry, Willy," Bruce said sincerely. "I can't imagine what that must have been like." Bruce waited for Willy to continue but he didn't. "Willy, you're alive for a reason. Maybe that reason is to bring the man responsible for their deaths to justice. Please tell me you still have that water bottle…."

"I do," Willy muttered, sighing and wiping the freely flowing tears from his face. "I've tried to drink it a dozen times, but I could never follow through." Willy looked up at Bruce and held his gaze. He cleared his throat before he continued. "I could have it for you here tomorrow, but I need your word this plan of yours is going to work out. That's the only thing I have left from…before."

Bruce sighed. "I can only promise you that I will do everything in my power to bring this to light and pursue those in power to act. You have to know that I'm literally putting my own head on the chopping block if this doesn't work."

Willy bowed his head. "Very well, then. I will leave tonight to go get it. I only ask two things in return. First, I want a copy of the report you are preparing for these Congressmen. I want a copy of the evidence and a copy of documentation from the testing lab. If something happens to you, I want to have options."

Bruce shook his head. "I already told you that if this didn't play out, I would send the information to the UN. The same procedure will be immediately acted upon by someone I trust if some accident befalls me in the meantime."

"Still," Willy insisted.

Bruce thought about it. "Willy, I have to go about this through the correct channels. If that information leaks out beforehand, or other incriminating actions I've taken over the last few months while fighting General Oates' agenda, it could cost me my command and more than likely end up with me dead."

"Still." Willy wasn't going to relent.

Bruce scratched at his head than rubbed his hand over his face in irritation. It was his turn to pace. Bruce noticed his men were studying him from a distance, so he stopped. "If the lab tests come back positive for something that can be traced back to General Oates, I will get you a copy of everything. But not until then."

"Very well," Willy conceded.

"And what's your second request?" Bruce asked, hoping it was something simple this time.

"Electricity and fuel for Tionesta and the other local towns."

Bruce shook his head discouragingly. "I wish I had that to give."

"Bah!" Willy dismissed the lie with a wave of his hand. "I know you have electricity here. I also know you got that refinery up and running. Trying to hide the tanker trucks in the convoy by fabricating metal boxes over them was a nice touch, I must admit. But, while you may be fooling some of the people along your route, you're not fooling me." Willy tapped his finger along the side of his nose indicating he knew Bruce's secret. "Besides, it's not for me. It's for the towns."

Bruce was dismayed at Willy's revelation and struggled on how to respond. Without an easy answer and not having time to consider a better response, Bruce settled on standing his ground. "I don't know what you're talking about, Willy."

"Okay, then." Without warning, Willy turned and started walking away.

"Willy?" Bruce called out with no response. "Willy, stop!" he said in a commanding voice. Willy stopped walking away, but he didn't turn and made no motion that he was going to return to the conversation. Bruce glanced back toward his men through the corner of his eye. They were still watching him. It was embarrassing. Now he'd have to walk over to Willy to finish their discussion. Bruce cursed under his breath and walked forward. Willy had a piece of tall grass in his hand, chewing on it indifferently.

"It sure is turning out to be a nice fall day, isn't it?" Willy said softly with a look up at the sky.

"Willy, what do you want from me?" Bruce asked, ignoring the question. Willy didn't answer. He just stood there staring off into the distance. Was he humming a song? Bruce took a step to the side, positioning himself directly into Willy's line of sight and then took a step closer until they were standing face to face. Bruce noticed his men over Willy's shoulder and they seemed to be growing nervous. One of the men started to walk forward. Bruce held up his hand in their direction before giving them a quick thumbs-up.

Bruce turned his attention back to Willy. "I cannot give you what you are asking, Willy. Nor can I even acknowledge its existence. If what you say is true, and I got caught doing what you ask—which I certainly would—I would end up in jail, or worse. Don't you understand? You don't think people are going to notice if Tionesta and Kane are the only towns in 1000 miles with electricity? The news would spread and those towns you love so much would get steamrolled by a larger looting group before year's end. Heck, there's even a raiding party nearby with thousands of people and fighters. They'd take over these towns in a heartbeat."

"You mean that group out of Chicago?"

"Yes, I mean that group out of Chicago!" Bruce said in exasperation. "I don't know where you are getting so much information, but if word spreads about some town in this area having electricity, including Warren, there's going to be bloodshed on a biblical scale. Willy, are you understanding what I'm saying?" Bruce demanded.

Willy nodded. "I understand you, Colonel. And after thinking about it, I agree that providing electricity to the towns in the current climate would likely be a bad thing. I also understand that if some military base were to obtain electricity, even that knowledge would have to be kept under tight wraps. A secret." Willy gave him a massive, big toothed grin. "I'm really good with secrets like that."

Bruce wasn't sure if he should laugh or cry. This mad man had him by the giblets and knew it. "I'm really trying to help here, Willy. I literally just finished having a meeting this morning with a general at the Pentagon, one that I trust. I'm trying to get permission to work more closely with the neighboring towns and help them where I can. I wasn't given official permission, as of yet, and it may be a few months before I can do so out in the open. But in the meantime, I'm still planning on helping out when and where I can. I plan to provide bus transportation and a security detail for those in Tionesta to go to this next flea market, swap meet, or whatever it is. I've also already promised both Tionesta and Kane to come to their aid if they are ever attacked. Willy, I've done a lot for the locals already, and I hope to be able to do more in the future. I want to help these people. I want to help rebuild this country." He paused briefly before adding. "And I want to help fix the wrongs I've done in the past by following orders and forcing people into Green Zones. It seemed like the best idea at the time, but Willy, I do feel bad for how it all turned out."

"Okay, what about fuel then?" Willy asked bluntly.

Bruce threw up his arms in exasperation and nearly screamed aloud in frustration. He had put himself out there and that surely wasn't the response he'd anticipated from the man. "What the hell, Willy? It's the same thing! If word spreads that some town has a bunch of fuel, let alone they are 'producing' fuel, that town becomes a big target!"

"See, I don't necessarily agree with that. Yes, some town having electricity would surely be noticed. But most small towns stored up and had access to fuel after the collapse. Most are running out of it now, but it's not something out of the ordinary. If you really wanted to help the locals, that would be huge for them. They could expand their growing fields with their tractors and implements and it would allow them to start travelling between the towns with vehicles. As it is now, no one can spare the gas for such a luxury."

"Willy, I can't get caught sharing my regiment's gas with the nearby town," Bruce said flatly. "If I got caught going off reservation and providing transportation and a security detail for a nearby town on their way to a swap meet, I'd likely get reamed out and written up by my superior, but that's all. If I drove a tanker truck of U.S. military-owned fuel into the center of Tionesta and refilled their gas tanks, I'd surely lose my command. Is that what you want?" Willy started to speak but Bruce cut him off. "Willy, I want to ask you a serious question. If I got caught doing this stuff and a different officer was sent up here to take my place, do you seriously think he would risk his command to help the locals?"

"Probably not," Willy conceded. He seemed to ponder something for a minute before adding, "I don't know why I like you Colonel, as I swore an oath to never trust anybody in the government ever again. But I do like you." There was that big toothy smile again. "I don't want you to lose your command and I don't want you to get in trouble. But I still think you could provide some gas to the local towns without getting caught."

Bruce was about to explode on the crazy little man, but Willy calmed him with another raised hand. "Hold on, Colonel. I'm not talking about delivering fuel into the center of town. Not long ago, I went on a scouting mission for Tionesta, checking to see if any of the local gas stations had fuel left in their tanks. Who's to say I wasn't wrong or maybe I didn't open every last access hatch and look inside? The locals wouldn't care where I found it if I suddenly located gas some place. They don't use a lot of fuel and it would probably last six months or more. The gas station I'm thinking of doesn't have anyone living nearby. No one needs to know how the gas arrived there in the middle of the night. Six months from now, you and I will find another rural gas station and drop off another load of fuel. Voila!" Willy snapped his fingers in front of Bruce's face. "Magic! With no one the wiser on where it came from. The only people that would know would be you and me. I could play off the first load as an oversight of mine. Most of the towns think I'm half-crazy anyway…." Willy trailed off but there was a bright twinkle in his eye.

"Was this whole 'crazy man' persona of his just an act?" Bruce wondered. If he found out that was true, he was going to be severely pissed at being hoodwinked. The man had a point though. This plan of his might actually work. Bruce would have to figure out how to finagle the numbers so the missing fuel wasn't discovered, but he could swing that. Sammy was the one who kept track of everything and made reports to HQ on the refinery's production numbers. He'd also shown interest in helping the local towns. Maybe not as much as Bruce, but the desire was still there.

Willy must have been watching the gears turning inside Bruce's head. "So, do we have a deal?"

Bruce sighed but smiled at the same time. He reached his hand out and Willy took it firmly.

"Victory!" Willy hollered out and he started to dance an Irish jig right in the middle of the street.

Bruce grabbed him by the arm with a smile. "Cut it out, Willy! My men are watching us."

"I know they are," Willy admitted as he stopped dancing. "That's half the fun. Now, we'll need to work out how and when you'll deliver the fuel so I know when it arrives. We'll have to set up a system so you can discretely let me know exactly how many gallons were delivered so I can ration it out between the various towns and groups equitably." Willy pulled out a folded piece of paper from his pocket and handed it over to Bruce discreetly. "There's a map on that paper for a gas station called Uni-Mart in the town of Tylersburg. It's not really a town; it's more of an intersecting of two country roads. I already checked, and all the houses in the area are abandoned. I also included the most discreet route for your men to get there without being seen."

Bruce unfolded the paper and looked at it. At the bottom, there was a note requesting two more small solar panel generators for his motorcycle and two more spare batteries for it. "What's this note down here at the bottom?" he asked.

Willy grinned. "Since you won't agree to provide the towns with electricity, that's my replacement offer. I'm going to need two more solar charging kits and extra batteries for my bike so I can extend my range to some new areas I'd like to check out."

Bruce just shook his head and scowled. He had just been played. "I'll see what I can come up with. No promises."

"I'll be back here at first light tomorrow morning, let's say 7:00 AM, to deliver my side of the bargain," Willy added with considerably less enthusiastically.

Bruce couldn't help but grin at the man. "Be careful out there, Willy. I'll see you tomorrow." Bruce placed the map inside his pocket and turned back toward his men who, to a one, wore bewildered faces. No one said a word as he passed through them and climbed into the Humvee.

Chapter 30

Bruce shifted uncomfortably in his rigid metal folding chair alongside three other men. They watched as a couple off-duty firemen washed one of the large fire engines parked outside the garage door of the firehouse. It was a surreal moment; the junior fire fighters joked and laughed with each other as if the world had never fallen apart. Today, Bruce was Major Earl Harris. He'd always disliked his middle name and very few knew it. After his meeting with General Duncan, it had been decided that he would go by his middle name and wear a different rank for his visit to meet Senator Epstein at the Raven Rock complex. If General Oates or his men were keeping tabs on who was visiting the complex, hopefully they wouldn't notice the name Major Earl Harris on the list.

Bruce drove down to Blue Ridge Summit, Pennsylvania, in the pre-dawn hours with a small convoy of MRAPs and up-armored Humvees. He'd wanted to just take a couple of Humvees, but since Willy's ambush maps didn't cover the southern part of the state, prudence dictated the extra manpower for the trip. The journey was largely uneventful; if they'd passed through any ambush locations, the looters hadn't made their presence known. The bulk of the convoy found a large parking lot just to the east of town and Bruce continued on alone in a single Humvee with just his personal security detail. They passed through the first checkpoint and front gate of the Raven Rock complex with his name verified on the visitor's log. They had been instructed to park at the Fire Department by a uniformed security guard who made no attempt to search their vehicle. Bruce surmised that military vehicles coming and going from the facility were commonplace, but he'd still expected a bit more screening by those guarding access to the President himself. When they parked the Humvee alongside the newly constructed firehouse, a different MP informed Bruce that he would be the only one admitted into the facility and the rest of his men would need to stay with the vehicle.

Bruce yawned and leaned back, trying to get comfortable in an uncomfortable chair. He closed his eyes, feeling like he hadn't slept for a week. He, along with three other civilians, was awaiting a transport vehicle to drive them into the complex itself, and they'd been waiting for over an hour now. Two of the men sitting next to him whispered in hushed tones, but Bruce wasn't paying attention to their conversation. In his mind, Bruce ran through the bullet points of his allegations against General Oates that he hoped to relay to the Senator.

Bruce snapped awake as he heard a vehicle pulling up, but it just turned out to be an older military pickup. He closed his eyes once more and leaned his head back against the concrete wall of the firehouse.

"Professor Hillman, Mr. Pilchek, Dr. Houseman, and Major Harris, please follow me." Bruce's eyes opened to find a teenaged private holding onto a clipboard with a look of utter boredom. Bruce stood with the others and fell in line as they followed the private to the pickup truck. "Three of you will have to squeeze in the back," he said unceremoniously as he walked to the driver's door without even a sideways glance in their direction. The four of them glanced at one another with uncertainty, likely wondering who should ride up front and who would be left to squeeze into the rear bench seat. The three men eventually settled their gazes on Bruce as he was the only one in uniform. One of the men clearly hadn't suffered any interruption to his pre-collapse diet, and Bruce motioned for him to take the front. That seemed to settle it.

A few seconds later Bruce found himself seated behind the driver pressed close to another man wearing what looked to be an expensive, though a bit wrinkled, suit. The older military pickup was stuffy in the mid-afternoon sun. Bruce apologized to the man beside him as he pushed against him to free up his left arm which had been pinned against the door. He rolled down his window and placed his arm on the door frame as they pulled away from the firehouse.

It was a short drive around the base of the mountain to the front blast doors leading into the facility, and Bruce had to admit he was a little amazed at the forty foot tall concrete doors that stood before them. They stood slightly ajar with what appeared to be only enough room for a couple people to walk through side by side. However, the driver didn't slow on approach, and for a brief moment Bruce thought for sure they were going to crash. It turned out to be an optical allusion and the opening seemed wider as they grew closer. The driver deftly navigated through the opening at thirty miles per hour with only a foot of clearance on each side of the truck. As they passed through, Bruce instinctively snatched his arm inside. Once through safely, he felt a little embarrassed and noticed the man next to him held a slight grin on his face, though he didn't say anything or look toward Bruce. Bruce felt a deep rumbling sound in his chest and glanced over his shoulder to see the large blast doors slowly closing behind them. As they sped forward, the vertical bar of light behind them narrowed and with a slight flash, the doors slammed home, leaving them in the dark. There was no turning back now.

They drove for nearly a half mile through a rounded tunnel with rough sides hewn directly out of the mountain bedrock. Bruce estimated it to be around thirty feet in diameter. Every so often smaller tunnel openings appeared on the left and right, and occasionally the tunnel "Y'd" in one direction or another. The driver maintained his speed as he veered left or right at each intersection, causing the men in the back to be briefly smooshed together as the truck changed course. The driver came to a stop in front of an imposing solid steel door with "Visitors" stenciled in large white letters over top. A single light bulb hanging in front of the sign and their otherwise dark surroundings gave Bruce the impression of a comic book scene in some gothic underworld like Gotham City.

"Here we are," their chauffer muttered over his shoulder. As soon as Bruce and the three other men exited the vehicle and the last door was shut, he quickly drove off, leaving them gawking in the middle of the dark, musty tunnel. One of the men seemed confident of the process and walked straight for the large steel door; the rest of them followed suit. As the two-foot-thick door slammed behind them, they entered a metal cage at the entrance of a long white hallway. There was a metal detector and conveyor belt set up in front of them with two guards seated behind a desk just outside the metal bars. Bruce heard the light scuff of a boot and looked over his shoulder to see a corporal with an M4 standing on a platform looking down into the cage. The whole scenario and what he was here to do made Bruce's heart begin to race.

"Have your pass and ID ready!" one of the guards at the desk said loudly. His terse command echoed off the concrete walls and Bruce reached into his back pocket, fishing for his ID. "If this is your first time here, there are no weapons of any kind permitted in the facility, including knives." He said the last peering directly at Bruce as he eyed his torso looking for a sidearm. The second guard behind the desk motioned the first man forward. He looked over the man's paperwork and studied his ID before looking the man up and down. When satisfied, he returned the man's paperwork through the metal bars and motioned him through the turnstile leading out of their cage. The guard motioned the next man forward.

By the time they got to Bruce, he realized that he didn't have any orders, paperwork, or a pass to offer the man and just handed over his

ID. "I wasn't given a pass or anything. I have a meeting scheduled with Senator Epstein." He hoped that would be enough.

The guard, dressed like an everyday policeman, took his military photo ID and looked Bruce up and down. "It says Colonel on here," he muttered.

"Yeah...," Bruce produced a fake grimace and cleared his throat noisily. "That's a bit of a long story and not really one I'd care to relive, young man."

The guard just nodded his head in an understanding way. The guard leaned back in his chair to the point of tipping over backwards and grabbed a clipboard off a hook on the wall behind him. He flipped through the first couple pages and Bruce watched his eyes scan down the list. "First name?"

"My first name is Bruce, though I typically go by my middle name, Earl." Bruce held his breath. He'd expected some extra scrutiny over his ID and name, and he'd even concocted a good story to explain why he'd been demoted two full ranks to Major, but now that he was under the microscope, he could feel his pores begin to leak. Without looking up, the man returned Bruce's ID and motioned him through the gate. He turned back to the other guard and they picked up on some conversation they must have been having before the foursome arrived.

Bruce stood patiently as the heavy-set man in front of him struggled to take off his shoes. His girth was getting in the way, forcing him to lean back against the x-ray machine for support as he pitched forward and untied his brown leather dress shoes. Bruce bent over to start unlacing his own boots when a tap on the machine next to his head made him look up. One of the men behind the conveyor belt into the x-ray machine shook his head at Bruce in a "don't worry about it" motion before rolling his eyes at the back of the heavy-set guy in front of Bruce. Bruce gave him a slight smile and offered a nod of thanks. He waited patiently for his three companions, and when Bruce finally walked through the metal detector, it squawked in loud condemnation. The guard who'd insinuated he didn't have to take off his boots walked over and quickly ran a wand over his body before motioning him forward to join the others.

A female Senior Airman in dress blues stood with a clipboard, patiently waiting for Bruce to join the others. She handed him a white plastic badge with a lapel clip and began her spiel. "A show of hands, please. Who hasn't been to this facility before?" Bruce and two of the others raised their hands. "Okay, I will be taking you gentlemen to the main dining facility to meet with your chaperones. You are not permitted to go anywhere outside of the dining facility without supervision, and I mean anywhere. If you are found wandering around without your chaperone, you will be arrested. Is that understood?" The four of them nodded their heads in unison. "You are required to wear and prominently display your visitor's badge at all times until you leave. If you are found wandering around without your visitor's badge, you will be arrested. Is that understood?" Again, they all nodded.

She gave Bruce a sideways glance and he quickly looked down at the badge before catching the clue and clipping it onto the breast pocket of his uniform. It was a plain white badge with "Visitor: Day Pass" printed at the top. Major Harris was written in bold marker in the center of the badge with Senator Trent Epstein scrawled in smaller handwriting on the bottom. Bruce also noticed a small card chip embedded on the pass, but he doubted it would open many doors for him.

"Follow me, please," she said politely, leading them down the long white hallway. They went through a set of revolving doors at the end of the hall that led into another long hallway, this one much wider. There were people milling about and walking in opposite directions on unknown tasks. Most wore military uniforms, but others wore suits or khaki pants. Bruce even noticed a woman pushing a baby stroller in their direction with a second child holding her hand. As they walked by, he heard the older child protesting something loudly. Their guide led them down a hallway to their right and before long there was a large opening on their left with a decorative sign reading "Cafeteria" over the entrance. She motioned them inside and handed her clipboard to another set of guards manning the entrance. These were also dressed as policemen similar to the men at the security entrance. "Enjoy your stay gentlemen," she said politely. "I'll let your contacts know that you're here. Feel free to ask Officer Bradley or Officer Manning if you have any questions." With that, she spun on her heel and walked away at a brisk pace.

The heavy-set man in front was quickly greeted by a man in a suit. "Professor Hillman, I'm so glad to see you. We've really got a serious situation on our hands. Do you think…." Their conversation trailed off as the two disappeared down the hallway in the direction they'd just come. Bruce turned back to find himself standing alone and the two police officers watching him casually. He gave them a friendly smile and stepped into the cafeteria. The cafeteria was physically shocking to Bruce's senses. The place smelled…clean. It looked like any cafeteria you might encounter at a large hospital before the collapse. There were hundreds of people of various backgrounds from military personnel representing every branch to civilians dressed in all manners, from business suits all the way down to a man wearing cargo shorts and a Hawaiian shirt. There were women and children moving about and men in construction outfits standing in line with their trays. It was as if the place was a time capsule and the people trapped inside never received the memo that the rest of the world was on fire. No one was skinny or dirty and when a Gunnery Sergeant carrying a tray walked in front of him, Bruce suddenly felt self-conscious that he hadn't starched and ironed his uniform before the trip.

How was he supposed to find this Senator he'd never met in all the hustle and bustle surrounding him? At first, Bruce stood near the cafeteria's entrance with his badge displayed prominently before realizing that maybe he shouldn't make himself so visible. General Duncan had said that General Oates was scheduled to be at the Pentagon today, but he was also known to show up at either location without warning. Bruce decided to sit in the back corner and watch for someone to enter the cafeteria looking around. He passed six checkout counters with computer-based point of sale machines and long lines of people waiting to pay. Everyone seemed to be paying with a credit card, though Bruce assumed it was likely some sort of internal ration card at the facility.

A loud whisking sound to his left startled Bruce, and he found a barista standing behind an espresso machine steaming some milk for a customer's latte. He was suddenly overwhelmed with feelings of both envy and hostility toward these people. They smiled, chittered amongst themselves, and generally acted as if they had no clue how the rest of the country was living. Standing in front of the coffee cart, with the smell of freshly ground coffee beans in his nose, Bruce suddenly had a hankering for a cup of coffee. He considered asking the barista how a visitor would go about obtaining one, but decided against it. Anyone that saw him surely had to be getting the impression that he was an "outsider." He realized that he'd been gawking at his surroundings. Bruce set his jaw, found a small two-person table near the back, and made for it. He wasn't sure what he'd expected to see when coming here, but this decadence hadn't been it.

Bruce sat at the table for what seemed like forever as he watched all manner of people come and go. There were a few times he saw people enter that seemed to be looking for someone. He would casually make his way in their direction but they always seemed to find who they'd been looking for. Bruce was beginning to wonder what he'd do if the senator never showed up. Would he leave? He didn't want to ask the policemen at the cafeteria's entrance, who were different now than the ones when he'd arrived. If he did, he wasn't sure how they would react. Bruce was tired. He was irritated at these carefree people, and he was starting to second guess this entire idea when a tall man in a deep navy pinstriped suit stepped in front of him. Bruce quickly stood and accepted the man's hand.

Senator Epstein motioned that they should sit and Bruce followed his lead, their knees awkwardly bumping together under the small table. "Major Harris, I'm sorry for making you wait so long. It's been a busy day for me." Bruce knew that whatever pretext General Duncan had set this meeting up under, it likely wasn't done with any secrecy. Duncan was obviously leaving it up to Bruce to handle the situation as he found it. Bruce noticed Senator Epstein flipping through a thick stack of papers in his hands as he spoke. "I hate to rush you, but we need to make this quick as I have a vote coming up soon." He glanced up briefly at Bruce with a friendly smile. "How can I be of assistance to you today, Major?" He'd no sooner finished asking the question when his gaze wandered back to the papers in front of him.

"Senator Epstein," Bruce began quietly.

"Trent."

What's that, sir?" Bruce asked.

"Just call me Trent. Senator Epstein was my father." He glanced up at Bruce again with another friendly smile. This time Bruce noticed the dark circles under his deep blue, piercing eyes.

"Yes, sir," Bruce answered formally. "Trent, is there somewhere private we could speak?"

Trent briefly glanced around at those seated next to them before answering. "I don't actually have my own office at this facility. We should be alright here. What's this meeting about?" He asked the last question as he again turned his attention back to his papers and it was starting to piss Bruce off.

"Senator Epstein, I have some classified and very important information about a serious crime that I need to share with you."

"Mmm, hmm."

"Senator Epstein!" Bruce said firmly yet quietly.

Senator Epstein looked up apologetically, and lowered the stack of papers onto the table. "I'm sorry, Major," he said sincerely. "I've had a long day but it's no excuse." He glanced briefly at his watch before turning his attention back to Bruce. "You were saying that you have information about some crime that's been committed? Have you taken this information up your proper chain of command yet?"

Bruce sighed. "No, sir, this isn't something I can take up the chain of command."

He didn't get a chance to finish as the senator cut him off. "Major Harris, I'm really sorry to interrupt you and I'm not trying to be rude, but I like I already mentioned, I have an incredibly busy day ahead of me. I don't know who set this meeting up and I didn't even know about it until this morning. I'm going to have to advise you to take up whatever information you have with your superiors first."

It was Bruce's turn to cut him off. He tossed the envelope containing Lt. Baier's report onto the senator's stack of papers. "Read it," he insisted firmly.

Senator Epstein seemed startled at Bruce's bluntness, but he finally nodded. He carefully opened the envelope and pulled out the papers inside. He read about halfway through the first page before quickly leafing through the other pages and scanning over them. His head came up and he looked Bruce in the eye. "Where did you get these?"

Bruce spoke slowly. "Sir, I really think we need to find someplace private to speak."

Trent looked around once more. "Yes. Yes. I do believe you're right." He placed the report back into the envelope and deftly slid it inside the breast pocket of his suit. Gathering up his own stack of papers, he stood. "Follow me."

As soon as they left the cafeteria, another man in a suit caught sight of the Senator. "Trent, where do you sit on the new energy bill?" the man asked aggressively over the heads of various people that were walking between them.

Senator Epstein didn't stop, but waved the stack of papers over his head and kept walking. "I'm still reading it."

"Trent, we need to know if you're with us! The vote is in two hours!" The man raised his voice this time to Senator Epstein's back as he continued walking. The man gave Bruce a quick unimportant glance.

"I'm still reading it," Trent replied without turning back.

"Trent?" The man nearly yelled over the thrum of people in the hallway.

It was awkward to say the least, and Bruce wondered if that type of exchange was normal here. Trent never slowed his pace. Bruce followed the senator down various passages, making too many turns to keep track of. The farther they travelled, the nicer the hallways became. There was drywall, wood trim, and paintings hanging on the walls in this newer section of the facility. Trent finally stopped in front of a small door and swiped his passkey card over the scanner mounted on the wall. There was an audible click and a small green light began to flash. Senator Epstein turned the handle. Bruce followed him into a small, dimly lit, eight-by-ten-foot room with a comfortable looking bed at the far end. It reminded Bruce of the small cabin on a cruise he'd once taken, but Trent's room was adorned with a deep red mahogany chair rail and ornate furnishings. Trent offered him the lone chair in the room and Bruce waved it off. The senator shrugged and lowered himself down into the chair.

"This is about as private as I can offer you, Major," Trent said awkwardly. "Would you like a drink? I have bottled water, Diet Coke, some lemonade...."

"A bottled water would be fine," Bruce answered.

Trent swiveled in the rich leather office chair and reached under his desk to open a mini fridge. He produced two ice cold bottles of water, handing one to Bruce. Setting his stack of papers onto the corner of his desk, he retrieved the Seal Team leader's report from his pocket.

"Senator Epstein, I feel we should probably speak before you read that. There is a lot of background information behind that report."

Senator Epstein swiveled the chair back to Bruce, placing his left foot across his opposite knee and reclining back. "You've got my full attention, Major," he said. This level of attention was a one hundred and eighty degree turn from his inattentiveness in the dining hall. "Please continue."

Bruce started from scratch, beginning with his real name and rank, and told the senator everything. Mostly everything; he left out a few details, including specifics of how Jenkins died and the current location of Mayor Reese. Bruce spoke for over an hour and the senator didn't interrupt. A few times Bruce found himself pacing the center of the small room, and when his water bottle was empty, Trent offered him another without saying a word. When Bruce was done speaking, Trent read through Lt. Baier's report and Mayor Reese's short message on General Oates' background. Trent nodded occasionally as he read.

"You've received some good intel here." He placed the note on the desk with the other papers. "And you say that General Duncan is the only other person that knows this information?" Bruce nodded. "And you have two bottles of drinking water from the Green Zone that I can send to the lab?" Bruce nodded again. Trent exhaled sharply. He spun his chair away from Bruce and reached up to a cabinet above his desk, pulling down a dark brown bottle of whiskey. He raised an eyebrow at Bruce who just shook his head. Senator Epstein poured himself a shot and swallowed it down in one gulp. He poured another and spun his chair back to Bruce.

"Major… uh, Colonel Harris. We've been trying to put something together on General Oates for six months, something that will stick. He's been our main opposition here in Congress and I don't just mean to the Republican Party. Two very outspoken opponents of his have already disappeared without a trace. We've been hearing rumors of things he's done since the very beginning, but we've never been able to gather any convincing proof. He's pretty well insulated. But if those tests come back positive and we can get his signature on the orders removing the substance from the storage facility…." He let the thought hang.

"Then what?" Bruce said, perhaps a little too demanding. "You say he's well insulated. I've risked my life to bring you this information. If he's still around after the smoke is cleared, I'm a dead man."

"As am I," Trent offered, raising the second shot glass toward Bruce in salute before draining it. "I don't know if you noticed the police presence in the halls outside. That was one of our main stipulations when they moved us here. We wanted civilian police oversight and not military. We control the security inside the facility here—not the President, and not General Oates. If those tests come back positive, I guarantee you that I'll have him arrested the second he steps foot inside this facility."

"I hate to be so bold, senator, but then what? How can I be assured he's going to be…dealt with? Do you plan on having a trial? I'm not sure you'd get very many witnesses to step forward, assuming you could even find them." He pointed at the Seal leader's report on the desk. "Even if you could prove it, couldn't the President just pardon General Oates as soon as he was found guilty?"

"Technically, yes. But I don't plan on putting him on trial." Senator Epstein paused briefly and thrummed his fingers on his desk a few times before continuing. "First off, I want to reassure you that all the information you shared will stay in this room and I'm going to handle this personally. Sitting on the intelligence committee, I'm one of only a handful of people alive in this country with the clearance to walk those samples into the facility to test them. I can also peruse their books and find out if any chemical or biological agents are missing. As of now, I'm clearing my schedule for tomorrow and plan to dig into this further and see where the rabbit trail leads. I'm going off the record here and this is just between you and me, but if those tests come back positive, I believe that General Oates is going to just disappear. I'm not going to say how, but let's just say that General Oates isn't the only person with underground assets. I imagine he might have himself an unfortunate accident while he's in detention."

Trent sighed. "I don't like the idea of handling things this way, but General Oates has been operating outside the laws that govern this nation for so long, it's about time he got a taste of his own medicine. Besides, removing him from the picture is the only way to get this country back on track. We literally can't get a single thing done in Congress without him pulling strings and having it all unravel. He needs to go away."

"What is it you guys are trying to do?" The question escaped Bruce's lips before he had the chance to consider his tone. "Please don't take this personally, Senator, but do you guys even have the first clue what's going on outside these walls?"

Senator Epstein frowned at him. "Yes, we get weekly reports and I've visited the Green Zones more than any other member of Congress…well, before they were abandoned. We're trying to come up with a plan to help what's left of the American people, but everything is in chaos right now. We're trying to keep millions of starving people fed with the limited shipments we're getting from the UN and, to be frank, it's not working out very well."

"Of course it's not working." Bruce rolled his eyes. "What you guys are trying to do is impossible! sir, I was in charge of perimeter security around Wilmington before being sent on my current mission. I've been part of the process from the beginning and I can assure you that, while done with the best intentions, feeding the mass population centers was never going to work. There are just too many starving people, too much chaos, and not enough food to go around. I'm not sure who's writing your weekly reports, but if I may offer some suggestions from someone who's actually been in the thick of things?"

Trent glanced down at his watch briefly before nodding to Bruce. "If you can keep it brief."

"Sir, what the government needs to do is triage who's left." Trent squinted his eyes and frowned at that. "This whole situation is a mass casualty event on an epic scale. Just like on the battlefield, you need to help the wounded you can help instead of wasting resources on people that aren't going to make it regardless of how much you try to help them. Congress needs to transition from their attempts to prevent things from falling apart any further and start focusing on shoring up the infrastructure that can be saved and beginning the process of rebuilding. Trying to find some way to feed the millions of starving people on the coasts is impossible, as you have now seen. There's just not enough food and medical assistance to go around.

"My recommendation is to start building in-roads with the small surviving towns and groups that are struggling to get by. Most of them are fairly self-sufficient and with the tiniest bit of help and resources made available to them, they could continue to grow and flourish. I have been working behind the scenes with some small towns and groups in my area and it's been a positive experience. There was considerable mistrust at first, but we've worked through that. The various towns in my area are beginning to work together now and share resources. I've actually been invited this weekend to attend their next group meeting. It would sure be helpful if I could provide them some reassurance and some aid from Congress. There's very little I can do for them by myself.

"I've been given the impression that Congress is just sitting back for now, watching to see how things play out. I'm here to tell you if you ignore middle America and don't help the small groups of survivors now, America is going to cease to exist and you'll never be able to rebuild. They'll never accept your oversight in the future. If you wait another year and then send some guy in a suit to engage these people, they're going to run that guy out of town. Pretty soon, this country is going to be made up of hundreds or thousands of tiny warring factions and getting control of it will be impossible.

"Kind of like this group up in Cleveland. They've apparently got some committees set up that are doing a good job of keeping law and order in the camp. I'll admit, they've got some serious issues and uphill battles ahead of them, but they're working together to overcome them. Why not send some people up there now? Don't ask anything from these people—no pledge of allegiance, no rules they have to live by or discussion of future tax policy—just see how you can aid them. Help them become more self-sustainable long term without having to raid cities to feed themselves. In fact, a few minor things like a little bit of fuel for their tractors, some seed to plant their own crops, and maybe some extra greenhouse material for those in the colder regions could go a very long way to helping these people not just survive, but thrive."

Bruce could tell that Senator Epstein was seriously pondering his ideas on how the government should react to the current situation, so he continued. "There's a guy in our area that travels between the various towns and groups carrying information and coordinating barters and aid between the towns. He calls himself 'The Postman.' You should seriously consider duplicating that on a larger scale across the country: help reunite the survivors out there and get them working together with aid from Congress. They're also longing for information from the outside world which could be your in. If you put a system together like this, you could actually help people begin to rebuild instead of spinning your wheels out her on the coasts. It's a horrible thing to consider, but the dwindling food shipments will eventually run out at some point. What tiny bit of food and help you are giving the masses on the coasts here is, in truth, just delaying the inevitable.

"It's triage," Bruce reiterated. "Help the people you can actually help and make sure when the government is strong enough to re-insert its authority over the country, there are actually people willing to trust you and listen to what you propose, people you've built relationships with and helped in the past."

Senator Epstein sat in his chair thrumming the tips of his fingers together in cadence. "That's actually quite an interesting perspective, Colonel, and one I haven't heard before. I like the idea of having regional representatives to coordinate between the surviving towns and help to coordinate the rebirth of the country. I think you may be on to something here." Trent rubbed at his chin thoughtfully. "You say you are meeting with your local towns this weekend?"

"Yes, sir," Bruce responded with a glimmer of hope.

"Let these people know that Congress would like to offer what help we can. Get a list of the most important items they need to aid their current self-sufficiency. We'll use this as an example for my colleagues of what can be accomplished by implementing your strategy. In the meantime, I'd like you to write down your recommendations in an actual policy paper and deliver it to me next weekend with the list of supplies requested by the towns."

"Who? Me?" Bruce asked, surprised.

Trent made a pretense of looking around for someone else in the room. "Yeah. You."

"Sir, I've never written a policy paper in my life and I wouldn't even know where to start."

"Colonel, what you just told me is a pretty good start," Trent said with an encouraging smile. "Start by relaying your prior experience in the Green Zones and your current experience out in no man's land. I think that experience makes you the perfect person to put a policy recommendation together." He paused to think. "In fact, we have a joint session of Congress scheduled for next weekend. The President is planning an address. I think it might make sense for you to come down here and deliver your report in person to both houses. Possibly take some questions on your ideas."

"Senator Epstein," Bruce interrupted, aghast.

Trent raised his hand. "I told you already: that's my dad. It's just Trent."

"Trent," Bruce began again, trying to contain his shock, "I'm not a politician; I'm a soldier. I really don't think I'm the guy for this."

"Of course you are. Colonel Harris, everyone has a role they need to play in rebuilding this country. I'm starting to think this may be yours." He spun his chair back to his desk, grabbed a Post-It note, and started to scribble numbers down. "This is my direct line, though it will likely be answered by my assistant. If you have any questions or need anything in the meantime, don't hesitate to call. I'm going to put myself at your disposal for now and see if we can get some traction on this idea of yours." He handed the small paper to Bruce and swiveled back to his desk. "What's your number up there in Warren? I'll keep you updated on what becomes of the General Oates situation."

Bruce gave Trent his number. "Sir, like I mentioned earlier, I believe General Oates may be monitoring communications. Is this wise for us to be talking via satphone?"

Trent waved off his concern. "We've suspected for a while that he's monitoring some of the calls down at the Pentagon. He doesn't have that capability at this facility. It's thoroughly hardened, and Congress maintains control and operation of the switchboard here." Bruce shrugged, but he couldn't hide his apprehension. Trent evidently noticed his concern. "You might be right. Better safe than sorry," he conceded. "If you need to call in, use the name Major Wilcox. That was my wife's maiden name. I'll also be careful what I say when I follow up with you on General Oates and we won't use his name or mention any specifics. How does that sound?"

Bruce nodded his head, a little overwhelmed at everything that had transpired since he'd entered the man's office. Trent slapped his thighs, signaling the end of the meeting, and stood to walk Bruce to the door. "Colonel Harris, I truly appreciate everything you've done to this point. I thank you for your service to this country and for your willingness to refuse the illegal orders you were given and risk your command to bring me this information. We need more men like you. Working together, hopefully we can salvage what's left of this country before it's too late. We'll get things back on the right track, you'll see." It sounded like politician's speech cut straight from some movie, but Bruce didn't mind. The man seemed genuine.

"Thank you, sir," Bruce said as he accepted Trent's handshake. "I hope you're right."

"Now, I've only got forty-five minutes left to finish going through this energy bill before the vote. We're desperately trying to figure out how to get what's left of the electrical grid up and running and I really need to focus on this," Trent explained. "I know I need to go with you to your vehicle to get those water bottles, and I hate to ask it, but do you mind waiting in the cafeteria for a couple more hours until I'm finished up here? I'll come and find you immediately after the vote."

Bruce chuckled lightly. "That's fine Senator. I don't mind." In truth, the idea of sitting in that dining room and watching all those clueless people coming and going did not appeal to him at all.

Trent offered his thanks and made to close the door before Bruce put his hand forward to stop its motion. Bruce's cheeks colored in embarrassment as he looked down the hallway. "Sir, I have no idea where I'm at and, uh, I'd rather not get arrested wandering around the halls."

Chapter 31

Bruce sat at his desk rubbing his temples. He'd spent four days since his trip to Raven Rock making notes and bouncing ideas off Sammy. He felt less confident now in his ideas for moving the country forward than he had when he'd shared them with Senator Epstein. Putting his rambling thoughts and plans on paper just reinforced his opinion that he wasn't the right guy to be making these recommendations to Congress. He'd raised more red flags and produced more questions than he had answers for. Regardless, he was due to return to Raven Rock in only four days to make a formal presentation to both houses of Congress.

Senator Epstein had advised him to come down a day early and he'd provide some interns to help Bruce type it all into a PowerPoint presentation. One day clearly wasn't going to be enough to organize all the chicken scratch he'd produced in the spiral notebook that mockingly stared back at him from his desk. He'd need a week to obtain answers to all the questions that had arisen in his planning, and he'd likely need another week just to organize that information. He only had four days to figure it all out, and he didn't even have that. Bruce would be spending the next three days escorting Tionestans to Brockway for their next market day and meeting with the attending towns' leadership. It wasn't something he could delegate to Sammy. He had to be there in person.

Bruce rubbed a hand over his face in exhaustion. If he continued on like this, he was going to kill himself—if Oates didn't get to him first. A knock at the door broke into his thoughts. Bruce dragged his bloodshot eyes off the notebook and looked up as Sammy stepped into the room and quietly shut the door behind him.

"Good Lord, Bruce!" Sammy said loudly with a look of disgust obvious on his face. "Did you stay up all night again? For Pete's sake, you're covered in sweat." Bruce didn't bother lying to his XO or making excuses as Sammy made his way over to the office windows and flung both of them wide open. A burst of bright morning sun blasted Bruce, and he was forced to turn his head and close his eyes. Little white specks danced behind his eyelids, and he felt the vise tightening around his temples. Was it really morning already?

"It smells like a French whore house in here," Sammy continued. "You need to go get a shower and take a break. You've been at it for 48 hours straight! If you show up at the meet-and-greet tomorrow looking like that, they're going to think you're a meth head."

"I can't," Bruce muttered, his voice cracking under the strain of speaking the words out loud.

"Well, you have to," Sammy insisted with his arms crossed in front of his chest. "If I have to, I'll get Sgt. Timms in here to drag you to the showers and confine you to your room."

Bruce's arm felt like it was made of jelly as he reached across his table and grabbed his water canteen. He took a couple long drags before setting it back down. "That's fine, Sammy. No need to get Sgt. Timms involved." He gave his friend a half-hearted smile. "But first, we need to discuss a couple things and I'm going to ask that you step away from that open window."

Sammy raised his eyebrow but didn't protest. He walked across the room and took his usual seat across from Bruce. "What's with the new orders I heard about this morning? You doubled our manpower at the checkpoints and increased our perimeter patrols. And is there some rationale you'd like to share with me on why I can't enjoy some crisp morning air?" Sammy said as he motioned toward the window.

Bruce sighed and leaned back in his chair, rubbing his temples once more. "I wanted to keep you clear of this, but it's probably time I bring you up to speed." Sammy sat forward in his chair as Bruce spent the next half hour going through all the details of the previous week's activities surrounding General Oates. "Two nights ago I received a call from Senator Epstein. He had the water from Willy's containers tested and it came back positive for some biological weapon code-named 'Black Thorn.' The orders for its release came from General Oates himself and you'll never guess who showed up to take possession and sign it out of the facility."

Sammy frowned. "Jenkins."

Bruce nodded. "No other biological or chemical agent had been checked out of the facility in the last two years and Black Thorn has never been authorized for release…ever."

"You'd think that would make it a pretty open and shut case," Sammy pointed out.

"It did," Bruce agreed. "The Capitol Police arrested General Oates immediately and had him before a judge the following day. The evidence was presented, and he was found guilty of treason, genocide, and a whole slew of other crimes. The judge sentenced him to death."

"Okay…then why all the extra security if Oates is out of the picture now?"

"He's not," Bruce spun his pen around his forefinger. "Someone helped him escape right after the sentencing. They killed a couple guards while breaking him out and no one has seen him since."

"Seriously?" Sammy stammered.

"Seriously," Bruce stood from his chair and stretched. Grabbing his now empty water canteen, he walked over to the corner of the room and refilled it from the pitcher of water next to the coffee pot. He considered brewing a pot but changed his mind. He needed sleep, not coffee.

"So, you're just now telling me this? What's our plan?" Sammy asked, not hiding his concern.

"I'm all out of plans, Sammy," Bruce answered as he walked back to the desk and collapsed in his chair. "Senator Epstein assures me they are scouring the countryside for Oates and he has access to a few off-the-books assets that are looking for him as well. They don't plan to arrest him again. One of those teams is scheduled to arrive here today. They're going to post up next door to my room and see if Oates turns up for revenge. Apparently, I've been promoted from colonel to carrot."

Sammy didn't laugh at the joke. "Bruce, this is serious. If General Oates' team can bust him out of Raven Rock, I'm sure they can waltz right into a little mountain town like this regardless of whether or not we increase our patrols."

"I'm aware of that Sammy," Bruce countered with more irritation in his voice than he intended. "However, I'm not going to make it easy for them, either." He pointed to the M4 leaning against the wall behind his desk, and for the first time Sammy noticed Bruce was wearing his sidearm.

"Bruce, we need to get you a 24-hour security team. Anybody could just waltz into your office like that Seal Team leader. Besides, I've spent time with you at the range with that thing."

Bruce didn't even have time to smile at Sammy's jest when there was a quiet knock on the door. A moment later the door swung open and a large man covered in road dust stepped inside, quickly shutting the door behind him. Sammy leaped to his feet, placing himself between Bruce and the intruder.

"Relax, Sammy!" Bruce ordered as he stood and walked around his desk. Lt. Baier eyed Sammy suspiciously as Bruce stepped in front of his XO and shook the lieutenant's hand. "We were just talking about you."

"I heard," Lt. Baier said disdainfully. "I thought we agreed to keep this between ourselves."

"We did," Bruce conceded. "But there have been some new developments and I'm going to need Major Samuelsson's help." Lt. Baier eyed the major up and down before giving Bruce a grudging nod. Bruce quickly introduced them and they gathered around his desk.

"In all seriousness, Lt. Baier, when we get done here, I'm going to have to insist that you tell me how you keep getting through our perimeter." The edges of Lt. Baier's lips turned up as he gave a small shrug. Bruce continued. "You look like hell. How was your trip?"

Lt. Baier snorted. "I look like hell? Colonel, have you looked in the mirror recently?" Bruce smiled as the lieutenant continued. "Our mission was unsuccessful. When we arrived in Cleveland, we snuck into the encampment the same way we did before. We spent a couple days kicking around a few ideas and trying to put a plan of attack together to take Skyler out. Unfortunately, he hardly ever left the control tower and when he did, there wasn't any pattern to it. On the third day, a plane arrived. We tried to get close, but the plane was pulled into a hangar before anyone departed. Word spread that an emergency council meeting was called. There were rumors that the President himself had sent a delegation to the group. The next thing you know, the entire encampment is mustered, and the leader of the delegation, a guy by the name of Ben Wetzer, gives a speech in front of everyone with Skyler and the entire council lined up behind him."

Lt. Baier shifted in his seat. "It was an amazing speech. It was very pro-America explaining the virtues of the US Constitution and how he's going to help them rebuild. He stated that he had the backing of Congress who is going to start sending the group aid and supplies to help feed them through the winter. They wouldn't need to raid any more cities." Bruce was growing more irritated the longer Lt. Baier spoke. Did Senator Epstein take his ideas and start implementing them without discussing it with him or developing a formal plan? Why was he wasting his time writing a policy paper?

"They were even getting an actual judge sent from D.C. to preside over criminal matters. The whopper was when he informed everyone that Skyler had volunteered to step down and Ben was going to be acting as mayor. It had been voted on unanimously by the council and Skyler would act as deputy mayor in charge of camp security."

"Based on what you told me before, that seems totally out of character for this Skyler guy to just step down like that," Bruce mused aloud.

"It sure is," Lt. Baier agreed, "except when you find out that Ben Wetzer isn't Ben Wetzer." Bruce and Sammy gave him a curious look. Lt. Baier frowned. "It was General Oates."

Bruce leaned back and squeezed the sides of his head. "You've got to be kidding me."

"Nope."

"What's the President thinking? He has to realize if he diverts food shipments to that encampment, Congress is going to start asking questions and eventually someone is going to recognize Oates up there. The President is already facing a subpoena to be questioned by Congress on his involvement with General Oates' previous actions. You'd think he'd hide General Oates in some deep, dark hole somewhere."

"You're assuming the President is in on this scheme," Lt. Baier pointed out.

"He has to be," Bruce insisted. "You heard rumors that he had a letter from the President with him when he met with the council. While it's easily possible that letter could have been forged, there is no way to fake getting food and supplies shipped in there. I can almost guarantee Congress isn't behind this, because they want Oates dead almost as badly as we do. And if he doesn't produce on his promise of aid, his term as mayor over that group is going to be really short-lived. General Oates isn't an idiot to make that big of a promise without being able to deliver. The only person I can think of that has the power to coordinate those kinds of food shipments would be the President himself."

"You're telling me that General Oates is heading up an army less than two hundred miles away…and you guys are worried about the politics behind it?" Sammy asked bluntly.

Lt. Baier ignored Sammy's comment. "We wanted to get back here as soon as possible and let you know what was going on."

"Well, it sure took you long enough to get here," Sammy said irritably.

Lt. Baier gave him a hard look before continuing his story. "After the speech, we regrouped and started discussing our options on how to take them both out. The following morning, we were confronted by one of the civilian security teams that patrolled the terminals. It didn't go well. Apparently, General Oates and Skyler had circulated our descriptions and half the people in the camp were on the look-out for us. Luckily, the civilian security patrols weren't armed. We tussled with them briefly and were able to incapacitate them before their reinforcements showed up. However, we had a hell of a time sneaking out of the camp. When we finally made it back to where we'd staged the Humvees, we nearly walked into an ambush."

Lt. Baier stretched his neck muscles. "In our haste to re-enter the camp, we didn't scout a new location to hide the Humvees. Apparently, Skyler was smarter than we thought and must have had us followed the last time we left camp. We got into quite a firefight before we were able to break contact and escape on foot into the forest. We spent the next six hours going through vacant houses until we were able to locate enough bicycles to make our way back here. We've been peddling for almost two days straight." He turned his icy gaze to Sammy. "So yes, it took us a while to get back." Sammy held out his palms apologetically.

"We plan to rest up a couple days, draw up a new plan of attack, and figure out some disguises. Hopefully, you can help us resupply.

After losing the Humvees, we're really low on ammunition and even lower on food. Another vehicle would be appreciated, as well."

Bruce cut him off with a raised hand. "Lt. Baier, even with disguises, it's a suicide mission for your men to go back in there."

Lt. Baier scratched at his beard. "I wouldn't call it a suicide mission, Colonel, but it definitely has its challenges. Besides, who else would be willing to try their hand at this?"

"I know a guy that would leap at the opportunity," Sammy offered with a tight grin.

Bruce stared at Sammy, and then it dawned on him who he was referring to. "Lieutenant, how soon could you put together an intel report on that encampment and draw us a map with precise detail of how your team snuck in and out of the airport?"

"Shouldn't take too long. I already have most of that put together. I'll just need to decode and transcribe it for you."

"Good. Why don't you take your team to the same building I put you up in the last time you were in town and get started on that report. I'll get some hot food and some fresh supplies sent over right away. I think we'll let someone else take a shot at this first. It's too risky for you and your men to go straight back into the lion's den, even in disguise. In the meantime, how would you feel about donning some 10th Mountain uniforms and letting me station you in a garrison we keep in one of the neighboring towns? You'd have to perform regular security patrols and watch details down there and you would have to spend some time on the town's gardening team, but it will get you out of the picture until we find out if this other avenue works out."

"Gardening team?" Lt. Baier mouthed the words with a confused look on his face. Bruce didn't explain as he was already halfway to the door. He opened it a crack and stuck his head out into the dim hallway. When he was certain there was no one else around, he bellowed down the hall. "Private Mason?" A second later the next door down flung open and his orderly careened into the hall, his hands frantically buttoning up his shirt. "Private Mason, I need you to go down to the comms truck and have them radio Tionesta. Get word to Willy that I need a meeting with him immediately. Make sure they radio back confirmation from Willy and what time he can meet me at the southwest checkpoint."

"Yes, sir," Private Mason said before turning away at a jog.

Bruce closed the door and walked back to his desk. He heard the sound of a twin engine plane off in the distance and fought the urge to walk over to the window and peer out. The security team from Epstein was arriving and he was starting to feel more awake now. Bruce took his seat and looked up to see Lt. Baier still staring at the floor with a confused look on his face.

Baier finally looked up and made eye contact with Bruce. "Gardening team?"

Willy lay prone only ten yards inside the tree line off route 62. He used his binoculars to scan the long concrete bridge crossing the winding Allegheny River. Someone had recently placed concrete barriers and multiple coils of razor wire at the entrance, blocking access across the river by anything larger than a motorcycle. Only a few days before, he'd crossed that bridge and met with Colonel Harris just south of Warren. The southeast checkpoint had been moved again, and Willy couldn't help but wonder why.

He studied the bridge once more. From his vantage point, he could make out an MRAP and Humvee on the far side of the bridge, both outfitted with 50-caliber machine guns on top. Willy had to admit, this was a far superior location to set up a roadblock than their previous location. There was a large distribution center on his side of the river with an expansive open field in front. It allowed the soldiers on the far side of the bridge to see potential threats approaching from a long way off. Anyone storming that checkpoint would need a tank to get through.

Willy could feel the hair on the back of his neck standing up. Colonel Harris hadn't arrived at the road block yet, and he was dreading the idea of making the long walk across the open ground with the two heavy machine guns pointed in his direction. If those trigger-happy soldiers didn't get the memo that he was supposed to be there....

Willy turned his binoculars toward the driveway entrance into the Blair distribution center. There was a five-foot-tall decorative concrete wall near the road with a bright blue sign attached, proudly announcing the company's name. Without being mowed over the last year, the grass around the sign and throughout the frontage had grown to nearly three feet high. He decided that would be his first point of cover. He studied the decorative stone wall and considered its construction. While it seemed to be made from large stacked boulders, he quickly surmised it was most likely a decorative, cultured stone façade covering a wood or block wall. Willy highly doubted it would stop the .50-caliber rounds from the MRAP and Humvee, but it was his only option.

He turned back to study the thick concrete barriers at the entrance to the bridge. They would provide better ballistic protection from the .50-caliber rounds, but he'd have to crawl through coils of razor wire to reach their protection. There were no good options. He'd have to trust Colonel Harris' intentions. Willy pondered the colonel briefly and the cautious friendliness he'd been feeling toward the man. After his wife and child's murder in the Newark Green Zone, Willy had sworn an oath to never trust someone from the government again. Colonel Harris chipped away at that oath each time they met. Bruce Harris seemed to be an honorable man with good intentions toward the local towns, yet the fact he'd engaged in helping round people up and place them in Green Zones still stuck in Willy's craw, regardless of his excuse of just following orders.

Willy's leg bounced nervously as he waited. Colonel Harris had reached out early that morning and requested an urgent meeting with him. It had been five days since he'd met with Colonel Harris and turned over the poisoned water bottles for testing. He'd spent the next couple days making his rounds to the various surviving groups and towns and coordinating the next meetup in Brockway. Upon his arrival back in Tionesta, two days ago, there'd been a cryptic message from the colonel waiting for him. All it said was, "It is done. 8k." Pastor Dan had passed it to him with a curious look and Willy just shrugged in response, though he knew perfectly well what it meant. Colonel Harris had delivered on his side of the bargain and delivered 8,000 gallons of gas to the Uni-Mart in Tylersburg. Willy informed Pastor Dan that he'd stopped at the gas station on his way back into town and discovered a manhole he'd missed on previous inspection which contained fuel. The elder Lutheran preacher turned Mayor had literally let out a loud "whoop" and clapped him on the shoulder with a heavy hand. It was the most emotion he'd ever experienced from the mayor and thinking back to the awkwardness of the moment still produced a smile on his lips.

Other than that message, he'd received no word on the outcome of the lab tests or the fate of General Oates. He could only assume that was the reason for the urgent meeting today. He was bursting with both anticipation and anxiety at what the colonel would reveal. What could be so urgent that it couldn't wait until tomorrow, when the colonel would be coming to Tionesta to escort most of the townspeople to Brockway? It couldn't be good news.

A few minutes later, Willy heard the faint sound of diesel engines echoing across the river and raised his binoculars once more. Three Humvees pulled up next to the MRAP across the bridge, and Willy could hear the sound of multiple up-armored Humvee doors slamming closed. A moment later, Colonel Harris and a small retinue of soldiers gathered in front of the MRAP. It was time.

Willy repositioned his pack behind the log he'd been using for cover and laid his M4 across it. He took off his pistol belt and laid it next to the pack. After a moment's hesitation, he reached back and pulled the Glock 17 from its holster and tucked it in the rear of his waistband. He considered grabbing a spare mag and let out a chuckle.

The handgun would be useless. He was being overly cautious and considered leaving the weapon behind. Yet caution had saved his life on more than one occasion. He kept the pistol on him. Willy settled his nerves as best he could and raised his head to the sky. "Angel, I'm coming to see you, but not today."

Willy stood and slowly picked his way down to the road. When he reached the asphalt, he picked up his stride and walked forward. As he reached the driveway entrance to the distribution center, he veered off the road and high-stepped his way through the tall grass to the decorative wall bearing the company's sign. As soon as he reached the short stone wall, he hopped up on top of it and took a seat with his legs dangling free over the edge. At the first sound of gunfire, he would pitch himself backwards off the wall and into the concealment of the high weeds. He would then be forced to low-crawl back to the tree line and his gear. He was being overly cautious and knew he would never make it.

Without his binoculars, it was hard to see Colonel Harris on the other side of the bridge and it looked as if he may be in a heated conversation with his men. Finally, the colonel strode forward with two of the men at his side. It took them a few minutes to cross the bridge, and when they reached the concrete barriers, Willy gave them a short wave. Colonel Harris spoke briefly with his men before taking a large plastic case and a huge duffle bag from one of his escorts. He heaved the heavy duffle bag up onto his shoulder with assistance from one of his men. Striding forward once more, Colonel Harris left the two men behind. Willy watched as they took positions behind the concrete barriers and scanned the woods behind him with their rifles. Willy waited patiently as Colonel Harris trudged the road in his direction and turned into the driveway. Picking his way through the high grass, he nearly tripped at one point and Willy heard him curse under his breath. Colonel Harris was always so concerned about his men watching him and what they saw. Willy could care less what anyone thought of him.

Colonel Harris stopped a few paces in front of the sign, dropping the massive Pelican case and duffle bag into the high weeds. He stayed bent over with his hands resting on his knees, his sides heaving from the exertion. The man needed some exercise…and some sleep. There were dark bags under the commander's eyes. "Hello, Colonel."

"Afternoon, Willy," Colonel Harris responded with difficulty, still bent over and breathing heavily. He cocked his head up to look at Willy and smiled. "You couldn't have done me a solid and met me half way?"

Willy returned the grin. "Nope. You look like you needed the exercise."

Colonel Harris chuckled. "You get my message?"

"Yep," Willy chirped, his legs swinging into open air as he looked down at the Colonel. "The town took six trips down to the Uni-Mart yesterday. Pastor Dan is appreciative, though he doesn't know it." Colonel Harris nodded his head as he leaned back, placing his palms into the small of his back and stretching.

"So, what's the urgent news?" Willy cut to the chase. "I'm sure you didn't have me drive all the way up here during daylight hours to discuss the weather. You know how I hate to travel during the day."

"I know you do. I received some news this morning that I felt you'd like to hear. Something that can't wait." Colonel Harris gave him a level stare.

"General Oates is still alive," Willy guessed. Colonel Harris gave a slight nod of confirmation. "And now he's coming after you, me, and everyone else in that report."

Colonel Harris shrugged his shoulders. "Not sure on that, though I don't think he's going to forget about us."

Willy frowned. "I'm sure he's not. What happened?"

Colonel Harris sighed and explained all that had happened since their last meeting. He spared a few details, but presented the facts as best he could, ending with the Seal Team's arrival and the information that was revealed.

"So, I'm guessing that team of special operations soldiers aren't going to be headed back there anytime soon?"

"They were planning on it. They'd already discussed a fresh plan of attack before they arrived at the gates this morning. They're willing and eager to head back out, but in good conscious, I'm having a hard time letting them go. They're wanted men at the camp with faces that will be recognized; they surely wouldn't come out of it unscathed. This is a mission for a single person who can blend in and stay hidden." Colonel Harris reached into his waist band and pulled out a large envelope. He reached his arm up to where Willy sat perched on the block wall and handed it over.

Willy accepted the envelope and opened it, pulling out a stack of papers. He thumbed through them quickly; finding maps, handwritten notes and diagrams. His anger began to rise as he looked up from the stack of papers. "This isn't the report you promised me."

"No, it's not," Colonel Harris conceded. "My report on everything that's happened and the test results from the lab are right here in this bag." He motioned his head toward the large black duffle bag at his feet. "At this point, I'm offering you one or the other. I had a feeling you'd want that one." He pointed to the stack of papers in Willy's hands.

Willy looked down at the stack of papers and started thumbing through them once more, studying them closer this time. "What are these?"

"It's a detailed intel report on the inner workings of General Oates' new army. There are maps of the surrounding areas, detailed instructions on how to sneak into the facility, descriptions of the personnel inside the camp and their security patrols, layout of the airport, the location of where their leadership has been staying, and nearly every other detail you might need."

Willy spent a few minutes looking through the information and Colonel Harris waited patiently for him to finish. When he was done,

Willy folded the papers and placed them back into the envelope, but he didn't hand it back. He had a feeling he knew where this was going.

"A team of spooks arrived this morning, sent by a Congressman I trust. They're sending in one of their men tomorrow to take out General Oates and his second in command, Skyler. If you head out now, you'll have an eight-hour head start on him. And just so you know, he'll have access to the same information you have in your hand."

Willy's mind was racing. He'd been mentally prepared to hear that General Oates had escaped justice. But this revelation had turned his brain to pudding and his thoughts where spinning around in circles. He'd dreamed about getting revenge for his family's death for a long time. He now had a legitimate opportunity to do just that, and he wasn't sure how he felt about it. "And the other report you promised me?"

"Like I said, it's one or the other." Colonel Harris shifted his feet. "I can't have you riding into the lion's den with my report in tow in case you get captured or killed. If you take the report in your hand, I'll hold onto the other one for now. If you find success on your journey, then your need for this one is nullified. If you're unsuccessful in killing General Oates, yet able to make it out alive, I'll provide you with my report under the same stipulations as before."

In Willy's mind, there was no decision to be made.

Colonel Harris continued. "I have an assortment of various gear for you to go through." Again, he motioned to the large duffel bag and over-sized Pelican case. "I have a Knight's Armament SASS sniper rifle. It's suppressed and outfitted with the latest X26 FLIR night vision scope. It's a backup rifle for one of my scout snipers and zeroed in at two hundred yards. I have his range book for the rifle as well. He'll let you borrow it, but he also said he'd like to have it back." He gave Willy a small smile which Willy didn't return so he moved on. "I can offer you a whole other assortment of goodies: ammunition,

MREs, smoke grenades, real grenades…whatever you'd like or think you would need."

Colonel Harris ran his hand through his hair and looked up, meeting Willy's eyes. "Willy, I want you to know that I'm not asking you to do this. I even considered not telling you anything until we returned from Brockway and I found out whether this other guy was successful in taking out the general. I'm providing this information to you as a friend, and I'd probably get in trouble for doing so. Based on the truly evil nature behind your wife and daughter's death, I feel you're entitled to an opportunity to serve justice in this matter…and this may be your last chance to do so. The last intel I received before Oates took over leadership of the camp was that they were preparing to relocate to Missouri within the next couple of days."

Colonel Harris paused for a moment, thinking. "I also know you've spent a lot of time spear-heading this meeting in Brockway. Maybe you should just—"

"I've done what I can there." Willy cut him off with a wave of his hand. "From here on out, it's up to you and the various towns to figure things out. If I don't return, you can coordinate future gas deliveries with Pastor Dan or Mayor Reese…or whoever." Willy looked deep into the colonel's eyes. "I want your word on it."

He quickly agreed. "You have my word, Willy." There was a long moment of awkward silence. "So, you're going to go after General Oates then?" Willy nodded. "Okay, I'll let the other operative know to keep his eye out for you in the camp. You want to go through this gear?"

Willy shook his head. "I'll take the MRE's but I've got my own rifle, if it comes down to that. I plan to do this face to face. I want to look into his eyes when he passes through the gates of hell." Willy said the last in a hard voice. He looked up to see a concerned look on Colonel Harris's face.

"Willy…."

Willy raised his hand. "Yeah, I know. He's really well guarded, I'm sure, and this is a death sentence in all likelihood. But this is personal, Colonel. I'm going to do it my way, even if it costs me my life."

Colonel Harris shuffled his weight again and looked down at his boots. "I understand. I'd probably want the same." Willy watched as the normally confident man before him seemed to be having some kind of inner struggle. The colonel opened his mouth to speak and then stopped himself. Willy sat on the block wall, looking down at the colonel and waiting. Eventually, Bruce bent over, unzipped the duffle bag, and produced half a dozen MREs. He handed them up one at a time and Willy stacked them on the wall next to where he sat. A look of uncertainty passed over Colonel Harris' face again and he hesitated before glancing over his shoulder toward his men. He bent over one last time and produced a small plastic grocery bag wrapped around something hard. He handed it over hesitantly.

"You can look inside, but don't open it."

Willy's fingers wrapped around a familiar item and his nervous fingers fumbled at the plastic knot of the bag. He glanced up at the Colonel who just stood there watching him. When he finally had it untied he slowly opened the top of the bag. Tears welled up in his eyes.

"That took a lot of begging and pleading for me to get back for you. The other one was kept by Congress along with my report as evidence of General Oates' crimes. Willy, it was made clear to me by the men who arrived today that if what's in that bag falls into the wrong hands, it's my ass on the line. Do you understand?" Willy wiped the lone tear from his cheek and nodded without taking his eyes off the bag's contents.

"I couldn't think of a more fitting end for General Oates. When you mentioned you wanted to do this face to face.... Well, just be careful and make sure no one else comes in contact with it." Willy reached his hand into the bag and gently ran his fingers over the pink stainless water bottle. He rotated it slightly inside the bag until the image of Hello Kitty and her small black eyes stared back into his soul. More tears fell. After moving it around in the bag, he got the sense that the water bottle was empty. He gave it a small shake and his premonition was confirmed. He looked up at Colonel Harris with blurry eyes.

"They decontaminated the water bottle at the lab. You're free to use it as you'd like…or not." Colonel Harris seemed uncomfortable. "In the bottom of the bag you'll find a small metal vial. The other operative that's heading up to Cleveland has an identical one. It was Senator Epstein's idea to get rid of Oates by giving him a taste of his own medicine…if the opportunity presented itself. Otherwise the operative is going to take him out at distance. There's only a few drops in there, but it will be more than enough to do the job. Just be sure you get rid of the contaminated water when you're done. Those couple drops mixed into a large enough container of water could kill a hundred men."

"I understand," Willy said, his voice raspy. He reached into the bottom of the bag and located a tiny metal vial, no bigger than a large vitamin pill. He rolled the cold metal between his fingers slowly.

He looked up again, making eye contact this time. "Thank you, Colonel."

"You're welcome, Willy." There was another moment of awkward silence. "Do you need anything else from me?" Willy shook his head, still rolling the small vial between his fingers. "Okay, I'm going to let my guys know to let you through the checkpoint when you're ready. How long do you need to get back to your bike? I assume you rode up here?"

With some effort, Willy maintained his composure in front of the colonel. "Fifteen minutes."

"Okay. I'll be waiting on the other side." Colonel Harris stood awkwardly for a moment before reaching his hand up and resting it on Willy's shin. "Be careful, Willy. Don't take any stupid chances. If you can't get close to him, just remember that we've got another guy on the same mission, and he's apparently quite proficient at what he does. Also, I'm putting together a plan for Congress to start helping the local towns and offering them aid. I want to be part of the rebuilding process with the locals and I'm going to need your help with that in the future. I need you to come back, alright?"

Willy simply nodded his head in response. He was surprised at the overwhelming emotions produced by holding that small water bottle in his hands once more. How many times over the past six months had he held it up to his mouth, his arm muscles wrestling against the signal from his brain to just drink it and end the pain. When he'd given it over to Colonel Harris to have tested, he'd assumed he'd never see it again. Yet here it was. His brain conjured up images of his little girl sitting at the small wooden table in their tiny room inside the Newark Green Zone.

Colonel Harris had obviously figured out that Willy was done talking. He bent over and heaved the heavy duffle bag up over his shoulder. Taking a knee, he picked up the large Pelican case containing the sniper rifle and let out a grunt as he stood. He turned toward his men and took two steps before stopping. "Goodbye, Willy," he said without turning back. There was a hint of finality to the words. Colonel Harris huffed as he fought his way through the tall grass and back to the road.

Willy watched him go with both of his hands wrapped around cold, smooth steel. When Colonel Harris reached his men and handed over his burden to younger shoulders, Willy hopped down from the wall. He stashed the small vial into his front pocket and stuffed as many MREs in the bag as he could. The rest he tucked under his arms, not wanting to let go of his daughter's water bottle clutched in his hands. He hustled back to his pack and rifle. He pulled the Glock 17 from his waistband, clipped his pistol belt around his waist, and holstered the weapon. He stuffed the MREs haphazardly into the top of his pack. After that, he spent a full five minutes struggling to release the water bottle. Eventually, he gently wrapped the plastic bag around it and placed it in the side pocket of his bag. Away from prying eyes, tears now streamed freely down his face.

He stood, slung the pack over both shoulders, and picked up his M4. Using his sleeve, he wiped away the tears from his face for the last time. He took in a few long, deep breaths to steady his nerves, exhaling them slowly. Willy smiled, turned his face up toward the heavens and whispered, "I'll be seeing you soon."

Epilogue

Bruce sat in the front passenger seat of his Humvee and struggled with his emotions on what he'd just done. Willy had proven his competence at staying alive on the open road these past six months, but sneaking into General Oates' camp and getting close enough to poison him was a completely different ball game. The quirky man had grown on Bruce since they met, and to say Bruce was concerned would be an understatement.

After the arrival of the team from Senator Epstein, and the revelation they'd be sending one of their men to kill General Oates, there really wasn't any need to send Willy. Bruce was now second-guessing his decision to even bring it up and could have just told Willy what was going on and left it at that. Bruce sighed. Out of the corner of his eye, he noticed his driver shot a quick apprehensive glance in his direction before quickly turning his gaze forward again.

"Are you sure he's coming?" Sammy asked from the back seat. This was the third time he'd asked the same question. "We've got a lot to do today and we've been sitting here for over thirty minutes now. Maybe he…"

Bruce cut Sammy off with a raised hand but said nothing. Willy had been more emotional over the water bottle than he'd expected, though he'd obviously tried to hide it. Never having a family himself,

Bruce couldn't fathom what it would be like to watch his loved ones die right in front of him. He could only imagine. If he'd been in Willy's shoes, he'd want revenge as well.

Movement from the turret of the Humvee in front of them caught Bruce's eye. The soldier manning the .50-caliber machine gun was waving someone forward. Seconds later Willy sped between the two checkpoint vehicles. He'd changed out of his UPS uniform and was now wearing a pair of khaki pants and an olive green soft shell jacket. His M4 was cinched tightly across his chest and he wore a large pack on his back. As the nearly silent, flat-black electric motorcycle whirred past the front of Bruce's Humvee, he waved to Willy through the front window. Willy didn't notice him, or if he did, he didn't acknowledge the gesture. His goggled eyes were focused on the road and he seemed to ignore the large trucks and soldiers he passed. He was on a mission.

"It's about time…," Sammy muttered.

Bruce gave his driver a slight nod and the Humvee's engine roared to life. He turned onto Route 62 north, away from the bridge, and pressed the gas. Bruce considered his current state of affairs. He was on his way to Brockway to meet with the leadership of the local survivors in the area. The results of that meeting could have far reaching consequences for the rest of the country. He was nowhere near prepared to address both houses of Congress in four days' time. He had a psychopath on the loose that was likely out for his blood, and he hadn't slept in two days. All he'd ever wanted was to be a soldier. Where was all this heading?

Bruce looked out the hazy window as the Humvee sped by the overpass for Route 6. He caught a brief glimpse of Willy as the motorcycle passed between the two MRAPs guarding the overpass and disappeared from view. "Happy hunting, Willy," Bruce muttered under his breath.

Sean set his pack down on the ground beside a large gnarly oak tree in the middle of Brockway's Taylor Memorial Park. To his left was a small decorative duck pond that lacked any winged creatures. If they hadn't been eaten already, they surely weren't going to make an appearance today with the multitude of people lounging on the grassy knoll nearby. A small stage had been set up on the edge of the park where a local bluegrass band was playing a song Sean recognized but couldn't name. He hummed along to the tune as he pulled his old Woobie blanket from the top of his pack and laid it out in the freshly mowed grass, a rare and noticeable luxury. Maria pulled two bright red apples out of her own pack and tossed one in his direction. Sean snatched it out of the air and gave her a wink.

They sat silently for a while, watching the band play. The sound of music was such a rare thing these days it literally captivated his attention. Even if it wasn't the genre of music Sean would have enjoyed in his previous life, he couldn't help but grin like a kid on Christmas morning. Eventually, Sean lay back on the blanket and stared up at the canopy of large tree limbs overhead, their leaves rippling in the soft breeze of late autumn. He felt Maria sidle up next to him and lay her head in the crook of his arm; he instinctively engulfed her, his hand softly rubbing her shoulder.

It had been a long day for Sean. He'd taken turns with his father and uncles manning their table at the market location in town. Sean had been surprised to find that very few people bought any of the extra guns their group had brought with them. The weapons, mostly deer rifles, handguns, and a few shotguns, were largely passed over by the milling throng of strangers that meandered through the tables. The only explanation Sean could come up with was those types of guns were all too common in these country towns. If somebody didn't already have one before the collapse, there were plenty of farm houses and vacant homes where a deer rifle or shotgun could be procured. However, the boxes of ammunition they'd brought with them had all been bartered for before noon, as had the two spare reloading kits the group had kept in storage. While these country folks might have plenty of guns, acquiring more ammunition for them was in high demand.

Maria was the first to break the silence. "How'd the meeting go?"

"It went well," Sean answered confidently. "The town council from Tionesta made some good trades, in my opinion, and everyone seemed even more eager this time around to enter into formal trade agreements and barter for future services. The delegation from Abbott mentioned they have a husband and wife team that are an emergency room doctor and a nurse. Emporium said they have a dentist in their group. Plans were made for them to travel between the towns for a week each month and offer their services. Colonel Harris even offered to send one of the 31st Regiment's medics to assist them and a security team to escort them while they travelled between towns."

"That was nice of him," Maria said as she shifted her body and moved her head down onto his chest.

"Yeah…it was," Sean agreed, but his reply included a note of apprehension as well.

"What's the matter with him offering his help?" Maria asked. She knew him all too well.

"Well, toward the end of the meeting, Colonel Harris addressed the entire assembly after being introduced by Pastor Dan. He offered his aid to the towns and asked for each group to put together a list of things they need: items that would help them become more self-sufficient and make life easier for them. He's apparently heading down to meet with Congress in a few days and he's going to try and convince them to start helping the locals rebuild."

"And…what's wrong with that?"

Sean sighed. "Nothing really. We know the colonel well enough and trust him, but the others…well, they're not so sure about him. I happened to be sitting next to the Emporium delegation and I overheard them discussing it afterwards. They're worried about the government finding out about their town and interfering in how they're doing things. While some of their delegation wanted to jump on the opportunity to ask for things like greenhouses, solar panels, and some other items the town needs, most others in the group wanted nothing to do with Colonel Harris or his help. I'm guessing by the tone of various conversations in the room that the other towns are similarly divided in their thinking."

"What do you think they'll do?"

"I don't know. He asked that they turn in their lists by tomorrow morning before we head back. I saw Pastor Dan making rounds after the meeting and talking to each group individually. I'm assuming he was trying to ease their fears by giving them some background on how Colonel Harris has helped Tionesta in the past and explain his support for the idea of receiving aid from the Feds. I can't be sure, but I don't think he was having a lot of luck. I guess we'll find out tomorrow morning."

Maria responded with a thoughtful, "Hmm." They returned to watching the band in silence.

Sean turned his head to where some of his family had taken over a spot in the grass near the pond. He sought out his son. He found James in the arms of his sister, Faith, whose head was bent over the bundle of blankets and making cooing faces. Sean smiled at the scene. His mother and father were there, as well as his brother Joshua with his wife Leah and their children. A small blur caught Sean's eye, and he watched a skinny young boy dash between his nephew's outstretched hands as they raced around the pond, weaving their way in and out of other revelers who'd set up blankets along the pond's edge. The children were playing tag and Joshua's older boys were being gracious to the young newcomer by letting him escape…for now. Sean tried to smile at the boys' carefree joy, but his lips refused to cooperate. The malnourished, five-year-old boy's name had also turned out to be James, just like his son.

James had been found by Major Samuelsson's men alongside his two-year-old sister when they'd searched the campsite down the road from Derrick Keefer's church after the gun battle. Major Samuelsson's retelling had depicted a scene of abject squalor inside the camp. Sean had been correct. The group of starving people living at the campsite had brought every able-bodied person to the fight…and they'd all died except the boy's mother. Almost a week after the attack, the woman was still in a coma with no signs of coming out of it. With the makeshift orphanage in Tionesta full to capacity, Sean's family had taken in the two children for the time being. The poor boy had no idea where his mother had gone and asked after her constantly.

At Tionesta's council meeting the day before leaving for Brockway, they had discussed what to do with the woman and how long they would try to keep her alive. She required twenty-four-hour care to feed and keep her bedding clean without a proper hospital bed and bed pan. Some wanted to bring James to his mother and see if his presence would pull her out of the coma, while others believed it would be cruel and heartbreaking for the small boy to know the truth of the situation. There were no easy solutions. Pastor Dan insisted they had a duty to keep the woman alive as long as possible and he would step down as mayor and care for the woman himself if it came to that. For the time being, it was decided to just keep things as they were and address the situation as new developments arose. Sean watched as the small boy grabbed onto the back of Samuel's legs, using them as a shield against his pursuers. Every time Sean looked at the boy, it was a reminder of how the world was still a very dangerous place.

The bluegrass band started up another tune, this one a slow song, and Maria gave his chest a little squeeze. "Did you hear anything else about Willy?"

Sean frowned. "No. I think everyone expected him to be here. He's the one common denominator in putting everyone together and nobody seems to know where he's gone."

"You've said before, he's really weird and unpredictable. I'm sure he'll turn up eventually."

Sean wasn't convinced. "I hope so. With the way he spoke the other day, I never would have guessed he would miss this, not for the world. I've got a bad feeling."

"You've always got a bad feeling," Maria chided him. She sat up and started fidgeting at something under the blanket. "Can you scoot over, please? I've got a root here digging into the middle of my ribs." Sean complied, and they resumed their positions with her head resting on his chest and his hand resting on her shoulder. She sighed and said, "That's better." Unfortunately, now *he* had something digging into his back through the blanket. He ignored it for the time being as best he could. It had been a long time since they'd had an opportunity to just relax and privately enjoy each other's company.

"So…," Maria began to say something but trailed off.

"Yes?" Sean finally urged her on, his curiosity piqued.

"So, I was with your mom early this morning when the vendors were still setting up. I made a trade for something that I haven't told you about yet."

Sean was a little irritated with her as they'd agreed on the drive down that they would discuss any potential trades or barters before going through with them. "What did you trade?"

"The Silky saw from my bug out bag," she said a tad sheepishly.

"What?" Sean said, unable to hide his irritation.

"Oh, come on!" Maria responded harshly. "You have the exact same one on your pack and I've never even used the thing."

"But still," Sean insisted. There was a moment of silence before he asked the inevitable. "So what did you get for it?"

There was another brief moment of silence before Maria turned over onto her stomach and propped on her elbows facing him. She was grinning ear to ear as her long raven hair pooled beneath her arms. She didn't say anything, just smiled. She was stunning and radiant to behold.

He was having a difficult time staying irritated with her and her contagious smile quickly induced a grin of his own. He turned onto his side facing her. His elbow on the ground, he rested his head onto his right palm, their faces only inches apart. "Well?"

Her eyebrows flicked up mischievously and her smile grew bigger, if that was possible. "I traded it for a pregnancy test."

Sean's initial reaction was shock. Not at what she'd bought. That point hadn't sunk into his brain yet. How could she trade a high quality, and practically new, hand saw for an item you could get at any pharmacy for a tenth of the price of the saw before the collapse? He didn't have time to bring it up, though, as his mind started to trudge through the other piece of information she'd imparted. Had she said "pregnancy test"? What would she need that for? She hadn't even had her first period yet. What had it been since James was born? Five months? Six? He thought he remembered her saying something about women not being able to get pregnant while still nursing.

His mind raced as reality set in. "And?" he forced his mouth to say.

"And what?" she played with him, flashing a devilish grin.

"And…what did it say?" he asked with an eagerness that surprised even himself.

"It said that Sean and Maria Marlin are going to have another baby!"

Characters

Allison – Sean's youngest sister
Andrew – Retreat member (original 5), banker
Beth Ann - Tionesta resident, Brody's wife
Brody – Retreat member (original 5), ex Special Forces
Bug – "little" Samuel, Sean's cousin, Uncle Lawrence's son
Caleb – Retreat member (original 5), former contractor
Captain "Shifty" Whalen - Commanding Officer, Delta Company, 31st Regiment
Captain Spears - Commanding Officer, Alpha Company, 31st Regiment
Captain Zrucky - Commanding Officer, Charlie Company, 31st Regiment
Colonel Bruce Harris - Commander, 31st Infantry Regiment, 10th Mountain Division
Corporal Lopez - 2nd Rifle Squad, First Platoon, Delta Company, 31st Regiment
Curtiss Eckley – Tionesta's Gardening Team Leader and city councilman
Damian – Retreat member (original 5), financier
Danny – Sean's cousin, Uncle Will's son
Darren – Doctor who becomes member of the retreat
Emily – Randy's wife
Faith – Sean's older sister
General Duncan - Commander, 10th Mountain Division
General Oates - Sits on Presidential Advisory Council
Hank Keefer - Tionesta resident, experienced with ham radios
Jackson – Sean's cousin, Uncle Lawrence's son
Joshua – Sean's older brother
Leah – Sean's sister in law, Joshua's wife
Lieutenant Aguilar - 2nd Platoon Commander, Third Battalion, 75th Ranger Regiment
Lieutenant Baier – 2nd Platoon Commander, Team Four, Navy Special Warfare Group
Lieutenant Jenkins - Instructed to eliminate Ranger Platoon, sent by General Oates
Major Dean "Sammy" Samuelsson - Colonel Harris's Executive Officer, 31st Regiment
Maria Marlin – Sean's wife
Mayor Kendall "David" Reese - Mayor of Kane, "Freedom America" radio broadcaster
Mr. Andrews – deceased wealthy executive, prior owner of North Homestead
Pastor Dan – Mayor of Tionesta
Peter – Elderly farmer, neighbor and friend of the retreat
Private Mason – Colonel Harris orderly
Randy – Retreat member (original 5), Sean's best friend
Richard – Sits on Tionesta City Council
Rose – Caleb's Wife
Samuel – Sean's father
Sean Marlin – Ex military Survival Instructor
Sergeant Timms - 2nd Rifle Squad, First Platoon, Delta Company, 31st Regiment
Skyler Benningfield – General Oates operative inside the looting army from Chicago
Tyler – Sean's brother in law, Faith's husband
Uncle Lawrence – Sean's uncle on his father's side
Uncle Nathan – Sean's uncle on his mother's side
Uncle Will – Sean's uncle on his mother's side
Willy – Newcomer to Tionesta, travels the open road connecting surviving groups

About the Author

Jonathan Hollerman is a former military S.E.R.E.(Survival, Evasion, Resistance, and Escape) Instructor and expert on survival and prepping. Jonathan currently offers his services as an Emergency Preparedness Consultant specializing in Survival Retreat design and has clients all over the world. He performs on-site survival retreat analysis and designs off-grid infrastructure for families working on a budget up to multi-million dollar compounds. Jonathan also provides his expertise through phone consultation and can be contacted via his company, Grid Down Consulting.

To contact the author or for personalized consulting please visit:

www.GridDownConsulting.com

You can follow ***Jonathan Hollerman*** on Facebook,
and on Instagram and Twitter **@GridDownPrepper**

81723551R00254

Made in the USA
Lexington, KY
20 February 2018